A MARMAC GUIDE TO NEW ORLEANS

Edited by
Cecilia Casrill Dartez

PELICAN PUBLISHING COMPANY
Gretna 2000

First edition, 1984
First Pelican edition, April 1988
Second Pelican edition, November 1991
Third Pelican edition, January 2000

ISBN: 1-56554-424-2
ISSN: 0736-8135

The Marmac Guidebook series was created and is directed by Marge McDonald of Atlanta, Georgia. As owner of a convention and sightseeing service in Atlanta for fourteen years, she learned from visitors and those relocating to Atlanta what information was important to them. She also served as President and CEO of the Georgia Hospitality and Travel Association for four years, and in 1978 was named Woman of the Year in Travel by the Travel Industry Association of America. She is president of Marmac Publishing Company.

Cecilia Casrill Dartez, a New Orleans native, is a Tulane University graduate with graduate study completed at Tulane and Princeton universities. She is also a retired New Orleans public school teacher, a currently licensed New Orleans tour guide for adults and children, a lecturer about New Orleans history and environs for adults and children, an author of children's books, and the former feature editor of the New Orleans edition of *Travel Host Magazine*. She also appears in the Louisiana State Library's 1998 *Louisiana Directory of Performing Artists*.

Much appreciation to Linda Lindsey for the extra typing, and to Estrellita for verifying many numbers. Another heartfelt thanks to the special people at the New Orleans Metropolitan Convention & Visitors Bureau.

Printed in the United States of America
Published by Pelican Publishing Company, Inc.
1000 Burmaster Street, Gretna, Louisiana 70053

CONTENTS

MAPS

KEY TO LETTER CODE

E	Expensive	CH	Entrance Charge
M	Moderately Expensive	NCH	No Charge
I	Inexpensive		

FOREWORD

The Marmac guidebooks are designed for the traveler who seeks comprehensive information in an easy-to-use format and who has a zest for the best in each city and area mentioned in this national series. We have chosen to include only what we can recommend to you on the basis of our own research, experience, and judgment. The inclusions are our reputation.

We first escort you into the city or area, introducing you to a new or perhaps former acquaintance, and we relate the history and folklore that is indigenous to this particular locale. Secondly, we assist you in "learning the ropes"—the essentials of the community, transportation systems, lodging and restaurants, nightlife and theater. Section three will point you toward available activities—sightseeing, museums and galleries, shopping, sports, and excursions into the heart of the city and to its environs. And, lastly, we salute the special needs of special people—the residents, international visitors, students and children, and senior citizens.

The key area maps are placed at the opening of each book, always at your fingertips for quick reference. Subsidiary maps include a downtown street map, in town and out-of-town touring maps, and special interest maps.

The Marmac guide serves as your scout in a new territory among new people or as a new friend among local residents. We are committed to a clear, bold, graphic format from our cover design to our contents, and through every chapter of the book. We will inform, advise, and be your companion in the exciting adventure of travel in the United States.

Please write with your comments and suggestions to Pelican Publishing Company, P.O. Box 3110, Gretna, Louisiana 70054-3110. We will always be glad to hear from you.

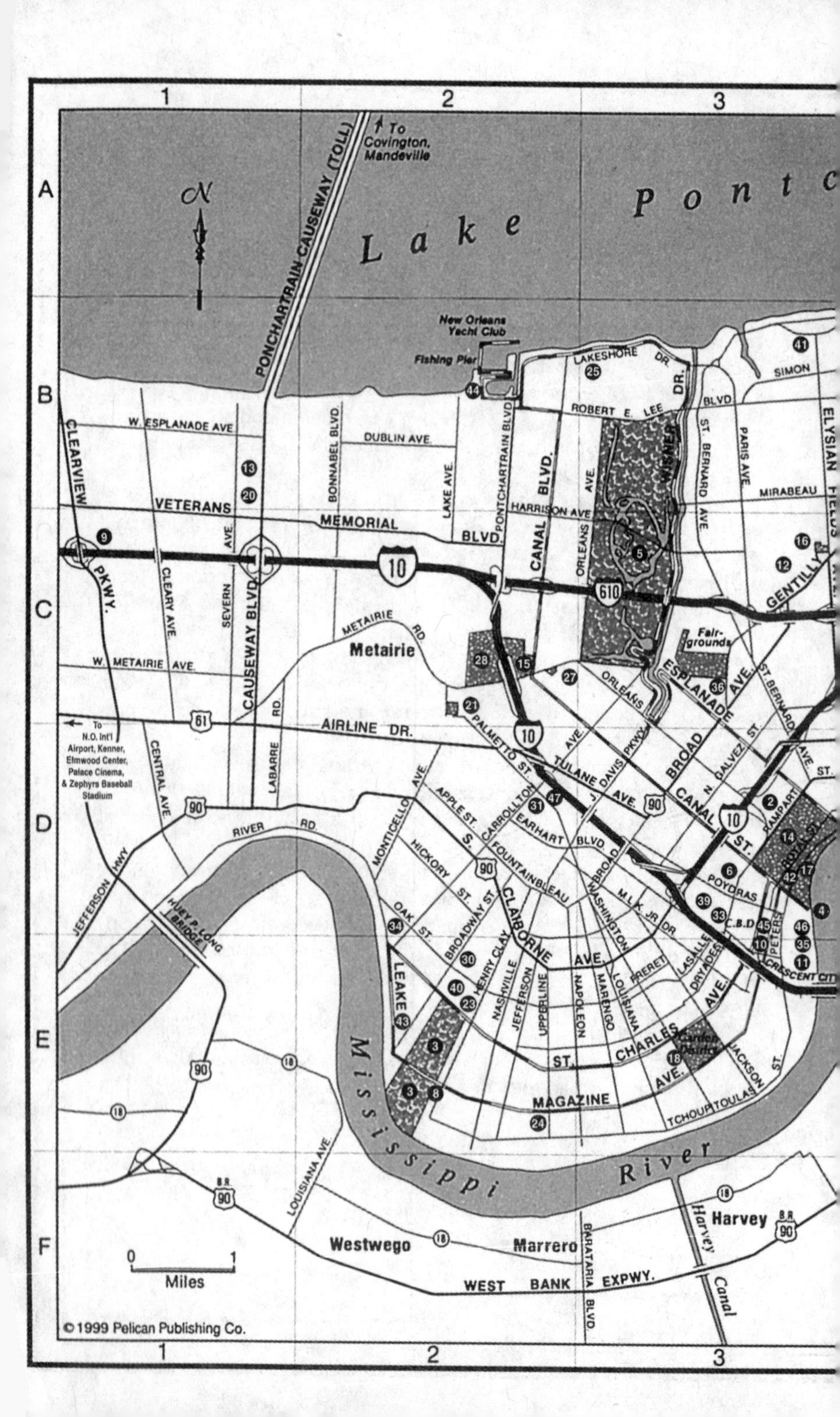

To Covington, Mandeville
Lake Pontc
PONCHARTRAIN CAUSEWAY (TOLL)
New Orleans Yacht Club
Fishing Pier
LAKESHORE DR.
ROBERT E. LEE BLVD
W. ESPLANADE AVE.
DUBLIN AVE.
BONNABEL BLVD.
LAKE AVE.
PONTCHARTRAIN BLVD
CANAL BLVD.
ORLEANS AVE.
WISNER
ST. BERNARD AVE.
PARIS AVE.
ELYSIAN FIELDS
SIMON
MIRABEAU
CLEARVIEW PKWY.
VETERANS MEMORIAL BLVD.
HARRISON AVE
GENTILLY
CLEARY AVE.
SEVERN AVE.
CAUSEWAY BLVD
METAIRIE RD.
Metairie
W. METAIRIE AVE.
LABARRE RD.
Fairgrounds
ESPLANADE AVE.
ORLEANS AVE.
DAVIS PKWY.
AIRLINE DR.
To N.O. Int'l Airport, Kenner, Elmwood Center, Palace Cinema, & Zephyrs Baseball Stadium
CENTRAL AVE.
PALMETTO ST.
TULANE AVE.
BROAD
N. GALVEZ ST.
ST. BERNARD AVE.
CANAL ST.
RAMPART
ROYAL ST.
RIVER RD.
MONTICELLO AVE.
APPLE ST.
CARROLLTON
S. CARROLLTON
EARHART BLVD.
FOUNTAINBLEAU
BROAD
WASHINGTON
M.L.K. JR DR
POYDRAS
C.B.D.
PETERS
CRESCENT CITY
JEFFERSON HWY
HUEY P. LONG BRIDGE
HICKORY ST.
BROADWAY ST.
CLAIBORNE AVE.
OAK ST.
LEAKE
HENRY CLAY
NASHVILLE
JEFFERSON
UPPERLINE
NAPOLEON
MARENGO
LOUISIANA
FRERET
LASALLE
DRYADES
AVE.
ST. CHARLES AVE.
Garden District
JACKSON
ST.
MAGAZINE
TCHOUPITOULAS
Mississippi River
LOUISIANA AVE.
Westwego
Marrero
Harvey
Harvey Canal
BARATARIA BLVD.
WEST BANK EXPWY.
Miles
© 1999 Pelican Publishing Co.

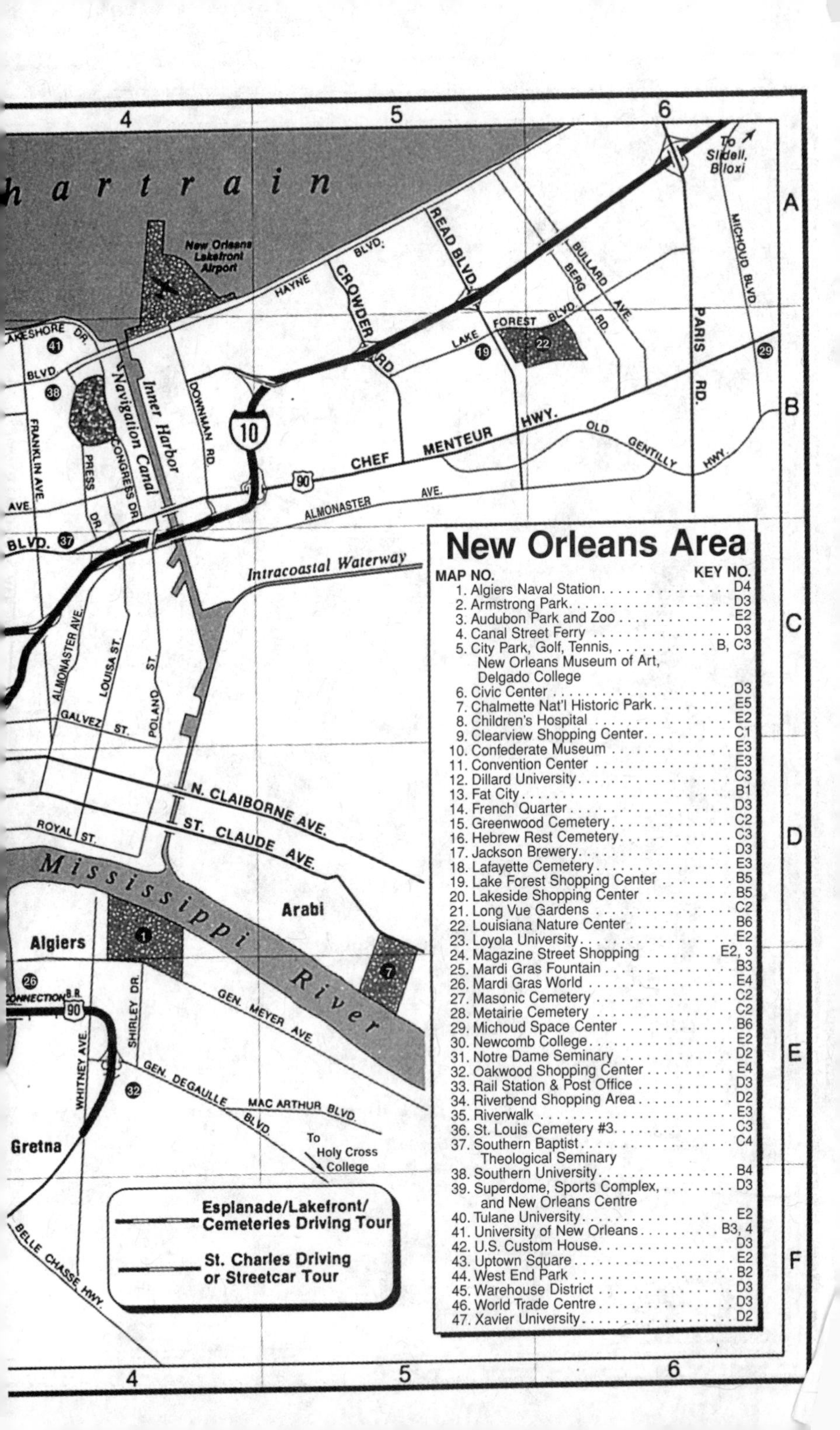

4
5
6
A
B
C
D
E
F
hartrain
New Orleans Lakefront Airport
To Slidell, Biloxi
HAYNE BLVD.
CROWDER RD.
READ BLVD.
BULLARD AVE.
BERG RD.
MICHOUD BLVD.
PARIS RD.
LAKE FOREST BLVD.
LAKESHORE DR.
BLVD.
FRANKLIN AVE.
PRESS DR.
CONGRESS DR.
Navigation Canal
Inner Harbor
DOWNMAN RD.
10
CHEF MENTEUR HWY.
OLD GENTILLY HWY.
90
ALMONASTER AVE.
AVE.
BLVD.
Intracoastal Waterway
ALMONASTER AVE.
LOUISA ST.
POLAND ST.
GALVEZ ST.
N. CLAIBORNE AVE.
ST. CLAUDE AVE.
ROYAL ST.
Mississippi River
Arabi
Algiers
CONNECTION B.R. 90
SHIRLEY DR.
WHITNEY AVE.
GEN. MEYER AVE.
GEN. DEGAULLE BLVD.
MAC ARTHUR BLVD.
To Holy Cross College
Gretna
BELLE CHASSE HWY.
Esplanade/Lakefront/ Cemeteries Driving Tour
St. Charles Driving or Streetcar Tour
New Orleans Area
MAP NO. KEY NO.
1. Algiers Naval Station D4
2. Armstrong Park D3
3. Audubon Park and Zoo E2
4. Canal Street Ferry D3
5. City Park, Golf, Tennis, New Orleans Museum of Art, Delgado College B, C3
6. Civic Center D3
7. Chalmette Nat'l Historic Park E5
8. Children's Hospital E2
9. Clearview Shopping Center C1
10. Confederate Museum E3
11. Convention Center E3
12. Dillard University C3
13. Fat City B1
14. French Quarter D3
15. Greenwood Cemetery C2
16. Hebrew Rest Cemetery C3
17. Jackson Brewery D3
18. Lafayette Cemetery E3
19. Lake Forest Shopping Center B5
20. Lakeside Shopping Center B5
21. Long Vue Gardens C2
22. Louisiana Nature Center B6
23. Loyola University E2
24. Magazine Street Shopping E2, 3
25. Mardi Gras Fountain B3
26. Mardi Gras World E4
27. Masonic Cemetery C2
28. Metairie Cemetery C2
29. Michoud Space Center B6
30. Newcomb College E2
31. Notre Dame Seminary D2
32. Oakwood Shopping Center E4
33. Rail Station & Post Office D3
34. Riverbend Shopping Area D2
35. Riverwalk E3
36. St. Louis Cemetery #3 C3
37. Southern Baptist Theological Seminary C4
38. Southern University B4
39. Superdome, Sports Complex, and New Orleans Centre D3
40. Tulane University E2
41. University of New Orleans B3, 4
42. U.S. Custom House D3
43. Uptown Square E2
44. West End Park B2
45. Warehouse District D3
46. World Trade Centre D3
47. Xavier University D2

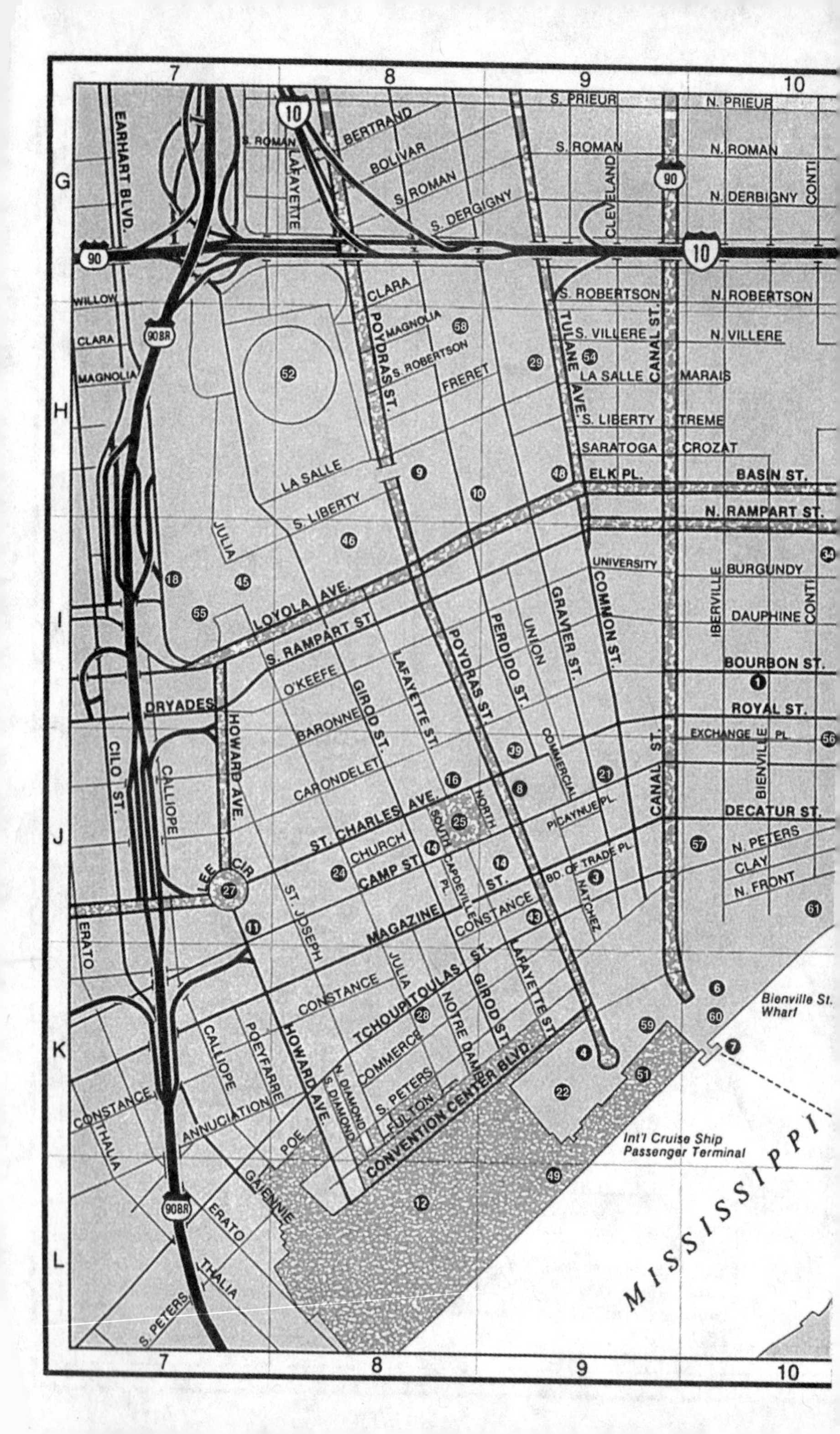

EARHART BLVD.
S. ROMAN
LAFAYETTE
BERTRAND
BOLIVAR
S. ROMAN
S. DERGIGNY
S. PRIEUR
S. ROMAN
CLEVELAND
N. PRIEUR
N. ROMAN
N. DERBIGNY
CONTI
WILLOW
CLARA
MAGNOLIA
CLARA
MAGNOLIA
POYDRAS ST.
S. ROBERTSON
FRERET
S. ROBERTSON
TULANE AVE.
S. VILLERE
LA SALLE
CANAL ST.
N. ROBERTSON
N. VILLERE
MARAIS
S. LIBERTY
SARATOGA
ELK PL.
TREME
CROZAT
BASIN ST.
N. RAMPART ST.
LA SALLE
S. LIBERTY
JULIA
LOYOLA AVE.
UNIVERSITY
BURGUNDY
DAUPHINE
IBERVILLE
S. RAMPART ST.
POYDRAS ST.
PERDIDO ST.
UNION
GRAVIER ST.
COMMON ST.
BOURBON ST.
ROYAL ST.
DRYADES
O'KEEFE
GIROD ST.
LAFAYETTE ST.
BARONNE
EXCHANGE PL.
BIENVILLE
CILO ST.
CALLIOPE
HOWARD AVE.
CARONDELET
COMMERCIAL
PICAYUNE PL.
DECATUR ST.
ST. CHARLES AVE.
SOUTH
NORTH
CHURCH
CAMP ST.
CAPDEVILLE PL.
BD. OF TRADE PL.
NATCHEZ
N. PETERS
CLAY
N. FRONT
LEE CIR
ST. JOSEPH
MAGAZINE
CONSTANCE
ERATO
CONSTANCE
JULIA
TCHOUPITOULAS ST.
GIROD ST.
LAFAYETTE ST.
NOTRE DAME
CALLIOPE
POEYFARRE
HOWARD AVE.
COMMERCE
Bienville St. Wharf
CONSTANCE
ANNUCIATION
N. DIAMOND
S. DIAMOND
S. PETERS
FULTON
CONVENTION CENTER BLVD.
THALIA
POE
GAIENNIE
Int'l Cruise Ship Passenger Terminal
ERATO
MISSISSIPPI
THALIA
S. PETERS

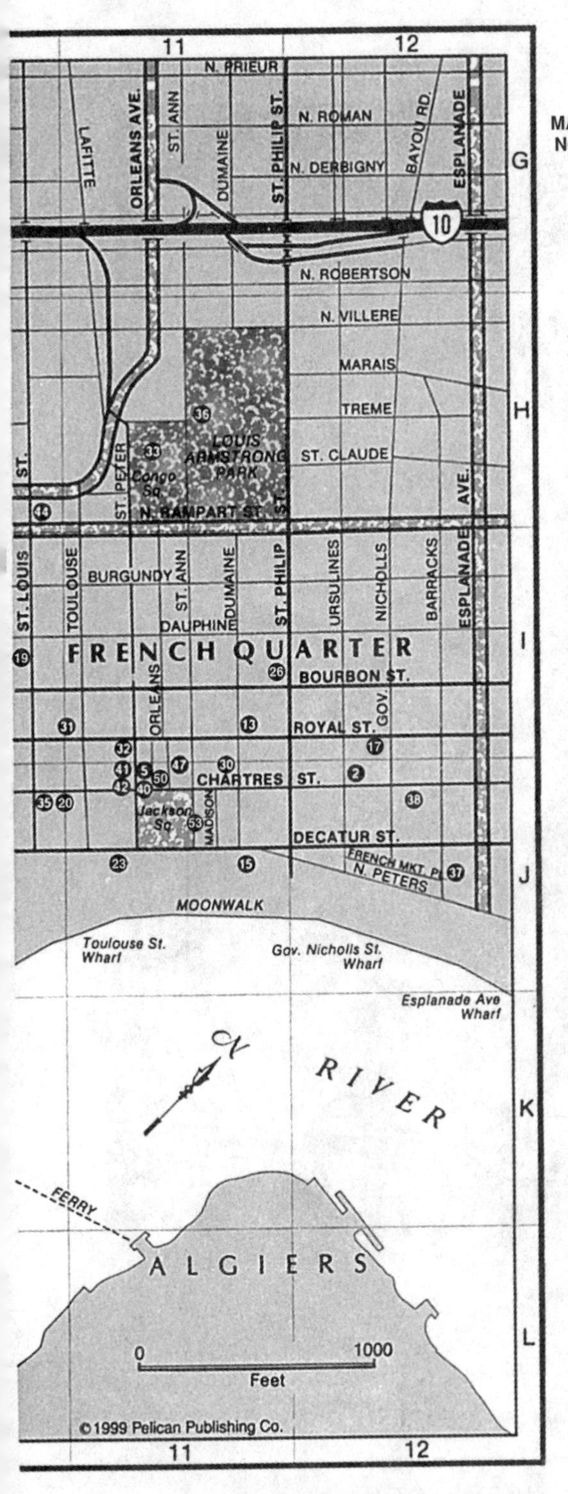

Downtown New Orleans

MAP NO.		KEY NO.
1.	Absinthe House	I10
2.	Beauregard/Keyes House	J12
3.	Board of Trade	J9
4.	British Plaza	K9
5.	Cabildo	J11
6.	Canal Place	K10
7.	Canal Street Ferry	K10
8.	Chamber of Commerce	J9
9.	City Hall	H8
10.	Civic Center	H8, 9
11.	Confederate Memorial Museum	J7
12.	Convention Center	L8
13.	Cornstalk Fence	I11
14.	Federal Complex	J8, 9
15.	French Market	J11
16.	Gallier Hall (Old City Hall)	J8
17.	Gallier Historic House	I12
18.	Greyhound Bus Terminal	I7
19.	Hermann-Grima House	I10
20.	Pharmacy Museum	J10
21.	International House	J9
22.	International Rivercenter	K9
23.	Jackson Brewery	J11
24.	Julia Row Renovation	J8
25.	Lafayette Square	J8
26.	Lafitte's Blacksmith Shop	I11
27.	Lee Monument	J7
28.	Louisiana Children's Museum	K8
29.	Louisiana State University Medical Complex	H9
30.	Madame John's Legacy	J11
31.	Merieuit House	I11
32.	Le Monnier House	I11
33.	Municipal Auditorium	H11
34.	Musse Conti (Wax Museum)	I10
35.	Napolean House	J10
36.	New Orleans Theater for the Performing Arts	H11
37.	Old U.S. Mint	J12
38.	Old Ursuline Convent	J12
39.	One Shell Square	J9
40.	Pedestrian Mall	J11
41.	Le Petit Salon	J11
42.	Petit Theatre du Vieux Carre	J11
43.	Piazza D'Italia	J9
44.	Police Station	H, I10
45.	Post Office and Federal Building	I7, 8
46.	Poydras Plaza	I8
47.	Presbytere	J11
48.	Public Library	H9
49.	Riverwalk	L9
50.	St. Louis Cathedral	J11
51.	Spanish Plaza	K9
52.	Superdome	H7, 8
53.	Tourist Information Center	J11
54.	Tulane Medical School	H9
55.	Union Passenger Terminal	I7
56.	U.S. Civil Courts Building	I10
57.	U.S. Customhouse	J10
58.	Veterans Adminstration Hospital	H8
59.	World Trade Center	K9
60.	Aquarium of the Americas and Imax Theatre	K10
61.	Woldenberg Park	J10

Dixieland jazz in a plantation gallery

Al Godoy, Louisiana State Tourist Commision

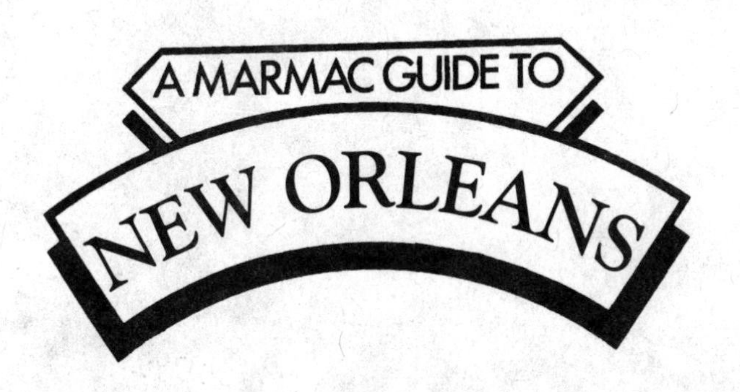
A MARMAC GUIDE TO
NEW ORLEANS

Bienville statue in its new French Quarter home Cecilia Castrill Dartez

NEW ORLEANS PAST

The first inhabitants of the "beautiful crescent" of the Lower Mississippi River were the Choctaws, an amiable Native American tribe living off the land and waterways. This fertile territory was passed by a succession of Spanish, French, and Canadian explorers probing into the heart of the new world via its main artery, the mighty Mississippi River. The first group of Europeans, survivors of Hernando de Soto's Spanish expedition in the mid-1500s, traversed downriver past the site that was to be New Orleans on their way to Mexico.

The French Claim

Over a century later, in 1682, Rene Robert Cavelier, Sieur de La Salle, turned this same bend in the river and claimed all of the land drained by the great river for Louis XIV, France's Sun King. He named the territory Louisiana.

In 1699 Canadian adventurers Pierre Le Moyne, Sieur d'lberville, and his eighteen-year-old brother Bienville floated past the future site of New Orleans. Bienville was to be the founder and governor of this new place that proved to be the pivot for control of the Gulf of Mexico, and also the southeastern access to the North American continent. As the Native Americans were displaced, or assimilated, the Spanish, French, and English all looked carefully at the colonization of New Orleans.

Bienville was sent from France by the Scotsman John Law—a gambler, mathematical whiz, womanizer, and promoter par excellence. Having fled England to France after a duel with an irate husband, this speculative genius talked his way into a position of prominence in the French Court. Law sold Philip, duc d'Orleans, regent for young Louis XV, on the idea of the Company of the West, a get-rich-quick scheme which was to save France from bankruptcy. The colony would be named after Philip . . . New Orleans.

Settling the Colony

On a May day in 1718, Bienville stepped ashore on a relatively high spot along the banks of the Mississippi River, with a French-drawn map of his "city-to-be" and a strange group of adventurers who were supposed to build it. The small clearing, chopped out of the thickets of river cane and willow, became the Place d'Armes (today known as Jackson Square) in the heart of the Vieux Carre (the French Quarter).

Bienville's well-planned city was far from an instant reality. His initial group, a motley crew of four other Canadians, six carpenters, and 30 convicts released by the French on condition that they come to the New World as laborers, took years to settle and become acclimated. Three years after the founding, only one warehouse, three houses, and a hundred huts had been built. Not one of these structures was according to Bienville's municipal plan.

In order to speed up the colonization effort, John Law relied on the process of deporting criminals from the jails of Paris and the French provinces. The population of all of Louisiana increased from about 400 in 1718 to 8,000 in 1721. The first large shipment of Negro slaves (147) arrived in 1720. The population of New Orleans and environs in 1721 was recorded at 1,700, almost half of which was slave labor.

Bienville protested the policy of deporting undesirables from France and the Regent agreed in 1720. John Law meanwhile had found another group of prospective colonists—German peasants weary of wars, landless, and attracted to a fresh beginning and new farms in a new country. These Germans brought a large measure of stability to the colonial effort, and those who did not speak French were given French surnames.

Hurricanes and Rebuilding

This odd mix of Native Americans, Europeans, and Negroes was hit hard by the first recorded tropical hurricane in the history of New Orleans. The orderly system of streets and structures which engineer Adrian de Pauger had laid out in 1721 was challenged by nature's forces. The Vieux Carre had been planned with a 4,000-foot river frontage and a military grid. Two-thirds of the houses were destroyed; therefore, complete and more substantial reconstruction was undertaken.

By 1743, the elegant regime of the Marquis de Vandreuil reaped the benefits of Bienville's long struggle to build New Orleans. Peace, prosperity, and pleasure were the signs of this first golden age. The sensual traditions of balls, banquets, fetes, carnivals, plays, opera, and ballet were established once and forever in the social fabric of the city.

The Spanish Regime

In 1762, as a result of one of many ill-conceived wars between France and Spain, Louisiana was given by Louis XV of France to his Bourbon cousin Charles III, king of Spain. The news of this change in ownership was evidently one of those messages that no one really wanted to deliver, for the citizens of New Orleans were not informed of the transfer for two years. Four years later, in 1766, the first Spanish governor arrived, only to be driven out in the Revolution of 1768 by a consortium of French civic and business leaders and the French military command.

The Spanish king retaliated, sending his favorite general, an Irishman named O'Reilly ("Bloody O'Reilly"), to chastise the leaders. Frenchmen Street was so named to immortalize the French men who were executed during this conflict. Spanish rule lasted from 1769 to 1803.

During the years 1788-94 New Orleans suffered two fires and three hurricanes, and a great majority of the French-built buildings in the city were demolished. Thus, most of the "French Quarter" that you see today was actually built by the Spanish.

The Acadian Influx

The largest trans-Atlantic migration in American colonial history occurred during the Spanish administration. In 1755, French Acadians had been expelled by the British from Nova Scotia and some had returned to France. Some of these exiles came to Louisiana via France as early as 1764. But in 1785, more than 1,600 Acadians were transported to Louisiana. Today, the word Acadian has been vernacularized to "Cajun" and is used to describe Cajun culture, Cajun people, Cajun houses, and even Cajun cookin'!

Another culture-shaping event during the Spanish regime was the production of the first profitable cane sugar crop. The cane was planted and the sugar produced on the plantation of Etienne de Bore, now the site of Audubon Park in Uptown New Orleans.

An American Territory

Although their tenure of 37 years had been a peaceful and beneficial one and the population had doubled, the Spanish could not win the deepest allegiance of New Orleanians. The delighted citizens thought for a month or so in the fall of 1803 that they would be French again. Spain returned New Orleans to France, but Napoleon decided to sell the territory. On December 20, 1803, documents were signed in the Cabildo, flags were raised and lowered in Jackson Square, and the Louisiana Territory officially became part of the United States.

The people of New Orleans had mixed emotions about this change. For years, the "Americans," or "Kaintucks" as they were more frequently and scornfully called, had been floating downriver on flatboats to sell their produce in New Orleans. New Orleanians were torn between wanting their business and abhorring their rowdy backcountry manners. This had created a reservoir of ill will within the French/Spanish community toward anything American. And now, not only did New Orleanians suddenly have an American flag flying in the Place d'Armes, but there were American soldiers marching around the city and English was the official language. The newly arrived Governor Claiborne didn't even speak French!

At the time of the Louisiana Purchase, New Orleans had a population of about 8,000. The city stretched for about one mile along the riverbank, from present-day Esplanade Avenue to Iberville Street. The streets were unpaved and sidewalks (banquettes) made of cypress boards were elevated above the streets because of frequent flooding. The more affluent citizens built their houses high off the ground on brick pillars (raised cottages) both as a safeguard against flooding and to provide storage space. Cellars were impossible in New Orleans because the water table was too high. Many of the houses were built with wood from the flatboats that the "Kaintucks" tore apart and sold when they reached New Orleans. By this time, the Saint Louis Cathedral and the Cabildo were completed and faced Jackson Square. The Presbytere was under construction. The first Protestant congregation in the Mississippi Valley was founded in 1805 by the Episcopal religion. By 1810 the census figures reflected the swell in population during the first seven years of American control. New Orleans had 17,242 inhabitants. American they were, but New Orleans still had a French heart.

Statehood for Louisiana

Louisiana became the 18th state in the United States of America in 1812. After considerable discussion, and still unsure it wanted to be an American city, New Orleans elected its first mayor, Monsieur Girod—who neither read, spoke, nor understood English.

Battle of New Orleans

The Battle of New Orleans, the first event that brought any cooperation between the Americans and the French/Spanish Creoles, was the last major battle of the War of 1812. After the British attacked

Washington, burned the White House, and fought at Fort McHenry in Baltimore, they sailed on to New Orleans. Here, the precisely trained and elegantly costumed British troops fought against a motley assemblage of "Kaintucks," Creole gentlemen, Cajuns from the bayou country, and a group of pirates on swampy terrain that was totally unfamiliar to them. Realizing that they were no match for Gen. Andrew Jackson and his "army," the British left their campfires burning and stole away to their ships during the night of January 18, 1815. Two thousand fifty-seven British troops were killed, including the commandant, General Pakenham. Seventy-one Americans were lost. The Battle of New Orleans was also the first military operation in which a steamboat took part.

One of the paradoxes of New Orleans history is that this battle was really unnecessary since the Treaty of Ghent, which ended the war, had been signed on January 8. However, communication was extremely slow in the 1800s. As a result of his leadership, Andrew Jackson became a national hero and later was elected president.

By the 1820s, the population of the city had increased to over 40,000—with an influx of French refugees from Santo Domingo and increasing numbers of indentured servants from Germany. The first railroad was being built and steamboats had arrived on the Mississippi River, vying with flatboats for space in New Orleans' ever bigger and busier port. The first theater was built in the French section of the city during this decade. In 1822, New Orleans replaced Mobile as the capital of the Louisiana Territory.

The Dueling Tradition

For years, dueling was the accepted way for gentlemen to settle their disputes in French New Orleans. It reached its height here from 1820 to 1840. Dueling pistols were a demand item for local gunsmiths. Fencing masters from France, Germany, and even the Balearic Islands and Santo Domingo opened academies on Exchange Alley. The protocol of dueling was strict, dependent not only on whom a gentleman may have insulted, but also on his status in society. As historian Stuart Landry says, "Only officers and gentlemen fought duels. A gentleman would not fight a duel with a man he wouldn't ask to dinner in his home."

Governor Claiborne's brother-in-law was killed in a duel when the length of the governor's mourning period for his late wife was challenged. Governor Claiborne himself fought a duel over a newspaper article that he felt attacked his administration. It later turned out that the newspaper account had been greatly exaggerated. Dueling was a romantic, but dangerous, means to settling disputes.

Growth in the 1830s

During the 1830s, the animosity that had always existed between the Creoles and the Americans burst forth anew. After a duel in which an American was killed, a Creole acquitted, and the judge attacked by a mob, the Americans succeeded in pushing through the legislature a provision to have the city divided into three municipalities—the American section above Canal Street, the French section below Canal (the French Quarter), and a section downriver from the Quarter known as the Faubourg Marigny. The commercial center of the city soon shifted from Chartres Street to the American section; new businesses blossomed and new buildings proliferated. In 1836 the St. Charles Hotel and the St. Louis Hotel, two of the early great hotels in America, were built with Greek detailing and Roman rotundas. These were followed in 1838 by the St. Charles Theater, the most elaborate theater in the country at that time.

The growth upriver began with the chartering in 1833 of the New Orleans and Carrollton Railroad, considered the third oldest railroad in the United States. The railroad followed the route of the present-day streetcars. The first residential area to blossom, both literally and figuratively, was the City of Lafayette, now called the Garden District. In American style, houses were now set back from the street on ample lots. The Americans also decided that they needed a proper seat of government for their second municipality, so in the late 1840s they built Gallier Hall, a fine example of Greek Revival architecture in the United States. The Creoles, keeping current with their upriver neighbors, added mansard roofs to the Cabildo and the Presbytere.

This very awkward and artificial division of the city lasted for 16 years. At the same time, tension was increasing between the northern and southern sections of the state of Louisiana, culminating in the removal of the capital from New Orleans upriver, first to Donaldsonville and then to Baton Rouge.

The Civil War and Reconstruction

In spite of friction between groups, New Orleans was at the height of its powers, enjoying a "Golden Age" both financially and culturally when the Civil War exploded across the nation. Because of New Orleans' strategic military location, it was bound to be a target of prime importance in the Civil War. The Mississippi River was blockaded and the once-busy port soon lay dormant. The city was captured in 1862 by Admiral Farragut and occupied by Gen. Ben Butler and his 15,000 Union troops. The general was soon christened "Spoons" Butler by the ladies of New Orleans because of his seemingly irresistible urge to commandeer everyone's silver.

Reconstruction in Louisiana, and particularly in New Orleans, was long, bitter, and very arduous. It wasn't until Rutherford B. Hayes was elected president that the rebuilding process began.

Turn of the Century

The last quarter of the 19th century was the heyday of the river steamer. The railroads thrived, competing with the steamboats for trade. In the 1870s, Capt. James B. Eads built a system of jetties at the mouth of the river, which opened the Port of New Orleans to ships of all sizes. Having been one of the first cities in the United States to be lit by gas, by the 1880s New Orleans was changing quickly to electricity.

In 1884-85, the Cotton Centennial Exposition was held on the site of what had been Etienne de Bore's sugar plantation—and what is now Audubon Park. This spectacular event was designed to prime the economic pump. It drew many visitors and helped heal the wartime breach between New Orleans and the north. The 1984 Louisiana World Exposition in New Orleans marked the 100th anniversary of the Cotton Centennial Exposition.

New Orleans has historically tended to wink at "little vices." Dueling didn't totally disappear until 1889. Horse racing has drawn crowds almost since the city was founded. Gambling has always flourished. By 1880, there were more than 80 gambling establishments in the city, as well as a lottery which was initiated during Reconstruction. Things became so lively that in 1897 an ordinance was passed limiting prostitution to a special section of the city. This "red light" district, known as Storyville, was located in the area of Canal and Basin streets. It was noted for some of the most elaborate "houses" and was serenaded by some of the greatest jazz musicians in the world. It lasted until 1917, when the Navy, with a base in the city, insisted it be closed down and the buildings demolished.

Cultural and Economic Center

New Orleans, in the early 20th century, was the center of cultural and economic life for the state. New Orleans jazz, which had grown out of the adapted European musical tradition of the Creole Negroes and the African chants and slave work songs, combined with the marching parade bands to produce a unique American music. Ragtime, jazz, and Dixieland from New Orleans were the new sounds drifting across the nation with increasing and permanent popularity. Today, jazz festivals are held all over the world.

In 1905, yellow fever was finally conquered when it was discovered that the lowly mosquito caused the disease. In 1914, an ingenious system of pumps was installed in the city, so well designed that they were copied to drain the Zuider Zee. Now, with the pestilence conquered by modern medicine and technology, New Orleans was both healthier and drier.

By 1915, there were five universities in New Orleans. Opera flourished until the unfortunate fire which burned the French Opera House in 1919. To the citizens of New Orleans, losing the Opera House was like losing a favorite relative; it was so much a part of the culture.

New Orleans sent some of its sons and daughters off to World War I. When they returned, the city became livelier than ever during Prohibition. Then came the Depression with Huey P. Long in power as the governor of Louisiana. In 1935, Long, Louisiana's most controversial governor, opened the bridge bearing his name that crosses the Mississippi River just upriver from New Orleans. This was a big boost for railroading into the city. For the first time, trains coming from the west did not have to be ferried across the river.

Just after World War II, the city elected its first "reform" mayor in many, many years, a handsome young war hero named de Lesseps S. Morrison, and entered into an exciting period of modernization and growth, along with a new emphasis on preservation of the good things from the past.

Today, the status of New Orleans' historic neighborhoods is becoming more secure with official historic designations. As a result, people are restoring and preserving our glorious past! Also, New Orleans is expanding its convention facilities to vie for the larger global conferences, as well as broadening its sports and entertainment facilities in the form of a new indoor sports complex and a recently proposed "Jazzland" themed amusement park for families. So, New Orleans continues to blend the old with the new and is ready to meet the new millennium with pride in its past and optimism for its future.

NEW ORLEANS TODAY

New Orleans, the magical name that conjures up visions of merriment, music, wonderful food, and drink! Rare it is for a visitor to visit only once. This fascinating city has the unique ability to blend old and new while mixing many traditions, cultures, and customs. It is a city embracing life, all of it, a city where streetcars still jostle daily back and forth along St. Charles Avenue and the Riverfront. It is also where you will find elegance and excitement in the most surprising places.

It is a kaleidoscope of colors, sounds, tastes, smells and feelings, a city loved by natives and enjoyed by travelers. Where else can one cross a mighty river, walk a quiet canal, fish in a lazy bayou, go crabbing and shrimping, sail the breezy lake, visit antique shops and used bookstores, shop in outdoor markets, and meander through a historic neighborhood all in a short visit?

New Orleans is a place where the dead are buried above the ground, with families sharing the same tomb; a city below sea level, whose buildings tower high above marshy land; a romantic place with a proud beginning, filled with fun-loving people able to change from informal to formal attire at the drop of an invitation. Happenings, from hurricane warnings to shopping sprees, are a potential party, and business in New Orleans always revolves around good food, Creole and Cajun cuisine, and good company.

The Changing Skyline

Until the late 1960s, there was a tacit understanding among architects and engineers that there was no way to build a highrise building in the marshy land of New Orleans. Technical advances since then have made the "impossible" feasible. The result has been an explosion of new highrise hotels and corporate buildings in the Central Business District. Poydras Street, fast becoming the business hub of the city, is the showcase for the "new" New Orleans. It is lined with sparkling new hotels, the New Orleans Centre shopping mall, and corporate centers built by Texaco, Exxon, Pan American Life, Shell, Freeport-McMoran, and Louisiana Land and Exploration Corporation. Poydras is crowned

Evening New Orleans skyline

William E. Majoue,
New Orleans Metropolitan Convention & Visitors Bureau

at one end by the Superdome, a one-of-a-kind sports arena, and at the other end by the New Orleans Convention center, the Mississippi River, and the lengthy Riverwalk shopping mall. This rapid growth is guided and supported by the Chamber of Commerce of New Orleans and the River Region, one of the most active and fastest growing chambers in the country.

Side by side with the new construction in the Central Business District is a resurgence of interest in preservation and restoration. Nineteenth-century warehouses and wholesale houses are being reincarnated as offices, restaurants, residences, and time-share condominiums . . . befitting the beginning of the 21st century.

Tourism

Tourists have always gravitated to New Orleans' French Quarter, where centuries-old buildings with ironwork and courtyards charm one into some of the nation's finest restaurants, nightclubs, and cafes. The Garden District also beckons with its charming Old South mansions and Louisiana cottages. The metropolitan New Orleans area boasts over 50,000 hotel rooms and a convention center with 1.1 million square feet of contiguous exhibit spaces (making it one of the prime convention centers of the South and the fourth largest in the U.S.). The city is a leading destination for international visitors to this country, surpassed only by New York and San Francisco.

The Port of New Orleans

New Orleans, being strategically situated approximately 100 miles from the mouth of the Mississippi River, is one of the largest ports in the United States.

New Orleans is at the junction of the 19,000 miles of inland waterways created by the Mississippi River, its tributaries, and the Gulf Intercoastal Waterways. Shippers as far north as Minneapolis, as far east as Pittsburgh and West Virginia, and as far west as Oklahoma and Nebraska have water access to international trade through the Port of New Orleans.

Major industries have developed along the banks of the Inner Harbor Navigation Canal, which was completed in 1925, linking the river to Lake Pontchartrain. Two other waterways join the canal, the Intercoastal Waterway and the Mississippi River-Gulf Outlet, which was built to provide an alternate route to the Gulf of Mexico, 40 miles shorter than the Mississippi River.

New Orleans and the Louisiana delta NASA *Space Center*

There are some important statistics you may consider as you walk along the riverfront parks or shipping areas. The Port of New Orleans is a $12-billion-a-year industry. It's also responsible for approximately 94,000 jobs. In addition, $261 million is generated statewide.

A new progressive project is now under way which will help the Port of New Orleans maintain its position as one of the great world ports, and as one of Louisiana's greatest assets. The project is being touted as the "New River Port—A Big, Bold, Beautiful Beginning." During the 1990s, $300 million was invested in new wharves, terminals, marshalling yards, cranes, and transportation infrastructure. In addition to handling products, the port sees approximately 200,000 passengers embark on cruises annually. These are all indications of the port's bold entry into the 21st century.

The port complex consists of a 2.01-mile-long quay between the Henry Clay Avenue and Milan Street terminals which can accommodate up to 15 vessels simultaneously and which is billed as the world's longest wharf. The port's France Road container terminal on the Inner Harbor Navigation Canal handles nearly 200,000 container units annually, and there is an 18-acre foreign-trade zone where foreign merchandise may be brought into the country without being immediately subjected to the usual U.S. Customs regulations.

The Port of New Orleans, one of the most modern and productive maritime centers of the world, continues to maintain its reputation as a port that meets the needs of changing industry with efficient, worldwide service. For up-to-the-minute port information, check their Internet address: http://www.portno.com.

International

Because of the fine port facility, New Orleans was one of the first cities in the United States to attract a significant volume of international business, and has been a center for consulates and foreign offices for years. In 1943, International House was founded as a pioneering trade association to provide a center for communication between foreign and domestic business people. The further expansion of foreign trade prompted a group of farsighted civic leaders to build the World Trade Center, a towering landmark on the banks of the Mississippi River, to consolidate the numerous maritime-related enterprises in the city. An upper floor is occupied by the Plimsoll Club, one of the unique private clubs of the world, named for the Plimsoll, the maximum load line on ships.

Ships of foreign navies frequently visit New Orleans and graciously invite the public aboard while in port. Check the newspaper's calendar of events for listings.

Also a boat trip on the river gives the tourist an opportunity to observe freighters from many countries; huge tankers, barely out of the water when full, high and swift when empty; and tiny tugs fighting the current while pushing massive rectangular barges. The pace of life on the Mississippi River is fascinating.

Educational and Cultural Center

The New Orleans community has historically been enriched by its colleges and universities. Three institutions of higher learning are all adjacent to each other in the uptown area of the city. Loyola University of the South, a Jesuit institution, faces St. Charles Avenue. Next door is Tulane University, formerly the University of Louisiana. Tulane was founded by Paul Tulane, a New Jersey-born philanthropist, in the late 19th century. Directly behind Tulane is the Sophie Newcomb College. Josephine Newcomb donated, then bequeathed, millions of dollars to the Board of Administrators of Tulane University for the founding of a college for women. Newcomb College is in memory of Josephine's only daughter, who died during adolescence.

Three predominantly black universities—Dillard, Xavier, and Southern University of New Orleans—contribute to the cultural milieu. An early-20th-century college, Our Lady of Holy Cross College, is convenient for students on the West Bank side of New Orleans. Then, there is the newest mid-20th-century addition to academia, the University of New Orleans (UNO), which is part of the Louisiana State University system. UNO is a modern campus on the shores of Lake Pontchartrain.

New Orleans is also a well-known medical center. Such institutions as the Tulane Medical School and Teaching Hospital, the Louisiana State University (LSU) Medical School, and the Ochsner Foundation Hospital are internationally respected.

The city is currently strengthening its vocational education opportunities, attracting manufacturers and technical businesses in addition to helping people earn associate's degrees. Delgado College on City Park Avenue and Nunez College in Chalmette are wonderful additions to the New Orleans educational scene.

The "Lively Arts" are very much alive in New Orleans—there are museums and galleries, theater groups, and community centers in all parts of the city. Key cultural facilities such as Le Petit Theatre du Vieux Carre, the Contemporary Arts Center, the St. Charles Avenue Jewish Community Center, the Lakefront Hellenic Center, the Jefferson Performing Arts Center, the Pontchartrain Center, and the St. Bernard Cultural Center all offer a wide variety of plays, musicals, concerts, exhibits, and classes.

New Orleans is extremely proud of its operatic tradition. The French Opera House was the first in the New World, and was the focal point of city life until it burned in 1910. From the seasons of 1806 to 1811, the French opera had given 374 performances of 92 operas. By 1836 the city had three opera companies in three languages: French, Italian, and English. Interest in opera did not lag with the loss of the opera house. New Orleans has continued to have its own opera company which performs regularly throughout the winter season. Each spring, New Orleans enjoys hosting the Metropolitan Opera Tryouts, which have been a vehicle for success for many of our talented local performers.

The Louisiana Philharmonic Orchestra (LPO) also has an extensive season. It performs in the magnificently renovated Orpheum Theater, across the street from the Fairmont Hotel in the business district, and in the Pontchartrain Center on Williams Boulevard in Kenner. Many concerts, ranging from jazz to chamber music, are offered in various places around the city each week.

Jazz, America's native music, born and bred in the streets and clubs of New Orleans, continues to belt out its rhythms everywhere, from Preservation Hall, up and down Bourbon Street, in street parades, funeral processions, and in the wild splendor of Mardi Gras. Jazz remains the heartbeat of metropolitan New Orleans.

Climate and Dress

Just as New Orleans mixes many cultures and many lifestyles, it also mixes many kinds of weather, often in the same day. The average high temperature of this subtropical city is 78 degrees, the average low temperature is 59 degrees, and the average total annual rainfall is 60 inches. While our weather is seldom very cold, it is always very changeable. In the winter, cold snaps seem to run in four- or five-day cycles. Rain brings one or two relatively cool days, followed by a gradual warming trend, coming full circle to the rain. Be aware that an increase in the humidity will make summer temperatures feel hotter and winter temperatures feel cooler.

Prepare to dress in layers, as the temperatures in the morning and evening may differ greatly from those in the middle of the day. Sweaters are worn outside in the winter and inside in the summer, due to over-exuberant air-conditioning. Rain gear is a must, and thanks to the tropical sun, umbrellas are popular rain or shine. Casual dress is most comfortable for touring, and acceptable all over town from April to October. However, many of the better New Orleans restaurants require that the gentlemen wear a coat and tie, and that ladies not wear jeans.

New Orleans and Its People

New Orleans is a progressive yet gracious old city inhabited by about a million people, an unusual potpourri of cultures and races—all speaking one language with as many different accents as there are neighborhoods and sections. Some older generations still speak French, Spanish, Italian, German, and Vietnamese.

In addition to the original settling families, new residents continue to flow into the city, being employed by the port, shipyards, Navy, and the oil, space, and tourism industries, all adding new traditions and flavors from other parts of the country and world.

Strong forces in all the varied communities join together in the tradition of civic service preparing for rapid growth in this old but forward-looking city in the United States. New Orleans, its people and its places, hold past and future in a present day-to-day excitement of living the good life.

MATTERS OF FACT

Whether you're visiting New Orleans or are a new resident, you are sure to have questions that arise. Some sources of help and information have been listed in the SPECIAL PEOPLE, FOR RESIDENTS, and TRANSPORTATION sections. Here we list some of the most basic places to get good answers. There may be a few repeats, but that is done to make life easier for you.

AAA—837-1080 (road service).
Ambulance—911 (New Orleans); 911 (Jefferson).
American Red Cross—586-8191.
Area Code, telephone—504.
Auto Pound, for towed cars—565-7236.
Automobile Registration, License, and Title—483-4610.
Better Business Bureau—581-6222.
Calendar of Events—
Times-Picayune.
New Orleans Magazine.
Gambit newspaper.
Where magazine (hotel concierge).
Community pages of telephone yellow pages.
City Hall—
Human Relations Commission; 565-7916.
TTY Deaf Information; 586-4475.
City Recreation Department (NORD); 826-1770.
Climate—Annual Averages
Mean temperature: 69.
Annual total rainfall: 60".
Clear days: 246.
Average humidity: 62%.
Dryest months: April, October, November.
Warmest month: August.
Coldest months: January, February.
Snow or ice: once every 10 years or so.
Consumer Information—Credit Bureau; 1-800-288-2585.
Consumer Product Safety Commission; 1-800-638-2772.
Dentist—
Dental Emergency Services; 349-5360.
Doctor—Orleans Parish Medical Society; 523-2474. Evenings or weekends, contact hotel physician or visit nearest hospital, see below.
Emergency Counseling—
DePaul Hospital and Community Mental Health Center; 899-8282.
The Greenhouse; 525-1333.
New Orleans Adolescent Hospital; 897-3400.

Parenting Center; 896-9591.
Traveler's Aid; 525-8726.

Emergency Road Service—837-1080.

Emergency Rooms—
Children's Hospital; 899-9511.
East Jefferson Hospital; 454-4000.
Ochsner Foundation Hospital; 838-3460.
Southern Baptist Hospital; 899-9311.
Touro Infirmary; 897-7011.
Veterans Hospital; 568-0811.

Environmental Compliance—443-8851.

Environmental Quality—471-2800.

Federal Bureau of Investigation—522-4671.

Federal Information Center—1-800-688-9889.

Fire—911 or 565-7833 (New Orleans); 911 (Jefferson).

Foreign Car Repair—Throughout the city; check telephone directory.

Gas Stations—Throughout the city; primary brands: Texaco, Chevron, Shell, Exxon, Spur, Amoco; most open 24 hours.

Hospitals—see Emergency Rooms and FOR RESIDENTS.

Law—Louisiana State Bar Association; 566-1600.

Legal—
Legal Aid Bureau, Civil Division; 523-2597.
Louisiana Legal Information Service; 525-3425.

Library, Public—New Orleans, Main Branch, 219 Loyola Ave.; 529-7323.

Local Laws—Drinking age, 21 (with ID). No open glass or metal containers on the street.

Louisiana Historical Society—588-9044.

Newspapers—
Times-Picayune (morning and evening).
Gambit (weekly).

Passport Offices—589-6728.

Pets—Society for Prevention of Cruelty to Animals; 944-7445.

Pharmacy—Located throughout the city; most open until 10 pm, many until midnight, a few 24 hours.

Police—911 or 821-2222 (New Orleans); 911 (Jefferson).

Population—Metro N.O.; 998,309.

Port of New Orleans—522-2551.

Post Office—Main Post Office; 589-1111/1112.

Radio Stations—

AM—

600	WVOG	Christian
640	KTIB	(Thibodaux) Oldies
690	WTIX	Talk/music
730	WASO	News/talk
750	KKNO	Christian
800	WSHO	Christian
830	WFNO	Spanish
870	WWL	News/talk
940	WYLD	Gospel
990	WGSO	CNN
1010	WCKW	Gospel
1060	WLNO	Christian
1230	WBOK	Inspirational
1280	WODT	Blues
1350	WSMB	News/talk
1450	WBYU	Nostalgia
1490	KJIN	Country
1510	KAGY	(Buras) Gospel
1540	KGLA	Spanish
1560	WSLA	News/talk

1600	KLEB	Country

FM—

88.3	WRBH	Reading for blind.
89.1	WBSN	Christian
89.9	WWNO	(NPR) Cultural
90.5	KTLN	(NPR) Cultural
90.7	WWOZ	Community
91.5	WTUL	Progressive
92.3	WCKW	Rock
93.3	WQUE	Urban
94.3	WTIX	Oldies
94.7	WYLA	Country
94.9	WADU	Beautiful
95.7	WTKL	Oldies
97.1	WEZB	Contemporary
98.5	WYLD	Urban
99.5	WRNO	Classic Rock
100.3	KLRZ	Classic Rock
101.1	WNOE	Country
101.9	WLMG	Contemporary
102.9	KMEZ	Contemporary
104.1	KHOM	Contemporary
104.7	WYLK	Country
105.3	WLTS	Contemporary
105.9	KBZE	(Thibodaux) Urban
106.1	WZRH	Country
106.3	KXOR	(Thibodaux) Country
106.7	KLJZ	Alternative
107.5	KCIL	Country

Social Secuity—1-800-772-1213.

Social Services—Volunteer and Information Agency; 488-4636.

State Patrol—471-2775.

Television Stations—
WWL, Channel 4 (CBS)
WDSU, Channel 6 (NBC)
WVUE, Channel 8 (Fox)
WYES, Channel 12 (PBS)
WHNO, Channel 20 (Ind.)
WGNO, Channel 26 (ABC)
WLAE, Channel 32 (PBS)
WNOL, Channel 38 (WB)
WPXL, Channel 49 (PAX)

Tickets—Ticketmaster Louisiana, Inc.; 522-5555.

Time and Weather—828-4000.

Time Zone—Central (daylight savings time April to October).

Tourist Information—
Tourism Offices; 568-5661, 566-5005, 246-5666.
Greater New Orleans Info—New Orleans International Airport; 464-0831.
Louisiana State Tourist Info; 568-6967, 568-5661.

Traffic Laws—May turn right on red, except where posted.
Switch on headlights when it is raining.
Seat belts must be worn.

Traveler's Aid—525-8726.

United States Customs—568-5661.

Veteran's Information—826-2385.

Weather—828-4000.

TRANSPORTATION

New Orleans has traditionally served as a bridge between the continental United States and South and Central America. It is the point of entry for many foreign travelers as well as the destination of many U.S. business people and fun-seekers. The following information should be of use to you in planning a trip to New Orleans and will help you around the city once you arrive.

TO NEW ORLEANS

Air

New Orleans International Airport is located on Airline Highway just west of New Orleans in the suburban city of Kenner. The airport is administered by the New Orleans Aviation Board (464-0831) and handles almost seven million passengers annually. Since New Orleans is a port of entry, the U.S. Customs Service (467-4319) has an airport facility and the Whitney National Bank in Jefferson Parish has a branch in the airport to facilitate currency exchange.

Automobiles enter from Airline Highway or from a specially marked ramp off of I-10 West that leads directly to the front of the airport. (This ramp exits from the right. Be aware, as the signs leading up to it give short notice.) Short-term parking is available in the multilevel parking garage. Long-term parking is available in two lots adjacent to the short-term parking lots. Additional long-term parking is available in several commercial parking lots across Airline Highway from the airport. These "off grounds" parking lots have shuttle buses which will take you and your luggage to the desired airport terminal.

Lakefront Airport, Lakefront at Inner Harbor Navigational Canal; main information number 243-4010. Individual companies to contact: Caudle—242-9496; General—241-2700; Million Air—241-2800; Air Reldan—241-9400.

The Lakefront Airport is a rare and valuable commodity—a full-service airport, with three runways (the longest being 6,879 feet) and an instrument-landing runway (ILS). There are fixed-based operators (FBOs), three flight schools, and a director of aviation. This is all within the city limits of New Orleans. The FAA air traffic control tower operates from 6 am to 10 pm. Also, there is a U.S. Customs and Agricultural Landing Rights Field. The airport's call sign is NEW. The fax is 504-243-9151; Web site is http://www.lakefront@gnofn.org.

The *Flight Deck Café* operates from 7 am to 5:30 pm and offers informal dining with daily specials. An additional treat here is watching planes take off and land while you comfortably dine behind a glass wall.

There are also facilities for private meetings and banquets. The Walnut Room is a beautiful Art-Deco facility available for receptions, large parties, and other special events.

The airport is administered by the Orleans Levee District. There are free shuttles available to a number of motels in New Orleans East.

Airlines serving New Orleans from New Orleans International Airport at Moisant Field:

Domestic

Aeromexico 1-800-237-6639
Air Tran 1-800-825-8538
American 1-800-433-7300
Continental 1-800-525-0280
Delta/Comair 1-800-221-1212
Lacsa 1-800-225-2272
Northwest Airlines 1-800-225-2525
Southwest Airlines 1-800-435-9792
Taca 1-800-535-8780
TWA 1-800-221-2000
United 1-800-241-6522
U.S. Air & Express 1-800-428-4322

International

Aerolineas Argentinas . . 1-800-333-0276
Aeromexico 1-800-237-6639
Air Canada 1-800-776-3000
Avianca 1-800-284-2622
Aviateca S.A. 1-800-327-9832
British Airways 1-800-247-9297
BWIA International
Airways 1-800-538-2942

Cayman Airways 1-800-422-9626
China Airlines 1-800-227-5118
Emirates Airlines 1-800-777-3999
Japan Airlines 1-800-525-3663
KLM Royal
Dutch Airlines 1-800-374-7747
Korean Air 1-800-438-5000
Lufthansa Airlines 1-800-645-3880
Mexicana Airlines 1-800-531-7921
Quantas Airways 1-800-227-4500
Singapore Airlines 1-800-742-3333
Swissair 1-800-221-4750
TWA 1-800-221-2000

Ground Services to and from New Orleans International Airport

Some hotels offer free airport transportation, so check with your hotel. If your hotel lacks this service, there are numerous alternatives. Limousine services are abundant, so just a few are listed. Rates and services do vary from company to company, but 24-hour service is available.

Airport Shuttle—"Official Ground Transportation"; 522-3500.
Passenger Express Transportation—Five or more passengers; 456-2118.

Limousine Service. All offer a variety of vehicles.
A Touch of Class—522-7565, 1-800-821-6352.
All Star Limousines—888-6746.
Blue Moon Limousine—595-8922.
Bonomolo Limousine—523-2666, 1-800-451-9258.
Cajun Transportation—246-7383.
Celebrity Limousine—888-5466.
Limousine Livery—561-8777, 1-800-326-1345.
London Livery—586-0700, 1-800-284-0660.
Rhodes Limousine Service—522-6010.

Taxi Service. There is a taxi stand at the airport, which is convenient to the baggage pick-up area. Fees vary with the company. The following fees are for delivery to the city center.

Metry Cab (835-4242) has a one-way fee of $21 for one to two passengers, or $8 per person for three to five occupants.

Yellow Taxi (525-3311), **United Cab** (522-9771), and **White Fleet** (948-6605) all have the same one-way rate of $21 for one to two passengers, or $8 per person for three to five people.

Bus Service. Greyhound (1-800-231-2222) runs between the airport and downtown hotels. Call for schedules and fees.

Automobile Rental

There are seven rental agencies with offices on the airport grounds on the lower level of the terminal. The phone numbers for their ticket counters are as follows:

Alamo 469-0532
Avis 464-9511
Budget 467-2277
Hertz 468-3695
National 466-4335
Payless 441-5700
Thrifty 467-8796

Airport and Tourist Information

Visitor Information Services are located in the West Lobby (464-2752), East Lobby (465-8852), West Baggage Claim (463-1020), and East Baggage Claim (463-1006). Each Information Counter is open from 8 am to 9 pm daily. All of the Visitor Information Service Representatives are bilingual or multilingual.

The **Traveler's Aid Booth** (464-3522), located in the East Lobby, provides tourist information and assists travelers in distress.

Translation Services are located in the West Lobby (464-2752), East Lobby (465-8852), West Baggage Claim (463-1020), and East Baggage Claim (463-1006). Each counter is open from 8 am to 9 pm daily. All of the Translation Service Representatives are bilingual or multilingual.

Passengers needing assistance in a foreign language not provided by Visitor Information Services can call the Red Cross Language Bank at 586-8191. This service is staffed with bilingual and multilingual volunteers and is available 24 hours a day.

Louisiana Tax Free Shopping is designed to promote international tourism to Louisiana by giving a refund on sales taxes. It applies to those who can show a passport and an international travel ticket and who will be in the country for less than 90 days. All shops in the airport have tax-free shopping. Refunds or further information can be obtained at (504) 527-6958 in New Orleans or at the Tax Free Shopping airport counter located in the ticket lobby between the bank and the Lacsa Ticket Counter (7 am—6 pm).

Aircraft Rental and Charter

There are over 30 air charter companies operating in the New Orleans area, with fixed-based aircraft, seaplanes, helicopters, and even air-ambulances ready to take you wherever you desire. Several companies offer all of the above-mentioned options and have 24-hour service: **Suwest Air Charter;** 242-4883, **Air Reldan;** 241-9400, **Flight Training Air Services;** 246-1020, **RFB Flying Services;** 242-8005, and **Executive Charters;** 246-6543. For additional local information call the New Orleans Lakefront Airport at 243-4010.

Automobile

I-10 leaves Mobile and the Mississippi coast, crosses Lake Pontchartrain, goes through the center of New Orleans, and continues west to Baton Rouge, Lafayette, and Houston. I-610 offers an alternate route from New Orleans East to Metairie, skirting the Central Business District.

From the northeast, I-59 joins I-10 near Slidell. Then, proceed south on I-10 to New Orleans.

From the northwest, I-55 ends as it meets I-10 at La Place. Then, proceed east on I-10 to New Orleans.

There are welcoming centers on I-10 just before the I-59 junction, and in Kenner at the Loyola Drive exit. These centers can supply you with maps, brochures, and a hearty New Orleans welcome.

Boat

You may choose to come to New Orleans by boat. Consider cruising down the Mississippi on the *Delta Queen, the Mississippi Queen*, or the newer, larger *American Queen* . . . the experience of a lifetime. Contact the **Delta Queen Steamboat Company,** Robin Street Wharf, 1380 Port of New Orleans Pl., New Orleans, Louisiana 70130-1890; 1-800-550-3007.

You may want to come to New Orleans on your personal or chartered boat. Plan your trip through the Intracoastal Waterway. Check with your reciprocating yacht club as to the availability of visitor's slips.

Also, check with the beautiful new South Shore Harbor Marina (adjacent to the Lakefront Airport), 6701 South Shore Harbor Blvd., 245-3152, for slip availability by the day or week. Rates and services are based upon the length of your boat.

Bus

Greyhound Bus Lines has a terminal in downtown New Orleans at 1001 Loyola Ave.; 525-6075. The suburban terminal is in Metairie at 3005 N. Causeway Blvd.; 828-3415.

Hotard/Grayline also has a local office at 2838 Touro St.; 944-0253, 1-800-553-4895; e-mail address: charters@hotard.com.

Rail

Amtrak National Rail Passenger Service has numerous trains that arrive and depart from the Union Passenger Terminal at 1001 Loyola Ave. Because of varied schedules, it's best to call for the correct information. For station information only, call 528-1610. For reservations and schedule information, call 1-800-872-7245.

AROUND NEW ORLEANS

Auto Rentals and Leasing

You will need a valid driver's license and a major credit card to rent a car. There are over 50 rental companies in the New Orleans area, offering everything from a limousine to an "oldie-but-goodie." A few suggestions are:

Alamo Rent-A-Car 1-800-327-9633
Avis Rent-A-Car 1-800-831-2847
Budget Car and Truck Rental . . . . 1-800-527-0700, 467-2277, TDD 1-800-826-5510
Enterprise Rent-A-Car 1-800-736-8222
Hertz Rent-A-Car . . . . 1-800-654-3131, TDD 1-800-654-2280
National Car Rental 1-800-227-7368

Limousine Charters

Take your choice of many companies. A few possibilities are **A Confidential Limousine Service**; 833-9999, **A Touch of Class Limousine Service**; 522-7565, 1-800-821-6352, **Celebrity Limousine Service**; 888-5466, 1-800-253-1991, **London Livery Limousine Service**; 586-0700, 1-800-284-0660, **New Orleans Limousine Service**; 529-5226, and **Nicoll's Limousine Service**; 522-5656.

Private Car

The streets in New Orleans follow the curve of the river. It is strongly recommended that you drive with a map in hand. It is easy to spot the main thoroughfares; they have "neutral grounds" (medians) in the middle. Street numbers change "hundreds" with every block. Cross streets begin at the river with 100 (or thereabouts, depending on how much the course of the river has shifted). Up and down streets start with 100 Canal St. The Uptown, or upriver, side of Canal Street will be 100 *South* Miro. The Downtown, or downriver, side will be 100 *North* Miro. The main arteries are Canal, Claiborne, St. Charles, Carrollton, Esplanade, Elysian Fields, and Robert E. Lee. I-10 and I-610 go right through town and, except at rush hour, offer quick routes to almost every section of town.

The speed limit, unless marked, is 35 mph. The State of Louisiana has a very strict law against driving while intoxicated, and includes permission to administer a "balloon test" to the driver.

Parking meters take quarters. Parking lots are plentiful all over town and many places of business stamp parking tickets. Be sure to inquire.

In case of emergency or when in need of assistance call:

AAA; 1-800-222-4357, **New Orleans Police**; 911, 821-2222, **Jefferson Parish Sheriff's Office**; 911, **State Patrol**; 471-2775, **Champion 24-Hour Emergency Locksmith**; 1-800-560-5011, **Highway Safety Hotline**; 1-800-259-4929, **Traveler's Aid Society**; 525-8726.

Public Transportation

Transportation in the New Orleans area is administered by the **Regional Transit Authority** (RTA). You can sightsee very comfortably in New Orleans using public transportation. Fare on buses and streetcars is $1.25, a transfer is 25 cents, express buses are $1.50, and the Riverfront streetcars in the French Quarter (affectionately called "Little Red Ladies" by many natives) are $1.50.

Exact fare is always required, or tokens can be purchased. A pack of 10 tokens is $12.50. Special passes are also available. A one-day *Visitour Pass* gives visitors unlimited rides for $5; a three-consecutive-day *Visitour Pass* is $12. Also available is a *Trans Pass*, $55 for unlimited rides for a month. Tokens and passes can be purchased at many major hotels, Whitney and Hibernia banks, and at some check-cashers' stores.

Buses and streetcars operate on 15-minute daily rotations but can take more than an hour at night. The St. Charles streetcar runs 24 hours daily, and the Riverfront streetcar only runs 6 am-midnight. For more information, maps, and schedules, call the RTA at 248-3900.

The **ferries** that cross the Mississippi at Canal Street, Jackson Avenue, downriver at Chalmette, and upriver at Luling are free to pedestrians and bicycle riders. However, any motor vehicle is charged a $1 fee when boarding the ferry on the West Bank side of the river. The Canal Street-to-Algiers ferry offers a tremendous view of New Orleans, from the World Trade Center to the historic Jackson Square and St. Louis Cathedral.

Taxis

There are many taxi companies in New Orleans. Some of the most reliable are **United Cabs;** 522-9771, **Metry Cab;** 835-4242, and **Yellow Checker Cabs;** 525-3311. There are taxi stands at all major hotels and taxis cruise Canal Street, Poydras Street, St. Charles Avenue, and the French Quarter regularly.

Tours

There are numerous professional tour companies in New Orleans. Check at your hotel for information. Individual and group tours are offered and multilingual guides are available for group tours.

A few suggested sightseeing companies are: **Gray Line Tours;** 569-1401, 1-800-535-7786, **Destinations New Orleans;** 524-4302, and **New Orleans Tours;** 592-0560, 1-800-543-6332. **The Friends of the Cabildo Museum,** 523-3939, offers walking tours of the French Quarter. In addition to adult tours, **Melody Tours, Inc.** now offers children's tours by a licensed tour guide, with children's perspectives in mind. For information call 361-5959 or 1-800-864-1332.

The **Jean Lafitte National Historical Park and Preserve** offers free walking tours of the French Quarter conducted by a park ranger.

St. Charles Avenue streetcar — *Michael Terranova, New Orleans Metropolitan Convention & Visitors Bureau*

Tickets for the daily tours are available from 9 am at the office at 916 N. Peters St. on a first-come-first-serve basis, with only one ticket per person. For more information, call 589-3882. Garden District walking tours are also available from the Ramada Plaza Hotel on St. Charles Avenue, 897-2030. Buggy tours of the French Quarter are marvelous fun. Just pick the one you like best and board on the Decatur Street side of Jackson Square.

During the two weeks after Easter, the Spring Fiesta Association offers house and courtyard tours throughout New Orleans and the surrounding area. For information contact New Orleans Spring Fiesta Association, 826 St. Ann St., New Orleans, LA 70130; 581-1367.

A variety of tours that are unique to New Orleans because of its diverse cultural background offer in-depth looks at other sides of this fascinating city. **Save Our Cemeteries, Inc.** takes you on tours of two of New Orleans' oldest cemeteries. See above-ground tombs in these "Cities of the Dead." For information, call 525-3377 or 1-888-721-7493. There's also **New Orleans Spirits Tours;** 566-9877, **Cemetery/Voodoo History Tours;** 947-2120, **Haunted History Tours;** 861-2727, **Vampire Tours;** 897-2030, and **Millennium Walking Tours;** 569-9002.

Riverboat tour cruises are a unique New Orleans experience that should definitely be in your plans. There are several companies that offer one-to-three-hour day or night Jazz Cruises: **Cajun Queen Riverboat River/Plantation/Harbor Cruise;** 524-0814, **John James Audubon Riverboat/Zoo Cruise;** 586-8777, **Steamboat Natchez,** an authentic stern-wheel steamboat with jazz lunch and dinner cruises; 586-8777, 1-800-233-BOAT, and **Creole Queen Dinner Jazz Cruise;** 524-0814.

Swamp boat tours offer a visit into the "back country" of Louisiana to observe the lush semitropical forests; the hidden swamps; untamed, unsettled land; and abundant wildlife—all from a safe vantage point. Companies that offer these tours are: **Jean Lafitte National Historical Park and Preserve Swamp Tours;** 589-3883, **Bayou Sauvage National Wildlife Refuge Swamp Tours;** 254-4490, **Honey Island Swamp Tours;** 641-1769, **Bayou Segnette Swamp Tours;** 561-8244, **Lil' Cajun Swamp Tours;** 689-3213, **Louisiana Swamp Tours;** 689-3599, 1-888-30-SWAMP, **Cypress Swamp Tours;** 581-4501, **Chacahoula Tours;** 436-2640, 1-800-299-7861, and **Crawfish Farm Tours;** 689-7600, 1-888-502-7600.

An airplane tour of the city is also fun. Call **Air Reldan,** 241-9400 or **Suwest Air Charter;** 282-4883.

Walking

Walking is a most satisfactory way to tour New Orleans since it permits closer inspection of architectural detail, flora, fauna, and people themselves. New Orleans sidewalks ("banquettes," as some locals call them) can be a challenge because of the shifting ground beneath them. As a result, sidewalks shift, lift, and drop—especially in treelined areas. The sidwalks may be concrete, flagstone, cobblestone, or brick; so wear comfortable walking shoes. We suggest that you do your walking during daylight hours and take taxis at night.

LODGING

Choosing a place to stay in New Orleans is like choosing from scrumptious desserts at a smorgasbord—the variety is overwhelming. You may prefer the elegance of one of the older, meticulously maintained hotels, such as the Pontchartrain or the Fairmont, or an intimate French Quarter inn, or any of a number of quaint bed and breakfasts, or your family situation may dictate the practical and equally pleasant atmosphere of a very modern hotel or motel. Whatever your preference, we feel sure that you will find the perfect place for you to stay in the following list.

Because rates sometimes change with the seasons we have included the following code:

E—Expensive, $100 and up for a double room.

M—Moderate, $85-$100 for a double room.

I—Inexpensive, less than $85 for a double room.

FP—Family Plan

Rates can fluctuate from season to season or even midweek to weekend. We advise that you ask for information about rate changes and discounts.

The Area Listing which follows will assist you in locating lodging in the area of your choice.

LODGING BY AREA

CENTRAL BUSINESS DISTRICT (CBD)

Ambassador Hotel, *I*.
Comfort Suites Downtown, M.
Courtyard by Marriott, M *to E*.
Days Inn—Canal, *I*.
Doubletree Hotel, *E*.
Embassy Suites Hotel, M.
Fairmont Hotel, *E*.
Four Points Sheraton, M.
Hampton Inn Downtown, M *to E*.
Holiday Inn Downtown Superdome, M.
Holiday Inn Select, *E*.
Hotel Inter-Continental N.O., *E*.
Hyatt Regency New Orleans, M *to E*.

International House Hotel, *E.*
International YMCA Hotel, *I.*
La Quinta Inn, M.
La Salle Hotel, *I.*
Le Meridien Hotel, *E.*
Le Pavillon, *E.*
New Orleans Hilton Riverside, *E.*
New Orleans Marriott, *E.*
Pallas Hotel, M.
Pelham Hotel, *E.*
Plaza Suite Hotel, *E.*
Queen & Crescent Hotel, M.
Radisson Hotel, *E.*
Sheraton New Orleans Hotel, *E.*
Westin Canal Place, *E.*
Windsor Court Hotel, *E.*
Wyndham Riverfront Hotel, *E.*

FAUBOURG MARIGNY

Claiborne Mansion, *E.*
Frenchmen, *I.*
La Maison Guest House, M.
Sweet Olive Guest House, M.

FRENCH QUARTER

Andrew Jackson Hotel, M.
Best Western Inn on Bourbon, M *to E.*
Bienville House Hotel, *E.*
Bourbon-Orleans, M.
Chateau Dupre, *I to* M.
Chateau Sonesta Hotel, *E.*
Cornstalk Hotel, M.
Creole House, *I.*
Dauphine Orleans Hotel, *I to* M.
French Quarter Courtyard Hotel, *I.*
Girod House, M.
Grenoble House, *E.*
Historic French Market Inn, *I.*
Holiday Inn Chateau Le Moyne, M *to E.*
Holiday Inn French Quarter, *E.*
Hotel De La Poste, M *to E.*
Hotel Maison de Ville, *E.*
Hotel Provincial, *I to* M.
Hotel St. Marie, *I.*
Hotel St. Pierre, *I.*
Hotel Ste. Helene, M.
Hotel Villa Convento, *I.*
Lafitte Guest House, M *to E.*
Lamothe House, M *to E.*
Landmark French Quarter Hotel, *I.*
Le Richelieu Hotel, *E.*
Maison Dupuy, *E.*
Melrose, *E.*
Monteleone Hotel, M.
New Orleans Guest House, *I.*
Nine-O-Five Royal Hotel, M.
Olivier House, M.
Omni Royal Orleans Hotel, *E.*
Place d'Armes Hotel, M.
Prince Conti Hotel, *I.*
Provincial Hotel, M *to E.*
Quarter House, *E.*
Royal Sonesta, *E.*
St. Ann Marie Antoinette Hotel, M *to E.*
Saint Louis Hotel, *E.*
St. Peter Guest House, M.
Soniat House, *E.*
Westin Canal Place, *E.*

LAKEFRONT

Rose Manor Inn, M.

LOWER ST. CHARLES

Avenue Plaza Hotel & Spa, M *to E.*
Best Western—Parc St. Charles, M.
Clarion—Grand Boutique Hotel, *E.*
Lafayette Hotel, *E.*
Marquette House N.O. International Hostel, *I.*
Old World Inn, *I.*
Pontchartrain Hotel, *E.*

Quality Inn Maison St. Charles, *M.*
Ramada Plaza Hotel—St. Charles, *M.*
St. Charles Guest House, *I to M.*
YMCA International Hotel, *I.*

METAIRIE/JEFFERSON

Best Western Airport All Suite Hotel, *M to E.*
Best Western Landmark Hotel, *M to E.*
Best Western N.O. Inn—Airport, *I.*
Brent House Hotel, *M.*
Days Inn—N.O. Airport, *I.*
Doubletree N.O. Lakeside, *M.*
Hampton Inn & Suites Elmwood, *M.*
Holiday Inn Metairie, *I to M.*
Holiday Inn N.O.—Veterans, *I.*
Holiday Inn Select N.O. Airport, *I.*
Howard Johnson Hotel, *M.*
KOA West, *I.*
La Quinta Inn Airport, *I to M.*
La Quinta Inn Metairie, *I to M.*
Landmark Hotel, *M.*
Marriott Residence Inn, *M to E.*
New Orleans Airport Hilton, *M to E.*
Park Plaza Inn, *M.*
Quality Hotel & Conference Center, *M.*
Radisson Inn N.O. Airport, *M.*
Ramada Limited Causeway, *I.*
Shoney's Inn, *I to M.*
Travelodge Hotel—N.O. Airport, *M.*

MID-CITY

Degas House, *M.*
Duvigneaud House, *M.*
Esplanade Villa, *E.*
Quality Inn—Midtown, *I.*

NEW ORLEANS EAST

Best Western—N.O. East, *I.*
Days Inn—Read, *I.*
La Quinta East, *I to M.*
La Quinta Inn Crowder, *I to M.*
Mardi Gras Camp Ground, *I.*
Parc d'Orleans Campgrounds, *I.*
Ramada Inn—N.O. Highrise, *I.*
Riverboat Travel Park, *I.*
Scottish Inns, *I.*

NORTH SHORE

Best Western Northpark Inn, *I.*
Courtyard by Marriott, *M.*
Days Inn, *I.*
Dixie Queen Bed & Breakfast, *M.*
Holiday Inn Covington, *I to M.*
KOA.
Ramada Inn, *I.*
Yogi Bear's Jellystone Park Camp Resort, *I.*

ST. BERNARD

Quality Inn Marina, *I.*

UPTOWN

Columns Hotel, *E.*
Hampton Inn St. Charles Avenue, *M to E.*
Park View Guest House, *I to M.*
Prytania Park Hotel, *I.*
St. Charles Inn, *M.*
Sully Mansion—Garden District, *M.*

WEST BANK

Holiday Inn N.O. West Bank, *I.*
Rodeway Inn Gretna, *M.*
Rosewalk House, *I.*
Travelodge Hotel N.O. West, *I to M.*
West Bank Tower Hotel, *I to M*

HOTELS AND MOTELS

AMBASSADOR HOTEL, 535 Tchoupitoulas St., New Orleans 70130; 527-5271; 1-888-527-5271. *I.* This hotel close to the Convention Center offers a restaurant and bar and a dataport in each room.

ANDREW JACKSON HOTEL, 919 Royal St., New Orleans 70116; 561-5881; 1-800-654-0224. M. This 22-room hotel is a charming accommodation within walking distance of major tourist attractions. It offers a complimentary continental breakfast.

AVENUE PLAZA HOTEL AND SPA, 2111 St. Charles Ave., New Orleans 70130; 566-1212; 1-800-535-9575; fax 525-6899. *M to E.* This hotel is on the St. Charles Avenue streetcar line and within walking distance of the Garden District. Suites are available; most rooms have a refrigerator and wet bar. Pool, Jacuzzi, sauna, sidewalk cafe, and lounge are amenities. *FP.*

BEST WESTERN HOTELS, 1-800-528-1234; www.bestwestern.com. *I to E.* This well-respected chain has a variety of lodgings in the New Orleans area.

Best Western Airport—All Suite Hotel, 2488 Veterans, Kenner 70062; 469-2800; 1-800-528-1234. *M to E.* There's a free airport limousine available, nonsmoking rooms, pool, sauna, Jacuzzi, modem-ready phones, and complimentary continental breakfast.

Best Western Inn on Bourbon, 541 Bourbon St., New Orleans 70130; 524-7611. *M to E.* For those who really want to be in the center of New Orleans' night life, this is a good place to stay. Balconied rooms overlook Bourbon Street activity. Cafeteria, piano bar, and pool are amenities.

Best Western Landmark Hotel, 2601 Severn Ave., Metairie 70002; 888-9500; 1-800-277-7575; fax 885-8474. *M to E.* Restaurant, lounge, nonsmoking rooms, and fitness center are amenities.

Best Western—New Orleans East, 12340 I-10 Service Rd., New Orleans 70128; 241-5100; 1-800-537-0834. *I.* This basic hotel offers a lounge, coffeemakers and microwaves in the rooms, and free continental breakfast.

Best Western New Orleans Inn—Airport, 1021 Airline Hwy., Kenner 70062; 464-1644; 1-800-333-8278; fax 885-8474. *I.* Pool, 24-hour restaurant, and modem-ready phones are amenities. Free parking. *FP.*

Best Western Northpark Inn, 625 N. Hwy. 190, Covington 70433; 892-2681; fax 893-0115. *I.* Swimming pool, nonsmoking rooms, cable

TV, restaurant, and complimentary continental breakfast are amenities.

Best Western—Parc St. Charles, 500 St. Charles Ave., New Orleans 70130; 522-9000. M. This more upscale hotel is considered a "boutique" hotel.

BIENVILLE HOUSE HOTEL, 320 Decatur St., New Orleans 70130; 529-2345; 1-800-535-7836; fax 525-6079. *E*. In the French Quarter, midway between Canal Street and Jackson Square, Bienville House is convenient to Excursion Boat Wharf, major tourist attractions, and shopping. It offers a patio pool and a tempting menu in its restaurant.

BOURBON-ORLEANS, 717 Orleans Ave., New Orleans 70116; 523-2222, 1-800-521-5338; fax 525-8166. M. Directly behind St. Louis Cathedral, the historic Quadroon Ballroom is part of this hotel. It was also, at one time, the convent of the Sisters of the Holy Family, a religious order of black Roman Catholic women. Pool, balconied rooms, bilevel suites, kitchenettes, valet parking, restaurant, and lounge are available.

BRENT HOUSE HOTEL, 1512 Jefferson Hwy., Jefferson 70121; 835-5411; 1-800-535-3986. M. This is an excellent facility for patients' families on the grounds of Ochsner Medical Center, with restaurants, beauty and barber shops, and gift shops. *FP*.

CHATEAU DUPRE, 131 Decatur St., New Orleans 70130; 569-0600; 1-800-285-0620; fax 569-0606. *I to* M. Luxurious suites and rooms with continental breakfast are available.

CHATEAU SONESTA HOTEL, 800 Iberville St., New Orleans 70112; 586-0800; fax 586-1987. *E*. This French Quarter hotel offers spacious suites and guestrooms with balcony and courtyard views. Indoor parking, restaurant, lounge, pool, and fitness center are on the premises.

CLARION—GRAND BOUTIQUE HOTEL, 2001 St. Charles Ave., New Orleans 70130; 558-9966; 1-800-976-1755; fax 571-6464. *E*. Beautiful Art-Deco decorated suites (with kitchenettes) are available at this hotel on the famed St. Charles Avenue streetcar line. It is in the same building as Straya's Restaurant.

COLUMNS HOTEL, 3811 St. Charles Ave., New Orleans 70115; 899-9308; fax 899-8170. *E*. This huge 19th-century mansion built by a New Orleans merchant was later the set for the film *Pretty Baby*. It has huge rooms, 14-foot ceilings, a spectacular stairway, excellent restaurant, and a popular Victorian Bar. It is located on the St. Charles Avenue streetcar line and is on the National Register of Historic Places. *FP.*

COMFORT SUITES DOWNTOWN, 346 Baronne St., New Orleans 70112; 524-1140; 1-800-528-5150; fax 523-4444. M. Close to the French Quarter and Convention Center, these are suites with kitchenettes. A free continental breakfast is also available.

COURTYARD BY MARRIOTT, 124 St. Charles Ave., New Orleans 70130; 581-9005; 1-800-321-2211; fax 581-6264. *M to E.* This hotel offers luxurious rooms in the heart of downtown on the St. Charles Avenue streetcar line. There's a restaurant, lounge, exercise room with whirlpool, and in-room coffeemakers, in addition to nonsmoking rooms.

COURTYARD BY MARRIOTT, 101 Northpark Blvd., Covington 70433; 871-0244; fax 867-9938. M. In addition to nonsmoking rooms, this hotel has hearing-impaired rooms. There's also an indoor pool, exercise room, lounge, meeting room, and in-room coffeemakers.

DAUPHINE ORLEANS HOTEL, 415 Dauphine St., New Orleans 70112; 586-1800; 1-800-521-7111; fax 586-1409. *I to* M. This French Quarter hotel is newly decorated and offers complimentary continental breakfast. Parking is available along with a pool, fitness center, lounge, and guest library. All rooms are "allergen and smoke free."

DAYS INNS OF AMERICA. *I.* These hotels are designed for budget-minded families or large groups traveling together. Days Inns maintain high management standards; most inns have outdoor pools, restaurants, and nonsmoking and handicap-accessible rooms. Free parking.

Days Inn, 1645 Gause Blvd., Slidell 70458; 641-3450; fax 641-3607. *I.* In addition to the aforementioned features, this inn has cable TV. *FP.*

Days Inn—Canal Street, 1630 Canal St., New Orleans 70112; 586-0110; 1-800-232-3297; fax 581-2253. *I.* This downtown inn is only a few blocks from the French Quarter, aquarium and IMAX, and Riverwalk and Canal Place shopping malls. *FP.*

Days Inn—New Orleans Airport, 1300 Veterans Blvd., Kenner 70065; 469-2531. *I.* This inn's additional features are a meeting room, beauty salon, and shuttle.

Days Inn—Read, 5801 Read Blvd. at I-10 East, New Orleans 70127; 241-2500; 1-800-331-6935; fax 245-8340. Convenient to the Lakefront Airport, University of New Orleans, Southern University, and NASA, this inn is 20 minutes from the French Quarter and Central Business District.

DOUBLETREE HOTEL, 300 Canal St., New Orleans 70130; 581-1300; 1-800-522-4100. *E.* This hotel has 368 rooms, 14 meeting rooms, an outdoor pool, and other amenities that assure a comfortable stay. Directly across from the French Quarter and aquarium and close to the World Trade Center, Convention Center, and Riverwalk and Canal Place shopping malls. The excellent on-site restaurant pleases a variety of tastes. *FP.*

DOUBLETREE NEW ORLEANS LAKESIDE, 3838 N. Causeway Blvd., Metairie 70002; 836-5253; fax 846-4562. M. This full-service deluxe hotel has indoor pool, health spa, lounge, nonsmoking rooms, and suites. Adjacent to a shopping mall and dining and entertainment areas. Also available are free French Quarter and airport transportation. *FP.*

EMBASSY SUITES HOTEL, 315 Julia St., New Orleans 70130; 525-1993; 1-800-362-2779; fax 522-3044. M. Newly renovated and close to the Convention Center, Riverwalk and Canal Place shopping malls, aquarium and IMAX, and World Trade Center, this hotel also offers extra services like two-hour cocktail receptions and complete breakfast. *FP.*

THE FAIRMONT HOTEL, University Place, New Orleans 70112; 529-7111; 1-800-527-4727. *E.* One of New Orleans' oldest and finest hotels, the Fairmont is located in the Central Business District, close to French Quarter shops, and world-famous Canal Street. The hotel, built in 1892 in Italianate style, was first named the Grunewald; in 1923 it was renamed for Teddy Roosevelt. Fairmont Hotels is now the proud owner. The Fairmont is famous for its good food, its sparkling gold holiday decorations, and two original cocktails—the Sazerac and the Ramos Gin Fizz. Its block-long lobby, in New Orleans fashion, begins at a church (Baronne Street) and ends at a theater (University Place). The Sazerac Dining Room is one of the finest restaurants in New Orleans, and an informal restaurant, Bailey's, offers tasty food for those on a schedule. The Fairmont also has two rooftop tennis courts and a swimming pool. Pay parking. *FP.*

FOUR POINTS SHERATON, 333 Poydras St., New Orleans 70130; 525-9444; 1-800-747-3279; fax 568-9312. M. This is close to riverfront attractions like the aquarium and IMAX Theatre, Riverwalk shopping mall, Convention Center, and French Quarter. *FP.*

FRENCH QUARTER COURTYARD HOTEL, 1101 N. Rampart St., New Orleans 70116; 522-7333; 1-800-290-4233; fax 522-3908. *I.* This small hotel boasts a beautiful courtyard and pool and provides a complimentary continental breakfast.

THE FRENCHMEN, 417 Frenchmen St., New Orleans 70116; 948-2166; 1-800-831-1781; fax 948-2258. *I.* This is an 1800s Creole townhouse transformed into a small hotel with a pool. Free parking.

GRENOBLE HOUSE, 329 Dauphine St., New Orleans 70112; 522-1331; 1-800-722-1834; fax 524-4968. *E.* This all-suite hotel was made from the historic restoration of three 1834 townhouses and is furnished with antiques and reproductions. There is a pool, Jacuzzi, and complimentary continental breakfast.

HAMPTON INNS. *M to E.* This national hotel company offers nice-sized guestrooms and suites, with all suites having kitchens. All Hampton Inns offer complimentary continental breakfast.

Hampton Inn & Suites Elmwood, 5150 Mounes St., Metairie 70006; 733-5646. *M.* Located in Elmwood Business Park and close to New Orleans International Airport.

Hampton Inn Downtown, 226 Carondelet St., New Orleans 70130; 529-9990; 1-800-292-0653; fax 529-9996. *M to E.* Located in the Central Business District close to the French Quarter, riverfront, and Convention Center.

Hampton Inn St. Charles Avenue, 3626 St. Charles Ave., New Orleans 70130; 899-9990. *M to E.* Located in the Garden District on the streetcar line. It is close to Tulane and Loyola universities and the Audubon Zoo and has an outdoor pool and patio area.

HILTON HOTELS. *M to E.* This premier international hotel company offers impressive accommodations, convenient sites, amenities for the business and pleasure traveler, and excellent service. Call 1-800-445-8667.

New Orleans Airport Hilton & Conference Center, 901 Airline Hwy., Kenner 70062; 469-5000; 1-800-872-5914; fax 465-1101. *M to E.* Directly across from New Orleans International Airport, this hotel offers a free shuttle to the airport and free on-ground parking. Shuttle service is also available to downtown New Orleans and the French Quarter. Close to the unique Esplanade Mall. Restaurant, pool, and excellent, ultramodern convention facilities.

New Orleans Hilton Riverside, 2 Poydras St., at the river, New Orleans 70140; 584-3999; 1-800-HILTONS; fax 584-3979. *E*. In the heart of the Central Business District, with the World Trade Center and Convention Center on one side, the Rouse Company's Riverwalk on another, and Canal Place Shopping Mall on another, the Hilton rises 29 stories above passing merchant ships. It houses fine restaurants and clubs, including *Pete Fountain's Jazz Club*, a swimming pool, and a free tennis club. Pay parking. *FP*.

HISTORIC FRENCH MARKET INN—A CLARION CARRIAGE HOUSE, 501 Decatur St., New Orleans 70112; 561-5621; 1-800-827-5621; fax 566-0160. *I*. This French Quarter hotel is close to Jackson Square and riverfront attractions. Complimentary continental breakfast is available, as is a free French Quarter walking tour. *FP*.

HOLIDAY INNS. *I to E*. This well-established chain will meet your expectations for excellent, moderately priced lodging. All properties have restaurants, pools, and entertainment. Call 1-800-HOLIDAY.

Holiday Inn Chateau Le Moyne, 301 Dauphine St., New Orleans 70112; 581-1303; fax 523-5709. M *to E*. This is a special Holiday Inn, located in the French Quarter and built to blend elegantly with the Quarter ambience; with a flagstone courtyard, pool, and restaurant.

Holiday Inn Covington, Highway 190, across Lake Pontchartrain Causeway from New Orleans, Covington 70433; 893-3580; fax 893-4807. *I to* M. Forty-five minutes from New Orleans, this inn has good meeting facilities, restaurants, pool, and interesting small antique and boutique-type shops in the restored area of old Covington. *FP*.

Holiday Inn Downtown Superdome, 330 Loyola Ave., New Orleans 70112; 581-1600; 1-800-535-7830; fax 586-0833. M. This hotel is across from the Civic Center in the Central Business District, within walking distance of the Superdome. It is close to Amtrak and bus terminals and the French Quarter as well as being convenient to the Supreme Court and Tulane and LSU medical schools. *FP*.

Holiday Inn French Quarter, 124 Royal St., New Orleans 70130; 529-7211; fax 566-1127. *E*. Just off Canal Street, this Holiday Inn with pool and restaurant is convenient to downtown tourist attractions and to public transportation.

Holiday Inn Metairie, 3400 S. I-10 Service Rd., Metairie 70001; 833-8201. *I to* M. Convenient to Lakeside Shopping Center, the Causeway, and about 15 minutes from downtown New Orleans, this highrise features pool and restaurant. Kennel. *FP*.

Holiday Inn New Orleans—Veterans, 6401 Veterans Memorial Blvd., Metairie 70003; 885-5700; fax 888-5815. *I*. Convenient to New Orleans Airport (with free shuttle) and Esplanade and Clearview shopping malls, this Holiday Inn also has a pool, lounge, restaurant, and exercise facilities. *FP.*

Holiday Inn New Orleans Westbank, 100 Westbank Expwy., Gretna 70053; 366-2361. *I.* This is on the West Bank and can be reached in about 15 minutes from the Central Business District and the French Quarter by way of the double-spanned Crescent City Connection across the Mississippi River (avoid peak traffic times). Also there is the Algiers Ferry, which launches from Canal Street. *FP.*

Holiday Inn Select, 881 Convention Center Blvd., New Orleans 70130; 524-1881. *E.* This new deluxe hotel is across from the Convention Center in the Central Business District and close to Riverwalk and Canal Place shopping malls, the arts district, riverfront, and French Quarter. Other features are a restaurant, lounge, and fitness and business centers.

Holiday Inn Select New Orleans Airport, 2929 Williams Blvd., Kenner 70062; 467-5611; 1-800-887-7371; fax 469-4915. *I.* Close to New Orleans International Airport, just off I-10 West, this inn has a Holidome—a glass-roofed family fun center with pool. It is about 20 minutes from the French Quarter and the Central Business District and is convenient to River Road plantation houses.

HOTEL DE LA POSTE, 316 Chartres St., New Orleans 70130; 581-1200; 1-800-448-4927; fax 523-2910. *M to E.* This hotel was designed to appear as old as the Quarter that surrounds it. De La Poste provides deluxe rooms with European courtyard views, an excellent restaurant, pool, and rooms for private parties. Located in the French Quarter, midway between Jackson Square and Canal Street, it is surrounded by antique shops, boutiques, and art galleries. *FP.*

HOTEL INTER-CONTINENTAL NEW ORLEANS, 444 St. Charles Ave., New Orleans 70130; 525-5566; fax 523-7310. *E.* This four-star luxury hotel on the St. Charles Avenue streetcar line is near the French Quarter and all riverfront attractions, including the Riverwalk and upscale Canal Place shopping malls. On-site are meeting facilities and excellent formal and informal restaurants. *FP.*

HOTEL MAISON DE VILLE, 727 Toulouse St., New Orleans 70130; 561-5858; 1-800-634-1600; fax 528-9939. *E.* This transformed 1840s townhouse furnished with antiques was once owned by Monsieur Peychaud, a Creole pharmacist who invented the cocktail in his Royal Street pharmacy. Also part of the hotel, just two blocks away, are the historic and luxurious Audubon Cottages. Complimentary continental breakfast, port and sherry service.

HOTEL PROVINCIAL, 1024 Chartres St., New Orleans 70116; 581-4995; 1-800-525-7922; fax 581-1018. *I to M.* This charming hotel is located in the heart of the French Quarter and offers on-site parking and courtyard pool. Cafe is open morning till night. *FP.*

HOTEL ST. MARIE, 827 Toulouse St., New Orleans 70112; 561-8951; 1-800-366-2743; fax 571-2802. *I.* This French Quarter hotel has 100 rooms surrounding a lush courtyard with pool. It also offers an on-site restaurant and bar. *FP.*

HOTEL ST. PIERRE, 911 Burgundy St., New Orleans 70116; 524-4401; 1-800-225-4040; fax 524-6800. *I.* This French Quarter hotel has two pools and complimentary coffee and doughnuts. Free parking. *FP.*

HOTEL STE. HELENE, 508 Chartres, New Orleans 70130; 522-5014; 1-800-348-3888; fax 523-7140. M. In an excellent French Quarter location, this hotel serves a complimentary continental breakfast in its courtyard.

HOTEL VILLA CONVENTO, 616 Ursulines St., New Orleans 70116; 522-1793; fax 524-1902. *I.* This quaint, small French Quarter hotel serves a continental breakfast and is very close to major French Quarter attractions.

HYATT REGENCY NEW ORLEANS, 500 Poydras Plaza, New Orleans 70113; 561-1234; 1-800-233-1234; fax 587-4141. *M to E.* This luxurious AAA four-star hotel is connected to the Superdome and the upscale New Orleans Centre mall. Complimentary shuttle service is provided to and from the riverfront and French Quarter. There is a pool, fitness center, sports bar, and four restaurants and lounges, including the Top of the Dome, which offers spectacular cityscapes from a revolving restaurant. This is one of New Orleans' prime convention facilities. Pay parking. *FP.*

INTERNATIONAL HOUSE HOTEL, 221 Camp St., New Orleans 70130; 553-9550; fax 553-9560; www.Ihhotel.com. *E.* This new elegant and modern hotel with 119 rooms is housed in the original International Trade Association building, the first world trade center in America. The Central Business District location is within walking distance of the World Trade Center, Convention Center, riverfront attractions, Riverwalk and upscale Canal Place shopping malls, and the French Quarter. Facilities include meeting and banquet rooms, full-service restaurant (the delightful Lemon Grass), bar, gift shop, nonsmoking floors, dataports, and fitness center. Some of the special amenities are complimentary continental breakfast, valet parking with 24-hour accessibility, 24-hour concierge, and Jacuzzis in the suites.

LA QUINTA INNS. *I to* M. La Quinta Inns have a national reputation for comfortable, clean rooms, nonsmoking areas, and meeting rooms. They are always near area restaurants and have pools and seniors' discounts. Call 1-800-687-6667.

La Quinta Inn, 301 Camp St., New Orleans 70130; 598-9977. M. Central Business District location near riverfront attractions.

La Quinta Inn Airport, 2610 Williams Blvd., Kenner 70065; 466-1401. *I to* M. Close to New Orleans International Airport, Esplanade Shopping Mall, and Pontchartrain Conference Center.

La Quinta Inn Crowder, 8400 Crowder Blvd. at I-10 Service Road, New Orleans 70127; 246-5800. *I to* M. Located near Louisiana Nature and Science Center, UNO, and Southern University.

La Quinta Inn East, 12001 I-10 Service Road at Bullard exit, New Orleans, 70128; 246-3003. *I to* M. Also located near Louisiana Nature and Science Center, UNO, and Southern University.

La Quinta Inn Metairie, 3100 I-10 Service Rd. at Causeway exit, Metairie 70001; 835-8511. *I to* M. Close to Lakeside and Clearview shopping malls and 20 minutes from the French Quarter.

LAFAYETTE HOTEL, 600 St. Charles Ave., New Orleans 70130; 524-4441; 1-800-733-4754. *E*. This elegant, English-country-style hotel is on the St. Charles Avenue streetcar line. It is also the home of Mike Ditka's Restaurant.

LANDMARK FRENCH QUARTER HOTEL, 920 N. Rampart St., New Orleans 70116; 524-3333; 1-800-535-7862; fax 522-8044. *I*. This intimate hotel on the edge of the French Quarter offers a complimentary Quarter shuttle. The hotel has a lounge and large courtyard with pool. *FP*.

LANDMARK HOTEL, 2601 Severn Ave., Metairie 70002; 888-9500. M. Located near Lakeside Shopping Mall off Causeway and I-10, this hotel has a beautiful ballroom and is popular with seniors' groups. French Quarter transportation is provided. Rooftop lounge with live music overlooks downtown New Orleans.

LE MERIDIEN HOTEL, 614 Canal St., New Orleans 70130; 525-6500; 1-800-543-4300; fax 525-8068. *E*. This casually elegant hotel on the edge of the French Quarter is close to Riverwalk and Canal Place shopping malls, the World Trade Center, and aquarium and IMAX. There's a rooftop pool, health and fitness center, and delightful bistro. *FP.*

LE PAVILLON, 833 Poydras St., New Orleans 70112; 581-3111; 1-800-535-9095; fax 522-5543. *E.* Le Pavillon is the centerpiece of New Orleans' center-of-business avenue, Poydras Street—with the Superdome at one end and the Riverwalk at the other end of this "street of the future." In this chic hotel with European ambience, enjoy spacious rooms or suites, good restaurants, and a heated rooftop swimming pool. There's also a new fitness center, nonsmoking rooms, 24-hour room service, and twice-daily maid service.

LE RICHELIEU HOTEL, 1234 Chartres St., New Orleans 70130; 529-2492; 1-800-535-9653; fax 524-8179. *E.* This elegant apartment hotel in the quiet residential area of the French Quarter is frequented by celebrities. It is just off Esplanade Avenue, with off-street parking provided. The main building is a restored Greek Revival mansion. It offers a lovely pool, patio, restaurant, and lounge.

MAISON DUPUY, 1001 Toulouse St., New Orleans 70112; 586-8000; 1-800-535-9177. *E.* This beautiful, locally owned, small hotel on the edge of the French Quarter features relaxing courtyards, a swimming pool, new fitness center, party and convention facilities, fine restaurant, interesting lounge, and rooms with private balconies. There are tables in the patio for romantic cocktails. The ambience is French Provincial; your stay will be luxurious. Suites with kitchenettes and dining rooms are available. *FP.*

MARRIOTT RESIDENCE INN, 3 Galleria Blvd., Metairie 70001; 832-0888; 1-800-331-3131; fax 832-4916. *M to E.* This new residential-style lodging facility is perfect for extended-stay travelers. This location features spacious suite studios and one- and two-bedroom suites, all with sleeper sofas as well. Suites contain many amenities, like dataports, voicemail, coffeemakers, irons, and ironing boards. Some on-site facilities are a pool, fitness center, and sport court. *FP.*

MONTELEONE HOTEL, 214 Royal St., New Orleans 70140; 523-3341; 1-800-535-9595; fax 528-1019. *M.* The elegant, locally owned Monteleone is in the heart of the French Quarter and offers good restaurants and shopping. A rooftop swimming pool and fitness center overlook the Mississippi River. An on-site lounge and non-smoking rooms are available. *FP.*

NEW ORLEANS MARRIOTT, 555 Canal St., New Orleans 70140; 581-1000; 1-800-228-9290; fax 523-6755. *E*. Towering 41 stories over Canal Street, the Marriott is one of the most popular convention hotels in New Orleans. It is at the beginning of the French Quarter, convenient to major tourist attractions and to public transportation. A pleasant pool area is located between the two hotel towers, and the popular *Riverview Restaurant*, known to the locals for its Sunday brunch, is on top of the hotel and offers a fine view of the city and the river. There are over 100 suites available as well as 80,000 feet of convention/exhibit area. Special convention rates and packages are available at certain times. Pay parking. *FP*.

NINE-O-FIVE ROYAL HOTEL, 905 Royal St., New Orleans 70116; 523-0219. M. Balcony suites with full kitchens are offered here.

OMNI ROYAL ORLEANS HOTEL, 621 St. Louis St., New Orleans 70140; 529-5333; 1-800-843-6664; fax 529-7089. *E*. One of the most elegant hotels in the city and the only Mobil "Four Star" hotel in the French Quarter, the Royal Orleans is a favorite of visitors. The first hotel built on this spot opened in 1936; the current establishment opened in 1960 and initiated a resurgence of restoration and appreciation of the unique quality of the French Quarter. The hotel is a gem which permits only the most tasteful furnishings, the best-trained staff, the finest restaurants, and the freshest flowers. There is a rooftop fitness center and pool area, popular for cocktails as well as swimming, with a view of the Quarter and the river. *FP*.

PALLAS HOTEL, 1732 Canal St., New Orleans 70112; 558-0201; 1-800-236-6119; fax 529-1609. M. Located next to the Central Business District and Tulane and LSU medical centers. Free shuttle service is provided to the nearby French Quarter and Superdome tourist areas, which are next to the New Orleans Centre and Riverwalk shopping malls.

PARK PLAZA INN, 2125 Veterans Blvd., Kenner 70062; 464-6464; 1-800-7275; fax 464-7532. M. Located close to Kenner's historic River Town and museums. Amenities include a pool, exercise room, nonsmoking rooms, and free continental breakfast.

PELHAM HOTEL, 444 Common St., New Orleans 70130; 522-4444; 1-800-659-5621; fax 529-9010. *E*. Located in the Central Business District, one block from the French Quarter, and close to riverfront tourist attractions and shopping. Luxurious rooms include terrycloth robes and English toiletries.

PLACE D'ARMES HOTEL, 625 St. Ann St., New Orleans 70116; 524-4531; 1-800-366-2743; fax 571-2803. M. Just off Jackson Square with on-site parking available, this is a perfect location for touring. Enjoy family accommodations, balconies, ceiling fans, patio, lounge, and free continental breakfast. Exhibit space is available. *FP.*

PLAZA SUITE HOTEL, 620 S. Peters St., New Orleans 70130; 524-9500; 1-800-770-6721; fax 524-2135. *E.* Fully equipped luxury suites are available in this French Quarter hotel within walking distance of riverfront attractions and the Convention Center.

THE PONTCHARTRAIN HOTEL, 2031 St. Charles Ave., New Orleans 70130; 524-0581; 1-800-777-6193; fax 529-1165. *E.* The Pontchartrain is a rare jewel in the world of hotels—a small family-owned hotel, supervised to perfection. Visitors are greeted with flowers and fruit in tastefully appointed rooms and suites. Service is impeccable. The hotel houses one of New Orleans' finest coffee shops, where New Orleanians meet for breakfast and lunch. The *Bayou Bar* is one of the city's favorites. The hotel is world famous and is a favorite stop for celebrities visiting New Orleans. The Pontchartrain is also the home of the famous "Mile High Ice Cream Pie." *FP.*

PRINCE CONTI HOTEL, 830 Conti St., New Orleans 70112; 529-4172; 1-800-366-2743; fax 581-3802. *I.* This quaint, small French Quarter hotel has a restaurant and bar and is close to jazz clubs. *FP.*

PRYTANIA PARK HOTEL, 1525 Prytania St., New Orleans 70130; 524-0427; 1-800-862-1984; fax 522-2977. *I.* This replica of a small European hotel is located in the Garden District on the St. Charles Avenue streetcar line. In-room microwaves and refrigerators and an on-site lunch cafe are offered. *FP.*

QUALITY INNS. *I to* M. This national chain has four conveniently located hotels in and around New Orleans. Senior citizens discounts, corporate and group rates available. Call 1-800-228-5151.

Quality Hotel and Conference Center, 2261 N. Causeway Blvd., Metairie 70001; 833-8211; fax 833-8213. M. Centrally located between the New Orleans Airport and French Quarter with a complimentary shuttle to both. Suites are also available, along with a fitness center, pool, sports bar, and Cajun restaurant. *FP.*

Quality Inn Maison St. Charles, 1319 St. Charles Ave., New Orleans 70130; 522-0187; 1-800-831-1783; fax 529-4379. M. Garden District location on the St. Charles Avenue streetcar line, with complimentary shuttle to the French Quarter and Convention Center. Courtyard, pool, and in-room coffeemakers.

Quality Inn Marina, 5353 Paris Rd., Chalmette 70032; 277-5353. *I*. Located on I-510 at the Gulf Outlet Marina and 20 minutes from the French Quarter. Deluxe rooms and suites, 24-hour cafe, banquet hall, and meeting rooms are available.

Quality Inn—Midtown, 3900 Tulane Ave., New Orleans 70113; 486-5541; 1-800-827-5543; fax 488-7440. *I*. Midtown location close to the Central Business District, Superdome, and New Orleans Centre Shopping Mall, with complimentary shuttle to the Quarter and Convention Center. Also available are a restaurant, lounge, and courtyard with pool and Jacuzzi. *FP*.

QUARTER HOUSE, 129 Chartres, New Orleans 70130; 523-5906; 1-800-736-5906; fax 593-0100. *E*. This hotel offers luxurious one- and two-bedroom suites, with equipped kitchens, whirlpool baths, and Victorian furnishings. The tropical courtyard has a pool.

QUEEN AND CRESCENT HOTEL, 344 Camp St., New Orleans 70130; 587-9700; 1-800-975-NOLA; fax 587-9701. M. This brand-new hotel in the Central Business District is within walking distance of the French Quarter, Riverwalk and Canal Place shopping malls, Convention Center, and riverfront attractions. Amenities include a fitness center, lounge, nonsmoking rooms, and in-room coffeemakers.

RADISSON HOTEL, 1500 Canal St., New Orleans 70112; 522-4500; 1-800-333-3333; fax 525-2644. *E*. This newly renovated hotel in the downtown area is close to riverfront attractions, the Convention Center, and French Quarter, with a free shuttle to the Quarter. Amenities include nonsmoking rooms, a fitness center, rooftop pool, and two restaurants and lounges.

RADISSON INN NEW ORLEANS AIRPORT, 2150 Veterans Blvd., Kenner 70062; 467-3111; fax 467-4634. M. Luxurious hotel in a suburban setting close to the airport, with free airport shuttle. Nonsmoking rooms are available, along with a restaurant, lounge, and outdoor pool.

RAMADA INNS. *I to* M. This moderate-priced motel chain is known for cleanliness, good management, and strategic location. Call 1-800-228-2828.

Ramada Inn, 798 E. I-10 Service Rd., Slidell 70461; 643-9960; fax 643-3508. *I.* This Northshore location also has nonsmoking rooms, on-site laundry, pool, restaurant, and lounge. *FP.*

Ramada Inn—New Orleans Highrise, 6324 Chef Menteur Hwy., New Orleans 70126; 241-2900; fax 241-5697. *I.* This full-service hotel just off I-10 has a lounge and pool. Free parking.

Ramada Limited Causeway, 2713 N. Causeway Blvd., Metairie 70002; 835-4141; fax 833-6942. *I.* This location is 15 minutes from the New Orleans Airport and the French Quarter. Features are nonsmoking rooms, a fitness center, pool, lounge, and free continental breakfast. *FP.*

Ramada Plaza Hotel—St. Charles, 2203 St. Charles Ave., New Orleans 70130; 566-1200; 1-800-443-4675; fax 581-1352. M. This beautiful boutique hotel in the Garden District is on the St. Charles Avenue streetcar line. The streetcar makes it only minutes to the French Quarter, Convention Center, Superdome, Tulane and Loyola universities, Audubon Zoo, and Riverbend. Also available are non-smoking rooms and a full-service restaurant and lounge.

RODEWAY INN GRETNA, 930 Westbank Expwy., Gretna 70053; 366-4311. M. Close to the double-spanned Crescent City Connection. Restaurant, pool, meeting room, and 10 minutes from the New Orleans Central Business District, French Quarter, and riverfront attractions. It is also 5 minutes from the Oakwood Shopping Mall.

ROYAL SONESTA, 300 Bourbon St., New Orleans 70130; 586-0300; fax 586-0335. *E.* A Bourbon Street location puts this grand hotel in the center of all business and tourist attractions. Luxurious suites and rooms with balconies have access to a heated pool and fitness center. There is an on-site gourmet restaurant, oyster bar, and bistro. It is only one block from Royal Street shopping, art galleries, and antique shops. *FP.*

ST. ANN MARIE ANTOINETTE HOTEL, 717 Conti St., New Orleans 70130; 525-2300; 1-800-535-9111; 1-888-535-9111; fax 524-8925. *M to E.* Another hidden treasure in the French Quarter, the St. Ann is a small, luxury hotel in the European tradition with an outdoor pool in the patio and tasteful rooms with balconies.

ST. CHARLES INN, 3636 St. Charles Ave., New Orleans 70115; 899-8888; 1-800-849-9908; fax 899-8892. *M.* The St. Charles Inn is well run and convenient to Tulane and Loyola universities, the Riverbend and Uptown Square shopping areas, Audubon Park and Zoo, and Garden District. It is on the streetcar and Mardi Gras parade routes, and the streetcar takes only minutes to the downtown area. Continental breakfast is provided. On one side of the inn is a restaurant; on the other side is a grill.

THE SAINT LOUIS HOTEL, 730 Bienville St., New Orleans 70130; 581-7300; 1-800-535-9111; 1-888-535-9111; fax 524-8925. *E.* Unsurpassed elegance in a number-one-rated French Quarter courtyard hotel, in the heart of the Quarter. The Saint Louis has been named one of the seven best hotels in New Orleans by Conde Nast. Nonsmoking rooms, valet parking, and a lounge are offered. This is also home to the world-famous and award-winning *Louis XVI* French restaurant. *FP.*

SHERATON NEW ORLEANS HOTEL, 500 Canal St., New Orleans 70130; 525-2500; 1-800-253-6156; fax 595-5550. *E.* A recent $25 million renovation has earned this full-service Central Business District hotel a four-star rating. It is adjacent to the French Quarter and has a pool, fitness center, concierge level, first-floor lounge, and second-floor cigar bar. *FP.*

SHONEY'S INN, 2421 Clearview Pkwy., Metairie 70001; 456-9081; 1-800-222-2222. *I to* M. Located off the I-10 at exit 226. Newly renovated with pool and nonsmoking rooms. Seniors, commercial, and AAA discounts are offered. *Shoney's* restaurant adjoins the inn. *FP.*

SONIAT HOUSE, 1133 Chartres St., New Orleans 70116; 522-0570; 1-800-544-8808; fax 522-7208. *E. Conde Nast Traveler* named this historic 1830s French Quarter townhouse one of the 10 best American small hotels. The *London Tattler* named it one of the 50 best in the world.

TRAVELODGE. *I to* M. Travelodge facilities are known nationwide for moderate prices and locations accessible to airports, tourist attractions, and business areas. Call 1-800-578-7878.

Travelodge Hotel—New Orleans Airport, 2240 Veterans Blvd., Kenner 70062; 469-7341. M. This Travelodge offers a complimentary shuttle to New Orleans Airport just minutes away. It is also 20 minutes from the French Quarter and has an on-site lounge. *FP.*

Travelodge Hotel New Orleans West, 2200 Westbank Expwy., Harvey 70058; 366-5311; fax 368-2274. *I to* M. Newly renovated, this AAA-approved, full-service hotel features a New Orleans-style courtyard and three pools. About 15 minutes from the French Quarter, with free transportation to the river ferry for crossing to major tourist attractions.

WEST BANK TOWER HOTEL, 100 Westbank Expwy., Gretna 70053; 366-8531; fax 362-9502. *I to M*. The Tower Hotel is about 15 minutes from the Central Business District and French Quarter by way of the double-spanned Crescent City Connection over the Mississippi River (avoid peak traffic times). It has a breakfast cafe.

WESTIN CANAL PLACE—HOTEL AND CONFERENCE CENTER, 100 Iberville St., New Orleans 70130; 566-7006; 1-800-228-3000; fax 553-5120. *E*. Completely renovated with spectacular city and Mississippi River views, this hotel is surrounded by the French Quarter, riverfront shopping, and the aquarium and IMAX Theater. A large, new conference center is here as well as a rooftop pool, fitness center, nonsmoking rooms, bar, and excellent restaurant overlooking the river. A hotel entrance to the upscale Canal Place Shopping Mall offers fine shops, small cafes, and a special-features cinema. *FP*.

WINDSOR COURT HOTEL, 300 Gravier St., New Orleans 70130; 523-6000; 1-800-262-2662; fax 596-4513. *E*. This hotel is one of the most elegant and exquisite in the city, and the only one with the AAA five-diamond hotel rating. It is situated in the Central Business District, so tourist attractions and convention facilities are easily accessible. Original artwork and sculptures decorate the hotel. Excellent restaurants and a popular place for traditional English afternoon tea. Lounge, entertainment, pool, health club, Jacuzzi, valet laundry, and parking. *FP*.

WYNDHAM RIVERFRONT HOTEL, 701 Convention Center Blvd., New Orleans 70130; 524-8200; 1-800-WYNDHAM; fax 524-0600. *E*. Brand-new luxury hotel located on the riverfront among all riverfront attractions, across from the Convention Center, and within walking distance of the World Trade Center and the French Quarter. An on-site restaurant and bar add to the convenience. Nonsmoking rooms are available as well as in-room coffeemakers, a fitness center, and business center. *FP*.

YMCA INTERNATIONAL HOTEL, 920 St. Charles Ave., at Lee Circle, New Orleans; 568-9622. *I*. An economical, clean, friendly place to stay, the "Y" is particularly suited to international visitors, families on a budget, and young travelers. The facilities of the YMCA, including gym and pool, are available to guests for a small fee. The YMCA Center is on the St. Charles Avenue streetcar route, on the Mardi Gras parade route, and close to Amtrak and bus terminals. Amenities include referral service, laundromat, tour desk in the lobby, and special Mardi Gras packages. *FP*.

HOTEL SAFETY RULES

As a public-safety service we include in this chapter the following guidance in case of a hotel fire. All information is taken from a publication of the National Safety Council.

Preliminary precautions start after you check into your hotel. Check the exits and fire alarms on your floor, count the doorways between your room and the exit, keep your key close to your bed, and take it with you if you leave your room in case you need to return. In case smoke blocks your exit, check the window latches and any adjoining buildings or decks for low-level escape.

In case of fire, take your key and crawl to the door. Don't stand; smoke and deadly gases rise.

If the doorknob is hot—do not open—stay in your room. Then open the window, phone for help, hang a sheet from the window to signal for help, turn on the bathroom fan, and fill the tub with water. Wet towels and sheets to put around doors if smoke seeps in. Make a tent over your head with a blanket at a partially opened window to get fresh air.

If the doorknob is not hot, leave, close the door to your room, proceed to the exit, counting doorways in the dark, and walk or crawl down to ground level. If blocked at lower levels, turn around, go up to the roof, and keep the roof door open to vent stairwell. Wait for help on the roof.

Do not use elevator. Remember to lie low to avoid smoke and gases.

ALTERNATIVE LODGING

Bed and Breakfast/Guest Houses

Bed and Breakfasts and guest houses have become extremely popular in the last few years. As a result, there have been many new additions to these classifications. Also, there are four agencies that provide complete listings, locations, prices, and available amenities. All accommodations have been carefully evaluated and most are near public transportation, are climate-controlled, and serve a continental breakfast. Tour information is available. Call, write, or fax for information.

AAA RESERVATION SERVICES, B&Bs, COTTAGES, APARTMENTS, 1740 Jackson Ave., New Orleans 70113; 522-1785; fax 566-0405. M. *FP.*

BED AND BREAKFAST ACCESS, LLC RESERVATION SERVICE, P.O. Box 1665, Metairie 70004; 834-7726; 1-888-766-6707; fax 834-2677.

BED & BREAKFAST, INC.—GUESTHOUSE & RESERVATION SERVICE, 1021 Moss St., New Orleans 70152; 488-4640; 1-800-729-4640. *M to E. FP.*

BED AND BREAKFAST OF NEW ORLEANS, 671 Rosa Ave., Metairie 70005; 838-0071.

A CREOLE HOUSE, 1013 St. Ann St., New Orleans 70116; 524-8076. *I.* Rooms include private bath, telephone, double beds, and period furnishings. Continental breakfast is served. Deposit is required with reservation; parking is on-street.

CLAIBORNE MANSION, 2111 Dauphine St., New Orleans 70116; 949-7327; 1-800-449-7327. *E.* This historic Greek Revival mansion has seven rooms and suites and a long-term-stay cottage. The uniquely decorated house exudes quiet elegance. The lush courtyard has a pool and waterfall. Amenities include complete breakfast, evening hors d'oeuvres, and cocktails.

CORNSTALK HOTEL, 915 Royal St., New Orleans 70116; 523-1515. M. Behind the famous cast-iron fence sits this pleasant guest house offering antique furnished rooms, with complimentary continental breakfast and morning newspaper served on the gallery overlooking Royal Street. Off-street parking is available.

DEGAS HOUSE, 2306 Esplanade Ave., New Orleans 70119; 821-5009; 1-800-755-6730; fax 821-0870. M. This historic house was French artist Edgar Degas's home during his 19th-century New Orleans visit. Complimentary tours and Creole breakfast are included. Located just minutes away from the New Orleans Museum of Art in City Park and from the French Quarter. *FP.*

DIXIE QUEEN BED & BREAKFAST, U.S. 90 at U.S. 190, Slidell 70459; 649-1255; 1-800-875-4287. M. This very interesting B&B offers a unique stay on a large river tugboat transformed into a houseboat with three comfortable rooms. Permanently docked at the edge of Honey Island Swamp, it is convenient to New Orleans and the Mississippi Gulf Coast.

DUVIGNEAUD HOUSE, 2859 Grand Route St. John, New Orleans 70119; 821-5009; 1-800-755-6730; fax 821-0870. M. On the National Historic Register, this restored 1834 French-style plantation home has spacious suites with full kitchens and cable TV and private courtyard. This house is just minutes from the New Orleans Museum of Art and the French Quarter.

ESPLANADE VILLA, 2216 Esplanade Ave. at Bayou Road, New Orleans 70119; 525-7040; 1-800-308-7040; fax 525-9760. *E*. This villa offers suites with Italianate detail and period furnishings, and all with cable TV, guest bar, and fridge. Other amenities are a gourmet breakfast and free parking. Located just minutes from the New Orleans Museum of Art and the French Quarter.

GIROD HOUSE, 835 Esplanade Ave., New Orleans 70116; 522-5214; 1-800-650-3323; fax 522-7208. M. This unique example of Creole architecture was built in 1833. It is impeccably restored, with all suites furnished with antiques. Breakfast is included.

LA MAISON GUEST HOUSE, 608 Kerlerec St., New Orleans 70116; 271-0228; 1-800-307-7179; fax 271-0228. M. This lovely 1805 Creole cottage is just three blocks from the French Quarter.

LAFITTE GUEST HOUSE, 1003 Bourbon St., New Orleans 70116; 581-2678; fax 581-2677. *M to E*. One block down Bourbon Street from pirate Jean Lafitte's famous Blacksmith Shop (now a well-known New Orleans bar) is Lafitte Guest House, a peaceful retreat in a historic French Quarter house, complete with courtyard, balconies, and continental breakfast. Free parking.

LAMOTHE HOUSE, 621 Esplanade Ave., New Orleans 70116; 947-1161; fax 943-6536. *Summer* M, *Winter E*. This meticulously restored antebellum home on what was once "the" street for Creole families contains period furnishings such as beautifully canopied beds and huge armoires. Complimentary breakfast is served in the formal dining room. There are numerous good restaurants in the neighborhood. Free parking.

MELROSE, 937 Esplanade Ave. at Burgundy Street, New Orleans 70116; 944-2255. *E*. This splendidly restored 1884 mansion on the edge of the French Quarter offers elegant double rooms and suites with a tropically landscaped courtyard with swimming pool. Standard amenities include limousine pickup at the airport, full breakfast, and evening cocktails and hors d'oeuvres.

THE OLD WORLD INN, 1330 Prytania St., New Orleans 70130; 566-1330; fax 566-1074. *I*. The Old World Inn offers an intimate, personal atmosphere with individually decorated rooms and gracious attention to the needs of its patrons. The Inn is one block from the St. Charles Avenue streetcar. Student rates are available.

OLIVIER HOUSE, 828 Toulouse St., New Orleans 70112; 525-8456. M. Next door to the site of the Old French Opera House, the house was built in 1836 by a music lover who wanted to be as close as possible to the opera. Enjoy fine individually decorated period rooms, some with kitchenettes, a restful courtyard with pool, and nearby parking.

PARK VIEW GUEST HOUSE, 7004 St. Charles Ave., New Orleans 70118; 861-7564; fax 861-1225. *I to* M. A beautiful Victorian home on the National Register of Historic Landmarks, this guest house is just across from Audubon Park, one block from Tulane and Loyola universities, and close to the free shuttle to the Zoo and Uptown Square and Riverbend shopping areas. The streetcar stops at the front door for a pleasant 20-minute ride to the French Quarter. Furnished with antiques, some rooms have balconies and some have connecting baths. Continental breakfast is served. Weekly rates are available.

ROSE MANOR INN, 7214 Pontchartrain Blvd., New Orleans 70124; 282-8200; fax 282-7283; www.rosemanor.com. M. This beautiful, antique-furnished bed and breakfast inn is located in an 1899 Lakefront-area mansion. Breakfast is served in an elegant, well-appointed dining room. Fresh fruit is available all day, and there is a happy hour for guests in the evening. There are six restaurants within a two-block radius of the inn. Separate sitting rooms and parlors are available for that special meeting. Rooms and suites are spacious, and the environment is very welcoming. *FP*.

ROSEWALK HOUSE, 320 Verret St., New Orleans 70114; 368-1500. *I*. Located in a National Historic neighborhood and close to the free ferry across the Mississippi River to the French Quarter and the CBD, this house has nonsmoking rooms, a courtyard, and airport transportation.

ST. CHARLES GUEST HOUSE, 1748 Prytania St., New Orleans 70130; 523-6556; fax 522-6340. *I to* M. Another of the delightful, affordable, husband-and-wife-run guest houses appearing in the Lower Garden District, the St. Charles is one block from the St. Charles Avenue streetcar and also has bicycles available for rent. Guests are provided with a front door key so they can come and go at will. They are invited to enjoy the pool and patio area. Continental breakfast is served each morning.

ST. PETER GUEST HOUSE, 1005 St. Peter St., New Orleans 70116; 524-9232; 1-800-535-7815. M. On the edge of the French Quarter, this 1850s townhouse with former slave quarters has been elegantly restored. Rooms have private baths and balconies facing street or courtyard. Decor is Victorian. Parking is on-street.

SULLY MANSION—GARDEN DISTRICT, 2631 Prytania St., New Orleans 70130; 891-0457. M. This charming circa-1890 mansion is in the heart of the Garden District. It is close to the St. Charles Avenue streetcar line for short rides to the Central Business District, French Quarter, or farther uptown to the University and Riverbend areas.

SWEET OLIVE GUEST HOUSE, 2460 N. Rampart St., New Orleans 70117; 947-4332. M. In historic Faubourg Marigny, these are quaint Creole cottages transformed into a lovely Bed and Breakfast. Each room is painted by a local artist to reflect the natural environs of New Orleans, such as the Magnolia Room. The guest house is within walking distance of the French Quarter.

Campgrounds

There are several campgrounds located within the city limits. They are all close to the intersection of I-10 East and Highway 90 (Chef Menteur Highway), about 15 minutes from downtown and the French Quarter, close to public transportation. All have sightseeing tours available.

MARDI GRAS CAMP GROUND, 6050 Chef Menteur Hwy., New Orleans 70126; 243-0085. *I*. This campground has showers, laundry, game room, swimming pool, and full hook-ups. It is also across the street from a public bus stop.

PARC D'ORLEANS CAMPGROUNDS, 7676 Chef Menteur Hwy., New Orleans 70126; 244-7434. *I*. Parking is available for motor homes, travel trailers, campers, and tents.

RIVERBOAT TRAVEL PARK, 6232 Chef Menteur Hwy., New Orleans 70126; 246-2628. *I*. Laundry and shower, pool, and game room are amenities.

For information on rates on motor home parking downtown, contact: **Allright Parking,** 522-9434; **Dixie Parking Service,** 523-4521; **Downtown Parking Service, Inc.,** 529-5708; **Superdome Parking,** 587-3663.

For campgrounds on the outskirts of the city we recommend the following:

FONTAINEBLEAU STATE PARK, Highway 190, Mandeville 70448; 624-4443. *I.* Trailer hook-ups, tent camping are on a first-come, first-served basis. There is also area reserved for Scout camping. This state park is on the north shore of Lake Pontchartrain, across the Causeway from New Orleans. Good restaurants are nearby. Fees are nominal.

KOA, Highway 433, Slidell; 643-3850.

KOA West, 11129 Jefferson Hwy., River Ridge 70123; 467-1792. *I.* Close to Kenner's River Town and all its museums and attractions.

YOGI BEAR'S JELLYSTONE PARK CAMP RESORT, Robert 70455; 542-1507; 1-800-558-2954. *I.* Accommodations include cabins, A-frames, facilities for motor homes, campers, and tent camping. Extras for kids of all ages include the waterslide, minigolf, paddleboats, canoes, skating rink, tubing, and special events. Ask about special rates. Exit 47 off I-12.

Hostels

MARQUETTE HOUSE NEW ORLEANS INTERNATIONAL HOSTEL, 2253 Carondelet St., off Jackson Avenue, New Orleans 70130; 523-3014; 1-800-909-4776 (Access Code: 09); fax 529-5933. *I.* An International Hostel one block from the St. Charles Avenue streetcar, Marquette House opens at 7 am and closes at 11 pm for check-ins. It is inexpensive, clean, and popular with young travelers.

RESORTS

The Mississippi Gulf Coast, the traditional family playground of New Orleanians, is just an hour's drive from New Orleans. The drive on U.S. Highway 90 from Bay St. Louis to Ocean Springs is one of the most beautiful in the United States. It is lined on one side with gracious homes, lovingly passed from one generation to another, and, on the other, with the beach and the waters of the Mississippi Sound. The beach is open to the public. There are also historic sites to visit, good restaurants, and boat trips to the barrier islands in the sound.

In the last few years, the official approval of Mississippi gambling has caused the Gulf Coast to become the hub of that state's tourist and gambling industries, and there has been a resort and casino building boom. There are now more nightlife spots, stage shows, big-name acts, boxing matches, places to eat, hotels, and resorts than ever before.

PRESIDENT CASINO—BROADWATER RESORT—GOLF CLUB & MARINA, 2110 W. Beach Blvd., Biloxi, MS 39533; 1-800-THE-PRES. *E*. This has been a traditionally popular resort for New Orleanians, for honeymoons, family trips, and boating. The Broadwater also features excellent tennis, golf, and swimming.

For additional Mississippi Gulf Coast information, call toll free 1-888-1-MS-GULF.

DINING

Food in New Orleans is a mixture of genius, tradition, romance, and creativity.

For most of its history, the city has held as tightly to its food traditions as it has to those concerning all other phases of the city's life. The original cuisine was, of course, French, but it was quickly mixed with the indigenous American Indian, which introduced filé, local seafoods, and native wild game. The Spanish added their lively flavors and colors, the Africans their new words (gumbo, okra) and thick stews, and the Cajuns their hot peppers, soups, and inventive seafood dishes (including alligator).

In general, the Creole is considered the more elegant city cooking, while the Cajun, although far more exotic than most local foods, is considered the "down-home" cooking of the country area. Recently, with the growth of the city and an influx of young Parisian-trained chefs introducing the "nouvelle cuisine," as well as restaurateurs from the world over, the restaurant scene has become considerably more cosmopolitan.

Be aware that there are more good restaurants in New Orleans than we can possibly list. These are some favorites.

Explore, enjoy, and leave your diet at home!

All categories below are based on an appetizer, entree, and dessert:

E—Expensive, over $30 per person.
M—Moderate, $15-30 per person.
I—Inexpensive, under $15 per person.
CS—Children's Specials.

The Children's Specials (CS) designation means everything from special children's menus, to table covers to draw and color on, to restaurant-inspired coloring books and pages, to masks and hats to make and color (all with containers of crayons provided). To find out more about these specials, see the CHILDREN chapter.

FOOD—ITS OWN LANGUAGE

You can get along without speaking French or Spanish in New Orleans, but you cannot reap the full enjoyment of your visit without learning the most useful language of all—*food*.

We will provide you with a working vocabulary. As you match each word with its own taste experience, the meaning will be imprinted indelibly and joyously in your mind. You will find it to be a tantalizing unforgettable language. Permit us to give you a first lesson.

Alligator—Popular in New Orleans in stews and soups as well as on shirts and sweaters. Try it—it's good! One of the most popular dishes served at the Jazz and Heritage Festival in the spring is Alligator Sauce Piquante.

Alligator pear—New Orleans' name for avocado, perhaps because of its green, bumpy skin.

Andouille—A hard, smoked, Cajun country sausage, good in gumbo or with eggs for breakfast and also great on an outdoor grill.

Beignets—Delectable square French doughnuts, fried in deep fat just until they puff into little golden-brown pillows, then covered with powdered sugar and served piping hot for the gods! Plan more than one stop at Cafe du Monde (at the Moon Walk end of the French Market) to enjoy coffee and doughnuts. Any time of day or night will do.

Bisque—A thick, spicy soup somewhere between a chowder and a gumbo.

Blackened—Take this term literally. Fillets of fish or fowl are specially seasoned, then allowed to blacken on both sides in a highly heated iron skillet.

Boudin—A Cajun sausage filled with anything from meat to crawfish, mixed with rice, and temptingly seasoned.

Bouillabaisse—Originally from Marseilles, the Louisiana version of this seafood delight is spicy and well laced with wine.

Cafe au lait—A half and half mixture of chicory coffee and rich, hot milk poured into the cup simultaneously, mixing thoroughly.

Cafe brulot—A potent after-dinner delight consisting of strong coffee and spices, laced with brandy, ignited at tableside, and served in special brulot cups.

Chicory—The root of the endive (most of it in the United States comes from Michigan) added to dark-roast coffee to make the Creole's favorite blend. Stories relate that chicory was first added to coffee during the Civil War because coffee was scarce. Most Creole coffee is made in a drip pot; real purists drip it slowly, sometimes spoonful-by-spoonful, until it is strong enough to "stand up without the cup."

Cocktail—One day in the early 1800s, a New Orleans pharmacist named Peychaud, whose establishment was at 437 Royal St., put together a tasty little drink that combined brandy and bitters. Needing something just the right size to serve it in, he seized upon an egg cup, *coquetier* in French. The Americans, who were just arriving on the scene, tried valiantly to pronounce the French word, but the closest they could get was "cocktail." Little did Mr. Peychaud or those Americans realize what they were starting! Peychaud's bitters is still used by New Orleanians for mixing their most special cocktails and sauces.

Court bouillon—A sumptuous stew of fish with tomatoes and spices served either with rice, or in a bowl with French bread as an accompaniment.

Crawfish—Looks like an immature lobster and is just as delicious, cooked in a variety of ways—bisque (a thick, highly seasoned soup), étouffée (a spicy stew served over rice), or boiled. The word is pronounced "crawfish"—to say it any other way immediately labels you as an outsider—as bad as saying "prayleen" instead of "prahleen."

Creole cream cheese—Similar to "clabber" or "pot cheese," it is sold in cartons in the dairy section of some grocery stores. It is delicious eaten with sugar and milk for breakfast or lunch, and is also used to make "frozen cream cheese," a popular local dessert.

Creole mustard—A spicy brown mustard, great on po' boy sandwiches and a necessary ingredient to a really good remoulade sauce. Take a jar of Zatarain's home with you!

Crepe—A light, thin French pancake, usually rolled and filled. They can be a main dish or a dessert. Crepes Suzettes is a festive way to end a New Orleans meal.

Dirty rice—Cooked in a heavy iron frying pan or Dutch oven, the rice is cooked in meat stock and seasoned with chicken livers, bits of meat, onions, garlic, and spices.

Doberge—An eight- or nine-layer cake, combining delicate buttery layers of gold cake with custard fillings, all covered by a creamy icing. This is New Orleans' favorite birthday cake. Small individual doberges are almost always served at teas and receptions.

Filé—Powdered leaves or dried sassafras first used in Louisiana by the Choctaw Indians. It is often used as a thickener for chicken gumbo.

Frog legs—Served in local restaurants fried in batter or sauteed in butter. There are "frog farms" in south Louisiana that pride themselves on the size and quality of the frogs' legs that they make available to seafood markets and restaurants.

Grillades—A local favorite for breakfast or dinner, made of round steak simmered until fork tender in a well-seasoned gravy.

Grits au gratin—Grits, that staple Southern accompaniment for eggs or grillades, is lifted to a new height when, after being boiled as usual, it is mixed with cheese, eggs, and a little garlic, and baked like a soufflé.

Gumbo—A thick, magnificently spiced soup made with seafood and/or chicken and sausage.

Jambalaya—An important Creole dish, made in an iron skillet, combining seafood, rice, ham or sausage, and the chef's choice of herbs and spices.

King cake—A ring-shaped cake, made of a yeast dough, decorated in Mardi Gras-colored sugar, and containing a bean or plastic baby. Whoever finds this prize in their piece of cake is the king or queen, and must have the next king cake party.

Make groceries—A colloquialism meaning "to go to the grocery," a literal translation from the French.

Mirliton—A pale green, pear-shaped member of the squash family, good either scalloped or stuffed.

Muffulettas—A large sandwich made on round Italian bread and filled with ham, Italian sausage, salami, mozzarella or provolone, and a marinated green olive salad. Half a muffuletta is a full meal. We recommend buying muffulettas at the Central Grocery (with maybe a piece of their delicious Greek baklava for dessert) or Progress Grocery and taking them to Jackson Square, the Moon Walk, Woldenberg Park, or on the Canal Street ferry for a picnic lunch.

Okra—A green pod-type vegetable usually used as a thickener in seafood gumbo.

Oyster loaf—A po' boy filled with fried oysters.

Pain perdu—Literally "lost bread," the local version of French toast.

Pecans—The last syllable of which is locally pronounced to rhyme with "on" rather than "an." Grown locally, these nutmeats are popular in Creole cooking..

Po' boys—Also known as poor boys. These are French bread sandwiches filled with anything from roast beef to fried oysters to soft-shell crabs. They come either "dressed" (with lettuce, tomato, mayonnaise, pickles) or "undressed" (either plain or buttered bread only). Most restaurants will sell you either a whole or a half po' boy.

Pompano—The fish that Mark Twain describes as "delicious as the less criminal forms of sin," often served baked in a paper bag (en Papillotte).

Praline—The first syllable of this word rhymes with "ma" not "may." This is a sugar and nut candy which, to be perfect, must be poured out on a marble slab to cool. It is the perfect ending to a Creole feast.

Red beans and rice—The national dish of South Louisiana, an integral part of the culture. In New Orleans, it is traditionally served on Monday. The red kidney beans are soaked overnight, then cooked slowly for hours with onions, garlic, bay leaf, pepper, and a ham bone and/or andouille. Every cook has his/her own version and there are endless conversations on the nuances of seasonings and methods of cooking. The beans are served over steamed rice.

Roux—The base for most Creole and Cajun gravies, sauces, and stews, made from a flour and fat mixture which is browned *very slowly* in an iron skillet. The ability to make a good roux is a main criterion by which Creole cooks are judged.

Snoball—New Orleans' favorite summer treat, a paper carton (choose your size) filled with shaved ice and your choice of a variety of delicious and colorful syrups.

Soft-shell crabs—Crabs which have just shed their hard shells, delicious boiled or fried, edible down to the last delicious claw (you eat the whole thing—do not try to remove the meat from shell). This is truly a gourmet delight!

Soupcon—A little bit, a small serving.

Trout meuniere—A tasty white fish, broiled or sauteed, and topped with a delicately seasoned brown butter sauce.

Turtle soup—A dark rich soup made with turtle meat and herbs, garnished with lemon slices and grated hard-boiled egg, and liberally laced with dry sherry.

RESTAURANTS BY AREA

CENTRAL BUSINESS/ WAREHOUSE DISTRICTS

Bailey's, American, M.
Bizou, French, M.
Bon Ton Cafe, Cajun, M.
Canal Place Food Court, Etcetera, *I*.
Christino's, Nouvelle Cuisine, M *to* E.
Emeril's, Nouvelle Cuisine, E.
Grill Room, Continental, E.
La Gauloise Bistro, Creole, M.
Le Petit Paris, French, M.
Michaul's, Cajun, M.
Mike Ditka's Restaurant, American, E.
Mother's, American, *I*.
Mulate's, Cajun, M.
New Orleans Centre Food Court, Etcetera, *I*.
Palace Cafe, Nouvelle Cuisine, M.
Praline Connection, Soul Food, M.
Riverview, Continental, M *to* E.
Riverwalk Food Court, Etcetera, *I*.
Sapphire, Continental, M *to* E.
Sazerac, Creole, M *to* E.
Smith and Wollensky, American, M *to* E.
Taqueria Corona, Mexican, *I*.
Top of the Dome, American, M *to* E.
Veranda, Regional, M.

CHALMETTE

Barrister's, Regional, *I to* M.
Bean Pot, Mexican, *I*.
Bubba John's, Regional, *I to* M.
China Ruby, Asian, M.
Franklin's Grill, American, *I*.
Piccadilly Cafeteria, Cafeteria, *I*.

Rocky and Carlo's, Italian, *I*.
Shoney's, American, *I*.
Styxx Asian Grille, Asian, *I to* M.

FAUBOURG MARIGNY

Cafe Brasil, Etcetera, *I*.
Feelings Cafe, Nouvelle Cuisine, M.
Flora's Coffee Cafe, Etcetera, *I*.
Jack Dempsey's Uptown Downtown Restaurant, Regional, *I to* M.
Mandich's, Regional, M.
P.J.'s, Etcetera, *I*.
Praline Connection, Soul Food, M.
Santa Fe, Mexican, *I to* M.
Snug Harbor, American, *I to* M.

FRENCH QUARTER

Acme Oyster House, Seafood, *I*.
Alex Patout's, Cajun, M.
Alpine, American, *I to* M.
Antoine's, French, M *to E*.
Arnaud's, French, M *to E*.
Bacco's, Italian, M.
Bayona, Nouvelle Cuisine, M *to E*.
Begue's, Continental, M *to E*.
Bella Luna, Italian, M *to E*.
Bistro at Maison de Ville, Nouvelle Cuisine, M *to E*.
Brennan's, Creole, M *to E*.
Broussard's, Creole, *E*.
Cafe du Monde, Etcetera, *I*.
Cafe Giovanni, Italian, M.
Cafe Maspero, American, *I*.
Cafe Sbisa, French, M.
Central Grocery, Etcetera, *I*.
Court of Two Sisters, Creole, M *to E*.
Crescent City Brewhouse, Regional, M.
Croissant d'Or, Etcetera, *I*.
Dickie Brennan's Steakhouse, American, *E*.
Felix's, Seafood, *I*.
Galatoire's, French, M *to E*.
Gumbo Shop, Creole, *I to* M.
Haagen Dazs Ice Cream Cafe, Etcetera, *I*.
Hard Rock Cafe, American, *I to* M.
House of Blues, American, *I to* M.
Jax Brewery Food Court, Etcetera, *I*.
Jimmy Buffett's Margaritaville Cafe, Etcetera, M.
K-Paul's, Cajun, M *to E*.
La Madeleine's, Etcetera, *I*.
La Marquise, Etcetera, *I*.
Landry's Seafood House, Seafood, M.
Louis XVI, French, *E*.
Lucky Cheng's, Asian, M.
Mike Anderson's, Seafood, M *to E*.
Mr. B's Bistro, Creole, M *to E*.
Napoleon House, American, *I to* M.
NOLA, Nouvelle Cuisine, M.
Old Coffee Pot, Creole, *I*.
Old Dog, New Trick, Vegetarian, *I*.
Original Papa Joe's, Regional, *I*.
Palm Court Jazz Cafe, Creole, M.
Panda's RiverView, Asian, *I to* M.
Patout's, Cajun, M.
Pelican Club, Nouvelle Cuisine, M.
Peristyle, Nouvelle Cuisine, *E*.
Petunia's Restaurant, Regional, M.
Planet Hollywood, Regional, M.

Progress Grocery, Etcetera, *I*.
Quarter Scene, Regional, M.
Ralph and Kacoo's, Seafood, M.
Red Fish Grill, Seafood, *E*.
Remoulade, Regional, *I*.
Rib Room, American, *E*.
Riverbend Grill, Continental, *E*.
Rue deLa Course, Etcetera, *I*.
Sclafani's, Nouvelle Cuisine, M.
Tony Moran's Italian Cuisine, Italian, M.
Tortorici's, Italian, M *to E*.
Tujague's, Creole, *E*.
Vera Cruz, Mexican, *I*.

LAKEFRONT

Amberjack's, Seafood, M.
Barataria, Seafood, M.
Breakwater, Regional, M.
Bruning's, Seafood, *I*.
Chateau Coffee Cafe, Etcetera, *I*.
China Rose, Asian, *I to* M.
Chinese King, Asian, *I*.
Deanie's, Seafood, *I to* M.
Fitzgerald's, Seafood, *I*.
Hong Kong, Asian, *I to* M.
Jaeger's, Seafood, *I to* M.
Joe's Crab Shack, Seafood, *I to* M.
La Cuisine's, Creole, M.
Lakeview Harbor, American, *I*.
Lovecchio's, Etcetera, *I*.
Midnight Star, Regional, *I*.
Plantation Coffeehouse, American, *I*.
R & O's Pizza Place, Italian, *I*.
Russell's Marina Grill, American, *I*.
Sidmar's, Seafood, *I*.
Steak Knife, Continental, *I to* M.
Tarby's Gourmet to Go, Etcetera, M.
Tony Angelo's, Italian, *I to* M.

LOWER ST. CHARLES

Cafe Pontchartrain, American, *I to* M.
Commander's Palace, Creole, *E*.
Delmonico's, Creole, M.
Houston's, American, *I to* M.
Kung's Dynasty, Asian, M *to E*.
Red Room, American, M.
Rue deLa Course, Etcetera, *I*.
Shoney's, American, *I*.
Straya's, Cajun, *I to* M.
Swiss Confectionery, Etcetera, M *to E*.
Uglesich's, Seafood, *I*.

METAIRIE

A & G Cafeteria, Cafeteria, *I*.
Andrea's, Italian, M *to E*.
Brick Oven Cafe, Italian, M.
Charlie G's, Nouvelle Cuisine, M *to E*.
Chili's, American, *I*.
Chuck E. Cheese, Etcetera, .
Copeland's, Cajun, M.
Crozier's, French, *E*.
Cuco's, Mexican, *I to* M.
Don's Seafood Hut, Seafood, M *to E*.
Esplanade Mall Food Court, Etcetera, *I*.
Foodies Kitchen, Deli and Cafe, Etcetera, *I*.
Golden Dragon, Asian, *I*.
Houston's, American, *I*.
La Madeleine's, Etcetera, *I*.
Lakeside Mall Food Court, Etcetera, *I*.
Martin Wine Cellar & Cafe, Etcetera, M *to E*.
Morning Call, Etcetera, *I*.
Pancho's, Mexican, *I*.
Piccadilly Cafeteria, Cafeteria, *I*.

Ralph and Kacoo's, Seafood, *I to* M.
Ruth's Chris Steak House, American, *E*.
Salvatore Ristorante, Italian, M.
Shogun, Asian, *I to* M.
Shoney's, American, *I*.
Sid-Mar's, Seafood, *I to* M.
Straya's, Cajun, *I to* M.
Swensen's, Etcetera, *I*.
Taj Mahal Indian Cuisine, Indian, *I*.
Taqueria Corona, Mexican, *I*.
Trauth's Lake House and Steamery, Seafood, *I*.

MID CITY

Angelo Brocato's, Etcetera, *I*.
Cafe Degas, Nouvelle Cuisine, M.
Chinese Kitchen, Asian, *I*.
Christian's, Creole, M *to E*.
Deutsches-Haus, German, *I to* M.
Dooky Chase, Soul Food, *I*.
Five Happiness Restaurant, Asian, *I*.
Gabrielle Restaurant, Creole, M.
Genghis Khan, Asian, *I to* M.
Lemon Grass Cafe, Asian, *I*.
Liuzza's, Creole, *I*.
Lola's, Spanish, *I to* M.
Mandina's, Creole, *I*.
Mona's Cafe & Deli, Middle Eastern, *I to* M.
New York Pizza, Italian, *I*.
Palmer's, Jamaican, *I*.
Piccadilly Cafeteria, Cafeteria, *I*.
Pizza Roma, Italian, *I*.
P.J.'s, Etcetera, *I*.
Ruth's Chris Steak House, American, *E*.
Semolina, Italian, M.
Shoney's, American, *I*.
Tavern on the Park, Nouvelle Cuisine, M.
Whole Foods Market, Etcetera, *I*.
Ye Olde College Inn, American, *I*.

NEW ORLEANS EAST/GENTILLY

Bally's All American Buffet, American, *I*.
East China, Asian, *I*.
Eddie's Restaurant and Bar, Soul Food, *I*.
Flight Deck Restaurant, American, *I*.
Jade East, Asian, *I*.
Kim Anh, Asian, *I*.
Sclafani's, Italian, *I to* M.

NORTH SHORE

Abita Brew Pub, Etcetera, *I*.
Abita Quail Farm, Regional, M *to E*.
Artesia, Nouvelle Cuisine, *E*.
Bechac's, Regional, M.
Benedict's, Creole, M.
Copeland's, Cajun, *I to* M.
Cracker Barrel, American, *I*.
Dakota's, Regional, M *to E*.
La Provence, French, *E*.
Trey Yuen, Asian, *I to* M.

UPTOWN

Back to the Garden, Vegetarian, *I*.
Brigtsen's, Creole, M.
Cafe Atchafalaya, Seafood, *I to* M.
Camellia Grill, American, *I*.
Casamento's, Seafood, *I to* M.
Charlie's Steak House, American, M.

Chef's Table, Nouvelle Cuisine, M.
Clancy's, Nouvelle Cuisine, M *to* E.
Copeland's, Cajun, M.
Cuco's, Mexican, *I to* M.
Franky and Johnny's, Creole, *I*.
Gautreau's, Nouvelle Cuisine, *I to* M.
Haagen Dazs Ice Cream Cafe, Etcetera, *I*.
Jacques-Imo Cafe, Creole, *I*.
Kelsey's, Nouvelle Cuisine, M *to* E.
Kokopelli's, American, *I*.
Kyoto, Asian, M.
La Madeleine's, Etcetera, *I*.
Louisiana Pizza Kitchen, Italian, *I to* M.
Martin Wine Cellar & Cafe, Etcetera, M *to E*.
New York Pizza, Italian, *I*.
Parasol's, Irish, *I*.
Pascal's Manale, Italian, M *to E*.
P.J.'s, Etcetera, *I*.
Rue deLa Course, Etcetera, *I*.
Semolina, Italian, M.
Taqueria Corona, Mexican, *I*.
The Upperline, Nouvelle Cuisine, M.

WEST BANK

China Doll, Asian, *I*.
Copeland's, Cajun, *I to* M.
Kim Son, Asian, *I to* M.
Louisiana Pizza Kitchen, Italian, *I to* M.
Mosca's, Italian, M.
Oakwood Center Food Court, Etcetera, *I*.
Pho Tau Bay Restaurant, Asian, *I*.
Piccadilly Cafeteria, Cafeteria, *I*.
Pupuseria Divino Corazon Restaurant, Mexican, *I*.
Shoney's, American, *I*.
Visko's, Seafood, M *to E*.

RESTAURANTS

American

Alpine, 620 Chartres St.; 523-3005. *I to* M. Casual dining in a quaint French Quarter environment, with very good food and helpful staff. CS.

Bailey's, Fairmont Hotel, 123 Baronne St.; 529-7111. M. This cozy bistro is a great late-night place for dinner or a snack. Casual patrons sit next to the more formal symphony and theater crowd, and everyone enjoys good New Orleans food and great cheeseburgers.

Bally's All American Buffet, 1 Stars and Stripes Blvd.; 248-3200. *I*. An incredible buffet! It features American and regional dishes with chicken, seafood, and beef; a variety of vegetables and salads; and an unbelievably large dessert bar. The restaurant building is totally separate from the casino boat. Breakfast, lunch, and dinner daily. CS.

Cafe Maspero, 440 Chartres; 524-8990. *I.* This quaint French Quarter cafe features overstuffed, world-famous po' boys and muffulettas seven days a week. Their breakfasts are also noted for generous portions. There's usually a line, but the wait is well rewarded. Casual.

Cafe Pontchartrain, Pontchartrain Hotel, 2031 St. Charles Ave.; 524-0581. *I to M.* Located on beautiful St. Charles Avenue in the Pontchartrain Hotel, this dining spot is just to the left of the hotel entrance. It is very popular for breakfast with the local business people, lunch with friends, and dinner with neighborhood residents. The Pontchartrain's famous blueberry muffins, piping hot and tasty, are a great addition to each meal. Lunch and dinner daily. Casual.

Camellia Grill, 626 S. Carrollton Ave.; 866-9573. *I.* The St. Charles street car stops almost in front of this favorite counter-top eating spot. The grill is always a New Orleans tradition with the university crowd and late-night stop for people on the go. Delicious burgers and large fancy sandwiches are served by friendly waiters dressed in white jackets and black ties. Try the orange or chocolate freeze and one of the fresh baked pies or cheesecakes. Crisp linen napkins are a trademark. Breakfast, lunch, and dinner daily. Very casual. No credit cards.

Charlie's Steak House, 4510 Dryades St.; 895-9705 or 895-9323. M. Charlie's is one of New Orleans' oldest and most popular steak houses. Dining is casual with emphasis on steaks rather than decor. Large steaks are served on hot sizzling platters, overflowing with fries or onion rings. Desserts and salads with blue cheese dressing are enough to satisfy any hungry lion. Lunch and dinner Tue-Sat.

Chili's, 4201 Veterans Blvd., Metairie; 885-1381. *I.* A cheerful, well-decorated restaurant with a varied menu. The different dining areas make this great for dates as well as families. CS.

Cracker Barrel, 790 I-10 East Service Rd.; 645-9631. *I.* Good country cooking for a family dining experience in a truly hospitable atmosphere. A unique gift shop connected to the restaurant is filled with goodies that adults and children will enjoy. CS.

Dickie Brennan's Steakhouse, 716 Iberville St.; 522-CHOP (2467); www.dbrennanssteakhouse.com. *E.* A steakhouse to rival all steakhouses, and only as a Brennan could accomplish. Only the best,

USDA prime steaks are served with a New Orleans touch. The ambience is elegant and the service excellent. Lunch and dinner daily.

Flight Deck Restaurant, Lakefront Airport, 6001 Stars and Stripes Blvd.; 241-2561. *I.* One entire wall of this restaurant is glass and faces the runway strips, offering a view of planes landing and taking off. A casual restaurant serving breakfast and lunch daily. Consistently good food, and extremely friendly and helpful staff. CS.

Franklin's Grill, 1515 E. Judge Perez Dr., Chalmette; 277-4007. *I.* Casual dining with really good food, and wonderful salad and baked potato bar. Lunch and dinner daily; friendly and helpful staff. CS.

Hard Rock Cafe, 440 N. Peter St.; 529-5617. *I to* M. Popular chain restaurant serving generous helpings of loud, taped rock music with music memorabilia on the walls. In addition to their huge burgers and good onion rings, there are daily fish specials. Daily 11:30 am to midnight. CS.

House of Blues, 225 Decatur St.; 529-2583. *I to* M. This outlet of the national chain is located in historic buildings with lots of character. The menu is varied and the food is good. Lunch and dinner daily. Sunday gospel brunch. Gift shop with logo-inspired items next to restaurant.

Houston's, 1755 St. Charles Ave.; 524-1578, 4241 Veterans Blvd., Metairie; 889-2301. *I to* M. Houston's is praised for its fresh food and consistency. A fun place for the family with a varied menu to meet all tastes—from hamburgers to ribs, chicken, and grilled fish. Absolutely delightful desserts. Lunch and dinner daily.

Kokopelli's, 3150 Calhoun St.; 861-3922. *I.* Grilled meat, seafood, and vegetarian dishes with an American Southwestern flavor. Lunch and dinner daily.

Lakeview Harbor, 911 Harrison Ave.; 486-4887. *I.* Serves some of the best burgers in the city, along with steaks and some seafood dishes. Lively atmosphere, and daily lunch and dinner specials.

Mike Ditka's Restaurant, Lafayette Hotel, 628 St. Charles Ave. *E.* On the St. Charles streetcar line, in the heart of the CBD, and in the lovely old Lafayette Hotel is a restaurant owned by New Orleans Saints football coach, Iron Mike Ditka, and partner Joe Carlucci. This restaurant is not for the fainthearted and features hearty dishes with names like Cowboy Oyster Shooter and Training Table Pot Roast. Carlucci describes the restaurant as having a "Chicago-style saloon atmosphere with a lot of New Orleans flavors." Call information for phone number and hours of operation.

Napoleon House, 500 Chartres St.; 524-9752. *I to M*. This age-old building located on a corner across the street from the Omni Royal Orleans Hotel is a welcome oasis for a glass of wine or beer and a tasty sandwich. The building dates back to 1797 and has interesting arched doorways and old stucco walls (see SELF-GUIDED TOURS, French Quarter Walking Tour). The po' boys are good; the background music is classical; the mood is relaxed. Lunch and dinner daily. Casual.

Plantation Coffeehouse, 5555 Canal Blvd.; 482-3164. *I*. Gourmet coffees and teas, a wide variety of regular and French pastries, salads, hot and cold sandwiches, light dinners, and vegetarian items are featured in this airy and cheerful cafe. It is popular with the after-theater crowd, and there's a classical guitarist on weekends. Breakfast, lunch, and dinner daily. *CS*.

Red Room, 2040 St. Charles Ave.; 528-9759. *M*. So aptly named because of the red-hued dining room, this excellent restaurant with a classic American menu even serves boar. Different types of live jazz are featured nightly. So, dress up and have fun.

The Rib Room, Omni Royal Orleans Hotel, 621 St. Louis; 529-7045. *E*. Excellent classic American food. The Rib Room is located in one of the Vieux Carre's luxury hotels, The Omni Royal Orleans. House favorites are succulent prime rib, homemade popovers, and a tempting dessert assortment, all served by red-coated waiters. The huge fan-shaped windows will give the relaxed diner a unique view of the bustling life of the French Quarter. Breakfast, lunch, and dinner daily. Sunday brunch. Reservations are required.

Russell's Marina Grill, 8555 Pontchartrain at Lake Marina Drive; 282-9999; fax 286-0707. *I*. Home of the original Onion Mum, a "don't miss it" dish to have as an appetizer or enjoy with your hamburger. Wonderful omelettes and even vegetarian items—really great food all served by a friendly and helpful staff. Breakfast, lunch, and dinner daily. *CS*.

Ruth's Chris Steak House, 3633 Veterans Blvd., Metairie; 888-3600, 711 N. Broad; 486-0810. *E*. Ruth's Chris Steak House is probably the Cadillac of steak houses in New Orleans. An old establishment which has satisfied New Orleans steak afficionados for years. Huge flavorful cuts of beef; entire menu is a la carte. Lunch and dinner daily. Reservations are required. Casual.

Shoney's Restaurants, 759 Veterans Blvd.; 835-9972, 8350 W. Judge Perez Dr.; 277-5758, 310 N. Carrollton Ave.; 488-7744, 1403 St. Charles Ave.; 525-1087, 4001 General de Gaulle Dr.; 362-5830. *I.* Many locations in the metro area, all with good food in a casual atmosphere. The extensive breakfast, soup, and salad bars are a delight. CS.

Smith and Wollensky, 1009 Poydras St.; 561-0770; www.smith&wollensky.com. *M to E.* Famous New York-based steakhouse serving only the best cuts of dry-aged USDA prime beef cooked to perfection. This large establishment has a variety of rooms to meet the needs of any size party. Lunch and dinner daily.

Snug Harbor, 626 Frenchmen St.; 949-0696. *I to M.* Serves some of the best hamburgers in town, along with steaks, seafood, and jazz. Dinner seven nights.

Top of the Dome, Hyatt Regency, 500 Poydras Plaza; 561-1234. *M to E.* Take the special elevator in the Hyatt up to the revolving glass room on the top of the building. The early evening to night view is enchanting, and on clear nights the bend in the river is spectacular. Seafoods, steaks, prime ribs, veal, and lamb are offered at dinner. A super place for cocktails, too. Reservations are necessary for dinner.

Ye Olde College Inn, 3016 S. Carrollton Ave.; 866-3683. *I.* This is another old-timer and old New Orleans tradition. Neighborhood people flock to this long-favorite eatery. The homespun, laid-back atmosphere is perfect for children or dining with the gang. The good food and low prices are hard to match. The big oyster loaf on French bread along with that old stand-by, red beans and rice, the chicken fried steak, and, of course, the cheeseburger, seem to capture both business people and university students and still rate a star or two. Lunch and dinner daily. Casual. CS.

Asian

China Doll, 830 Manhattan Blvd.; 366-1111. *I.* Chinese cuisine with a three-star rating by local restaurant critic Tom Fitzmorris, "Mr. Food." Excellent food with friendly service. Lunch and dinner Mon-Sat.

China Rose, 125 Robert E. Lee Blvd.; 283-2800. *I to M*. This well-established Lakeview restaurant is a favorite among locals, known for its wide variety of Cantonese-prepared seafood. Beautifully decorated, and excellent food presentation. Lunch and dinner daily.

China Ruby, 3604 Campagna Dr., Chalmette; 271-3125. M. Freshly prepared, very good Chinese cuisine in an authentic and friendly Chinese setting. Lunch and dinner daily.

Chinese Kitchen, 3327 S. Carrollton Ave.; 482-1122. *I*. This is a quick and convenient place to dine, and is also popular with students. This homestyle Oriental dining room has only a few small tables very close together. The Chinese Kitchen has the usual soups, fried rice, and egg rolls, plus a varied Oriental menu. Prices are good and food is tasty. Lunch and dinner daily. Casual.

Chinese King, 6158 Elysian Fields Ave.; 288-8833. *I*. Excellently prepared Chinese cuisine with the freshest ingredients. Close to the Lakefront and the UNO campus, it is popular with locals, including students. Special orders are welcomed. Lunch and dinner Mon-Sat.

Five Happiness Restaurant, 3605 S. Carrollton Ave.; 482-3935. *I*. This neighborhood restaurant specializes in Mandarin and Szechuan dishes, with many entrees of poultry, beef, pork, seafood, and vegetarian dishes. Take out orders are also available. Lunch and dinner daily. Reservations are needed. Very casual.

Genghis Khan, 4053 Tulane Ave.; 482-4044. *I to* M. Genghis Khan offers out-of-sight Korean-Japanese cuisine in a small neighborhood-type restaurant. Winner of "Best of the Best" Award. There is wonderful entertainment while you dine—live classical music with a violinist, pianist, and even opera singers. Dinner daily. Casual.

Golden Dragon, 4417 Veterans Blvd.; 887-6081. *I*. Fine little restaurant across from Clearview shopping center. Friendly and family operated. Golden dragon cutouts on the walls and a scattering of Oriental lanterns decorate the interior. The Szechuan and Hunan dishes are tasty, but the specialty is the moo-su-pork, and it is the best in town. Lunch Mon-Fri, dinner Fri-Sun. Reservations are needed. Casual.

Hong Kong, 7400 Lakeshore Dr.; 282-1511. *I to* M. Having dinner at the Hong Kong is almost like dining on board ship. The dining room is over the water and the power- and sailboats pass in view. There is a beautiful view of the yacht harbor. Many colorful Oriental silk lanterns cast a lovely soft romantic light. Each Cantonese or steak dish is steaming and delicious. The sailors and boat people come for late-night chopstick treats. The coconut ice cream is especially good. Lunch Mon-Fri, dinner daily. Casual.

Jade East, 7011 Read Blvd.; 243-1671. *I*. This Oriental eating establishment is located off I-10 in a small shopping center and is a 15-minute ride from downtown. The friendly atmosphere and pleasant decor set the mood for a relaxing meal. Many of the dishes are Szechuan or Hunan, hot and spicy. Lunch and dinner daily. Casual.

Kim Anh, 4952 Bullard Ave.; 244-8293. *I*. Excellent, authentic Vietnamese cuisine with a wide variety of selections. Owned and operated by a friendly, helpful Vietnamese family. There are special karaoke nights. Lunch and dinner daily except Wed. Casual.

Kim Son, 349 Whitney Ave. at West Bank Expressway; 366-2489. *I to* M. Vietnamese restaurant with friendly and helpful personnel. The menu features Vietnamese and Chinese dishes, and some are prepared in clay pots. Wonderful rolls and even baked crabs. Lunch and dinner Mon-Sat, dinner Sun.

Kung's Dynasty, 1912 St. Charles Ave.; 525-6669. *M to E*. Excellent Chinese cuisine in an elegant setting with friendly service; on historic St. Charles Avenue. No MSG used in any of the Mandarin, Hunan, Szechuan, or Cantonese dishes. Whole roast pig (advanced order) with accoutrements for special gatherings. Lunch and dinner daily.

Kyoto, 4920 Prytania St.; 891-3644. M. Cheerful Japanese restaurant with sushi bar. Lunch and dinner Mon-Sat.

Lemon Grass Cafe, 216 N. Carrollton Ave.; 488-8335. *I*. Exciting Vietnamese dishes prepared by the chef/owner, and, yes, some dishes with the lovely lemon grass. Dinner nightly.

Lucky Cheng's, 720 St. Louis St.; 529-2045. M. Asia-Creole cuisine with a four-star rating. The colorful Storyville-type decor and atmosphere are spiced up by the drag-queen waitresses. Be prepared for lots of fun during this dining experience. Dinner nightly. Sunday brunch.

Panda's RiverView, Jax Brewery, 600 Decatur St., fifth floor; 523-6073. *I to* M. Dine on Szechuan, Hunan, and Mandarin cuisine with a spectacular view of the Mississippi River. Does some delivery in the downtown area. Lunch and dinner daily.

Pho Tau Bay Restaurant, 113C Westbank Expwy., Gretna; 368-9846. *I.* Authentic Vietnamese dishes. The extensive menu is especially strong on vegetarian selections. Breakfast, lunch, and dinner daily.

Shogun, 2325 Veterans Blvd., Metairie; 833-7477. *I to M.* Interesting, small Japanese restaurant. If you are dining alone or with a friend, you may enjoy being seated at the sushi bar and watching the chefs prepare your meal. Tables are available. The experience begins with a drink and a warm damp hand towel to clean the diners' fingers. Service is good and food presented on small Japanese trays should please every age. The Oriental method of frying shrimp, pork, beef, or chicken in a light batter is truly delicious. Informal friendly dining. Lunch and dinner daily. Casual.

Styxx Asian Grille, 535 E. Judge Perez Dr., Chalmette; 276-2742. *I to M.* This new restaurant already has quite a following because of its use of a variety of fresh seasonings, spices, roots, and other Asian ingredients. Taste, color, aroma, and nutrition are all kept in mind during the preparation of dishes that hail from several Far East lands as well as fusion dishes. Always excellent with wonderful service. Lunch and dinner Tue-Sun except dinner only Sat.

Trey Yuen, Causeway Boulevard, Mandeville; 1-626-4476. *I to M.* Drive across the Causeway and enjoy the sunset before dining, then enjoy a fine Asian meal. Menu consists of Cantonese, Szechuan, and some Formosan creations. Good seafood dishes. Lunch Wed-Sat, dinner Mon-Sat, dinner Mon-Sat. Casual.

Cajun

Alex Patout's, 221 Royal St.; 525-7788. M. This renowned chef and cookbook author heralds from New Iberia—Cajun Country. Casually elegant restaurant with freshly prepared dishes. Seafood au gratin, shrimp and crawfish dishes, eggplant pirogue, and roast duck are just some of the delectable choices. Dinner nightly. Reservations are recommended.

Bon Ton Cafe, 401 Magazine St., just off Poydras Street; 523-8410. M. New Orleans' oldest Cajun restaurant, this wonderful cafe uses traditional family Cajun recipes. It began as a small cafe frequented by business people. This family-type restaurant is noted for catfish and complete crawfish dinners with several tasty courses. The stuffed eggplant and the bread pudding are among the best in the city. Mixed drinks are excellent. Lunch and dinner Mon-Fri. Reservations are recommended. Casual.

Copeland's, 4338 St. Charles Ave. on streetcar line; 897-2325, 701 Veterans Memorial Blvd.; 831-3437, 1001 S. Clearview Pkwy.; 733-7843, 1700 Lapalco Blvd.; 364-1575, 1337 Gause Blvd.; 643-0001. *I to* M. Lively atmosphere and decor serving excellent Cajun/American food. Traditional red beans and rice, fluffy buttermilk biscuits, pasta shrimp, and a wide range of seafood, chicken, and beef dishes. Lunch and dinner daily. Wonderful Sunday jazz brunch. Casual.

K-Paul's, 416 Chartres St.; 524-7394. M *to E*. Southern hospitality and authentic Cajun cuisine in Chef Paul Prudhomme's signature restaurant. The freshest ingredients are used in excellent dishes such as gumbo, blackened fish, crawfish etouffee, sweet potato pie, and many more. Lunch and dinner specials featured daily. Dinner reservations available.

Michaul's, 840 St. Charles Ave.; 522-5517. M. Live music in this large Cajun dancehall, and wonderful food, too, *cher*. This Cajun music restaurant is a good place to learn Cajun dance steps and experience popular Cajun cuisine with flair. Dinner and dance nightly Mon-Sat. CS.

Mulate's, 201 Julia St.; 522-1492. M. Specializes in Cajun cooking, live music, and dancing for the entire family; across from Convention Center. Taste of Cajun culture with dishes such as frog legs, stuffed crabs, fried catfish, and boiled crawfish—to name a few. Casual for lunch and dinner seven days. CS.

Patout's Restaurant, 501 Bourbon St.; 524-4054. M. Patout's is the result of three generations of Cajun cooking. Authentic Cajun cuisine with live Cajun music nightly. This new location has a balcony overlooking busy Bourbon Street. Lunch and dinner daily.

Straya's, 2001 St. Charles Ave.; 593-9955, 4517 Veterans Blvd.; 887-8873. *I to* M. Al Copeland's famous California-Cajun restaurant offers culinary excitement and generous portions. The St. Charles Avenue location offers a lovely view of the traveling historic streetcars. Lunch and dinner seven days.

Continental

Begue's, 300 Bourbon St.; 586-0300. *M to E.* Located in the Royal Sonesta Hotel, this beautifully decorated dining room is as popular with locals as it is with the many visitors who enjoy the fine Continental and Creole cuisine. Eggs Benedict and delicious crepes are favorites. Each day of the week features a special menu to tempt the appetite. Breakfast, lunch, and dinner daily.

Grill Room, Windsor Court Hotel, 300 Gravier St.; 523-6000. *E.* This well-appointed restaurant offers magnificent, sophisticated, inspired cuisine. Service is impeccable. It has one of the best brunches in the city, complete with live chamber music. After a truly fine meal, walk through the connecting corridors to view the hotel's art collection. Breakfast, lunch, and dinner seven days. Sunday brunch.

Riverbend Grill, Westin Hotel, 100 Iberville St., 11th floor; 553-5082. *E.* Dine in a garden setting with a spectacular view of the Mississippi River. A variety of dishes makes this dining experience worth repeating. Breakfast, lunch, and dinner daily. Excellent Sunday jazz brunch.

Riverview, atop the Marriott Hotel, 555 Canal St.; 581-1000. *M to E.* Forty-one stories above New Orleans, the view is something special and so is the Continental cuisine. Before dinner, or after, enjoy cocktails in the Riverview Bar. Breakfast and lunch Mon-Fri, dinner daily. Superb Sunday jazz brunch. Reservations are recommended. Jackets are required.

Sapphire, 228 Camp St.; 571-7500. *M to E.* A dynamic restaurant boasting very good, special dishes such as lacquered duck with Costa Rican pineapple. Breakfast, lunch, and dinner daily.

Steak Knife Restaurant, 888 Harrison Ave.; 488-8981. *I to M.* Wonderful food in a relaxed, casually elegant setting. This restaurant has been a Lakeview mainstay for many years, and was so successful it moved to larger facilities. Live jazz on weekends. Dinner seven days. CS.

Creole

Benedict's, 1144 Lovers' Ln.; 1-504-626-4557. M. Local Creole specialties are served in a quaint 19th-century home. Dinner Tue-Sat. Sunday brunch.

Brennan's, 417 Royal St.; 525-9711. *M to E.* A New Orleans landmark established in 1949 and situated in a beautiful, historic building with one of the loveliest courtyards in the French Quarter. "Breakfast at Brennan's" is a time-honored tradition, unhurried, fantastic, and served until 2:30 pm. Specialties are eggs benedict, sardou, or hussarde. Each of the dining rooms is decorated in a different color scheme, some overlooking the patio. Superb French and Creole cuisine features seafood, veal, and beef entrees and the flaming desserts are a dramatic conclusion to a memorable meal. This is where bananas foster originated. Brennan's has been managed by generations of the Brennan family, a long line of creative New Orleans restaurateurs. Breakfast, lunch, and dinner daily. Reservations are recommended.

Brigtsen's, 723 Dante St.; 861-7610. *M.* The chef hails from K-Paul's and has very good command of the full-bodied Cajun-Creole style. Rabbit is a specialty, and the chef's style also shines in the steak, chicken, and fish dishes. Situated in the charming Riverbend area of uptown New Orleans. Dinner Tue-Sat.

Broussard's, 819 Conti St.; 581-3866. *E.* Beautifully redecorated, this 1920s restaurant offers elegant dining rooms and features outstanding French and Creole dishes, including Creole fish, veal oscar, bananas foster, and broussard crepes. Late-night dinners here following the ballet or opera are a New Orleans tradition. Live piano music is featured, and validated parking is available. Dinner Mon-Sun. Jackets are required and reservations are recommended.

Christian's, 3835 Iberville St.; 482-4924. *M to E.* The uniqueness of the 1914 church building adds a great deal to this restaurant's appeal. Old pews are used as side seats, and the stained-glass windows have been retained. The menu is French Creole New Orleans cuisine, prepared by chefs who have been trained in the Quarter's outstanding restaurants. Sauces and desserts are exceptional. In season, buster crabs are excellent. Make reservations and take a 10-minute cab ride from Canal Street. Lunch and dinner Tue-Fri, dinner Sat. Reservations are required.

Commander's Palace, 1403 Washington Ave.; 899-8221. *E.* This gracious 1880s Victorian mansion built in the Garden District by Emile Commander has been restored and decorated by the Brennan family. It is one of New Orleans' finest restaurants. The lush, green patio is a favorite spot for before-dinner drinks and to enjoy the jazz band that plays on Saturdays and Sundays. Usually, one of the Brennans will greet you during the evening meal. Try the delicious well-seasoned Creole dishes and famous flaming desserts served at tableside. Valet parking.

Lunch Mon-Fri, dinner nightly. Sat-Sun jazz brunch. Jackets and reservations are required; tie for gentlemen preferred during dinner and Sunday jazz brunch.

Court of Two Sisters, 613 Royal St.; 522-7261. *M to E*. Located in a lovely historic house with a pretty courtyard. The nightly dinner menu is a la carte Creole and seafood. Daily jazz brunch.

Delmonico's, 1300 St. Charles Ave.; 525-4937. M. Located on the historic St. Charles streetcar line, and in the same historic building since 1895. A major, elegant renovation has just been completed by the famous Chef Emeril Lagasse, and Delmonico's is again serving classic Creole cuisine under his expert and fantastic direction. Expect excellent, freshly prepared meals presented the old-fashioned way with friendly service. Lunch Mon-Fri, dinner nightly. Sunday brunch.

Franky and Johnny's, 321 Arabella St.; 899-9146. *I*. There's always a hungry lunch crowd here waiting for the delicious fried seafood or one of Franky and Johnny's famous neighborhood po' boys. Lunch and dinner daily. Very casual.

Gabrielle Restaurant, 3201 Esplanade Ave.; 948-6233. M. Friendly service and excellent traditionally prepared Creole cuisine are offered here. This delightful bistro is situated in a former gas station! Very popular, so reservations are recommended. Dinner Tue-Sat.

Gumbo Shop, 630 St. Peter St.; 525-1486. *I to* M. Located in a restored 18th-century building, and serving some of the best gumbo in the city. The varied menu includes seafood, chicken, sandwiches, and salads. Lunch and dinner seven days.

Jacques-Imo Cafe, 8324 Oak St.; 861-0886. *I*. Quaint uptown cafe with friendly service, known for its great gumbo. Dinner daily. Closed for the month of August.

La Cuisine's, 225 W. Harrison Ave.; 486-7664. M. This Lakeview restaurant is quite popular with the local crowd. Excellently prepared French/Creole cuisine is served with neighborhood friendliness. Free parking. Lunch and dinner Tue-Sun.

La Gauloise Bistro, Hotel Meridien, 614 Canal St. M. Located on the hotel's mezzanine level overlooking Canal Street. A varied menu of good food with surprising touches. Lunch and dinner seven days.

Liuzza's, 3636 Bienville St.; 482-9120. *I.* Neighborhood-type restaurant with excellent roast beef po' boys and daily changing plate lunches. The food is consistently good. Lunch and dinner daily. Cash only.

Mandina's, 3800 Canal St.; 482-9179. *I.* The bright, noisy, crowded little dining room in this neighborhood restaurant is a meeting and eating place for many local politicians and business people. The food is a mix of Italian and Creole cuisine. The special of the day may be red beans and rice, a staple for Orleanians. The seafood a la carte is succulent; the shrimp salad is fit for royalty. No frills here, just food. Lunch and dinner daily. Cash only.

Mr. B's Bistro, 201 Royal St.; 523-2078. *M to E.* This exciting bistro is owned by the famous Brennan family and operated by the younger Brennans. A chic "in" place to go for lunch or dinner, the oysters en brochette are the best in town. Specialties include smoked redfish, seafood, pasta dishes, good desserts, and a delicious milk punch. Lunch and dinner daily. Wonderful Sunday brunch.

Old Coffee Pot, 714 St. Peter St.; 524-3500. *I.* This small, quaint restaurant with a lovely courtyard has been a favorite spot for locals for many years. The Creole cuisine here is absolutely wonderful. Breakfast, lunch, and dinner seven days.

Palm Court Jazz Cafe, 1204 Decatur St.; 525-0200. M. Wonderful Creole fare with traditional jazz every night. You can try the Creole feast or some of the newly created dishes. Dinner Wed-Sun.

Sazerac, Fairmont Hotel, 123 Baronne St.; 529-4733. *M to E.* The Sazerac is one of New Orleans' most lavish dining rooms. Fresh flowers, strolling musicians, waiters in elegant livery, and the fine menu, featuring a different specialty each day, make this a superlative dining experience. Rack of lamb, lobster tails, salmon, and caviar are some of the delectables. Also try the decadent desserts. Lunch Mon-Fri, dinner daily. Sunday jazz brunch. Reservations are required.

Tujague's, 823 Decatur; 525-8676. *E.* Across from the French Market, this 1860s Creole cuisine landmark has a dependably good reputation. In a true Creole fashion, the six-course dinner is sheer pleasure. There is also a three-course luncheon menu. A la carte menu items are available too, and everything is excellent. Lunch and dinner daily. Reservations are recommended.

French

Antoine's, 713 St. Louis; 581-4422. M *to* E. Antoine's is considered the oldest restaurant in North America, and generations of the same family have operated this internationally renowned French/Creole restaurant since 1840. The cuisine is excellent and the service is impeccable! The old-world ambience provides a unique dining experience. Oysters Rockefeller or Crawfish Cardinale is a good way to begin, and the puffed fried souffle potatoes are a must as is the Baked Alaska. Ask the waiter to show you the wine cellar and look into one of the private dining rooms, the Rex, Proteus, and Mardi Gras rooms. Don't expect to hurry! Lunch and dinner Mon-Sat. Reservations are recommended and jackets are a must.

Arnaud's, 813 Bienville St.; 523-5433. M *to* E. This restaurant is one of New Orleans' oldest, dating back to 1918. The menu is French and traditional Creole New Orleans cuisine in an old New Orleans atmosphere. The restaurant was founded by Count Arnaud Cazeniave, and is noted for the Shrimp Arnaud, Oysters Bienville, Trout Meuniere, and Creole Bread Pudding. Lunch Mon-Fri, dinner daily. Sunday jazz brunch. Reservations and jackets are required.

Bizou, 701 St. Charles Ave.; 524-4114. M. The chef was born in France and has worked with Parisian chefs and in local prominent restaurants. When he later opened this sophisticated restaurant, it quickly earned an excellent reputation. It offers classic French cuisine, prepared in an unhurried manner and always exceptional. Chef Daniel Bonnot also prepares several traditional dishes for the local French community or visiting French, when given 48 hours' notice. Lunch and dinner Mon-Fri, dinner Sat, late-evening desserts.

Cafe Sbisa, 1011 Decatur St.; 522-5565. M. A very chic French Quarter dining spot since 1899. Some of the chef's specialties include delicious smoked redfish, salmon, and other seafood creations, as well as unique soups. Marble-top tables and ceiling fans create a relaxed Quarter ambience. The cafe is a popular supper spot after the ball or theater. Dinner daily. Sunday brunch.

Crozier's, 3216 W. Esplanade Ave., Metairie; 833-8108. *E*. This fine restaurant's husband and wife proprietors are from Lyon, France. The decor is simple and inviting, with the feeling of country French. Cream of vegetable soup, the pate and fowl dishes, and steak and pork entrees are delicious. Truly friendly service. Dinner Tue-Sat. Reservations are required.

Galatoire's, 209 Bourbon St.; 525-2021. *M to E*. Four generations of the same family have operated this famous restaurant since 1905. It is popular with locals and visitors alike. French/Creole specialties are served in a brightly lit dining room. It is totally New Orleans, with friendly service and excellent cuisine. Lunch and dinner Tue-Sun, with reservations available for Tue-Thu only. Jackets are required for dinner and Sunday.

La Provence, 25020 Hwy. 190, Lacombe; 1-626-7662. *E*. It is well worth the hour's drive across the Lake Pontchartrain Causeway (at the end of which you turn right onto Highway 190, and follow it to Lacombe, Louisiana) to dine at this most renowned restaurant. It is presided over by one of the finest chefs in an area of fine chefs. The sophisticated French and Greek food and the relaxed, rustic setting in which it is served are an unexpected and unbeatable combination. Be sure to make a reservation. Lunch Sun, dinner Wed-Sun. Jackets are required.

Le Petit Paris, 731 Common St.; 524-7660. M. The French-born owner/chef Angele operates this small cafe with extremely good, basic French cuisine, which is quite popular with the downtown business crowd. Angele learned her cooking and management skills in France, and her hot lunches—*plats du jour*—have that slow-cooked goodness. Breakfast and lunch Mon-Fri.

Louis XVI, 730 Bienville St.; 581-7000. *E*. Elegant dining, excellent service, and presentation of a classic French menu are found here, where each table has fresh flowers and is beautifully set with lovely china and crystal. The ambience is of old Europe. Cold salad buffet and oyster souffle are popular luncheon specialties. There are very good hot hors d'oeuvres, a fine rack of lamb, and excellent Beef Wellington. This small restaurant is in the St. Louis Hotel and is a grand place to celebrate a special occasion. Breakfast and dinner daily.

German

Deutsches-Haus, German Club, 200 Galvez St.; 522-8014. *I to M*. Fantastic, authentic German food. The best time to go here is during Oktoberfest, from the end of September through October. During this time, Friday-Sunday, enjoy great food, dance to German music, and sample fine beer in a true party atmosphere. Other times of the year, Wednesday-Friday, only "short" snacks, German sandwiches, and drinks are served.

Indian

Taj Mahal Indian Cuisine, 923 Metairie Rd.; 836-6859. *I.* Excellent food with perfect Indian seasonings. Grilled or fried seafood, fowl, beef, lamb, or vegetarian dishes are all offered. A lunch buffet is featured (expanded on Sun). Lunch and dinner Tue-Sun. CS.

Irish

Parasol's, 2533 Constance St.; 899-2054. *I.* This small neighborhood restaurant is known as the pride of the Irish Channel. Most of the locals come to relax and see friends while waiting for a delicious, huge New Orleans-style po' boy or another sandwich rich with meat and gravy, enough for two. St. Patrick's Day is a must at this Irish heaven—green beer is an annual tradition. Lunch and dinner Mon and Wed-Sat. Very casual.

Italian

Andrea's, 3100 19th St. at Ridgelake, Metairie; 834-8583. *M to E.* Serving excellent Northern Italian and Continental cuisine in a friendly atmosphere. Chef Andrea is a familiar nightly sight, preparing special dishes at tableside. Freshly prepared food has made Andrea's one of the area's most popular restaurants—even the pasta is homemade. Lunch Mon-Fri, dinner nightly. Sunday brunch.

Bacco's, 310 Chartres St.; 522-2426. M. Another successful Brennan family restaurant, here Italian cuisine is served with a New Orleans twist. The crawfish cannelloni and "Creole Country" andouille cream sauce are excellent examples of their special dishes. The pasta is homemade and the Italian wine list is enviable. Breakfast, lunch, and dinner daily.

Bella Luna, 914 N. Peters St.; 529-1583. *M to E.* The restaurant's name—"beautiful moon"—was inspired by the view that diners see when the full moon is shining beautifully over the Mississippi River. Maine lobster, local seafood, and wonderful pastas are featured on the varied menu with some dishes having a Southwest touch. Dinner nightly.

Brick Oven Cafe, 2805 Williams Blvd.; 466-2097. M. Very popular Kenner cafe featuring unique dishes. One example is the *costoletta di vitello liberta*—a veal chop stuffed with prosciutto—and there are very good sauces and pastas. One of their proud features is a big wood-burning oven, in which a large selection of gourmet pizzas is cooked. Lunch and dinner daily.

Cafe Giovanni, 117 Decatur St.; 529-2154. M. A romantic, elegant atmosphere for dining or drinks at the cocktail bar, enhanced by live music and late-night jazz on the weekends. Delicious, unique Italian dishes with Asian influences featuring duck, local seafood, and a variety of pastas. Dinner nightly.

Louisiana Pizza Kitchen, 615 S. Carrollton Ave.; 866-5900, 2112 Belle Chasse Hwy.; 433-5800. *I to M*. Pizzas baked in a wood-burning oven, which yields thin, crackly crusts. In authentic Italian style, each pizza serves one person. Whole-wheat or white-crust pizzas are now offered. Pizzas with unique ingredients, vegetarian pizzas, and pasta dishes are featured. Lunch and dinner daily.

Mosca's, Highway 90, Waggaman; 436-9942. M. On the West Bank of the Mississippi River across the Huey P. Long Bridge in such an unpretentious building that you'll drive right by if you don't look hard to your left, Mosca's has been luring New Orleans upriver for good food and drink for many years. The seafood dishes are superb. Try the oysters Italian style. Expect delicious food and a rustic dining room. Dinner Tue-Sat. Casual. No credit cards.

New York Pizza, 208 N. Carrollton Ave.; 482-2376, 5201 Magazine St.; 891-2376. *I*. In addition to great pizzas, there are Italian dishes, po' boys, muffulettas, and more than 50 beer choices. Lunch and dinner Tue-Sun. Casual.

Pascal's Manale, 1838 Napoleon Ave.; 895-4877. *M to E*. This popular neighborhood dining spot dates back to 1913. Always crowded, you'll find people jamming into the "waiting bar" to sample one of the bartender's specialties or feast on oysters. Italian and Creole seafood dishes are the specialties. Be sure to sample the seasoned barbecued shrimp (served with a huge bib) or lump crabmeat and shrimp salad. Lunch Mon-Fri, dinner daily. Reservations are recommended. Casual.

Pizza Roma, 4840 Bienville Ave.; 483-9949. *I*. Exceptional pizzas and a wide variety of Italian dishes and salads are freshly prepared upon your order at this quaint neighborhood cafe. Takeout and delivery service. Lunch and dinner daily.

R & O's Pizza Place, 216 Old Hammond Hwy.; 831-1248. *I*. This casual cafe not only serves pizza but a variety of Italian dishes and fresh seafood in comfortable surroundings. Lunch and dinner Wed-Mon.

Rocky and Carlo's, 613 W. St. Bernard Hwy., Chalmette; 279-8323. *I*. An old established St. Bernard landmark, Rocky and Carlo's has a homespun atmosphere, serving excellent home-style meals, good sandwiches, fine seafoods, delicious salads, and desserts. Breakfast, lunch, and dinner daily. No credit cards. CS.

Salvatore Ristorante, 3226 N. Arnoult Rd.; 455-2433. M. Marvelous Italian food cooked and served to perfection. Excellent wines are available to accompany your meal, as well as a variety of homemade breads. Transportation to this Metairie restaurant is never a problem. When you make your reservations by phone, you can arrange for Salvatore's to send its own limousine to your hotel for personal pick-up service to and from this fine restaurant.

Sclafani's, 9900 Hayne Blvd.; 241-4472. *I to* M. Excellent Italian restaurant with well-seasoned dishes. Some Creole dishes are also on the menu. Very friendly, New Orleans-style service. Lunch Tue-Sat, dinner Thu-Sat.

Semolina, 3242 Magazine St.; 895-4260, 5080 Pontchartrain Blvd.; 486-5581. M. This chain of international pasta restaurants features unbelievable dishes such as Shrimp Bangkok. Lunch and dinner daily.

Tony Angelo's, 6262 Fleur de Lis Dr.; 488-0888. *I to* M. Tony Angelo's, not far from the Lakefront, has a wooden interior which lends a casual warm atmosphere. The Sicilian/Creole menu is very extensive. The favorites are the lasagna, one of the famous veal dishes, the soups and salads, and the delicious homemade desserts. There is no rush to come and go, so the meal may be long; it's worth the wait. Dinner Tue-Sat. Reservations are recommended.

Tony Moran's Italian Cuisine, 240 Bourbon St.; 523-3181. M. Located on the second floor of the legendary Old Absinthe House. Moran's has traditionally offered some of the finest Northern Italian cuisine in the city. Lunch and dinner daily.

Tortorici's, 441 Royal St.; 522-4295. *M to E*. This authentic New Orleans Italian restaurant has been serving Orleanians for almost 100 years with its friendly, wonderful service. A marvelous treat and excellent sampling of its special cuisine is the Tortorici's Trio—shrimp scampi with special pasta, a beef tenderloin medallion with mushroom sauce, and a chicken fillet with Creole crawfish topping. Piano music. In the heart of the French Quarter, and within walking distance of much entertainment. Dinner nightly. Casual.

Jamaican

Palmer's, 135 N. Carrollton Ave. at Canal Street; 482-3658. *I.* A great neighborhood-type restaurant celebrating Caribbean cuisine. Some specialty beers, such as Red Stripe, and taped reggae music accompany downhome island dishes. Lunch and dinner Tue-Fri, dinner Sat.

Mexican

Cuco's, 5048 Veterans Blvd.; 454-5005, 3000 Veterans Blvd.; 837-1900, 1340 S. Carrollton Ave.; 861-3322. *I to M.* Consistently good, zesty Mexican cuisine, with even a "Heart Healthy Menu." Lunch and dinner daily. *CS.*

Pancho's Mexican Buffet, 3780 Veterans Blvd.; 885-2432. *I.* A truly festive atmosphere for the whole family, with typical—always good—Mexican fare. Order freshly prepared dishes from the buffet line, and serve yourself from the extensive salad and dessert bars. Lunch and dinner daily. *CS.*

Pupuseria Divino Corazon Restaurant, 2300 Belle Chasse Hwy., Gretna; 368-5724. *I.* Cozy cafe with wonderful Mexican and Central American dishes, all homemade with the freshest ingredients. Lunch and dinner Thu-Tue.

Santa Fe Restaurant, 801 Frenchmen St.; 944-6854. *I to M.* Excellent Southwest/Mexican cuisine in one of the Faubourg Marigny's beautiful old houses with high ceilings; overlooking Washington Square. Marvelous thin, crisp nachos and special salsa are served when you are seated. Good stop during Faubourg Marigny tour. Lunch and dinner Mon-Fri, dinner Sat.

Taqueria Corona, 5932 Magazine St.; 897-3974, 857 Fulton St.; 524-9805, 3535 Severn Ave., Metairie; 885-5088. *I.* Good Mexican dishes served in an intimate atmosphere. The authentic recipes featuring marinated and roasted meats are very popular with the local crowd. Lunch and dinner daily.

Vera Cruz, 7537 Maple St.; 866-1736. *I.* Classic Mexican/American food, plus a standard steak, fish, and chicken menu for the less adventuresome is the selection here. Offering generous portions, Vera Cruz also makes good drinks, with popular happy hour specials. A gathering place for the college crowd and young professionals. Lunch Sat-Sun, dinner Wed-Sun. Very casual.

Middle Eastern

Mona's Cafe & Deli, 3901 Banks St.; 482-7743. *I to M.* This delightful surprise in Mid City offers wonderful Lebanese food with friendly service. Lunch and dinner daily.

Nouvelle Cuisine

Artesia, 21516 Hwy. 36, Abita Springs; 504-892-1662. *E.* This is a Creole mansion in an elegant country setting of oak trees and azaleas. Wonderful, unique French-Louisiana dishes make this restaurant a real treat. Call for directions. Lunch and dinner Wed-Sat. Sunday brunch.

Bayona, 430 Dauphine St.; 525-4455. *M to E.* This nationally acclaimed restaurant run by Chef Susan Spicer is situated in a quaint 1790s Creole cottage with a lovely courtyard. Wonderfully creative dishes with Mediterranean flavors. Many New Orleans favorites are also featured. Lunch and dinner Mon-Fri, dinner Sat.

Bistro at Maison de Ville, 733 Toulouse St.; 528-9206. *M to E. Gourmet* magazine in 1996 voted the Bistro as one of "America's Top Tables." Very elegant, intimate Franch-style bistro featuring many New Orleans favorite dishes with a Mediterranean flair. Quite popular with the locals. Reservations. Lunch and dinner Mon-Sat. Sunday brunch.

Cafe Degas, 3127 Esplanade Ave.; 945-5635. M. Casual, intimate dining, similar to a cafe in the south of France. This is named for French Impressionist Edgar Degas, who lived and worked in this neighborhood for five months. Tables are placed in a unique, temperature-controlled, covered deck, making this a nice romantic spot. Daily specials along with consistently good dishes. Chocolate lovers will enjoy the dessert specials. Lunch and dinner daily. Sat-Sun brunch.

Charlie G's, 111 Veterans Blvd.; 837-6408. *M to E.* This grill offers creative seafood, beef, chicken, or duck dishes cooked over hickory or mesquite. Nightly live entertainment. Lunch and dinner daily. Sunday brunch.

Chef's Table, 2100 St. Charles Ave.; 525-2328. M. This intimate, romantic restaurant also has a cozy piano room which adds to the bistro-like ambience. International flavors give wonderful New Orleans classic dishes a twist. Lunch Tue-Fri, dinner Mon-Sat.

Christino's, Omni Royal Crescent Hotel, 228 Camp St.; 527-0897 or 527-0006. *M to E.* Creative dishes with Mediterranean flavors. Extensive choices range from light fare to hearty meals. Breakfast, lunch, and dinner daily.

Clancy's, 6100 Annunciation St.; 895-1111. *M to E.* A small corner restaurant hidden away in the uptown area near Audubon Park, Clancy's has a clublike bar and intimate dining ambience. The menu is interesting, with several entrees from the grill. Some of the best Oysters Rockefeller in town are served here. Good fish and rabbit entrees and a delicious dessert cart, prepared by a young chef with new ideas, are also wonderful. Lunch Tue-Fri, dinner Mon-Sat.

Emeril's, 800 Tchoupitoulas; 528-9393. *E.* Chef Emeril Lagasse of cookbook and cable TV's Food Network fame adds wildly imaginative concepts to marvelous food creations. An old manufacturing plant has been transformed into an elegant restaurant with large windows and exposed brick. Lunch and dinner Mon-Fri, dinner Sat-Sun.

Feelings Cafe, 2600 Chartres St.; 945-2222. M. Located in the Fabourg Marigny (beyond the French Market), this old building on a corner lot has a second-level dining room and a balcony overlooking the patio piano bar. The downstairs dining room has exposed old brick walls and intimate little tables and chairs. There is an exciting menu featuring the new, New Orleans cuisine which has been introduced by a number of young chefs. Be sure to try the peanut butter pie. Lunch Fri, dinner nightly.

Gautreau's, 1728 Soniat St.; 899-7397. *I to* M. Although small in size, Gautreau's is big in tasty well-prepared imaginative foods. A family-owned drugstore has been remodeled and given a new role. Don't miss the brownie pie—sinfully good! The Tournedos Lafitte, Veal Milanaise, and Oysters en Brochette are outstanding. Dinner Mon-Sat.

Kelsey's, 3923 Magazine St.; 897-6722. *M to E.* In the heart of uptown, Chef-Owner Randy Barlow applies various international flavors to classic New Orleans dishes to create a wonderful new cuisine. Some examples are duck breast with provolone and jalapeno, and a curry-spiked shrimp Bombay pie. Lunch and dinner Tue-Fri, dinner Sat.

NOLA, 534 St. Louis St.; 522-6652. M. Renowned chef Emeril Lagasse has created a bistro-type restaurant which features his special cuisine, in addition to gourmet pizzas prepared in wood-burning ovens. This informal atmosphere is fun for the entire family, and allows everyone the opportunity to sample marvelous regional and contemporary Creole dishes "a la Emeril's." Lunch Mon-Sat, dinner nightly. CS.

Palace Cafe, 605 Canal St.; 523-1661. M. The renowned Brennan family's Parisian-style grand cafe serves excellent New Orleans-style dishes. The menu is a blend of classic and contemporary Creole and Cajun dishes, with fresh twists to delight your palate. The andouille-encrusted fish and white-chocolate bread pudding are perfect examples. Lunch and dinner daily. Sunday live blues brunch.

Pelican Club, 312 Exchange Alley; 523-1504. M. This elegant and stylish restaurant has gained an excellent reputation for creating imaginative Louisiana cuisine by blending diverse international styles. Expect the best in seafood and steak dishes. The Christmas *réveillon* menu is quite popular. Dinner nightly, with "Early Dinner" specials.

Peristyle, 1041 Dumaine St.; 593-9535. *E*. This is the restaurant of New Orleans' new star chef, Anne Kearney. It has received much attention nationally. It offers specialized and unique dishes prepared with home-grown Louisiana ingredients. Elegant presentations. Lunch Fri (two seatings: 11:30 and 1:30), dinner Tue-Sat. Reservations are strongly recommended!

Sclafani's, 301 Dauphine St.; 524-5475. M. Beautiful French Quarter courtyard dining is now offered. Since the 1940s, the Sclafani family has been serving creative cuisine such as steak Dauphine and fish Bienville, and the restaurant continues to evolve positively. Breakfast, lunch, and dinner daily. Sunday brunch.

Tavern on the Park, 900 City Park Ave.; 486-3333. M. This lovely art-deco-style restaurant across the street from one of the country's largest urban parks serves creative New Orleans cuisine. Wonderful service in a beautifully renovated old building. Lunch and dinner Tue-Fri, dinner Sat.

The Upperline, 1413 Upperline St.; 891-9822. M. A small, but exciting, intimate dining spot, this is consistently good. The decor is art deco. The huge wooden bar covers one wall completely and is a popular place to gather. For appetizers, the pasta salad with seafood and oyster/artichoke au gratin are hearty beginners. The charcoal-grilled chicken, redfish, or shrimp are recommended. Lunch Sun, dinner Wed-Sun.

Regional

Abita Quail Farm, 23185 Hwy. 435, Abita Springs; 504-892-5176. M *to* E. Wonderfully prepared food in the Louisiana tradition is served here. Excellent service and beautiful surroundings. Call for directions. Dinner daily, and special events.

Barrister's, 2120 Pakenham Dr., Chalmette; 271-2500. I *to* M. This new restaurant serves excellent New Orleans cuisine. One of the chefs hails from a well-established North Shore restaurant and his reputation and experience help to create a truly local dining experience. Fresh ingredients and wonderful service. Lunch and dinner daily, breakfast Sat-Sun.

Bechac's, 2025 Lakeshore Dr., Mandeville; 504-626-8500. M. This "tried and true" restaurant overlooking the north shore of Lake Pontchartrain is popular with locals. Consistently good food with fresh native ingredients. Lunch and dinner Fri-Mon, lunch Tue. Sunday brunch.

Breakwater, 8550 Pontchartrain Blvd.; 283-8301. M. Casual and patio dining at the Lakefront next to the marina. Consistently good local food. Lunch Mon-Fri, dinner nightly.

Bubba John's, 9212 W. Judge Perez Dr., Chalmette; 279-1589. I *to* M. Good New Orleans-type food complete with down-home atmosphere and jukebox. Very popular family restaurant. Lunch and dinner Wed-Sat, dinner Sun-Mon. CS.

Crescent City Brewhouse, 527 Decatur St.; 522-0571. M. Special monthly brews are featured along with a variety of Louisiana-style entrees, sandwiches, and pizzas. Daily live entertainment features local musicians who play jazz, swing, and rhythm and blues. Balcony seating offers wonderful views of the Mississippi River. Lunch and dinner daily.

Dakota's, 629 N. Hwy. 190, Covington; 504-892-3712. M *to* E. This comfortable, elegant restaurant serves contemporary Louisiana cuisine. *Gourmet* magazine named it one of metro New Orleans' top 20 restaurants. Lunch Mon-Fri, dinner nightly.

Jack Dempsey's Uptown Downtown Restaurant, 738 Poland Ave.; 943-9914. *I to* M. Jack Dempsey's is almost a New Orleans institution! Dishes are excellently prepared in the Louisiana tradition. All seafood is fresh and fantastic with generous portions. During peak times, expect a line outside, but not if you go early. There is even a jukebox with many '50s tunes. Lunch and dinner Tue-Fri, dinner Sat.

Mandich's, 3200 St. Claude Ave.; 947-9553. M. This nicely decorated neighborhood restaurant has been serving extremely good New Orleans cuisine since the 1940s. It is a favorite among professionals and nonprofessionals. Lunch Tue-Fri, dinner Fri-Sat.

The Midnight Star Cafe, 7224 Pontchartrain Blvd.; 282-6241. *I.* Quite lively with a family atmosphere. Good local food and popular dishes. Live jazz band Fri-Sat. Lunch and dinner Tue-Sat. Sunday jazz brunch. CS.

Original Papa Joe's, 600-610 Bourbon St.; 529-1728. *I.* Enjoy great New Orleans food at affordable prices: po' boys, fried seafood, gumbo. Both table and barside diners are offered full views of the Bourbon Street excitement. Lunch and dinner Thu-Mon.

Petunia's Restaurant, 817 St. Louis St.; 522-6440. M. A favorite of locals, in a lovely Creole cottage. Traditional and original Creole and Cajun dishes very well prepared. The specialties are the excellent "world's largest crepes" with a variety of wonderful fillings. Breakfast, lunch, and dinner daily.

Planet Hollywood, Jackson Brewery Brewhouse, 620 Decatur St.; 522-7826. M. This popular restaurant chain now offers special New Orleans dishes in addition to its regular menu. There is much activity, with recorded music and a myriad of screens flashing celebrity interviews and movie excerpts. Walls are filled with costumes and other memorabilia from past and present movies. Merchandising shop also in restaurant. Lunch and dinner daily. CS.

Quarter Scene, 900 Dumaine; 522-6533. M. One of the few 24-hour restaurants in town, and only closed on Tuesday evenings. The restaurant is intimate and casual and offers consistently good food and excellent service—all with delightful Quarter ambience. Varied menu with many traditional New Orleans dishes—and breakfast (wonderful omelettes).

Remoulade, 309 Bourbon St.; 523-0377. *I.* This is a casual offshoot from the renowned Arnaud's restaurant, offering some popular New Orleans dishes along with burgers, pizzas, and po' boys. The fried seafood is wonderful, as are the Arnaud's soups. Lunch and dinner daily.

Veranda Restaurant, Hotel Inter-Continental, 444 St. Charles Ave.; 525-5566. M. It has been stated that the Veranda Restaurant captures the feeling of both an old New Orleans home and a Southern plantation. This is thanks mainly to the talents of local chef Willy Coln. Its celebrated New Orleans food is excellent, and even a "heart-healthy" menu is available. Breakfast, lunch, and dinner daily. Sunday champagne jazz brunch.

Seafood

Acme Oyster House, 724 Iberville St.; 522-5980. *I.* This is a favorite luncheon spot for many of the downtown business people who enjoy the relaxed surroundings of this typical marble-topped oyster bar and casual dining room. Acme's is a French Quarter landmark which has been serving fresh oysters in a variety of ways since 1910. There are also many other excellent seafood offerings and even something for nonseafood people. Crispy fresh French bread is always used. Lunch and dinner seven days.

Amberjack's Down Under, 7306 Lakeshore Dr.; 283-2096. M. Very casual restaurant with a view of the marina. Fresh seafood, pizzas, and some other Italian dishes are on the menu. Lunch Sun, dinner nightly.

Barataria, 900 Harrison Ave.; 488-7474. M. Barataria's offers a marvelous "Louisiana proud" menu, complete with fresh oysters farmed in oyster beds owned by Chef Ralph Pausina's family. Lunch Tue-Fri; dinner nightly.

Bruning's, West End Park on Lake Pontchartrain; 282-9395 or 288-4521. *I.* This family seafood institution began in 1859, and some locals will eat seafood only at Bruning's. It has a beautiful view of Lake Pontchartrain, a back dining room that juts out over the lake, and a variety of excellent seafood dishes. Lunch and dinner seven days. CS.

Cafe Atchafalaya, 901 Louisiana Ave.; 891-5271. *I to* M. Cafe

Atchafalaya, a neighborhood restaurant, combines casual atmosphere and reasonable prices. The seafood is prepared in the Cajun style. Bring the family and enjoy the daily chef's seafood special. Breakfast Sat-Sun, lunch and dinner daily.

Casamento's, 4330 Magazine St.; 895-9761. *I to M*. This tiny, spotlessly clean seafood spot has been owned and operated by the same family for years. The interior is done in decorative white tile, in the Sicilian tradition. Locals flock here for lunch and dinner. The oyster bar is a must while waiting to be seated. Fried oysters on thick buttered toast is a favorite. Lunch and dinner Tue-Sun. Casual.

Deanie's Seafood, 1713 Lake Ave.; 831-4141. *I to M*. Home of giant-portion-wonderfully-prepared seafood dishes. Fried seafood platters are the specialty. Arrive at this Bucktown institution extremely hungry. Lively, crowded family-type restaurant, with even little pizzas for children. Brunch, lunch, and dinner daily. CS.

Don's Seafood Hut, 4801 Veterans Memorial Blvd.; 889-1550. *M to E*. Restaurant and oyster bar. Good selection of fresh Louisiana seafood prepared Cajun style, fried, broiled, and boiled. Etouffees, bisques, and gumbos. Steaks and chicken, too. Children's menu available. Free parking. Lunch and dinner daily. Casual. CS.

Felix's, 739 Iberville St.; 522-4440. *I*. Well known for its excellent oysters on the half-shell and delicious sandwiches, this informal cafe, loud and boisterous, attracts many downtown business people for lunch. There are other good seafood dishes on the menu, but the oyster is the superstar. Lunch and dinner seven days.

Fitzgerald's, West End Park Boulevard; 282-9254. *I*. For years this seafood eating establishment has occupied the same over-the-water location right on Lake Pontchartrain. Fitzgerald's has all types of seafoods prepared in a variety of ways. Purists tackle a huge tray of boiled crabs to pick and eat right out of the red shells. The less adventuresome have a crabmeat salad. It's delicious either way. Roll up your sleeves and have a grand time. Lunch and dinner Tue-Sun. Very casual. CS.

Jaeger's, West End Park; 282-9149. *I to M*. A traditional New Orleans seafood restaurant, owned by the same family for generations, Jaeger's features fried or broiled fish, crawfish, oysters, and soft-shell crabs in season. This West End location offers diners beautiful Lake Pontchartrain sunsets and views of passing boats. Live music also featured. Lunch Sat-Sun, dinner Wed-Sun. CS.

Landry's Seafood House, 400 N. Peters St.; 558-0038. M. In this bright, bustling restaurant overlooking French Quarter activities, New Orleans seafood is the specialty. Excellent menu items, with even non-seafood items and fantastic desserts. Lunch and dinner seven days. CS.

Mike Anderson's, 215 Bourbon St.; 524-3884. *M to E.* Complete menu of fresh south Louisiana seafood and an oyster bar. Seafood is fried, boiled, broiled, and char-broiled; gumbos, etouffees, and bisques are also available. Friendly service and children's plates in a pleasant, casual, nautical atmosphere. Discount parking. Lunch and dinner daily.

Ralph and Kacoo's, 519 Toulouse St.; 522-5226, 601 Veterans Blvd.; 831-3177. *I to* M. "The seafood restaurant with the Cajun accent." Traditional favorites like sumptuous seafood platters of Cajun specialties and authentic Louisiana hush puppies are some of the offerings on its extensive menu. Lunch and dinner daily. CS.

Red Fish Grill, 115 Bourbon St.; 598-1200. *E.* Another successful restaurant from the Brennan family, offering excellently grilled seafood. The tastefully decorated restaurant has a wonderful variety of seafood prepared many ways. Lunch and dinner daily. Sunday brunch.

Sid-Mar's, 1824 Orpheum; 831-9541. *I to* M. Some of the best boiled seafood in town is served in this old, but classic, seafood establishment. Good po' boys and dinner all served in a nautical-style dining room and on a porch overlooking Lake Pontchartrain in historic Bucktown. Lunch and dinner Tue-Sun. CS.

Trauth's Lake House and Steamery, 3700 Williams Blvd., Kenner; 443-6488. *I.* Very informal with good food, and an "all you can eat catfish and chicken" offer. Very popular with families. Lunch and dinner daily. CS.

Uglesich's, 1238 Baronne St. near Lee Circle; 523-8571. *I.* A neighborhood restaurant with neighborhood hospitality serving good ol' New Orleans home cooking with all fresh ingredients. Well known for its fried local seafood, freshly shucked oysters, and wonderful po' boys. Lunch Mon-Fri.

Visko's, 516 Gretna Blvd.; 366-1516. *M to E.* A West Bank family landmark, Visko's serves delicious fresh seafoods and steamed lobsters. There is a variety of seafood prepared for you—steamed, fried, or broiled—oysters on the half-shell, and even grilled steaks. Atmosphere is pleasant and homelike with artwork and lovely antiques. Oyster bar and patio too. Lunch and dinner daily. Reservations are needed. Casual.

Soul Food

Dooky Chase, 2301 Orleans Ave.; 821-0600. *I*. Dooky Chase has the reputation of being one of the best soul Creole eating spots in the city. The gumbo, chicken, or seafood dishes would please any gourmet's tastebuds. Although claimed as a fine eating and meeting place by the black community, Leah Chase's restaurant has become popular with people from all walks of life. Lunch and dinner seven days. Casual.

Eddie's Restaurant and Bar, 2119 Law St.; 945-2207. *I*. Eddie's, located in the old Gentilly section of the city, is known for its "soul food" atmosphere. It is close to Dillard University—your cabbie can drive you there. Lunch Mon-Fri, dinner Fri-Sat. Sunday brunch.

Praline Connection, 542 Frenchmen St.; 943-3934, 907 S. Peters; 523-3973. M. New Orleans soul, home-style cooking with a varied menu to please all tastes. As the name implies, this is also a good dessert place. Wonderful pralines and pastries can be purchased in a pastry shop section of the Faubourg Marigny restaurant. This is a great stop when you are doing the Faubourg Marigny walking tour. Lunch and dinner seven days. Sunday gospel brunch at the Warehouse District location.

Spanish

Lola's, 3312 Esplanade Ave.; 488-6946. *I to* M. A Spanish chef serves authentic paellas and many other wonderful dishes from his homeland. Friendly and comfortable atmosphere. You are welcome to bring your own bottle of wine, as alcohol is not available on the menu. No reservations or credit cards are accepted. Dinner Tue-Sun.

Vegetarian

Back to the Garden, 920 St. Charles Ave.; 522-8792. *I*. Located on Lee Circle in the YMCA Hotel, this restaurant serves lots of wonderful, fresh dishes. Breakfast and lunch Mon-Sat.

Old Dog, New Trick Cafe, 307 Exchange Alley; 522-4569. *I*. In a casual setting just off Canal Street in the French Quarter. The unique combination of fresh ingredients with invigorating seasonings yields healthy and delightfully tasty dishes. Lunch and dinner daily. Sat-Sun brunch.

ETCETERA

Abita Brew Pub, 72011 Holly St., North Shore; 504-892-5837. *I.* A Louisiana microbrewery with most of its fare designed to complement its standard brews. Good food does make this also a family restaurant, where kids have their own menu. Lunch and dinner daily. CS.

Angelo Brocato's, 214 N. Carrollton Ave.; 486-1465. *I.* A beloved New Orleans tradition, Angelo Brocato has been making the best Italian ice cream, ices, cannoli, and cookies in town since he began in the French Quarter almost 100 years ago. The move to Carrollton Avenue hasn't changed things a bit. The aroma of strong Italian coffee greets you at the door and lures you in to savor one or more of the delightful sweets. Don't miss it. Open daily. Casual. CS.

Cafe Brasil, 2100 Chartres St.; 949-0851. *I.* This coffee house cafe has a variety of coffees, pastries, and drinks. Very casual and informal. Afternoons and evenings.

Cafe du Monde, French Market at Jackson Square, 800 Decatur St.; 525-4544. *I.* Nobody leaves New Orleans without having made a ceremonial trip to Cafe du Monde for "coffee and doughnuts." But these are not your ordinary coffee and doughnuts. The coffee is "cafe au lait," strong Creole coffee with chicory, well laced with hot milk (they are poured simultaneously into the already hot cup). The doughnuts are the French beignet (ben-yay), scrumptious squares of deep-fried dough, puffed like pillows and golden brown in color, topped with mountains of confectioners' sugar. It is one of the most popular spots to begin the day or end an evening. Open 24 hours daily. Very casual. CS.

Canal Place Food Court, 333 Canal St.; 523-4158. *I.* A variety of restaurants and cafes in a casually elegant atmosphere. CS.

CC's Gourmet Coffee Houses, 630 S. Carrollton Ave.; 865-0027, 701 Metairie Rd., Metairie; 831-1449, 941 Royal St.; 581-6996. *I.* Pastries and good, freshly brewed coffees and teas. These cafes are popular with the student and young business crowds. Several other locations citywide. Open daily.

Central and Progress Grocery and Sandwich Shops, 923 Decatur St.; 523-1620, 915 Decatur St.; 525-6627. *I.* These two old-fashioned Italian grocery stores produce the best (and authentic) muffulettas in the city. The muffuletta is similar to a po' boy . . . except it's on seeded round loaves, filled with Italian cold cuts and cheeses, and slathered with a special olive salad. Locals have strong favorites, so try both to see which one you prefer. Great place for Riverfront picnic shopping. CS.

Chateau Coffee Cafe, 139 Robert E. Lee Blvd.; 286-1777. *I.* Gourmet coffees and teas, a variety of pastries, salads, sandwiches (hot and cold), the new "wraps," and even vegetarian items are featured in this neat cafe. Breakfast, lunch, and dinner daily.

Chuck E. Cheese, 7000 Veterans Memorial Blvd.; 454-5959, 3701 General de Gaulle Dr.; 364-1214. *I.* A great family place for informal, inexpensive, entertaining meals. Games, video games, and live entertainment for the kids. Private parties welcome. Lunch and dinner seven days. CS.

Croissant d'Or Patisserie, 617 Ursulines St.; 524-4663. *I.* The chef hails from France and all baking is done on the premises. Authentic French croissants and enormous selection of marvelous pastries and coffees. Light lunches. True French Quarter environment complete with fountain and courtyard. Breakfast and lunch daily. CS.

Esplanade and Lakeside Mall Food Courts, 1401 W. Esplanade Ave., Kenner; 468-6116, 3301 Veterans Memorial Blvd.; 835-8000. *I.* Potpourri of restaurants and cafes as branches of many New Orleans restaurants. Typical suburban-type food courts—light, airy, and busy. CS.

Flora's Coffee Cafe, 2600 Royal St., corner of Franklin; 947-8358. *I.* A variety of coffees, teas, pastries, veggie and meaty sandwiches, smoothies, and breads. Poetry readings are presented, and classic and alternative movies are shown on a 56-inch screen. Seating consists of couches and chairs. Breakfast, lunch, and dinner daily.

Foodies Kitchen, Deli and Cafe, 720 Veterans Memorial Blvd.; 837-9695; www.foodieskitchen.com. *I.* This is many concepts rolled into one—deli, cafe, bakery, florist, wine cellar, grocery—but definitely a place to pick up a gourmet meal to take home and enjoy. There are 100-plus takeout restaurant-style meals; numerous desserts; gourmet, salad, and sandwich bars; at least 20 different freshly baked breads; and beautiful fresh produce. Children will also savor the variety of choices and the tasting stations. The dining area is open and airy and features entertaining "food sayings" of some interesting people. CS.

Haagen Dazs Ice Cream Cafe, 621 St. Peter St.; 523-4001, 8108 Hampson; 861-1005. *I.* Haagen Dazs ice cream is the "creme de la creme" of desserts and a fine way to end any of your meals in the Quarter, Riverbend, or other locations in the city. Rest, relax, and have dessert in the afternoon before beginning your next Quarter tour or shopping spree. Many different flavors and taste treats. Open daily. Casual. CS.

Jax Brewery Food Court. *I*. Includes food stands from traditional New Orleans restaurants. Relaxed, informal, with riverview tables available. Open seven days. CS.

Jimmy Buffett's Margaritaville Cafe, 1104 Decatur St.; 592-2565. M. Island-inspired menu featuring shrimp, ribs, Jamaican chicken, and Mexican corn,. Live music is offered daily at 3 pm, with an occasional visit from Buffett himself. Lunch and dinner daily.

La Madeleine's, on Jackson Square, 547 St. Ann St.; 568-0073, 601 S. Carrollton Ave.; 861-8662, 3300 Severn Ave., Metairie; 456-1624. *I*. Wonderful French bakery-cafe with many pastry selections. Brioches and breads baked in-shop. Light meals also. Casual. Breakfast, lunch, and dinner daily. CS.

La Marquise, 625 Chartres St.; 524-0420. *I*. For the visitors who savor a cup of coffee and a French pastry early in the morning before touring the Quarter, this is the place to find such a treat. It is also a nice place for an afternoon sweet "pick up" and a cup of coffee. There is also a delightful courtyard with Old World charm. Open daily. CS.

Lovecchio's, 872 Harrison Ave.; 482-4616. *I*. Small neighborhood cafe and catering service with huge takeout menu. There are daily specials, homemade dinners, numerous po' boy selections, fried seafood, and and wonderful desserts. A local favorite since the 1970s. Lunch and dinner Mon-Sat.

Martin Wine Cellar & Cafe, 714 Elmeer Ave., Metairie; 896-7300, 3827 Baronne St.; 899-7411. *M to E*. Delightful cafe for some gourmet sampling and traditionally a place for locals to prepare for special parties with an array of fine wines, party platters, pates, cheeses, and foods from around the world.

Morning Call, 3325 Severn Ave.; 885-4068. *I*. Originally in the French Market for generations. Counters, stools, and mirrors along with the magnificent chicory coffee (cafe au lait) and beignets have moved to the suburbs. Casual. 24 hours. CS.

New Orleans Centre Food Court, 1400 Poydras St.; 568-0000. *I.* Two levels of a variety of New Orleans eating establishments, including Cafe du Monde. Entire centre connects to the Hyatt Regency via enclosed mall. CS.

Oakwood Center Food Court, 197 Westbank Expwy.; 362-1900. *I.* All types of New Orleans food and typical fast food in a suburban mall setting.

P.J.'s, 5432 Magazine St.; 895-0273, 7624 Maple St.; 866-7031, 637 N. Carrollton; 486-8862, 634 Frenchmen St.; 949-2292. *I.* Good freshly brewed coffee and pastries. Popular with the student crowd. Many other locations citywide. Open daily.

Riverwalk Food Court. *I.* A potpourri of food sold at individual stands with menus posted on the wall above. Tables inside and out have great river views. Great for conventioneers. Informal, inexpensive. Open seven days. CS.

Rue de la Course, 1500 Magazine St.; 529-1455, 3128 Magazine St.; 899-0242, 217 N. Peters; 523-0206. *I.* Classic coffee house which features a large selection of specialty and gourmet coffees and teas. Accompany your coffee or tea with any of the variety of pastries, desserts, and even king cake, along with a game of Scrabble or street watching. Breakfast, lunch, and dinner daily. No credit cards.

Swensen's, 3301 Veterans Blvd.; 831-7442. *I.* Some of the best ice cream and variations served anywhere. Open daily. CS.

Swiss Confectionery, 747 St. Charles Ave.; 522-7788. *M to E.* An excellent place from which to order all sorts of specialty cakes and pastry shells. This is the place that generations of brides and grooms have used for wedding and shower cakes; they have the best wedding cake recipe in the city. Mon-Sat mornings and afternoons.

Tarby's Gourmet to Go, 312 Harrison Ave.; 486-7500. M. Described as a place for "upscale home replacement meals"; also offering a catering menu for a variety of events. Fully prepared healthful meals can be picked up on the way home from work. Lunch and dinner Mon-Sat. CS.

Whole Foods Market and Deli, 3135 Esplanade Ave.; 943-1626. *I.* A visit to the Whole Foods Market is worth the trip wherever you live. Beautiful fresh fruits, vegetables, and produce to suit any gourmet's kitchen are sold here. Located in the store's rear is a take-out or "eat and shop" deli. Many cold cuts, cheeses, salads, and some baked items and desserts. Outside tables overlooking Esplanade Avenue. Open daily. CS.

CAFETERIAS

A & G Cafeteria, Clearview Shopping Mall, Metairie; 885-0182. *I.* Open seven days. CS.

Piccadilly Cafeteria, 3800 S. Carrollton Ave.; 482-0775. *I.* CS.

Piccadilly Cafeteria, 3200 Paris Rd., Chalmette; 271-6860. *I.* CS.

Piccadilly Cafeteria, 8908 Veterans Memorial Blvd., Metairie; 467-4224. *I.* CS.

Piccadilly Cafeteria, 533 Lapalco Blvd., Gretna; 391-1063. *I.* CS.

Piccadilly Cafeteria, 1701 Barataria Blvd., Marrero; 341-7525. *I.* CS.

Piccadilly Cafeteria, 2222 Clearview Pkwy., Metairie; 454-6271. *I.* CS.

Piccadilly Cafeteria, 2609 Jefferson Hwy.; 834-2695. *I.* CS.

BRUNCH

Sunday brunch has long been one of New Orleans' favorite ways to entertain. The traditional menu is a milk-punch, free-flowing champagne, or some other alcoholic beverage, grillades and grits au gratin, and cafe brulot. Some restaurants have enormous buffets, with seemingly endless choices of entrees, side dishes, and desserts. Background music is furnished by a live band—and if the drink is plentiful enough the band lively enough, brunch may last through suppertime!

Today, many fine local restaurants have their own variations on this theme. Following is a list of just a few that are special. We suggest reservations. All brunches also have special rates for children.

Cafe Sbisa, 1011 Decatur St.; 522-5565. Sunday brunch with live jazz in the heart of the French Market.

Commander's Palace, 1403 Washington Ave.; 899-8221. Traditional weekend jazz brunch in this beautiful Victorian mansion and courtyard.

Court of Two Sisters, 613 Royal St.; 522-7261. Traditional daily brunch. Outdoor patio seating. True French Quarter feeling.

Hotel Inter-Continental—Veranda Restaurant, 444 St. Charles Ave.; 585-4383. Sunday champagne jazz brunch.

House of Blues, 225 Decatur St.; 529-2583. Sunday gospel brunch. Tickets must be purchased in advance.

Kabby's, Hilton Hotel, 2 Poydras St.; 561-0500. Champagne jazz brunch.

Mr. B's Bistro, 201 Royal St.; 523-2078. Traditional Sunday brunch. Beautiful bar setting, live music. The spot where Quarter people meet.

The Rib Room, Omni Royal Orleans Hotel, 621 St. Louis; 529-5333. Traditional Sunday brunch. Great people-watching spot.

Riverview, atop the Marriott Hotel; 581-1000. Sunday champagne jazz brunch. Extensive and superb. Tremendous view of the river.

Sazerac, Fairmont Hotel, 123 Baronne St.; 529-4733. Traditional jazz brunch. Home of the Sazerac cocktail.

Westin Hotel—Riverbend Grill, 100 Iberville St.; 566-7006. Sunday jazz brunch. Magnificent view of the river.

PERFORMING ARTS

Music and New Orleans just go together. From the first opera house on this continent to the first notes of Dixieland jazz and the blues, all kinds of music are part of the soul of the city. Opera, in 19th-century New Orleans, wasn't a luxury. It was a necessity of life. The arias were the pop music of the day. A Frenchman, short on funds, would give up his dinner to buy a ticket for the evening's performance. Even ladies who were "in the family way" went to the opera, sitting in the loges-grillees, boxes that were shielded by lattice work from the rest of the audience.

Then came jazz. Born about 1900, mothered by the blues, it permeated every strata of New Orleans society and then spread to the rest of the world. Legendary ambassadors such as Louis Armstrong, Sidney Bechet, and Papa Celestin have done more to promote understanding between peoples of the world than many career diplomats.

Theater and dance groups have also proliferated here. By 1840, there were theaters in New Orleans offering plays in French, German, and English (in the American sector). Today, there are numerous local performing groups. The Theatre of the Performing Arts, situated in Louis Armstrong Park, is an active arena for the performing arts. Broadway shows visit the Saenger Theater regularly, and the universities have active drama departments. We trust that, in the following listings, you will find many ways to spend an entertaining evening.

Overture to a Cultural Season; 611 Gravier St.; 522-8464. Interested patrons of the arts formed this group to help raise money for the performing arts and to foster community interest in the arts. The group opens "the Season" with a large black tie affair in the Central Business District. They call the gala "Overture to a Cultural Season." Currently, the subscriptions are at a premium. The number of patrons has grown, and the evening is one of the most popular fall social events.

PERFORMING ARTS BY AREA

CENTRAL BUSINESS DISTRICT

Contemporary Arts Center, Theater

Louisiana Philharmonic Orchestra, Music

New Orleans Ballet Association, Dance

Orpheum Theatre, Music, Theater
Saenger Performing Arts Center, Theater
Salem Community Theater, Theater
Southern Repertory Theater, Theater
Symphony Chorus, Music

CHALMETTE

Chalmette Cultural Center, Dance, Music

FAUBOURG MARIGNY

Snug Harbor, Music
NOCCA (New Orleans Center for Creative Arts), Dance, Music, Theater

FRENCH QUARTER

Creole Queen Paddlewheeler, Music
French Quarter Fest, Music
French Quarter Weekend Concerts, Music
Le Petit Theatre du Vieux Carre, Theater
Louisiana Vocal Arts Chorale, Music
New Orleans Opera Association, Music
O'Flaherty's Folk Concerts, Music
St. Louis Cathedral, Music
Steamboat Natchez, Music
Theatre of the Performing Arts, Music, Theater

LAKEFRONT

Louisiana Vocal Arts Chorale, Music
University of New Orleans Arena, Music
University of New Orleans Performing Arts Center, Music, Theater

METAIRIE/KENNER

Carlone's Dinner Theater, Theater
Delta Festival Ballet, Dance
Jefferson Ballet Theatre, Dance
Jefferson Performing Arts Society, Dance, Music, Theater
Kenner Little Theater, Theater
Louisiana Philharmonic Orchestra, Music
New Orleans Children's Chorus, Music
Pontchartrain Center, Dance, Music, Theater
Rivertown Repertory Theatre, Theater

MID CITY

Delgado Community College Arts Center, Music, Theater
Dillard University, Theater
Greater N.O. Suzuki Forum, Music
Xavier University, Music

NORTH SHORE

Slidell Little Theater, Theater
Southeastern Louisiana University, Dance, Music, Theater

UPTOWN

Ballet Hysell, Dance
Christ Church Cathedral, Music
Jewish Community Center, Dance, Theater
Junior Philharmonic Society, Music

Louisiana Vocal Arts Chorale, Music
Loyola Ballet, Dance
Loyola College of Music, Music
Loyola Theater, Theater
Newcomb Dance Company, Dance
Newcomb Music, Music
Rogers Chapel—Newcomb/Tulane, Music, Theater
Shakespeare Summer Festival, Theater
Summer Lyric Theater, Theater
Trinity Artist Series, Music
Tulane University, Dance, Theater

DANCE

Ballet Hysell, 1527 Harmony St.; 895-3113. Ballet Hysell is a local company that offers interesting presentations during the winter season and workshops in the summer. Call for schedule.

Chalmette Cultural Center, 8245 W. Judge Perez Dr.; 278-1508. The cultural center of St. Bernard Parish has brought dance companies to this area neighboring New Orleans.

Delta Festival Ballet Co., 3850 N. Causeway Blvd.; 836-7166. Louisiana's only resident professional dance company, which has a school and a junior company. Presents wonderful productions throughout the year in the tri-parish cultural centers. Check the newspaper calendar or call for information.

Jefferson Ballet Theatre, 3621 Florida Ave., Kenner; 468-1231. Its goal is the understanding and appreciation of classical ballet. Performances are held at Loyola University's Roussel Hall and at the Pontchartrain Center. Call for schedule.

Jefferson Performing Arts Society (JPAS), 400 Phlox Ave., Metairie; 885-2000. Conducts many dance performances throughout the year. Call for schedule, or check a local publication calendar.

Jewish Community Center, 5342 St. Charles Ave.; 897-0143. Holds performances throughout the year. Call for schedule and information.

Loyola Ballet, Loyola University Campus, 6363 St. Charles Ave.; 865-2778. Contemporary and classical performances throughout the school year.

Newcomb Dance Company, Newcomb/Tulane University Campus, 6823 St. Charles Ave.; 865-5106 or 865-5789. Performances are held during the school year and feature advanced student dancers and visiting artists.

New Orleans Ballet Association, 305 Baronne St.; 522-0996. Committed to making dance accessible to the community. Hosts performances throughout the year.

NOCCA (New Orleans Center for Creative Arts), St. Ferdinand by the river; 523-7708 or 899-0055. Creative school for the arts with students attending part time from high schools in a nine-parish area. The new facility will provide for a larger student body and for performances by students and visiting artists.

Pontchartrain Center, 4545 Williams Blvd.; 465-9985. Beautiful, new facility on Kenner's lakefront which presents local and touring performances.

Southeastern Louisiana University (SLU), Hammond; 504-549-2341. Annual Fanfare production brings dance from around the world to Louisiana.

Tulane University, 6823 St. Charles Ave.; 865-5267. Performances by student artists along with seasoned professionals.

MUSIC

Chalmette Cultural Center, 8245 W. Judge Perez Dr.; 278-1508. The well-equipped cultural center of St. Bernard Parish frequently presents musicians.

Christ Church Cathedral, 2919 St. Charles Ave.; 895-6602. Cathedral Concerts Program presents concerts throughout the year in a variety of musical genres. There are also postconcert receptions to meet performers.

Creole Queen Paddlewheeler, Canal Street Dock at Spanish Plaza; 524-0814. Nightly dinner cruise with a Dixieland jazz band.

Delgado Community College Arts Center, 615 City Park Ave.; 483-4168. Vocal and instrumental recitals, offered free of charge, are held regularly in the drama hall.

French Quarter Fest, April throughout the French Quarter; 522-5730.

Free performances by hundreds of local musicians on a multitude of stages.

French Quarter Weekend Concerts, Saturday and Sunday afternoons at Decatur and St. Philip streets and Decatur and Dumaine streets. Check calendar in local publications.

Greater N.O. Suzuki Forum; 733-3159. Monthly workshops and performances are held throughout the year by qualified teachers in the metro area. Annual institute at Delgado Community College. Call for schedule or check local publications.

Jefferson Performing Arts Society (JPAS), 400 Phlox Ave., Metairie; 885-2000. Conducts many musical performances year round. Call for schedule or check a local publication calendar.

Junior Philharmonic Society, Tulane University's Dixon Hall; 895-7253. Elementary- through college-aged performers present a variety of concerts free of charge.

Louisiana Philharmonic Orchestra (LPO), Orpheum Theatre, 129 University Pl.; Pontchartrain Center, Metairie; 523-6530. One of only two full-time orchestras in the U.S. Concerts are held throughout the year and include jazz and American favorites, some with a Latin flavor. There is also the Classic Series, Casual Classic Series, Family Discovery Series (wonderful fun and educational for families with children), Southern Serenades Plantation Concerts, Beethoven and Blue Jeans Concerts, Christmas Concerts, and open-air spring concerts in area parks. Internationally known guest artists perform regularly with the orchestra. You have not "heard" New Orleans until you have heard its orchestra.

Louisiana Vocal Arts Chorale, University of New Orleans; 482-6338. Composed of professional singers and those for whom the chorale is an avocation. Concerts are held at St. Charles Avenue Presbyterian Church and the St. Louis Cathedral.

Loyola College of Music, 6363 St. Charles Ave., Roussel Hall; 865-3492. The Montage Performance Series encompasses many musical genres including jazz, opera, choral, ballet, symphonic, chamber, and concert music and solo recitals. There is also a Lagniappe Performance series of free concerts.

New Orleans Children's Chorus, 787 Harrison Ave.; 488-5973. This local group has even presented a solo concert at Carnegie Hall, and performed at St. Peter's Basilica in Rome. The five choirs of children range in ages from 8 to 18, and also perform with the LPO. Concerts are held during the school year.

New Orleans Opera Association, Theater of the Performing Arts, 801 N. Rampart; 529-2278. The Opera Association continues the tradition which began when the famous French Opera House was built. There is a fall and spring season annually with a strong community following. The Women's Opera Guild also conducts an opera orientation and appreciation series.

Newcomb Music, Tulane University's Dixon Hall and Rogers Memorial Chapel; 865-5267. Music students present a "Music at Midday" concert series.

NOCCA (New Orleans Center for Creative Arts), St. Ferdinand by the river; 523-7708 or 899-0055. Creative school for the arts with students attending part time from high schools in a nine-parish area. The new facility will provide for a larger student body and for performances by students and visiting artists.

O'Flaherty's Folk Concerts, O'Flaherty's Irish Channel Pub, 508 Toulouse St.; 529-1317. Authentic music of Ireland by resident band "The Celtic Folk," local Irish luminaries, and touring Irish musicians and balladeers. The pub also assists with the annual Fall Celtic Festival.

Orpheum Theatre, 129 University Pl.; 524-3285. Beautiful, refurbished old theater with original ornate work and fantastic acoustics; the downtown home for the Louisiana Philharmonic Orchestra. The Classic and Family Discovery series are held here.

Pontchartrain Center, 4545 Williams Blvd.; 465-9985. Beautiful, new facility on Kenner's lakefront which presents local and touring performances. The center is also the Jefferson Parish home for the Louisiana Philharmonic Orchestra.

Rogers Chapel—Newcomb/Tulane, 1229 Broadway; 865-5422. "Music at Midday" series performed by dedicated music students.

St. Louis Cathedral, Jackson Square; 525-9585. Vocal and instrumental concerts on some Sundays.

Snug Harbor, 626 Frenchmen St.; 949-0696. Traditional and contemporary jazz in a cafe-like setting.

Southeastern Louisiana University (SLU), Hammond; 504-549-2341. Annual Fanfare production brings music from around the world to Louisiana.

Steamboat Natchez; 586-8777. Nightly dinner/jazz cruises on the Mississippi River. Board the boat at 6 pm; return at 8:30 pm. There is limited free on-the-wharf parking.

Symphony Chorus; 365-3056. The principal chorus of the Louisiana Philharmonic Orchestra, which performs several concerts each season.

Theatre of the Performing Arts, 801 N. Rampart; 565-7462 or 565-7470. Contemporary-style performance hall used for numerous cultural events.

Trinity Artist Series, Trinity Episcopal Church, 1329 Jackson Ave.; 522-0276. Classical and chamber music on Sunday evenings.

University of New Orleans Arena, 6801 Franklin Ave.; 286-7222. This Lakefront arena hosts many prominent touring musicians. Call for schedule or check local publications.

University of New Orleans Performing Arts Center, Lakefront at Elysian Fields; 280-6381. Department of Music features a Musical Excursions series with local, national, and international artists.

Xavier University, 7325 Palmetto St.; 483-7597. During the school year, the Music Department presents student and faculty/artist performances.

THEATER

Carlone's Dinner Theater, 100 N. Labarre Rd., corner of Airline Highway; 838-9906. This new dinner theater has a wonderful stage with exceptional lighting and sound, and presents quality theatrical productions.

Contemporary Arts Center, 900 Camp St.; 523-1216. A showcase for avant-garde plays, very informal readings, and truly contemporary art displays.

Delgado Community College Arts Center, 615 City Park Ave.;

483-4168. A variety of plays and musicals are held throughout the school year.

Dillard University, 2601 Gentilly Blvd.; 286-4762. Four productions are offered during the school year.

Jefferson Performing Arts Society (JPAS), 400 Phlox Ave., Metairie; 885-2000. Will soon celebrate its silver anniversary. Many high-quality musicals and theatrical productions are offered throughout the year.

Jewish Community Center, 5342 St. Charles Ave.; 897-0143. The Jewish Community Center is located uptown on the St. Charles Avenue streetcar line and presents periodic theater presentations.

Kenner Little Theater, 467-4508. This young people's theater group presents family-oriented plays, and tours Jefferson Parish schools, parks, and libraries. The group has proven to be highly successful and has a dedicated following.

Le Petit Theatre du Vieux Carre, 616 St. Peter St.; 522-9958. Le Petit, New Orleans' oldest theater group, has several productions a year. Tickets are available by subscription or individually. The children's theater is located in the same building, has three productions (the traditional Christmas play and two in the summer), as well as puppet shows and workshops. Auditions are held in September and casts for all productions are selected. Works by local artists are exhibited in one of the downstairs rooms, and are displayed during the year.

Loyola Theater, Loyola University, 6363 St. Charles Ave.; 865-3840. The drama and speech departments offer several productions during the school year.

NOCCA (New Orleans Center for Creative Arts), St. Ferdinand by the river; 523-7708 or 899-0055. Creative school for the arts with students attending part time from high schools in a nine-parish area. The new facility will provide for a larger student body and for performances by students and visiting artists.

Orpheum Theater, 129 University Pl.; 524-3285. Beautiful, refurbished old theater with original ornate work and fantastic acoustics. Theatrical productions involving music.

Pontchartrain Center, 4545 Williams Blvd.; 465-9985. Beautiful, new facility on Kenner's lakefront which presents Mardi Gras balls and local and touring theatrical performances.

Rivertown Repertory Theatre, Fourth and Minor streets, Kenner; 468-7221. Theater group with very successful local productions.

Rogers Chapel—Newcomb/Tulane, 1229 Broadway; 865-5422. Summer theatrical performances by the Lyric Theater and children's plays by Patchwork Players.

Saenger Performing Arts Center, 143 N. Rampart St.; 524-2490. Outstanding Broadway plays and concerts are presented during the year, along with a special holiday production at Christmas. The Saenger is one of the beautiful old theaters in the city—refurbished and restored. Subscriptions or individual tickets are available at the Box Office, 143 N. Rampart, or through Ticketmaster outlets.

Salem Community Theater, 4212 Camp St.; 895-3773. Small, new theater with a few productions.

Shakespeare Summer Festival, Tulane University's Lupin Theater; 865-5105. Excellent productions performed by students and professionals.

Slidell Little Theater, 2024 Nellie Dr.; 504-641-0324. New North Shore theater with several annual performances.

Southern Repertory Theater, Canal Place; 861-8163. Wonderful productions from a small group which bills itself as emphasizing the "performance of actors and the language of Southern regional cultural diversity."

Southeastern Louisiana University (SLU), Hammond; 504-549-2341. Annual Fanfare production brings performers from around the world to Louisiana.

Summer Lyric Theater, Tulane University's Dixon Hall; 865-5269. A talented group of national and local performers and some apprentice students present top-notch productions during the summer months: musicals and operettas with beautiful sets and costumes.

Theatre of the Performing Arts, 801 N. Rampart; 565-7462 or 565-7470. Contemporary building with enormous crystal-chandeliered lobby; presents touring and resident theater productions.

University of New Orleans Performing Arts Center, Lakefront Campus; 280-6381. This performing arts center has productions throughout the year, some classics, some avant garde.

NIGHTLIFE

New Orleans rarely sleeps. No matter what time you walk in the Quarter your ears will pick up jazzy tunes flowing into the streets, enticing you to come inside for the entertainment. There is no still time; even at daybreak, the sounds and smells of the Quarter are very much alive and present.

Most of the downtown hotels and guest houses have quiet piano lounges or small three-piece jazz groups. The bars along St. Charles Avenue, neighborhoods, and the university area have their own following when the sun goes down. Bourbon Street, of course, is the most lively place. Take a deep breath and a long afternoon rest and prepare to join the night owls as you explore the after-dark madness of New Orleans. (All music in the following listing is live music by local or touring talent.)

NIGHTLIFE BY AREA

CENTRAL BUSINESS DISTRICT

Fairmont Court, Music for Listening and Dancing
Howlin' Wolf, Music for Listening and Dancing
Hotel Inter-Continental, Music for Listening and Dancing
Jazz Meridien, Bars
Michaul's, Music for Listening and Dancing
Mulate's, Music for Listening and Dancing
Pete Fountain's Jazz Club, Music for Listening and Dancing
Polo Club Lounge, Music for Listening and Dancing
Riverbend Grill, Music for Listening and Dancing
Sazerac Bar, Music for Listening and Dancing
Tips Big Room, Music for Listening and Dancing
Top of the Mart, Music for Listening and Dancing

CHALMETTE

Beach Bar, Music for Listening and Dancing, Karaoke

FAUBOURG MARIGNY

Cafe Brasil, Music for Listening and Dancing

Jazz band for a paddlewheeler — *New Orleans Metropolitan Convention & Visitors Bureau and Riverview Photography*

Dream Palace, Music for Listening and Dancing
Feelings Cafe, Bars
Snug Harbor Jazz Bistro, Music for Listening and Dancing

FRENCH QUARTER

Arnaud's Cigar Bar, Bars
Bombay Club, Bars
Can Can Cafe, Music for Listening and Dancing
Carousel Revolving Bar, Music for Listening and Dancing
Chris Owens Club, Music for Listening and Dancing
Creole Queen Riverboat, Music for Listening and Dancing
Crescent City Brewhouse, Music for Listening and Dancing
Donna's Bar and Grill, Music for Listening and Dancing
Famous Door, Music for Listening and Dancing
Fritzel's European Jazz Pub, Music for Listening and Dancing
Funky Butt, Music for Listening and Dancing
Gazebo Cafe & Bar, Music for Listening and Dancing
House of Blues, Music for Listening and Dancing
Jimmy Buffett's Margaritaville Cafe, Music for Listening and Dancing
Lafitte's Blacksmith Shop, Bars
Maison Bourbon Nite Club, Music for Listening and Dancing
Market Cafe, Music for Listening and Dancing
Maxwell's Toulouse Cabaret, Music for Listening and Dancing
Molly's at the Market, Bars
Mystic Den, Bars
Napoleon House, Bars
Natchez Steamboat, Music for Listening and Dancing
O'Flaherty's Irish Channel Pub, Music for Listening and Dancing
Old Absinthe House, Bars
Old Opera House, Bars
Palm Court Jazz Cafe, Music for Listening and Dancing
Pat O'Brien's, Music for Listening and Dancing
Patout's Cajun Corner, Music for Listening and Dancing
Praline Connection Gospel and Blues Hall, Music for Listening and Dancing
Preservation Hall, Music for Listening and Dancing
Storyville District, Music for Listening and Dancing
Tipitina's—French Quarter, Music for Listening and Dancing
21 Supper Club, Music for Listening and Dancing

LAKEFRONT

Amberjacks, Music for Listening and Dancing
Bally's Lakefront Casino, Music for Listening and Dancing
Jaeger's Beer Garden, Music for Listening and Dancing
Midnight Star Cafe, Music for Listening and Dancing
Parlay's, Bars
Plantation Coffee House, Music for Listening and Dancing
Spanky's Bar and Grill, Bars
Steak Knife, Music for Listening and Dancing

METAIRIE/KENNER

Bengal Lounge, Music for Listening and Dancing
Billy K's Encore, Music for Listening and Dancing
Callahan's, Music for Listening and Dancing
Critic's Choice, Music for Listening and Dancing
Jefferson Orleans North, Music for Listening and Dancing
Kenny's Key West, Music for Listening and Dancing
Lager's International Ale House, Bars
Pinnacle Lounge, Music for Listening and Dancing
Treasure Chest Casino, Music for Listening and Dancing

MID CITY

Acadian Beer Garden, Bars
Dixie Tavern, Music for Listening and Dancing
Mid-City Lanes, Music for Listening and Dancing

UPTOWN

Bayou Bar, Bars
Bulldog, Bars
Carrollton Station, Music for Listening and Dancing
Cooter Brown's Tavern, Bars
Dante Street Deli Cafe, Music for Listening and Dancing
Dos Jefes Uptown Cigar Bar, Music for Listening and Dancing
Jimmy's, Music for Listening and Dancing
Le Bon Temps Roule, Music for Listening and Dancing
Maple Leaf Bar, Music for Listening and Dancing
Mermaid Lounge, Music for Listening and Dancing
Parasol's Bar, Bars
Red Room, Music for Listening and Dancing
Samuel's Avenue Beer Pub, Bars
Tipitina's, Music for Listening and Dancing
Victorian Lounge, Bars

WEST BANK

Boomtown Casino, Music for Listening and Dancing
Four Columns, Music for Listening and Dancing
Junkyard Night Club, Music for Listening and Dancing

Bars

Acadian Beer Garden, 201 N. Carrollton Ave.; 483-9003. Very casual with many featured bands.

Arnaud's Cigar Bar, 813 Bienville St.; 523-5433. Wide selection of fine and rare tobaccos, and superb variety of liquors and liqueurs.

Bayou Bar, Pontchartrain Hotel, 2031 St. Charles Ave.; 524-0581. A beautiful piano bar, and a popular meeting place for locals and tourists. Live piano music nightly.

Bombay Club, 8 Conti Street; 586-0972. Magnificent martinis with piano accompaniment. This piano/martini bar is decorated with authentic artifacts from the Duke and Duchess of Windsor. Also, wide selection of liqueurs and liquors.

Bulldog, 3236 Magazine St.; 891-1516. In addition to a variety of cigars and scotches, there are approximately 200 draught or bottle beers available. A nice selection of bar food is also offered.

Cooter Brown's Tavern, 509 S. Carrollton; 866-9104. One of the Riverbend area's favorite neighborhood taverns, with a selection of 200 draught and bottle beers. Good bar food is also offered.

Feelings Cafe, 2600 Chartres St.; 945-2222. Feelings Cafe has a cozy indoor piano bar patio surrounded by dining tables and an overhead gallery.

Jazz Meridien, 614 Canal St.; 525-6500. Authentic New Orleans music background for good French hotel bar, in Le Meridien Hotel.

Lafitte's Blacksmith Shop, 941 Bourbon St.; 523-0066. Considered to be the oldest bar in North America. A blacksmith shop on this site was supposedly used as a reputable "front" for Lafitte and his pirates many years ago. A favorite bar for many . . . and its dark, pirate-like ambience does have a mysterious air.

Lager's International Ale House, 3501 Veterans Memorial Blvd.; 887-9923. A place for beer lovers with—literally—a worldly selection of tap beers.

Molly's at the Market, 1107 Decatur St.; 525-5169. Has become the traditional afterwork place for local and visiting media personnel.

Mystic Den, Royal Sonesta Hotel, 300 Bourbon St.; 586-0300. Good place to relax and chat. Renowned pianist Ronnie Kole is regularly featured.

Napoleon House, 500 Chartres St.; 524-9752. Enjoy a variety of drinks in the genuine Old World atmosphere of this 200-year-old building, with recorded classical music only.

Old Absinthe House, 240 Bourbon St.; 523-3181. This bar is unique in its decor and has long been a tourist attraction. The walls are papered with calling cards and photos of famous visitors.

Old Opera House, 601 Bourbon St.; 522-3265. A variety of drinks and live music.

Parasol's Bar, 2533 Constance St.; 897-5413. Year round a regular local meeting place, but this is the place to be for St. Patrick's Day celebrations.

Parlay's Bar and Lounge, 870 Harrison Ave.; 482-4700. Popular local meeting place open till the wee hours.

Samuel's Avenue Beer Pub, 1628 St Charles Ave.; 581-3777. A pub on historic St. Charles Avenue with nearly 200 beers from which to choose.

Spanky's Bar and Grill, 5243 Canal Blvd.; 488-0100. Spacious, with TV screens throughout broadcasting all types of sports. Cigars, drinks, and food add to the lively atmosphere.

Victorian Lounge, Columns Hotel, 3811 St. Charles Ave.; 899-9308. Pleasant and cozy Victorian atmosphere with background music.

Music for Listening and Dancing

Amberjacks, 7306 Lakeshore Dr.; 282-6660. Live music and even a weekly comedy night.

Bally's Lakefront Casino, 1 Stars and Stripes Blvd.; 248-3200. A variety of live music, entertainment, and comedy acts.

Beach Bar, 7617 W. Judge Perez Dr.; 271-9002. Popular, casual bar for locals, with weekend karaoke and bands.

Bengal Lounge, 4612 Quincy St.; 456-0986. Live music and big dance floor.

Billy K's Encore, 3400 Hessmer Ave.; 780-2266. Live music and dancing.

Boomtown Casino, 4132 Peters Rd., Harvey; 366-7711. Live music includes '50s and '60s oldies, big-band sound, and country with country line-dance lessons.

Cafe Brasil, 2100 Chartres; 947-9386. Live music nightly ranges from jazz to rock to Latin bands.

Callahan's, 3213 Kingman St.; 888-9898. Live music with special dance-lesson nights that range from line dancing to West Coast swing dance. There's even a comedy night.

Can Can Cafe, Royal Sonesta Hotel, 300 Bourbon St.; 586-0300. Live Dixieland jazz band, premium-brand liquors, and a variety of coffee-and-spirits creations.

Carousel Revolving Bar, Monteleone Hotel, 214 Royal St.; 523-3341. An authetic revolving carousel is the bar's centerpiece. Live music, and a good selection of vintage ports and single-malt scotches.

Carrollton Station, 8140 Willow St.; 865-9190. Popular with the college crowd for good R&B as well as rock and Cajun.

Chris Owens Club, Bourbon Street at St. Louis; 523-6400. This is one of New Orleans' all-time favorite night spots. The superstar of the Quarter puts on a lively dance revue nightly. This is a must for visitors.

Creole Queen Riverboat, Poydras Street Wharf; 524-0814. Listen and second line to jazz during the nightly dinner cruise.

Crescent City Brewhouse, 527 Decatur St.; 522-0571. An upbeat brewpub featuring handcrafted brews and live music nightly.

Critic's Choice, 4725 Quincy St.; 887-9809. Live music and dancing.

Dante Street Deli Cafe, 736 Dante St.; 861-3634. Lively Sunday jazz brunch.

Dixie Tavern, 3340 Canal St.; 822-8268. Live music and dancing.

Donna's Bar and Grill, 800 N. Rampart St.; 596-6914. Lots of good New Orleans music, brass bands, and jazz jams.

Dos Jefes Uptown Cigar Bar, 5535 Tchoupitoulas St.; 891-8500. Live music and a selection of more than 40 premium-brand cigars. The upscale bar offers a variety of liqueurs, liquors, and single-malt scotches.

Dream Palace, 534 Frenchmen St.; 945-2040. Varied live music for dancing that ranges from Latin salsa to jazz to funky blues.

Fairmont Court, Fairmont Hotel, 123 Baronne St.; 529-7111. Elegant piano bar; jazz bands too.

Famous Door, 339 Bourbon St.; 522-7626. This is a Quarter jazz landmark and the original home of the Dukes of Dixieland. Listen for a few minutes on the street corner and then go inside for an evening of New Orleans Dixieland jazz and cocktails. R&B also featured.

Four Columns, 3711 Westbank Expwy., Harvey; 340-4109. Live Cajun music.

Fritzel's European Jazz Pub, 733 Bourbon St.; 561-0432. Traditional jazz pub offering a full lineup of jazz bands.

Funky Butt, 714 N. Rampart St., across from Armstrong Park; 558-0872. The mellow atmosphere of this club is the perfect setting for authentic jazz and blues, starting at 9 each night.

Gazebo Cafe & Bar, 1018 Decatur St. in the French Market; 522-0862. Contemporary or traditional jazz in an outdoor patio setting.

Hotel Inter-Continental, 444 St. Charles Ave.; 525-5566. Music and dancing in an elegant hotel setting.

House of Blues, 225 Decatur St.; 529-2624. The funky and spacious New Orleans branch of this national chain, complete with balcony seating, attracts local and national music groups.

Howlin' Wolf, 828 St. Peter St.; 523-2551. A variety of music, from alternative and jazz to blues and rock, is featured from local and touring bands. There's even an open-mike acoustic night.

Jaeger's Beer Garden, West End Park; 283-7585. Large dance floor. The "oldies but goodies" and other music are featured from live bands.

The Jefferson Orleans North, 2600 Edenborn Ave.; 454-6110. Ballroom dancing to the big-band sound.

Jimmy Buffett's Margaritaville Cafe, 1104 Decatur St.; 592-2565. Live music nightly in Key West-themed club featuring city's top acts—even Jimmy Buffett when he's in town.

Jimmy's, 8200 Willow St.; 861-8200. Across from Carrollton Station—try both! Jimmy's brings nationally known R&B, reggae, rock, etc., to New Orleans.

Junkyard Night Club, 350 Douglas Lane, Marrero; 371-4643. Live music, Cajun-music nights, and "Lagniappe" party nights.

Kenny's Key West, 3012 N. Arnoult Rd.; 456-9500. Live local music.

Le Bon Temps Roule, 4801 Magazine St.; 895-8117. A regular crowd pleaser with live music, daily drink specials, and "free oysters on the half shell" Fridays.

Maison Bourbon Nite Club, 641 Bourbon St.; 522-8818. Maison Bourbon is one of the havens for authentic Dixieland jazz on Bourbon Street. It jumps with music lovers and is inexpensive.

Maple Leaf Bar, 8316 Oak St.; 866-9359. Good drinks and live music played by New Orleans' best young musicians make for relaxing, fun evenings in this uptown location. Poetry readings on Sundays.

Market Cafe, 1000 Decatur St.; 527-5000. Open-air cafe featuring live jazz daily along with Cajun and Creole cuisine.

Maxwell's Toulouse Cabaret, 615 Toulouse St.; 523-4207. Jazz sessions nightly.

Mermaid Lounge, 1102 Constance St.; 524-4747. Local music geared toward a younger crowd . . . contemporary jazz and alternative rock.

Michaul's Live Cajun Music Restaurant, 840 St. Charles Ave.; 522-5517. Cajun music, and even on-the-floor dancing lessons, all week. Families welcomed.

Mid-City Lanes Rock 'n Bowl, 4133 S. Carrollton Ave.; 482-3133. A funky entertainment venue featuring rockin' zydeco and Cajun bands and varied local talent alternating on two stages with a dance floor in between. You can even bowl in the vintage 1941 bowling alley, and snack at the food counter.

Midnight Star Cafe, 7224 Pontchartrain Blvd.; 282-6241. Catch the sounds of live jazz on the open-air porch of this neat cafe.

Mulate's, 201 Julia St.; 522-1492. Live Cajun music all week with dancing. Even on-floor dancing lessons. Families welcomed.

Natchez Steamboat, Toulouse Street Wharf, across from Jackson Square; 586-8777. On Tuesday through Sunday nights, enjoy dinner and the sounds of the Steamboat Stompers and Dukes of Dixieland on a relaxing river trip, with optional buffet. Limited parking on wharf.

O'Flaherty's Irish Channel Pub, 514 Toulouse St.; 529-1317. Enjoy the authentic music of Ireland, with guest and resident musicians/balladeers, along with your favorite ale or lager. Irish public-house atmosphere; some "pub grub" available.

Palm Court Jazz Cafe, 1204 Decatur St.; 525-0200. Excellent place to listen to traditional jazz.

Pat O'Brien's, 718 St. Peter St.; 525-4823. Whether it's music, drink, or fun people you're seeking, look no further! After one of the famous Hurricanes (the cool, sweet, rum drink served in the huge glass) you're sure to sit back and sing old favorites with the crowd. It is rare not to see college students and granny types all having fun under one roof. There is a quiet patio in the rear just in case the party is too loud inside.

Patout's Cajun Corner, 501 Bourbon St.; 529-4256. Spirited live Cajun music nightly.

Pete Fountain's Jazz Club, Hilton Hotel, 2 Poydras St.; 561-0500. One of New Orleans' favorite native sons is now at home at the Hilton, complete with his clarinet and classic jazz band. Don't miss this highly entertaining Dixieland jazz show.

Pinnacle Lounge, top of Landmark Hotel, 2601 Severn Ave.; 888-9500. Variety of live music with large dance floor, and distant lovely view of New Orleans skyline.

Plantation Coffee House, 5555 Canal Blvd.; 482-3164. Enjoy your favorite type of coffee with a French pastry to the beautiful sound of a classical guitarist.

Polo Club Lounge, 300 Gravier St.; 523-6000. Pianist performs solo or in trio; repertoire includes jazz, dance music, and show tunes.

Praline Connection Gospel and Blues Hall, 907 S. Peters St.; 523-3973. Lively gospel, blues, and jazz are served during evenings and Sunday brunch.

Preservation Hall, 726 St. Peter St.; 522-2841. This is the best place in the whole United States to hear hot traditional jazz in a no-frills surrounding. No drinks, just music. The musicians who play here have toured the world.

Red Room, 2040 St. Charles Ave.; 528-9759. Supper club in a structure that used to be a restaurant in the Eiffel Tower. A different musical genre is presented each night for dancing pleasure.

Riverbend Grill, Westin Hotel, 100 Iberville St.; 568-0155. At the top of the hotel, this room has a spectacular view of the river. A jazz trio provides entertainment.

Sazerac Bar, Fairmont Hotel, 123 Baronne St.; 529-7111. Experience soft sounds and the world-famous Sazerac cocktail (supposedly the world's first cocktail).

Snug Harbor Jazz Bistro, 626 Frenchmen St.; 949-0696. Jazz and cocktails, along with New Orleans' favorite dishes, are available in this club located in historic Faubourg Marigny. Rated the city's best jazz club by *Esquire* magazine.

Steak Knife, 888 Harrison Ave.; 488-8981. Enjoy live jazz bands while you drink and dine.

Storyville District, 125 Bourbon St.; 410-1000, www.thestoryvilledistrict.com. Live jazz and marvelous food—two of New Orleans' passions—are combined to create a wonderfully unique place. The Ralph Brennan Restaurant Group and Jazz Fest founder Quint Davis have joined talents to create a special environment for lunch, dinner (till midnight), and Sunday brunch with a variety of jazz bands.

Tipitina's, 501 Napoleon Ave.; 897-3943. The original legendary club where the late Professor Longhair played. It remains a popular showcase for local and touring bands.

Tipitina's—French Quarter, 233 N. Peters St.; 897-3943. Some of the best music in town can be heard in this new branch of the well-known club.

Tips Big Room, 310 Howard Ave.; 568-1702. Tipitina's spacious, modern complex in the Warehouse District with state-of-the-art sound and lighting systems. Enormous dance floor.

Top of the Mart, World Trade Center, 2 Canal St.; 522-9795. The most beautiful revolving cocktail lounge in New Orleans, overlooking the World's Fair Exposition site and the Mississippi River, offers nightly entertainment and some of the best drinks in town.

Treasure Chest Casino, 5050 Williams Blvd.; 443-8000. A variety of live music and entertainment.

21 Supper Club, 615 Toulouse St.; 598-2121. Ambience reminiscent of yesteryear's opulent cabarets. Experience traditional or modern jazz, a "swing show," or other local music.

DOWNTOWN RIVERFRONT

The Downtown Riverfront is a "people place," the most exciting area of new development in the city. The key to its appeal is the Mississippi River itself. For generations it was cut off from view by levees, floodwalls, and wharves. Now it is suddenly accessible, to mesmerize native and visitor alike with its size, power, and constantly changing panorama of water traffic.

The area runs from the Moon Walk, adjacent to the French Quarter, to Julia Street near the twin Mississippi River bridges. It includes New Orleans' huge—and still growing—Convention Center, fine hotels, Canal Place for elegant shopping, major corporate offices, the World Trade Center, lively nightlife, excursion boat terminals, urban picnic spots, Algiers Ferry Landing, Aquarium of the Americas, IMAX Theatre, and Riverwalk shopping mall. Within the Jackson Brewery Complex on the French Quarter side of Canal Street, and the Riverwalk on the other end, there can be found every imaginable variety of food, drink, shopping, music, entertainment, and—always—spectacular views of the river, the French Quarter, and the city beyond.

This area is equally good for family visitors and adult conventioneers. After dark, it offers some of the liveliest night spots in the city, even the world's ninth Hard Rock Cafe in the Jax Marketplace, the Planet Hollywood Restaurant with its movie memorabilia, and the Aquarium of the Americas. Some popular clubs in this area include the Top of the Mart at the World Trade Center and Mulate's Cajun music restaurant (good for families). Every New Orleans night on the town must end, no matter how late—or early—with coffee and doughnuts (beignets) at Cafe du Monde on Decatur Street at Jackson Square.

Beginning at the Moon Walk, Riverfront attractions include a landing for steamboats *Natchez* and *Jean Lafitte*, Jax Brewery, Jax Millhouse, and Jax Marketplace. These are all part of the $150-million development of the original Jax Brewery buildings, most of which date from 1890. Open seven days a week, they combine a historic facade with a glitzy interior full of Creole and Cajun crafts, cooking schools, hats, jewelry, clothes, and toys. There is ample parking for cars and tour buses. Other sites along the Downtown Riverfront include the following:

Canal Place, Westin Hotel (see SHOPPING, HOTELS). Public parking.

Algiers Ferry Landing. A ride across the Mississippi River and back, either by car or on foot. Great views.

World Trade Center. Consular offices and shipping companies and a great outside elevator ride to the top. Public parking with entrance on Poydras Street. (New hotel to be added by 2000.)

Spanish Plaza is a happy urban picnic spot with landings for the excursion boats *Creole Queen*, *Cajun Queen*, and *Cotton Blossom*. Take time to enjoy the beautiful, tiled Spanish coats-of-arms which surround the fountain.

Riverwalk. A festival marketplace developed by the Rouse Company on the site of the 1984 World's Fair. It runs the gamut from elegant to trivial. Open seven days, frequent live entertainment, great river views, and the riverside promenade with explanatory markers citing interesting Mississippi River lore.

Hilton Hotel (see HOTELS, RESTAURANTS, NIGHTLIFE). Public parking.

New Orleans Convention Center is so enormous that the annual Bacchus and New Orleans Orpheus Mardi Gras parades can roll through on their routes to delight the crowds—regardless of the weather. Adjacent to the Riverwalk Marketplace, the Convention Center (also called the Morial New Orleans Convention Center) will meet the 21st century with completed additions that will consist of three million square feet, with two luxurious ballrooms, 140 upper-level meeting rooms, a conference auditorium to seat 4,000, expanded contiguous exhibit spaces of 12 combinable halls for almost 6,000 exhibit booths, a 400-seat restaurant, small-group dining areas, and two full-service kitchens capable of serving 20,000 meals in a 24-hour period—all with the most advanced and sophisticated convention services.

Aquarium of the Americas. Realistic recreations of the aquatic environments in the western hemisphere. Thousands of specimens and thousands of gallons of watery habitat. There's even an "underwater tunnel" walkway.

Entergy IMAX Theatre, next to the aquarium, screens magnificent, giant visual productions.

Woldenberg Park is a beautiful green space next to the river which connects the aquarium and the Jax Brewery Complex. This park with its indigenous trees and plants is wonderful for picnics and an ideal place for children to run off some of their extra energy.

SIGHTS

Allow as much time as possible to sample the super-abundant smorgasbord of sights that New Orleans has to offer. Almost every visitor begins where the city began, in the French Quarter. This is a wise decision. But time permitting, be sure to savor the elegance of the Garden District, the pastel potpourri of the uptown area, the pastoral calm of the city's great parks and curving lakefront, and the ranks of shimmering glass buildings, New Orleans' version of the "Hall of Mirrors" which leads down Poydras Street to the Superdome. Every area has its quiet cafes where you can stop to relax along the way. Also, all of these sights are family- and children-friendly, fun places. So plunge in and enjoy! We wager that before you're done, you'll be planning your next trip to the Crescent City. Refer to the SELF-GUIDED TOURS chapter for explicit tours and complementary maps.

SIGHTS BY AREA

CENTRAL BUSINESS/ WAREHOUSE DISTRICTS

Aquarium of the Americas
Board of Trade Plaza
The Canal Street Ferry
Civic Center
Confederate Museum
Gallier Hall
The International Plaza
Lafayette Square
Louisiana Children's Museum
Maritime Museum
National D-Day Museum
Riverwalk Promenade
St. Charles Streetcar
St. Patrick's Church
The Superdome and Sports Complex
United States Custom House
World Trade Center

CHALMETTE

Jackson Barracks
Jean Lafitte National Historical Park—Chalmette Battlefield and Isleno Units
Steamboat Houses

FAUBOURG MARIGNY

Royal and Burgundy Street Shotgun Houses
Saints Peter and Paul Church
Washington Square
W. C. C. Claiborne Mansion

FRENCH QUARTER

French Market
Gallier House
Hermann-Grima House
Historic New Orleans Collection
Jackson Square
Jazz Museum
Louis Armstrong Park
The Louisiana State Museum Complex: Cabildo, Presbytere, Old U.S. Mint
The Lower Pontalba, 1850 House
Madame John's Legacy
Musee Conti Wax Museum
Old Absinthe House
Our Lady of Guadalupe Church
Pharmacy Museum
St. Louis Cathedral
Woldenberg River Park

KENNER/METAIRIE

Rivertown, LaSalle Landing
Zephyrs' Baseball Stadium

LAKEFRONT/MID CITY

Bucktown
City Park
Lake Pontchartrain
Lake Pontchartrain Causeway
Longue Vue Gardens
Pitot House
St. Louis Cemetery No. 3

NEW ORLEANS EAST

Jazzland Theme Park
Louisiana Nature and Science Center

UPTOWN

Audubon Park and Zoo
Cornstalk Fence and Garden District
Lafayette Cemetery
Opera Guild House
St. Charles Streetcar

WEST BANK

Blaine Kern Mardi Gras World
Jean Lafitte National Historical Park—Barataria Unit

Aquarium of the Americas. Mississippi River at Canal Street, 581-4629 or 1-800-774-7344. The two-story aquarium is home to more than 7,500 specimens of marine life, representing 395 species. Includes rare white alligators. Exhibits are: Mississippi River and Delta Habitat, Gulf of Mexico, Amazon Rainforest Habitat, and the Caribbean Reef Environment.

Audubon Park and Zoo, 6400 Magazine St.; 581-4629 or 1-800-774-7394. Audubon Park, which houses one of the top five zoos in the country, is located in the uptown area, across from Tulane and Loyola universities. Located on the site of Etienne de Bore's plantation, where sugar was first granulated in 1794, it delights visitors and locals alike with acres of blooming flowers, century-old moss-covered oaks, and winding lagoons. Between Magazine Street and St. Charles Avenue, the park is devoted to picnicking, golf, biking, swimming—or just sitting and watching the world go by. The zoo is a well-designed, cageless home for many endangered species, as well as a learning center for thousands of Louisiana schoolchildren. A relaxing stroll or tram ride through the zoo enables the visitor to view the animals in their natural habitat.

The zoo's well-placed snack bars offer light refreshment and the two Zootique shops provide interesting shopping. There are birds-of-prey and elephant shows. The young (and young at heart) enjoy the Children's Zoo, where they are not only able to pet the animals, but also learn about animal diets and ways.

There are daily paddlewheel boat trips from the foot of Canal Street to the zoo that enable the visitor to enjoy seeing the Mississippi River on the way. The Magazine Street bus line goes from Canal Street to the zoo and back. A free shuttle also departs from the St. Charles Avenue streetcar line stop #36 and brings guests to the zoo's main gate.

Blaine Kern Mardi Gras World, across the Mississippi River in Algiers, 233 Newton St., 361-7821. Free parking is available, and there's also a shuttle bus and ferry. A chance for both visitors and residents to see the backstage workings of Mardi Gras, how parades are planned and floats are constructed. There is also a small theater showing a documentary about Mardi Gras, a gift shop, and a snack bar.

Board of Trade Plaza, 400 Magazine St. An oasis in the Central Business District welcomes tired tourists and locals alike. It was originally part of Bienville's plantation (see NEW ORLEANS PAST). In 1833, the Banks Arcade was erected, designed by Charles Zimple, a well-known New Orleans architect.

The St. James Hotel, established on this site a few years later, was used by Federal forces as a hospital during the Civil War in May 1862. The Board of Trade Building, just to the rear, was erected in 1885 to house the Produce Exchange.

When the Plaza was restored in 1967, the cast-iron columns and arches from the old lobby of the St. James Hotel were preserved and now shade the entrance to the Board of Trade Building. Interesting murals by H. Alvin Sharpe were painted around its domed ceiling depicting phases of local industry. In 1889, the building became the Board of Trade. The hotel was torn down. This is a grand place to rest or picnic while touring.

Bucktown. There is a small canal off Lake Pontchartrain that runs between Orleans and Jefferson parishes toward the old Hammond Highway. Years ago, this was an established residential boating community which supplied much fresh seafood to the New Orleans area. Today, many active fishing boats can still be seen lining the canal, and there are several wonderful seafood restaurants in Bucktown—on shore.

The Canal Street Ferry, Canal Street and the Mississippi River. You may either drive or walk on the ferry. Enjoy the ride across the river; then just stay on and ride back. If you are driving, be prepared to move your car to the other side of the boat when it docks on the Algiers side of the river. You will have a grand view of the city skyline, traffic on the river, the Crescent City Connection, Jackson Square, the big curve in the river after which "the Crescent City" is named, and the levees which protect the city from flooding. Don't miss this ride, but plan to go during off-peak hours as many commuters use the ferry daily to go back and forth to work. *CH* for cars.

City Park, bounded by Bayou St. John and City Park Avenue, Marconi Drive, and Robert E. Lee Boulevard (see SELF-GUIDED TOURS, Esplanade/Cemeteries Tour). An excellent place to relax and daydream, or for activity to fish, boat ride, play tennis, golf, or bicycle (see SPORTS). There are peaceful lagoons with romantic arched bridges, beautiful rose gardens, children's Storyland and amusement park, the Last Carousel, stadiums for football and soccer, and even the training academy for the city's mounted police.

Civic Center, 300 and 400 blocks of Loyola Avenue; 586-4311. The Civic Center surrounds a welcome green space called Duncan Plaza. The Civic Center also includes New Orleans City Hall on the corner of Loyola and Poydras, the Louisiana State Office building, the State Supreme Court Building, with the statue of Oliver Wendell Holmes, a chief justice of the United States Supreme Court and a native Louisianian, and the New Orleans Public Library on the corner of Loyola and Tulane avenues.

W. C. C. Claiborne Mansion, 2111 Dauphine St. In the Faubourg Marigny Historic District, this unique mansion was built in 1855. This was the home of the son of Gov. W. C. C. Claiborne, Louisiana's first American governor. Private residence.

Confederate Museum, 929 Camp St., just off Lee Circle; 523-4522. Civil War enthusiasts will love it! The museum contains an extensive collection of uniforms, flags, medical equipment, weapons, and portraits. The collection is housed in a Romanesque building donated by philanthropist Frank Howard. Jefferson Davis lay in state here after he died in New Orleans in 1893. Built in 1890, this building is on the National Register of Historic Places.

Cornstalk Fence and Garden District, 1448 Fourth St. The Short House, an Italian villa-style house, is a private residence. The custom-made, cast-iron cornstalk and morning glory fence is the only one of its kind in the Garden District. The elegant Garden District was an area settled by wealthy Americans after the Louisiana Purchase.

French Market. This is a site that was used by the Indians for bartering their products. The market buildings were constructed in stages in 1813, 1822, and 1872. The French Market area houses restaurants, boutiques, a praline shop, a toy shop, souvenirs, the Farmers' Market, and Flea Market.

Gallier Hall, 545 St. Charles Ave.; 565-7457. Built between 1845 and 1850 and the city hall of the American sector of the divided city, Gallier Hall maintained the seat of government after the city was reunited in 1853. It was designed by James Gallier, Sr., and is one of the best examples of Greek Revival architecture in the United States. Today, the main floor has been lovingly restored and is available for private parties. Gallier Hall is always decorated for the holidays. Cultural and recreational departments are housed in the building. It is also the site for toasts with Mardi Gras "royalty."

Gallier House, 1118-32 Royal St.; 525-5661. This is the home of James Gallier, Jr., architect par excellence, as was his father, and designer of the French Opera House along with many other notable buildings. The home has been lovingly restored and filled with period furnishing so as to create, as nearly as possible, the feeling of what it was like to live in New Orleans in the mid-1800s. There are also films and exhibits as well as a small gift shop. The Gallier House interior is in different "dress" depending on which season you visit. In summer months, chairs are slip-covered, and floors are covered with straw carpets. During winter, heavy drapes and carpets replace the summer "dress." Group and special children's tours available.

Hermann-Grima House, 820 St. Louis St.; 525-5661. Built in 1831 by German immigrant Samuel Hermann, and named for the two families who lived in this elegant Federal-style mansion, this house is beautifully and authentically furnished to reflect the city's golden era. There is a lovely courtyard garden, the only horse stable left intact in the Quarter, a servant building, and a totally functional outdoor kitchen which is the site of 19th-century cooking demonstrations.

In addition to informational and fun tours, wonderful seasonal and specialized tours are offered based on local historical holiday traditions and decorations. Children's tours, programs, and workshops are also

Gallier House *Gallier Historic House Museum*

Hermann-Grima House *Hermann-Grima Historic House Museum*

available, focusing on 19th-century lore, archeological digs, or the making of ornaments, cookies, valentines, Easter bonnets, summer potpourris, and much more!

Historic New Orleans Collection, 533 Royal St.; 523-4662. Many documents, including the original of the 1812 Louisiana Constitution, paintings, rare books, and other important memorabilia, are on display in 11 galleries. Guides are available to tour you through this late 1700s house. A research library is also available for special study. Gift shop. *CH*.

The International Plaza in downtown New Orleans is a complex of plazas devoted to each country which has had a particular influence on the city's past and present history.

British Place, located at the foot of Poydras Street, is a glassy circle centered with a fine statue of Sir Winston Churchill.

Plaza de Espana, located between the World Trade Center, #1 Canal St., and the Mississippi River, has interesting tile work, a large fountain, and benches which make it ideal for rest or picnicking on pleasant days.

Place de France, in front of the World Trade Center building, was landscaped around a gilded statue of Joan of Arc, which was dedicated by French President Charles de Gaulle during his visit in 1960. A new street has been built in this area, and the Joan of Arc statue is being moved to the French Quarter.

Plaza d'Italia, Poydras and Tchoupitoulas streets, has an intriguing design that gives the feeling of wandering from one imposing stage set to another. This is the site of large celebrations on Columbus Day, the second Monday in October, and on St. Joseph's Day, March 19.

Jackson Barracks, 6400 St. Claude Ave., on the way to Chalmette; 278-8242. The main buildings date from 1834 and a military museum is housed in the old powder magazine (Mon-Fri 7:30 am-4 pm; Sat 10 am-4 pm). This is the headquarters for the Louisiana National Guard; 271-6262.

Jackson Square. The emotional center of the city, Jackson Square is always festive, always interesting. What was once a bare parade ground is now a formal garden constantly astir with a variety of activities. It is a joyous place, a year-round outdoor art gallery filled with tourists, locals, musicians, working artists, street entertainers, and bordered by interesting shops and historic buildings. You will find yourself drawn back to the Square frequently just to relax and enjoy the ambience. Every so often a large ship is visible on the Mississippi; then the marvelous

Jackson Square and St. Louis Cathedral at twilight *Ron Calamia, New Orleans Metropolitan Convention & Visitors Bureau*

steam calliope on the *Delta Queen* is heard tuning up in salute. If the breeze is right, the wonderful aroma of the coffee and doughnuts at Cafe du Monde floats across the Square to tempt you. This is one of the showplaces of the world.

Jazz Museum (see SIGHTS, The Old U.S. Mint).

Jazzland Theme Park, intersection of I-10 and I-510 in New Orleans East; 522-3911 or 1-888-522-5299. This 140-acre amusement park showcasing the unique Louisiana culture is scheduled to open in spring 2000. It will be a total family experience featuring 23 amusement rides, food, the Great Lawn for live entertainment, and areas known as "Jazz Place," "Cajun Country," "Gospel Garden," "Pontchartrain Beach," "Mardi Gras," and a special "Kids' Section."

Jean Lafitte National Historical Park, French Quarter Unit Information Station, 916-18 N. Peters St.; 589-3719. Isleno Unit, St. Bernard LA; 682-0862. Chalmette National Historical Park, 8606 W. St. Bernard Hwy.; 589-4428, and the Barataria Unit, Marrero; 589-2330. The Isleno Unit contains an educational exhibit telling the tale of the group of Canary Islanders sent by the king of Spain to colonize the Lower Mississippi. Open daily.

Chalmette Park is six miles from Canal Street. This is the site of the famed Battle of New Orleans, which, although fought after the War of 1812 was officially over, made Andrew Jackson a hero and later president. It also helped unite the city. The battlefield is well marked; there is a 110-foot memorial monument and cemetery. The Beauregard Plantation House, an 1840 design of James Gallier, Sr., is filled with interesting exhibits. A walk up the levee affords a grand view of the Mississippi River (which is about 35 feet closer to the house than it was when the battle was fought).

The Barataria Unit is a section of undeveloped swamp, where visitors can indulge in guided walking and canoe tours. The park helps represent how south Louisiana looked before it was developed, and it is one of the best-preserved natural marshlands in the entire National Park System.

Lafayette Cemetery. Corner of Washington Avenue and Prytania Street. In 1833, this above-ground cemetery was laid out by the Garden District's original residents. For its first 20 years, the occupants were yellow fever victims. Note how the house-like tombs serve the same family for generations. The cemetery is open to the public, and, at times, small art classes set up easels inside to paint some of Lafayette's uniqueness.

A quiet street in a New Orleans cemetery invites the living to sit and visit a while — *Cecilia Casrill Dartez*

Lafayette Square, opposite Gallier Hall in the 500 block of St. Charles Avenue. The second oldest public park area in New Orleans, this is the site of the famous funeral for three—Clay, Calhoun, and Webster—in the 1850s. A promenade leads from Lafayette Square to the banks of the Mississippi River.

Lake Pontchartrain. One of the largest and most shallow of the world's freshwater lakes, Lake Pontchartrain is 40 miles long, 25 miles wide, and averages 16 feet in depth. Because it is so shallow, waves blow up quickly in a storm, making it a challenge to all boaters. Many long-distance sailing races begin at the Southern Yacht Club in New Orleans and follow a course through Lake Pontchartrain and Lake Borgne to the Gulf of Mexico. From that point they sail on to the Mississippi Gulf Coast, to Florida, or to Mexico.

Lake Pontchartrain Causeway. This is the longest bridge in the world, approximately 24 miles long. The bridge spans the middle of Lake Pontchartrain from north to south. Toll is $3 for southbound autos.

Longue Vue Gardens, 7 Bamboo Rd., off Metairie Rd.; 488-5488. Longue Vue Gardens is a magnificent estate built by Edgar and Edith Stern, which has been left in trust to enrich the lives of all who visit. There are eight acres of incomparable gardens with fountains, sculptures, live oaks, boxwood, rosebushes, and seasonal plantings. The Stern home is a Greek Revival stucco over brick "cottage" filled with art and antiques and some unusual china collections. Films, concerts, and outdoor ballet performances are often presented. Special adult and children's gardening programs are also conducted. Call for schedule. Gift shop. *CH*.

Louis Armstrong Park; 901 N. Rampart St. This centerpiece of the arts complex has on one side the Municipal Auditorium, on the other the Theatre of the Performing Arts. The park itself is named in honor of Louis Armstrong, who grew up an orphan child in New Orleans and became one of the best-known jazz musicians of all times. The park was originally an Indian camp. Later it was known as Congo Square, the place where slaves were allowed to gather and dance on Sunday afternoon. The dances were crowded, exuberant, often interspersed with fights, and became wilder and wilder as the afternoon went on. The whole celebration ended when sunset sent the briefly free spirits back into subservience. *NCH*. Daylight hours in large groups only, please, and with caution.

Louisiana Children's Museum; 428 Julia St.; 523-1357. Child-centered programs and tours available in an interesting renovation of an old warehouse. Hands-on exhibits include: Big City Port, Body Shop, Raceways, Bubbles, Animation Workshop, Science Center, Water Works, Kids' Cafe, Cajun Cottage, Channel 4 Kid Watch Studio, Challenges, and First Adventures. Live entertainment is also presented in a kid-sized theater setting. Gift shop. Tue-Sat 9:30 am-4:30 pm; Sun. noon-4:30 pm. *CH*.

Louisiana Nature and Science Center; 246-5672. Located in Joe Brown Park in New Orleans East. Take I-10 East to Read Boulevard, right on Read Boulevard, enter the park on Nature Center Drive about 1/4 mile down, and follow drive to LNSC. This is about an 18-minute drive from downtown and well worth the trip for the entire family. This science museum and nature preserve are dedicated to the enjoyment and discovery of Louisiana nature. There are hands-on exhibits, a working beehive, Discovery Loft, Interpretive Center, film presentations, and planetarium which has laser shows. Nature guides take you on fascinating nature trails which wander through 86 acres of Louisiana wilderness. Tue-Fri 9 am-5 pm; Sat-Sun noon-5 pm. *CH*.

The Louisiana State Museum Complex; 568-6972 or 568-6968. The Louisiana State Museum preserves and displays the state's unique cultural heritage. The museum's enormous collections consist of over 3 million artifacts (for example, Napoleon's death mask), documents, memorabilia, paintings, photos, prints, etc. Some of these collections are housed in the three following buildings.

The Cabildo, Chartres Street on Jackson Square, was built in 1795 with money and labor donated by Don Andres Almonaster y Roxas, whose only request was to be buried in the St. Louis Cathedral. The Confederate States and the United States of America have governed from within this building. Also, the Louisiana Purchase, which doubled the size of the U.S. in 1803, was signed on the Cabildo's second floor.

The Presbytere, Chartres Street on Jackson Square, was also built with the generous funds of Don Andres in 1785-91. It was to be an exact copy of the Cabildo and built to house the clergy for St. Louis Cathedral. It was, however, never used for that purpose. Some of the exhibits are: "The Battle of New Orleans," antique toys, "Uptown New Orleans," "Folklife in Louisiana Photography," Mardi Gras jewelry and costumes. Gift shop. Tue-Sun 9 am-5 pm. *CH*.

The Old U.S. Mint, 400 Esplanade Ave. Fort San Carlos, one of the city's five forts, stood here in the 1700s. This mint was completed by the U.S. government between 1835 and 1839, and its last production time was 1879-1910; it produced $5 million in coin per month during its peak production. This building houses the Jazz and Mardi Gras museums, with Armstrong's cornet, other jazz greats' instruments, and Mardi Gras jewelry and costumes. Also, the "Streetcar Named Desire" sits peacefully in the garden facing the French Market. Gift shop. Tue-Sun 9am-5 pm. *CH*.

The Lower Pontalba, The 1850 House, 523 St. Ann St. on Jackson Square; 568-6972. These apartments were built by the Baroness Pontalba, whose father financed the St. Louis Cathedral, the Cabildo, and the Presbytere. One section, called the 1850 House, is a restoration of a street-level shop with two-story residence upstairs. The upstairs town house, with its many "modern" conveniences, was very advanced for its time. Tue-Sun 9 am-5 pm. *CH*.

Madame John's Legacy, 632 Dumaine St. Built after the Good Friday Fire of 1788, this building was at one time the home of Madame Marie Louise Roman, whose son built the well-known Oak Alley Plantation house (see SELF-GUIDED TOURS, ONE-DAY EXCURSIONS). The second floor houses an exhibit telling the history of the home. The second floor, the kitchen, and the garconniere have been meticulously restored. The patio, planted entirely with native plants, is one of the most beautiful in the French Quarter.

Musee Conti Wax Museum, 917 Conti St.; 525-2605. Designed for family viewing, the only wax museum of its kind in America brings to (seemingly) life the legends of Louisiana: Napoleon in his bathtub, New Orleans' historic incidents, Mardi Gras, voodoo, and jazz greats. There is even a Haunted Dungeon with more than 20 "monsters." A delightful, fun way for the family to learn about New Orleans history. Programs in French, German, Spanish, Japanese, and Italian. Group rate available. Daily 10 am-5:30 pm. *CH*.

National D-Day Museum, corner of Magazine and Howard streets; 525-1544. Scheduled to open June 2000, this museum is dedicated to the pivotal events of the 20th century—the Allied invasions of World War II. It will commemorate the valor of the men and women who made the Allied victory possible.

Old Absinthe House, 240 Bourbon St. The house was built in 1806. The name refers to the liqueur, absinthe, which was served here until it was later outlawed. The Old Absinthe House remains a popular bar in the French Quarter (see NIGHTLIFE).

Opera Guild House, 2504 Prytania St.; 899-1945. This house was built in 1859 for an American merchant. The interior is decorated in Victorian style and is open for tours. Mon 1-4 pm; bus tours by appointment any day.

Our Lady of Guadalupe Church, 411 N. Rampart St.; 525-1551. This historic church was built in 1827 and dedicated by Pere Antoine as the mortuary chapel for the St. Louis cemetery. This was done because there were hundreds of funerals held for victims of the yellow fever and cholera epidemics. It was then believed that the corpses sent off a "noxious miasma" which infected the living. There were so many deaths during these epidemics that families had to stand in line beside the chapel to wait their turn, and rioting often broke out among overwrought groups as they waited. In 1903, when the Dominicans arrived, the name was changed to St. Anthony of Padua Church, and it became the parish for Italian Catholics. Then the Storyville district of permissible prostitution was created by the city. The church was in the middle of this notorious area, so the Dominicans moved St. Anthony's to the end of Canal Street. As Our Lady of Guadalupe Church, it now contains the International Shrine of St. Jude, and is a monument to New Orleans' firefighters and police officers who have died in the line of duty. It is also called St. Jude's Church.

Pharmacy Museum, 514 Chartres St.; 565-8027. Enter a real apothecary shop as it was in the early 1800s, as well as medical and voodoo exhibits and a beautiful patio to relax in after your tour. Tue-Sun 10 am-5 pm. *CH*.

Pitot House, 1440 Moss St.; 482-0312. Rescued and restored by the Louisiana Landmarks Society, the house and adjoining 30-acre plantation were bought originally in 1810 by James Pitot, Louisiana's first democratically elected mayor. It is a typical Louisiana adaptation of West Indies architecture. There are costumed guides to make your visit more authentic and enjoyable. It is also the office for the Louisiana Landmarks Society. Wed-Sat 10 am-3 pm. *CH*.

Rivertown and LaSalle Landing, 405 Williams Blvd.; 468-7231. This historic miniature Victorian town is located on the Mississippi River in Kenner. The delightful architecture creates a bygone-era ambience. Rivertown consists of: specialty shops, tea houses, the Louisiana Wildlife and Fisheries Museum, the New Orleans Saints Hall of Fame, Louisiana Toy Train Museum, Kenner Historical Museum, the Freeport McMoRan Daily Living Science Center, Planetarium and Observatory, the Cannes Brulee Native American exhibit (with live, authentic demonstrations), Rivertown Repertory Theatre, Mardi Gras Museum, and Children's Castle with children's live entertainment. LaSalle Landing is a grassy park on the levee with a spectacular view of the Mississippi River. Gift shops. About 20 minutes from downtown during off-peak traffic. Take I-10 West, exit at Williams Boulevard, and continue left on Williams to Rivertown. Tue-Sat 9 am-5 pm, Sun 1-5 pm. *CH*. Special discount tickets may be purchased, and all museums can be visited for quite a bargain price.

Riverwalk Promenade, 1 Poydras St.; 522-1555. This is the wharf section of the Riverwalk mall which offers magnificent views of the Mississippi River and its boat traffic. The walkway is dotted with entertaining plaques which convey river lore.

Royal Street Shotgun Houses, in the Faubourg Marigny Historic District. A shotgun house, as the story goes, is a house in which, with the front and back doors open, a shot can travel through without hitting any walls (the rooms are arranged one behind the other). Number 2228 Royal St. is an 1880s single-frame shotgun house. At 2216-18 is an 1850s double-frame shotgun house in the Greek Revival style. Private residences.

St. Charles Streetcar. Board the historic streetcar at Canal and St. Charles for a delightful ride to view the mansions that wealthy Americans built after the Louisiana Purchase.

St. Louis Cathedral, Jackson Square. Built in 1795 with the generous funds of Don Andres Almonaster y Roxas, and considered the oldest cathedral in the U.S. It is still an active church with a dedicated congregation. Guided tours (donation optional) are given when mass is not being conducted, so check the times. View the beautiful stained glasses which depict the life of King Louis. Gift shop.

St. Louis Cemetery No. 3, Esplanade Avenue near Bayou St. John. This above-ground cemetery is a typical "City of the Dead." The streets were planned, named, and laid out in 1854, very similar to the planning of a small city. Here is the famous monument to architect James Gallier, Sr., and his wife, who were lost on an ocean voyage. The cast-iron entrance gates were fabricated by Francis Larges. An information booklet can be purchased from the office. Daily 9 am-4 pm.

St. Patrick's Church, 724 Camp St.; 525-4413. In 1983, the church celebrated its 150th anniversary, and is the second oldest parish church in New Orleans. The Latin mass is still celebrated at St. Patrick's each

Sunday morning. James Gallier, Sr., assisted in designing the church, which was inspired by Yorkminster in England. Murals behind the altar were painted in 1840 by Leon Pomerade. Call for schedule. *NCH*.

Saints Peter and Paul Church, 2300 block of Burgundy in the Faubourg Marigny Historic District. This congregation was founded in 1848. Architect Henry Howard designed this beautiful brick church, which was built in 1860. It was built to meet the needs of the Irish, German, and French Catholic population, and contains the original floor-to-ceiling elegant, multicolored stained-glass window scenes.

Steamboat Houses, 400 and 503 Egania St., downriver from Canal Street. Inspired by steamboats, these distinctive private homes, each with a pilot house on top, were built in the early 1900s by a river pilot father and son. Not open to the public.

The Superdome and Sports Complex, 1500 Poydras St.; Superdome 587-3663; Sports Complex 522-7825. Situated on a nine-acre site like a huge space mushroom, the Superdome is the architectural spectacular of the Central Business District. This colossal sports arena, the home of the New Orleans Saints, the Tulane Green Wave, and many Super Bowls and Sugar Bowls, is also used for concerts, religious and business conventions, trade shows, exhibition baseball games, and even a Mardi Gras parade. The Superdome seats over 95,000. Football plays and replays are shown on six giant overhead TV screens. The plush private boxes are located midway up the three levels, and have private seating, televisions, living, dining, and bath facilities. General ticket sales are on the ground floor. There are guided tours daily from 9:30 am to 4 pm. *CH*—except during some events.

The new 18,000-seat sports arena next to the Dome is the home of the New Orleans Brass hockey team.

United States Custom House, 423 Canal St. Fort San Luis, one of the five forts built by the Spanish to protect the city, was originally on this site. A customs office has operated here since 1792. The present building was started in 1848, finished in 1880, and legend has it that it is built on cotton bales.

Washington Square, exactly one square block bounded by Frenchmen, Dauphine, and Royal streets and Elysian Fields Avenue. A haven from the harried life, this area has traditionally been the playground and park for Faubourg Marigny families.

Woldenberg River Park. Wonderful 12-acre riverfront park from Canal Street to St. Peter Street, connecting the Aquarium and the

Jackson Brewery. There are approximately 600 trees, 1400 shrubs, and lots of open, grassy area for children to run off some "pent-up" energy. Many walkways from which to view river traffic and the city skyline.

World Trade Center, #2 Canal St.; 529-1601. This superbly designed building rises like an exclamation point where Canal Street meets the Mississippi River, reminding residents and visitors alike that international trade is the key to the New Orleans economy. The Center houses many of the consular, import-export, and international banking establishments in the city. International art exhibits are frequently held in the lobby.

The glass elevator on the outside of the building rises 34 floors, affording an ever-changing view of the city with the river winding dramatically below.

Zephyrs' Baseball Stadium, 6000 Airline Hwy., Jefferson; 734-5155. This is the home of the Zephyrs triple-A baseball team and nutria mascots Boudreaux and wife Clotile. Baseball games here are quite an event and include activities such as musical entertainment and fireworks. It is a real treat for the entire family.

VISUAL ARTS

Art and architecture are top priorities in New Orleans. Artists have always been drawn by a combination of the easy climate, the accepting attitude of the people, and the wealth of interesting subjects to paint.

Architecturally, careful planning and supervision have allowed the city to maintain a pleasing balance between the dignity of the old and the excitement of the new. Visual treats abound. Anywhere in the city you may find easels set up or photographers catching their subjects at just the right angle.

Currently, New Orleans is home for an elite group of artists who work in a variety of mediums, ranging from oils to silver to papier mache, and whose works are represented in collections throughout the United States. To see the works of prominent, national artists on display is a special treat for visitors.

MUSEUMS

New Orleans Museum of Art, City Park; 488-2631; hearing impaired 488-9562. The New Orleans Museum of Art is one of the busiest and most vital of the museums of the South. It is housed in a neoclassic building designed by Chicago architect Samuel Marx and surrounded by the huge live oaks and placid lagoons of City Park. The site was chosen and the original museum endowed by Isaac Delgado, a wealthy sugar broker. He made three stipulations in his grant: the museum would house his own extensive collection; it would have an active board of directors; and it would be called the Isaac Delgado Museum of Art (which it was until the 1970s). When it opened in 1911, Mr. Delgado was too ill to attend the festivities, and he died a year later.

Today's permanent collections include a Kress Foundation gift of Italian Old Master paintings, the pre-Columbian collection, a representative group of impressionist and modern paintings, sculpture, glass, a fine photography collection, now numbering over 8,000 prints, and a Faberge egg exhibit. Tours, lectures, and movies are offered regularly. Call for exact times. Museum hours: Tue-Sun 10 am-5 pm. Museum shop. *CH*.

The Contemporary Arts Center, 900 Camp St.; 523-1216. The Contemporary Arts Center has sponsored avant-garde offerings of all kinds, exhibits, installations, and performances by both national and local artists. There are even changing exhibits of work by local K-12 creative-art students. Call or check local publications for current exhibits and fees.

Ogden Museum of Southern Art, 615 Howard Ave.; 539-9600. This museum is scheduled to open in 2000 in the architecturally magnificent 1889 Howard Building on Lee Circle. Oil man Patrick F. Taylor is credited with the purchase and continued preservation and restoration of this incredible building. When New Orleanian Roger H. Ogden donated his personal Southern art collection to the University of New Orleans Foundation, the UNO/Ogden Museum of Southern Art was created. The educational museum will delve into the evolution of visual arts in the South through a variety of methods such as internships, lectures, film and video programs, and docent tours—all based on the Odgen permanent collection and other changing exhibitions. Visitors will be in for a truly double treat here: fantastic exhibits in a fantastic building.

GALLERIES

The **Arts Council of New Orleans,** 225 Baronne St., keeps a current list of the galleries and their current shows. For information, call the Arts Council at 523-1465.

Some representative galleries are:

Academy Gallery, 5256 Magazine St.; 899-8111. Nationally known artists who happen to be local residents. Paintings, sculpures, prints. Located in the New Orleans Academy of Fine Arts. Mon-Fri 9 am-4 pm; Sat 10 am-4 pm.

America's Gallery for Animation and Cartoon Art, 532 Royal St.; 586-0801. Collections of animation and art collectibles from Warner Bros. and Disney Studios. Mon-Thu 10 am-6 pm; Fri-Sat 10 am-9 pm; Sun 11 am-5 pm.

Arthur Roger Gallery, 432 Julia St.; 522-1999. Contemporary fine arts and installations. Mon-Sat 10 am-5 pm.

Bergen Galleries, 730 Royal St.; 523-7882. Fine-art posters, limited-edition graphics, sports art, Louisiana festival posters, oil-industry graphics. Mon-Sat 10 am-5 pm.

Bernard K. Passman Gallery, Riverwalk, Poydras Street at the Mississippi River; 525-4581. Black coral sculpture. Same hours as Riverwalk.

Bruno Galleries, 910 Julia St.; 525-4288. The exclusive representative of the British royal family's favorite crystal, Royal Brierly Crystal. Call for hours.

Carmen Llewellyn Gallery, 240 Chartres St.; 558-9859. Latin American art with some North American artists. Call for hours.

Carol Robinson Gallery, 840 Napoleon Ave.; 895-6130. Contemporary paintings, sculpture, graphics. Tue-Sat 10 am-5:30 pm.

Casell Gallery, 818 Royal St.; 524-0671 and 1-800-548-5413. Variety of Louisiana art with framing, packaging, and shipping available. Daily 10 am-6 pm.

Cynthia Sutton, 429 Royal St.; 523-3377. Beautiful gallery with an impressive selection of fine oil paintings. Also wide selection of fine porcelains. Mon-Sat 9 am-5 pm; Sun 10 am-5 pm.

Davis Gallery, 3964 Magazine St.; 897-0780. African art. Tue-Sat 10 am-5 pm.

DeVille Books and Prints, 344 Carondelet St.; 525-1846. Group shows of works. Mon-Fri 9:30 am-5:30 pm; Sat 10 am-4 pm.

Didier, Inc., 3439 Magazine St.; 899-7749. 19th-century American furniture, American paintings and prints, specializing in ornithological prints. Mon-Sat 10 am-5 pm.

Dixon and Dixon Antiques and Art Galleries, 237 Royal St.; 524-0282 and 1-800-848-5148. 18th- and 19th-century European paintings and Oriental rugs. Mon-Sat 9 am-6 pm.

Dyansen Galleries, 433 Royal St.; 523-2902. Originals, graphics, and bronzes by national and international artists. Daily 10 am-6 pm.

Enoch's Gallery, 4001 Baronne St.; 897-2603. Original watercolors by Walter Anderson and others. Call for hours.

Fine Arts Gallery of New Orleans, 220 Chartres St.; 522-0691. 17th- to 20th-century fine art by American and European artists.

Fischer-Gambino, 637 Royal St.; 524-9067. Art selections in mixed media by American artists. Mon-Sat 10 am-10 pm; Sun 10 am-7 pm.

Galleria Veronese, 623 Royal St.; 523-5195. Antiques and art gallery.

Gallerie Simone Stern, 518 Julia St.; 529-1118. Contemporary paintings, prints, sculpture. Tue-Sat 10 am-5 pm.

A Gallery for Fine Photography, 332 Royal St.; 568-1313. An extensive inventory of fine photographs including from the early 19th and 20th centuries. Mon-Sat 10 am-6 pm; Sun 11 am-6 pm.

A Gallery in the Woods, 13401 River Rd., Lower Coast Algiers; 392-5359. Quaint gallery of Louisiana artists which also conducts art workshops. Call for hours.

Gallery on the Bayou, 1324 Moss St.; 488-2659. Louisiana artists display works in a lovely raised shotgun cottage overlooking Bayou St. John. Parking lot next door. Call for showings and hours.

Hanson Galleries, 229 Royal St.; 524-8211. Original graphics, sculpture, paintings, tapestries, rare prints. Mon-Sat 10 am-7 pm; Sun 11 am-5 pm.

Kurt Schon, Ltd., 523 Royal St.; 524-5462. Paintings by Royal Academy artists and others. Call for hours.

LaBelle Gallerie, 309 Chartres St.; 529-3080. African-American art. Call for hours.

LeMieux Galleries, 332 Julia St.; 522-5988. Louisiana artists. Mon-Sat 10 am-5:30 pm.

Marguerite Oestreicher Fine Arts, 626 Julia St.; 581-9253. Master drawings from the 17th, 18th, and 19th centuries to contemporary art by Louisiana natives. Tue-Sat 10 am-5 pm.

Nahan Galleries, 540 Royal St.; 524-8696. Representation of major international and American artists, including Calder, Chagall, Dali, Miro, Rockwell. Daily 9:30 am-6 pm; Sun 11 am-6 pm.

906 Gallery, 906 Royal St.; 525-4527. Custom prints, etchings, and silkscreens. Historical battle scenes and etchings by Mexican artists. Mon-Sat 10 am-6 pm; Sun noon-6 pm.

Peligro! Folk Art, 305 Decatur St.; 581-1706. Call for hours.

Photo Works, 839 Chartres; 593-9090. Vivid images of New Orleans in black and white or color by local photographers. Daily 10 am-5 pm.

Rodrigue Gallery of New Orleans, 721 Royal St.; 581-4244. Louisiana artists, paintings, prints, books.

St. Charles Gallery, 1 Poydras St.; 523-0112. Fine paintings, prints, portraits, restorations, old and rare books and maps. Mon-Fri 10 am-5 pm.

Southwest Designs, 230 Chartres St.; 522-4345. Art by Native American and contemporary artists of the West. Call for hours.

Thomas Mann Gallery, 1804 Magazine St.; 581-2113. Contemporary metals from American and international artists and sculptors. Call for hours.

Vincent Art, 631 Decatur St.; 522-2773. 19th- and 20th-century impressionists and post-impressionists for collectors and investors. Tue-Sat 10 am-5 pm or by appointment.

Vincent Mann Gallery, 713 Bienville St.; 523-2342. Excellent selection of paintings by the late-19th- and 20th-century French impressionists. Mon-Sat 10 am-5 pm.

University Galleries

There are also changing exhibits at **Delgado Fine Arts Gallery** (483-4048); at **Dillard University Art Gallery** (286-4711); at **Tulane University,** at the **Newcomb Art School Gallery,** the **Howard-Tilton Memorial Library** (865-5604), and the **Newcomb Women's Gallery** (865-2780); at **Loyola University Danna Center Gallery** (865-3622); at the **University of New Orleans Fine Arts Gallery** (286-6493); and at **Southern University** (286-5267).

Fine Crafts Galleries

Many artists and craftsmen enjoy national reputations as well as local fame.

Bonhage, J. B., Jr., 1332 Washington Ave.; 899-6767. Metal floral sculpture.

Creative Native, 3137 Magazine St.; 899-6484. Variety of Louisiana artists' handcrafts.

Faget, Mignon, 710 Dublin St.; 865-7361. Fine jewelry and boutique.

Importicos, 5523 Magazine St., 891-6141; 736 Royal St., 523-3100. Indonesian pottery and woodcrafts.

Mercury Gallery, 4204 Magazine St.; 897-6666. Glassworks, metalwork, sculpture, stone carvings, and mixed-media art.

New Orleans School of Glassworks and Printmaking Studio, 727 Magazine St.; 529-7277. Tours and daily demonstrations.

Nuance/Louisiana Artisans Gallery, 728 Dublin St.; 865-8463. Original glass-blown works.

Shadyside Pottery Shop, 3823 Magazine St.; 897-1710.

Vision Quest, 1034 Royal St.; 523-0920. Native American prints and artifacts.

ART IN PUBLIC PLACES

New Orleans is noted for its sculptures, which are found in every section of the city and include every style, from the most classic to the most contemporary.

Margaret. The first statue in the United States to honor a woman is located where Camp and Prytania streets come together. The sculptor was Alexander Doyle of New York. The statue, of Carrara marble, depicts the unselfish Irish lady who, after her husband and child died, devoted her life to helping the orphaned and destitute of the community. She is one of the few women who openly defied Gen. Ben Butler, the Union general who occupied New Orleans.

At St. Charles Avenue and Lee Circle, there are two visual treats, the *Robert E. Lee Statue* (see SELF-GUIDED TOURS, St. Charles Driving Tour) and the *K&B Plaza*, across the street at 1055 St. Charles Ave. The latter is a fine contemporary building by Skidmore, Owings, and Merrill surrounded by contemporary sculptures from the Virlane Foundation. Since the works are outside, they are on view at all times. There is also an art exhibit inside the building. When the building is open, there are pamphlets inside describing the collection. Call 586-2007 for times. Also, 30 major works from this collection will be on view in a Sculpture Garden in City Park (see below). *NCH*.

Jackson Square is the country's largest year-round outdoor art gallery and, amazingly, the whole thing is put away every night and put up again every morning. Plan to be there for at least one of those times—it's interesting to watch—a good time to engage the artists in conversation.

Farther down Decatur, toward Canal Street, is a truly dynamic monument. At the end of the Jackson Brewery Complex, Decatur Street seems to split into another street—North Peters Street. In this Y split is a triangular neutral ground (median) which is dedicated to our founder. Here is a powerful work by Angela Gregory, a New Orleans native who has accepted commissions in many parts of the world. This is New Orleans' official monument to its founder, *Jean Baptist LeMoyne, Sieur de Bienville*. Ms. Gregory also did the monument marking the site of Bienville's last dwelling place in Paris.

The Central Business District offers the following sculptural treats:

At 1515 Poydras St., just across from the Superdome, don't miss Ida Kohlmeyer's kinetic sculpture, *The Krewe of Poydras*. Ms. Kohlmeyer, who is known nationally for her abstract paintings, has fashioned the colorful "members" of her krewe from sheet steel, welded into bold, intriguing shapes, mounted on 40-foot steel poles which revolve in strong winds.

The building at 1515 Poydras also boasts 15 large paintings by artist Krista Jurisich, which are hung in the building's elevators! She calls this series *Sky Lift*.

At Poydras and Camp streets, in the plaza between the Hale Boggs Building and the Fifth Circuit Court Building, there are a number of interesting contemporary sculptures.

Along Basin Street, from Canal Street to St. Louis Street, there is a row of statues which pay tribute to New Orleans' strong ties to Latin America. At Canal Street is Abel Valmitjana's granite statue of *Simon Bolivar*, a gift to the city from the people of Venezuela. Bolivar was the hero who was responsible for freeing most of Latin America from Spain.

Just beyond the Bolivar statue is a monument to *Benito Juarez*, the great Mexican hero who once lived in New Orleans, and who, in the latter part of the 19th century, freed Mexico from the rule of the Emperor Maximillian.

At Basin and St. Louis streets is a monument to *Gen. Francisco Morazon*, a Central American revolutionary hero who was executed by Costa Rican rebels in 1842. It was given by the peoples of Honduras and El Salvador.

The *Louisiana Land and Exploration Co. Building* at 909 Poydras St. shows a work by sculptor Enrique Alferez.

There is also much statuary of note in the parks of New Orleans (including even the benches in the *City Park Rose Garden* with their Richard Koch-designed whimsical creatures lurking beneath). Stop to enjoy them as you tour. In City Park, adjacent to the New Orleans Museum of Art, there will be a Sydney and Walda Bestoff Sculpture Garden, consisting of nearly 50 sculptures by major 20th-century European, American, Israeli, and Japanese artists—all gifts from the Bestoff Foundation.

For those who may have occasion to visit the *Ochsner Foundation-Medical Complex* while in New Orleans, the long hallway which links the buildings in the complex is lined with an excellent collection of contemporary graphic art. *Touro Infirmary*, in uptown New Orleans, cheers patients and visitors with a fine display of contemporary paintings and graphics.

Children's Hospital, 200 Henry Clay, has some fine original Louisiana art to brighten the hallways.

Other facts of note to those interested in the visual arts:

The Arts Quarterly, an excellent publication, is sent to members of the New Orleans Museum of Art. For information, call 488-2631.

The Arts Council of New Orleans has completed an arts directory. For information, contact Arts Directory, Arts Council of New Orleans, 225 Baronne St.; 523-1465. The directory gives lists of organizations, museums, galleries, and companies involved in the arts in New Orleans.

SHOPPING

A shopping spree in New Orleans is part exploration of the city, part a hunt for treasure, and always a day filled with good food and good cheer. There is Canal Street, the main downtown shopping thoroughfare, one of the widest main streets in the world. There are, as in other cities, fine shopping malls. However, the most fun to be had shopping in New Orleans comes in wandering through the quaint and interesting shopping areas where behind a battered clapboard facade you may find a valuable antique, an elegant piece of handmade jewelry, or a new outfit for your child. Plan time for leisurely "poking around," and be sure to wear comfortable shoes.

The Magazine Street Bus, the St. Charles streetcar, the riverfront "Red Ladies" streetcars, and the Vieux Carre minibuses make most interesting shopping areas of the city accessible to the visitor who may be without a car.

SHOPPING DISTRICTS

Downtown

The downtown shopping center, Canal Street, the French Quarter, and Poydras at the Hyatt Regency are the hub for shopping. Most of the department stores, music stores, and branches of fine New York stores are located in downtown malls: Canal Place, New Orleans Centre, the Riverwalk Marketplace, and the Jax Brewery.

One Canal Place and Riverwalk, on either side of the World Trade Center, are two of the newest complexes including such fine stores as Saks Fifth Avenue, Brooks Brothers, Laura Ashley, Gucci, and Abercrombie and Fitch. One Canal Place features office towers and lodging as well as retail space. The New Orleans Centre, situated between the Hyatt Regency and the Superdome, includes such fine stores as Lord & Taylor, Macy's, Ballin's, Gentlemen's Quarter Ltd., Ann Taylor, and Victoria's Secret on its three levels. The downtown malls offer free and reduced-fee parking.

French Quarter

The French Quarter offers a tremendous variety of shopping: the Jackson Brewery (a renovated 1891 brewhouse) overlooking the Mississippi River, the Brewhouse Malls, the French Market shopping area, and the quaint Quarter shops, boutiques, art and antique galleries, and poster and souvenir shops that line Decatur, Chartres, and Royal streets. There is a Royal Street Merchant Guide.

St. Charles Avenue Shops

Many specialty shops are located on the St. Charles streetcar line a few blocks from Lee Circle. They offer art galleries, fine fabrics, beautiful clothes, Oriental rugs, modern furniture, and restaurants in which to rejuvenate yourself.

Garden District

Located in the Garden District on Prytania Street is "The Rink," a collection of several specialty shops under one roof. It was, indeed, an old-fashioned skating rink which is now happily recycled.

Magazine Antiques

Magazine Street is filled with many blocks of quaint antique and gift shops, a favorite place of native New Orleanians. Be sure to pick up the Magazine Street Merchant's Association brochure to guide you in your wanderings. The Magazine Bus runs the length of the street, from Canal Street to the Audubon Zoo.

Uptown Square

Located on Broadway, right at the Mississippi River and Leake Avenue, is the Uptown Square Shopping Center. A variety of clothing, gift, specialty shops, and restaurants are located in this replica of a medieval village. There is often entertainment in the courtyard on weekends.

Riverbend

In the Carrollton section of uptown New Orleans is another group of shops, restaurants, and specialty stores, including the Dante/River Shopping Center. These shops are within walking distance of the St. Charles streetcar line. You will find fine clothing, restaurants, jewelry, craftspeople, antiques, and more.

Suburban Malls

Clearview Shopping Center on Veterans Boulevard and Clearview Parkway is in Metairie. Dillard's and Sears are the larger stores at Clearview. There is an A & G Cafeteria with live piano music.

The Esplanade, 1401 W. Esplanade Ave., Kenner; 468-6116. The newest and most innovative design of New Orleans' suburban malls, a multilevel, upbeat family spot anchored by Dillard's on one end and Macy's on the other, with almost 130 shops in between.

Lakeside Shopping Mall, with its large parking facility and many movie houses, is a popular place to be casual, bring small children, and shop in the comfort of air conditioning. There are two large department stores, Dillard's and J. C. Penney's, and a variety of other stores.

Oakwood Shopping Mall is across the Crescent City Connection and is more convenient to the downtown area, the Garden District, or those residents who live on the West Bank. Many restaurants, lounges, and places of business have located here since the 1950s, including Sears and Dillard's.

Slidell Factory Outlet Mall; 504-646-0756. This mall consists of about 30 stores owned and operated by the manufacturers. The stores sell quality merchandise at reduced prices. Only 20 minutes from New Orleans in off-peak traffic. Factory stores can be reached via Interstates 10, 12, and 59. Take Exit #263, I-10.

Tanger Factory Outlet; 2200 Tanger Blvd., Gonzales; 1-800-406-2112. This outlet mall 45 minutes from New Orleans boasts 57 stores sellings clothing, shoes, perfumes, toys, electronics, kitchenware, and more. There are even two restaurants.

SHOPPING BY AREA

CENTRAL BUSINESS/ WAREHOUSE DISTRICTS

Adler's, Jewelry
B. Dalton Booksellers, Books
Banana Republic, Clothing
Brooks Brothers, Clothing
Cambias Office Equipment, Office Supplies
Days of Wine and Roses, Tobacco
DeVille's, Books
Flowers Unlimited By Jesse, Florists
Gucci, Clothing
Koslow's Furs, Clothing
Laura Ashley, Clothing
Lord & Taylor, Clothing
Motherhood Maternity, Clothing
Porter-Stevens, Clothing, Shoes
Pottery Barn, Home Furnishings
Rapp's, Leather
Rubenstein Bros., Clothing
Saks Fifth Avenue, Clothing
Serio's Mike Po-Boys & Deli, Foods
Swiss Confectionery, Foods
World's Best Toys, Toys

FRENCH QUARTER/ FAUBOURG MARIGNY

The Acorn Shop, Jewelry
Arcadian Books and Prints, Books
Art Accent, Eclectic-Novelty
Beckham's Book Shop, Books
Black Butterfly, Miniatures
Bookstar, Books
Christmas in October, Eclectic-Novelty
Cohen, James H. and Sons, Coins and Stamps
Dixon & Dixon, Antiques, Prints and Paintings
Doerr Furniture, Furniture
Eastern Onion Singing Telegrams, Eclectic-Novelty
Epitome in Fine Tobacco, Tobacco
Faubourg Marigny Bookstore, Books
Faulkner House Books, Books
Feet First, Discount Stores and Factory Outlets
Fleur de Paris, Clothing
The French Market, Markets
French Quarter Florist, Florists
Friends of the Cabildo, Books
Gentlemen's Quarter, Clothing, Shoes
Hello Dolly, Toys
Historic New Orleans Collection, Books
Hurwitz-Mintz, Furniture
Keil's Antiques, Antiques, Jewelry
La Cuisine Classique, Home Furnishings
La Marquise Pastry Shop, Foods
La Petite Fleur, Jewelry
Lawrence's Bakery, Foods
Le Petit Soldier Shop, Toys
Librairie Book Shop, Books
The Little Toy Shoppe, Gift Shops and Accessories, Toys
Manheim Galleries, Antiques
Moliere's Antique Shop, Jewelry

Moss Antiques, Jewelry
Old Children's Books, Books
Quarter Stitch, Crafts, Hobbies, and Needleworks
Rau's Antiques, Antiques
Rothschild's, Antiques
Royal Antiques, Antiques, Jewelry
Sports Art Gallery, Prints and Paintings
Stern Antiques, Antiques
Sutton's, Linens
Tower Records, Videos, & Books, Music and Videos
Trashy Diva, Discount Stores and Factory Outlets
Virgin Megastore, Music and Videos
Waldhorn & Adler Antiques, Antiques, Jewelry
Raymond H. Weil Co., Coins and Stamps
Ye Olde Pipe Shoppe, Tobacco

GARDEN DISTRICT/ LOWER ST. CHARLES

Calico Corners, Fabrics
Home Furnishing Store Ltd., Home Furnishings
Joy Balloons, Balloon Bouquets
Lylian Shop, Clothing, Lace, Linens
MGM Costume Rentals, Costumes
Mignon, Clothing
On Stage, Eclectic-Novelty
Promenade Fine Fabrics, Costumes, Fabrics
Sarouk Shop, Rugs
Scheinuk, Florists
Smith's Record Center, Music and Videos
Town and Country Shop, Clothing, Linens

LAKEFRONT

Charlie's Deli, Foods
John Jay's, Skin Care
Lakeview Fine Foods, Foods
Lakeview Florist, Florists
Little Miss Muffin, Gift Shops and Accessories
Movietime Video, Movies
University of New Orleans Bookstore, Books
West Marine, Boating

MAGAZINE STREET

A Antiques, Antiques
Antebellum Antiques, Antiques
Antiques by Nina Sloss, Antiques
As You Like It Silver Shop, Antiques
Ballunacy, Balloon Bouquets
Beaucoup Books, Books
Blackamoor Antiques, Antiques
Chez Nous Charcuterie, Food
Crescent City Market, Markets
Didier Inc., Prints and Paintings
Dombourian Oriental Rugs, Rugs
Dos Jefes Uptown Cigar Shop, Tobacco
Feet First, Discount Stores and Factory Outlets, Shoes
George Herget Books, Books
Hobby Shop, Crafts, Hobbies, and Needleworks
Irwin's Flower Salon, Florists
Magazine Arcade Antiques, Antiques
Perlis Men's Shop, Clothing
Persian Cat, Crafts, Hobbies, and Needleworks
Probst Decorating, Fabrics
Stan Levy Imports, Antiques

METAIRIE/JEFFERSON

Adventure Sports, Sports Equipment
Angelo's Bakery, Foods
Animal Crackers, Clothing
Bagel Factory, Foods
Balloons Unlimited, Balloon Bouquets
Baltazor Bridal Fabrics & Laces, Lace
Banana Republic, Clothing
Barnes & Noble Booksellers, Books
Beach Bros., Furniture
Bennett's Camera and Video, Photographic Supplies
Blue Diamond Kiln Co., Crafts, Hobbies, and Needleworks
Borders Books & Music, Books
Chocolate Soup, Clothing
Connie's Sit N' Knit, Crafts, Hobbies, and Needleworks
Designs in Jewelry, Jewelry
Edwin Watts, Sports Equipment
Eric's of Metairie, Crafts, Hobbies, and Needleworks
Foodies Kitchen, Foods
Gambino's Bakeries, Foods
Gary's Arts Craft & Needlework, Crafts, Hobbies, and Needleworks
Hancock Fabrics, Costumes, Fabrics
Harrie J's Maternity Fashions, Clothing
Haydel's, Foods
Humbug Costumes, Costumes
Juanita's Name Brand Discount Shoes, Shoes
Kirschman's, Furniture
Lakeside Camera & Imaging, Photographic Supplies
Langenstein's, Foods
Le Jouet, Toys
Lynley Designs, Discount Stores and Factory Outlets
Maple Street Book Shop, Books
Marshall's, Discount Stores and Factory Outlets
Martin Wine Cellar, Foods
Massey's, Sports Equipment
Maternite, Clothing
Men's Wearhouse, Discount Stores and Factory Outlets
Metairie Fabric Shop, Costumes, Fabrics
Mothertime, Clothing
Nevada Bob's, Sports Equipment
Nutrition Fair, Foods
Oriental Merchandise, Eclectic-Novelty
Oshman's Sports, Sports Equipment
Southern Coins, Coins and Stamps
Sports Authority, Sports Equipment
Stein Mart, Discount Stores and Factory Outlets
Toys R Us, Toys
US Office Products, Office Supplies
Video Blast, Music and Videos
Waldenbooks, Books
Werlein's for Music, Music and Videos

MID CITY

Armadillo South Architectural Salvage, Antiques
Costume Headquarters, Costumes
Gambino's Bakeries, Foods
Moldaner's, Photographic Supplies

New Orleans Museum of Art, Books
Ricca Demolishing Corp., Antiques
Whole Foods Market, Foods

NEW ORLEANS EAST/ CHALMETTE

Ally's Hallmark & Gift Shop, Gift Shops and Accessories
Balloons by Fascination, Balloon Bouquets
Baptist Book Store, Books
Bon-Faye's, Florists
The Fruit Basket, Foods
St. Bernard Sporting Goods, Sports Equipment

UPTOWN/RIVERBEND

Albert Brown Salon, Skin Care
Alice Designs, Clothing
J. Aronson's, Gift Shops and Accessories
Athlete's Foot, Sports Equipment
Bagatelle, Clothing
Ballin's, Clothing
Body Joys, Skin Care
The Camera Shop, Photographic Supplies
Catholic Book Store, Books
Dante Street Deli, Foods
Dunbar & Company, Discount Stores and Factory Outlets
EarthSavers, Skin Care
Encore Dress, Discount Stores and Factory Outlets
Gae-Tana's/Maple St. Clothing, Discount Stores and Factory Outlets
Gentry's, Clothing, Gift Shops and Accessories
M. Goldberg, Clothing
Haase's Shoe Store and Young Folks Shop, Clothing, Shoes
Junior League Thrift Shop, Discount Stores and Factory Outlets
Kid's Stuff, Toys
LaBonbonniere European Pastry Shop, Foods
Langenstein's, Foods
Lollipop Shoppe, Clothing
Lulu Buras, Skin Care
Magic Box, Toys
Maple Street Book Shop, Books
Mariposa, Discount Stores and Factory Outlets
Martin Wine Cellar, Foods
Meisel Fabrics, Fabrics, Lace
Mignon Faget Ltd., Clothing, Jewelry
On the Other Hand, Discount Stores and Factory Outlets
Party Basket, Gift Shops and Accessories
Pippin Lane, Clothing
Quilt Cottage, Inc., Crafts, Hobbies, and Needleworks
Rapp's, Leather
Rohm's Floral Designs & Greenhouses, Florists
St. Germain, Shoes
Scriptura, Gift Shops and Accessories
Simply Gold, Jewelry
Sound of Music, Gift Shops and Accessories
Stationer of New Orleans, Gift Shops and Accessories
Stein Mart, Discount Stores and Factory Outlets
The Sun Shop, Gift Shops and Accessories
Symmetry Jewelers, Jewelry
Tulane Book Stores, Books

Uptown Square Winery, Foods
Uptowner Antiques, Antiques
Video Connection, Music and Videos
Yvonne LaFleur, Clothing

WEST BANK

Academy Sports & Outdoors, Sports Equipment
Bayou Books, Books
Books-A-Million, Books
Dillard's, Clothing
Men's Wearhouse, Discount Stores and Factory Outlets
Oakwood Mall
Toys R Us, Toys
Waldenbooks, Books

ANTIQUES

New Orleans is a heaven for antique lovers for there are hundreds of shops, all catering to different tastes and pocketbooks. Shops range from very expensive to classic junque, and everything in between.

Many families have operated antique shops for generations in the same Quarter locations; but recently, some of the dealers have moved uptown to Magazine Street. The antique rage has also crossed the Causeway/Lake Pontchartrain and many shops have opened in the Covington/Mandeville and Slidell areas. Take time to browse, for there are always treasures in New Orleans looking for a new home.

A Antiques, 5423 Magazine St.; 899-3001. An uptown shop that buys and sells antique furniture, rugs, and glass items. A Antiques also has old photographs and albums.

Antebellum Antiques, 2011 Magazine St.; 558-0208, 558-0221. Furniture and decorative art of 19th-century American, French, and English design.

Armadillo South Architectural Salvage, 4801 Washington Ave.; 486-1150. Original architectural salvage for historically correct renovations.

As You Like It Silver Shop, 3021 Magazine St.; 897-6915. This shop has almost every silver pattern, old and new. You can find Grandmother's outdated silver pattern.

Blackamoor Antiques, Inc., 3433 Magazine St.; 897-2711. The shop itself is beautifully decorated with fine English and French furniture for sale. A fun place to get ideas—don't miss it.

Dixon & Dixon, 237 and 318 Royal St.; 524-0282. Oriental rugs, estate jewelry, porcelains, rare paintings, and furniture in three galleries.

Keil's Antiques, 325 Royal St.; 522-4552. English and French antiques as well as crystal, china, and chandeliers are sold at Keil's Antiques.

Magazine Arcade Antiques, 3017 Magazine St.; 899-5451. This arcade is the antique buff's dream with 10 little antique shops under one roof. Furniture, china, and art deco items can be found here.

Manheim Galleries, 409 Royal St.; 568-1901. These period antiques are housed in a beautiful historically famous French Quarter landmark, with museum-type pieces and an outstanding collection of jade, art objects, and Boehm birds the specialty.

Rau's Antiques, 630 Royal St.; 523-5660. Antique collectors may get delightfully lost in this extensive French Quarter shop; fine jewelry, sterling flatware, china, cut glass, chandeliers, clocks, and many rooms of furniture.

Ricca Demolishing Corp., 511 N. Solomon; 488-5248. Here you will find antique building materials and architectural finishings such as brass hardware.

Rothschild's, 321 Royal St.; 523-2281. This shop is more like a museum, the true collector's delight. Fine antiques.

Royal Antiques, 307-9 Royal St.; 524-7033, 524-7035. A large selection of English antique furniture—chests, tables, and chairs—is available here, with estate jewelry and some reproductions.

Stan Levy Imports, 1028 Louisiana St.; 899-6384. Plan to spend all day looking in Stan Levy's for the shop has endless rooms of antiques and collectibles.

Uptowner Antiques, 3828 Magazine St.; 891-7700. Uptowner Antiques shows English antiques by appointment.

Waldhorn & Adler Antiques, 343 Royal St.; 581-6379. One of the oldest and most interesting buildings in the Quarter, Waldhorn & Adler has fine porcelains, crystal, and furniture. Some of the finest jewelry in the South is here.

BALLOON BOUQUETS

Balloons by Fascination, 9053 W. Judge Perez; 277-3818. Unique bouquets; citywide delivery.

Balloons Unlimited, 3401 W. Esplanade Ave.; 833-6666, 779-9090. Bouquets, talking balloons, decorating service, delivery.

Ballunacy, 4843 Magazine St.; 897-9003. Elegant gifts and party decorations, delivery.

Joy Balloons, 1522 Chippewa St.; 522-8194. Sponsored by St. Michael's Special School, who suggest that you "send a bouquet of joy today," delivery.

BOOKS

Several antique shops and quaint bookstores in New Orleans have rare, old books. Many national booksellers are located in shopping malls. There are also good neighborhood shops, downtown book dealers, and full-service independent bookstores.

The Symphony Book Fair held every year in the spring by members of the symphony's volunteer group is a wonderful opportunity to find rare or first edition books mixed between the paperback and hardback donations.

Arcadian Books and Prints, 714 Orleans St.; 523-4138. Nestled within the row of antique shops, Arcadian Books has old books and art prints which are suitable for framing.

B. Dalton Booksellers; 837-2868. A national chain having several shopping mall locations throughout the city.

Baptist Book Store, 2939 Gentilly Rd.; 282-2626. The Baptist Book Store has a wide assortment of Bibles, religious, and children's books as well as devotional and teaching aids.

Barnes & Noble Booksellers, 3121 Veterans Blvd.; 455-4929. This large, two-level bookstore offers CDs, stationery, and coffee in addition to national and regional books and an impressive children's section. Poetry readings and children's activities are frequently scheduled.

Bayou Books, 1005 Monroe St., Gretna; 368-1171. Bayou buys and sells books and has a search service with rare out-of-print books and new and used books for sale. This is a very cozy shop across the Mississippi River on the West Bank.

Beaucoup Books, 5414 Magazine St.; 895-2663. Along Magazine Street enjoy this bookstore for its variety and personal attention.

Beckham's Book Shop, 2281 Decatur St.; 522-9875. This is a second-hand and antiquarian bookshop, "a two-story treasure trove of old books."

Books-A-Million, Oakwood Shopping Center; 364-1070. This is quite a large bookstore with regular and many discount titles and a big children's section with special activities.

Bookstar, 414 N. Peters; 523-6411. This two-level bookstore in the French Quarter carries best sellers and a wide variety of Louisiana books for adults and children.

Borders Books & Music, Causeway and Veterans; 835-1363. This large, two-level bookstore features a coffee shop and music section as well. It also has a large children's section and a variety of regional titles. The store conducts a range of adult and children's activities—all related to books and music.

Catholic Book Store, 8039 Fig St.; 861-7504. Located in the Carrollton section, the shop has a fine selection of religious materials, books, and paperbacks as well as gift books.

DeVille Books and Prints, 344 Carondelet; 525-6846. DeVille's is a large bookstore with many regional titles which also offers a free book-find service, antiquarian books, and appraisals.

Faubourg Marigny Bookstore, 600 Frenchmen St.; 943-9875.

Faulkner House Books, 624 Pirates Alley; 524-2940.

George Herget Books, 3109 Magazine St.; 891-5595.

Historic New Orleans Collection, 533 Royal St.; 523-4662. Antiquarian and secondhand books.

Librairie Book Shop, 823 Chartres St.; 525-4837. Antiquarian and secondhand books.

Maple Street Book Shop, uptown university section, 7523 Maple St.; 866-4916. Children's Book Shop, 7529 Maple St.; 861-2105. Old Metairie Book Shop, 200 Metairie Rd.; 832-8937. New paperbacks and hardback best sellers are available here, with a variety of children's books in a separate Victorian cottage at the Maple Street location, including children's Louisiana lore books with two local characters—Gaston the Alligator and Jenny Giraffe. The stores always have signed copies of books for special gifts.

Old Children's Books, 734 Royal St.; 525-3655. This is a delightful small bookstore.

Tulane Book Stores, Tulane University; 865-5913.

University of New Orleans Bookstore, University Center, Lakefront; 280-6373.

Waldenbooks; 888-1275. A national chain having several New Orleans locations in shopping malls, Waldenbooks has a large selection of books and magazines.

CLOTHING

New Orleans' fine department stores, Macy's, Dillard's, Sears, and Penney's, all have fine collections of clothing for all ages, sexes, and sizes. More specialized shops are listed below.

Women's Clothing

All of the Canal Street stores and mall shopping centers have fine ladies' wear.

Alice Designs, 8200 Hampson St.; 865-7950. Fine fabric and custom-made formal, bridal, and casual clothes. Also, "Color Me Beautiful" consultations are available by appointment.

Bagatelle, Uptown Square; 861-3341. Designer clothes, blouses, sweaters, and formal gowns.

Ballin's, 721 Dante St.; 866-4367, and New Orleans Centre. Children's, teens', and ladies' designer clothes, jewelry, and accessories.

Banana Republic, Riverwalk at 1 Poydras Pl.; 523-6843, Lakeside Mall, Metairie; 832-9294, and Esplanade Mall, Kenner; 469-5570. Clothes for men and women that will take you from an African safari to a Yuppie happy hour.

Fleur de Paris, 712 Royal St.; 525-1899. Unique beautiful clothing. Also has a millinery with special ready-mades, or assist in designing your own hat and have it made there just for you.

Gucci, One Canal Place; 524-5544. The Italian designer shop is a favorite representative of haute couture in New Orleans.

Laura Ashley, One Canal Place. The British shop brings its country-print fashions, petticoats, and Old World look to New Orleans.

Lord & Taylor, New Orleans Centre; 581-5673. Everything from sporty, business, dressy to elegant gowns for the ball or prom.

Mignon Faget Ltd., 710 Dublin St.; 865-7361. Original design, small boutique shop.

Perlis Men's Shop, 6070 Magazine St.; 895-8661. Uptown's favorite men's shop has women's and boys' traditional clothes, too!

Saks Fifth Avenue, One Canal Place; 524-2200. The famous New York store.

Town and Country Shop, 1432 St. Charles Ave.; 523-7027. A landmark on the Avenue. Bridal, formal, and complete ladies' wear. Gift and children's items.

Yvonne LaFleur, 8131 Hampson St.; 866-9666, and Riverwalk and Esplanade malls. Old laces, chic hats, shoes, handbags, fine lingerie, gifts, and cosmetic items.

Maternity

There are several really fine stores for the ladies in waiting throughout the city and in nearby malls.

Harrie J's Maternity Fashions, Inc., 1213 N. Causeway Blvd., Metairie; 834-0231. They've dressed mothers-to-be since the 1960s. Complete stock including needs for nursing mothers.

Maternite, Lakeside Mall; 831-9551.

Motherhood Maternity, Esplanade Mall, Kenner; 443-9634.

Mothertime, Esplanade Mall; 466-6255.

Men's Clothing

New Orleans' men, because of Mardi Gras, wear evening clothes more often than most. These are some of their favorite shops for day and evening wear.

Banana Republic, Riverwalk at 1 Poydras Pl.; 523-6843, Lakeside Mall, Metairie; 832-9294, and Esplanade Mall, Kenner; 469-5570.

Brooks Brothers, One Canal Place; 522-4200. Clothing for the executive. Complete men's furnishings.

Gentlemen's Quarter, 232 Royal St.; 522-7139. Specialty shop for men. Unusual designer clothing and sportswear.

Gentry's, Uptown Square, 200 Broadway; 866-8608. Men's clothing. Gifts, furnishings, cards, gourmet kitchen items.

M. Goldberg, Uptown Square; 866-1116. Men's and boys' clothing. The complete men's and boys' shop.

Perlis Men's Shop, 6070 Magazine St.; 895-8661. Home of the crawfish shirt. All types of men's shoes, clothing, gifts, and formal wear (to buy or rent).

Porter-Stevens, Lakeside Mall, Veterans and Causeway; 834-3771. Complete men's clothing and shoes.

Rubenstein Bros., 102 St. Charles Ave.; 581-6666. Complete men's wear. Mall location at Lake Forest Plaza; 242-2880.

Children's Clothing and Gifts

Animal Crackers, 240 Metairie Rd.; 837-2333. Clothing, shoes, and gifts.

Ballin's, 721 Dante St.; 866-4367. Tots', children's, teens', and moms' chic clothing too. Mall location at New Orleans Centre.

Chocolate Soup, 2030 Metairie Rd.; 837-8314. Nice selection of children's better and designer clothing. Their own label hosts a can of what else? Chocolate Soup!

Haase's Shoe Store and Young Folks Shop, 8119 Oak St.; 866-9944. A favorite place with uptown mothers for children's clothes and shoes.

Lollipop Shoppe, 8125 Hampson St.; 865-1014. Gifts and clothing for the tots and children.

Lylian Shop, 1514 St. Charles Ave.; 525-2020. (see Lace)

Mignon, 2727 Prytania St., The Rink shopping center; 891-2374. Delightful place to shop for children's clothing, accessories, gifts, toys, and books. They even have the children's Louisiana lore books of two local characters—Gaston the Alligator and Jenny Giraffe.

Pippin Lane—A Children's Emporium, 2929 Magazine St.; 269-0106. Features imported children's clothing and linens, shoes, toys, and custom hand-painted furniture.

Area malls also have children's sections in the large department stores.

CRAFTS, HOBBIES, AND NEEDLEWORKS

Blue Diamond Kiln Co., 2009 S. Hullen St., Metairie; 835-2035. Kilns for the potters are sold at Blue Diamond Shop.

Connie's Sit N' Knit, 1818 Veterans Blvd., Metairie; 835-2832. All types of knitting and needlepoint needs, pictures, rugs, or canvas to work are available.

Eric's of Metairie, 4310 Waverly St., Metairie; 455-9339. This is one of the largest craft supply shops in New Orleans.

Gary's Arts Craft & Needlework, 3221 N. Causeway; 834-5258, and 3109 18th St., Metairie; 834-5258.

Hobby Shop (National Art and Hobby), 5835 Magazine St.; 899-4491. Painting and art supplies, model planes, wood carving, and all kinds of hobby needs are available here.

Persian Cat, 8211 Hampson St.; 864-1908. Complete handiwork supplies are available here.

Quarter Stitch, 630 Chartres; 522-4451. On Jackson Square in the French Quarter, this shop specializes in original needlepoint designs.

Quilt Cottage, Inc., 801 Nashville St.; 895-3791. Everything to begin your family quilt is here: fabric, books, patterns, and quilt workshops.

COINS AND STAMPS

Cohen, James H. and Sons, 437 Royal St.; 522-3305. For the war buffs, this shop specializes in pre-1898 collector items, firearms, swords, guns, and coins.

Southern Coins, 474 Metairie Rd.; 837-1711. A wide variety of coins, gold, bullion, and some jewelry can be found here.

Raymond H. Weil Co., 407 Royal St.; 581-7373. Raymond H. Weil Co. specializes in rare Confederate and American stamps.

COSTUMES

Costumes are an important part of life in New Orleans. We've listed shops at which you can buy or rent costumes, and places to buy fancy trims to make your own.

Costume Headquarters, 240 Iris Ave., Jefferson; 488-9523. Costumes and makeup for all occasions can be bought or rented.

Hancock Fabrics, 8726 W. Judge Perez Dr., Chalmette; 271-3574.

Humbug Costumes, 2707 Williams Blvd., Kenner; 469-3339. This store carries all sizes in costumes, makeup, and masks.

MGM Costume Rentals, 1617 St. Charles Ave.; 581-3999. Thousands of Hollywood costumes can be found here; also wigs, masks, and makeup.

Metairie Fabric Shop, 480 Metairie Rd., Metairie; 833-6209. Metairie Fabric Shop supplies costume materials, trims, and Mardi Gras throws.

Promenade Fine Fabrics, 1520 St. Charles Ave.; 522-1488. This store carries a wide variety of very fine fabrics, buttons, and ribbons.

DISCOUNT STORES AND FACTORY OUTLETS

Ladies' Clothing

Feet First, 5500 Magazine; 899-6800, and 518 Chartres; 566-7525, and two other city locations. Ladies' shoes at discount prices.

Gae-Tana's/Maple St. Clothing, 7732 Maple St.; 865-9625. Designer clothes for ladies at discount prices.

Marshall's, Elmwood Village, 1300 S. Clearview Pkwy., Harahan; 734-1151. Discount department store for the whole family.

Stein Mart, 5300 Tchoupitoulas; 891-6377, and 2805 Veterans Hwy.; 469-2530. Wonderful variety of clothing, shoes, jewelry, and gifts.

Men's Clothing

Marshall's, Elmwood Village, 1300 S. Clearview Pkwy., Harahan; 734-1151. Discounts for the whole family.

Men's Wearhouse, 197 Westbank Expwy.; 362-3114, and 3033 N. Causeway Blvd.; 837-4295. Great bargains on men's suits.

Stein Mart, 5300 Tchoupitoulas; 891-6377, and 2805 Veterans Hwy.; 469-2530. Wonderful variety of clothing, shoes, and gifts.

Children's Clothing

Lynley Designs, 2628 Jefferson Hwy.; 833-7667. Manufacturer's outlet clothing for children.

Marshall's, Elmwood Village, 1300 S. Clearview Pkwy., Harahan; 734-1151. Discount department store for the whole family.

Stein Mart, 5300 Tchoupitoulas; 891-6377, and 2805 Veterans Hwy.; 469-2530. Wonderful variety of clothing, shoes, and gifts.

Recycled and Vintage Clothing

Now popular with men and women of all ages and incomes, these shops are filled with both everyday finds and collector's items. They are also full of good ideas for Mardi Gras costumes.

Dunbar & Company, 8209 Hampson St.; 866-0820. Vintage clothing and accessories from the 1890s to the 1950s.

Encore Dress Shop, 7814 Maple St.; 861-9028. Quality clothes on consignment to benefit the New Orleans Symphony.

Junior League Thrift Shop, Inc., 4645 Freret St.; 891-1289. Good source of lovely clothes for the family as well as formal wear and, sometimes, costumes.

Mariposa, 2038 Magazine St.; 523-3037. Unique selection of vintage clothing and accessories.

On the Other Hand, 8126 Hampson; 861-0159. Exclusive resale boutique.

Trashy Diva, 829 Chartres St.; 581-4555. Marvelous place to shop. Vintage clothing from the 1850s (for special collections) to 1960s. Accessories and shoes, also.

ECLECTIC-NOVELTY

Christmas in October, 1025 Decatur St.; 581-5820. Christmas decorations from the world over. Shop in July or anytime. Open 7 days, 10 am-5 pm.

Eastern Onion Singing Telegrams; 831-1319. Guaranteed to liven things up—singing telegrams for all occasions; male and female dancers.

Habeba Singing & Dancing Telegrams, nationwide; 947-1057.

On Stage, Kenilworth Mall; 246-5292. All types of dance shoes and clothing.

Oriental Merchandise Co., 2636 Edenborn Ave., Metairie; 888-3191. Decorations, lanterns, Mardi Gras and party supplies.

FABRICS

Calico Corners, 1820 St. Charles Ave.; 522-0005. Upholstery, decorator seconds, drapery fabric, and slipcovers are tantalizingly displayed.

Hancock Fabrics, 8726 W. Judge Perez Dr.; 271-3574. Several locations sell fabrics for home and everyday use, trims.

Meisel Fabrics, 8225 Oak St.; 866-9438. Fine fabrics and drapery materials, trims, and ribbons can be found here.

Metairie Fabric Shop, 480 Metairie Rd., Metairie; 833-6209. This is a complete shop meeting fabric needs and offering costume supplies.

Probst Decorating, 3300 Magazine St.; 895-2094. Drapery and upholstery fabric and home needs are taken care of; drapes are made to order.

Promenade Fine Fabrics, 1520 St. Charles Ave.; 522-1488. Promenade has a complete selection of dressmaking fabrics, imported silks, laces, formal fabrics, trims, imported braids, and ribbons.

FLORISTS

Plants or flowers are always the special way to please. Most florists have FTD (Florist Telegraph Delivery) service and local delivery.

Bon-Faye's Florist, 6023 Chef Menteur Hwy.; 241-5104. Well-established florist and balloon-bouquet shop. Arrangements with a personal touch.

Flowers Unlimited By Jesse, 201 St. Charles Ave.; 524-6567. Beautiful selection of flowers for all occasions.

French Quarter Florist, 223 Dauphine St.; 523-5040. Open 24 hours for service and special arrangements.

Irwin's Flower Salon, 4238 Magazine St.; 897-1313. A true artist in floral art, Irwin's specializes in receptions and large parties.

Lakeview Florist, 6246 General Diaz; 486-3719. Arrangements with a personal touch. Complete wedding floral designs.

Rohm's Floral Designs & Greenhouses, 8333 Maple St.; 861-3611. Beautiful church and debut arrangements. Potted plants and cut flowers or small vase items.

Scheinuk, 2600 St. Charles Ave.; 895-3944. This florist is an Avenue landmark, especially with the outdoor Easter bunny exhibit. Flowers for large or small parties.

FOODS

Bakeries

New Orleans has a fine chain of McKenzie's bakeries scattered throughout the city, noted for birthday cakes, Prussians, coffee cakes, and King Cakes. The main office can be reached at 944-8771.

Angelo's Bakery, 1507 Metairie Rd., Metairie; 834-1116. Angelo's meets any type of bakery need; novelty cakes, birthday, or wedding cakes to order.

Bagel Factory, 3113 N. Causeway Blvd., Metairie; 837-8707, and 7901 St. Charles Ave.; 866-1521. This is a kosher bakery, with all types of kosher breads. Wedding and party cakes may be ordered.

Gambino's Bakeries, 3609 Toledano; 822-3340. Several locations in the city. The doberge cakes are a tradition.

Haydel's, 4037 Jefferson Hwy., Jefferson; 837-0190 (also in Kenner). Haydel's has really good cakes, pastries—noted for their King Cakes.

La Marquise Pastry Shop, 625 Chartres St.; 524-0420. La Marquise makes the best croissants in town, as well as delicious French pastries to take out or eat in.

LaBonbonniere European Pastry Shop, 1114 S. Carrollton St.; 866-2760. This is a small shop with a mouth-watering selection of European pastries and cakes.

Lawrence's Bakery, 5228 Elysian Fields Ave. at Filmore; 288-4262. Known as Mr. Wedding Cake, Lawrence specializes in doberge varieties, tortes, cocktail and party baked goods, and petit fours.

Swiss Confectionery, 747 St. Charles Ave.; 522-7788. The most beautiful wedding cakes are made to special order. Swiss has become a wedding tradition in New Orleans—their wedding-cake recipe is one of the best in the city. There is a huge selection of special-order and novelty cakes. This new, larger location has a wedding planner room.

Delis

Charlie's Deli, 515 Harrison Ave., Lakeview; 486-1766. Overstuffed sandwiches, lox, and bagels can be bought here to eat in or take out. Open 7 days a week.

Chez Nous Charcuterie, 5701 Magazine St.; 899-7303. Chez Nous Charcuterie specializes in gourmet dinners, desserts with exotic ingredients.

Dante Street Deli, 736 Dante St., at the river; 861-3634. Sandwiches are sold to eat in or out; dinners, cheese, and relishes also available.

Serio's Mike Po-Boys & Deli, 133 St. Charles Ave., in the Central Business District; 523-2668. Serio's is a good lunch spot.

Health Food Stores

Nutrition Fair, 4409 Veterans Blvd., Metairie; 885-5000. Nutrition Fair has a large supply of vitamins and all-natural food.

Whole Foods Market, 3135 Esplanade Ave.; 943-1626. A complete supermarket and deli section is here, with a tremendous selection of organically grown foods, foods without preservatives, vitamins, minerals, and herbs.

International and Gourmet Foods

Everyone has favorites, and listed below are a few of the neighborhood hideaways to get you started.

Chez Nous Charcuterie, 5701 Magazine St.; 899-7303. A small specialty shop housed in an old Victorian cottage, Chez Nous offers home-cooked meals for take-out. Gourmet desserts, imported cheese, chocolates, and coffee beans are specialties.

Dante Street Deli, 736 Dante St.; 861-3634. Many imported coffee beans, candies, canned goods, and cheeses.

Foodies Kitchen, 720 Veterans Blvd.; 837-9695. Gourmet food store for takeout or eat in. A plethora of freshly prepared gourmet dishes, salads, sandwiches, entire meals, desserts, breads, and fruits and vegetables. It also features a wine cellar, cheese section, coffees, teas, and a flower section. It is a food lover's dream.

La Marquise Pastry Shop (see Bakeries).

LaBonbonniere European Pastry Shop (see Bakeries).

Lakeview Fine Foods, 801 Harrison Ave.; 482-7333. Deli, selection of fine wines, and gourmet and Cajun foods.

Langenstein's, 1330 Arabella St.; 899-9283, and 800 Metairie Rd.; 831-6682. Live lobsters, rabbit, quail, shrimp, duck, and other special cuts of fine aged meats can be bought here. Groceries, imported items, and prepared meals.

Martin Wine Cellar, 3827 Baronne St.; 899-7411, and 714 Elmeer Ave., Metairie; 896-7300. Largest selection of fine wines in the city. Many gourmet foods, gift baskets, and deli.

Uptown Square Winery, Uptown Square, 200 Broadway; 866-2791. Specialties are imported beer, cheeses, pate, and gourmet items.

Whole Foods Market (see Health Food Stores).

FURNITURE

The following locally owned and operated furniture stores offer tremendous variety and competitive prices and put on wonderful annual sales.

Beach Bros., 3627 Airline Dr.; 831-4137. Furniture, appliances, and personal service.

Doerr Furniture, 914 Elysian Fields Ave.; 947-0606. Totally family owned and operated, with tremendous personal service. "Largest selection of solid wood furniture in the South." In business since 1938.

Hurwitz-Mintz, 211 Royal St.; 568-9555, 1-800-597-9555. "The South's largest selection of fine furniture." Also has an interior-design studio.

Kirschman's, 5800 Veterans Blvd.; 889-2770. Large variety of home furnishings, electronics, and appliances. In business since 1914.

GIFT SHOPS AND ACCESSORIES

There are many beautiful shops in the French Quarter and throughout the city. Listed are a few suggestions to spur you on.

Ally's Hallmark & Gift Shop, 8400 W. Judge Perez Dr., Chalmette; 271-3480. Large selection of various occasion and seasonal cards. Unique gifts and candies.

J. Aronson's, Uptown Square, 200 Broadway; 865-1186. Wedding and anniversary gifts. China, crystal, and household gifts.

Gentry's (see Men's Clothing).

Little Miss Muffin, 785 Harrison Ave.; 482-8200. Some cards, stationery, and many gift items for the home and children.

The Little Toy Shoppe, 900 Decatur St.; 522-6588. Large selection of toys, souvenirs, puppets, and books for children. They even have the children's Louisiana lore books of two local characters—Gaston the Alligator and Jenny Giraffe.

Party Basket, 734 Nashville Ave.; 891-0045. Cards, birthday items, party supplies.

Scriptura, 5423 Magazine St.; 897-1555. Features fine handmade paper products with either formal or unusual touches. A variety of stationery items, journals, wax seals, embossers, writing instruments, and many other items are available to indulge in written communication.

Sound of Music, 3141 Calhoun St.; 861-2215. Greeting cards, stationery, and small gift items are the standard fare here.

Stationer of New Orleans, Uptown Square; 866-0093. Beautiful stationery and fine papers of all kinds are sold here.

The Sun Shop, 7722 Maple St.; 861-8338. American Indian art and beadwork, imported and local handicrafts are the unusual items found at The Sun Shop.

HOME CLEANING

Maid Brigade; 738-5849. General cleaning in the metropolitan area.

HOME FURNISHINGS

Home Furnishings Store Ltd., 1600 Prytania St.; 566-1707. Finished or unfinished furniture and sofas and home fabric can be bought here.

La Cuisine Classique, 439 Decatur St.; 524-0068. Gourmet kitchen items.

Pottery Barn, Canal Place; 568-0011. Large selection of home furnishings—dishes, linens, glassware, and home decor.

JEWELRY

Most of the department stores have fine jewelry departments in all locations. Adler's is a New Orleans landmark. Boudreaux's is a tradition.

Designs in Jewelry, 3315 Severn Ave., Metairie; 888-0713. Have your jewelry custom designed in gold or silver.

La Petite Fleur, 534 Royal St.; 522-1305. Beautifully unique jewelry, some antique. Personal service.

Mignon Faget Ltd., 710 Dublin St.; 865-7361. Mignon Faget Ltd. designs unique gold and silver creative jewelry.

Simply Gold, 7713 Maple St.; 866-5433. Fine jewelry, gold, and diamonds are found here.

Symmetry Jewelers, 8128 Hampson St.; 861-9925. Gold engraving and gold creations are displayed at Symmetry.

Antique

Keil's Antiques (see Antiques).

Moliere's Antique Shop, 612 Chartres St.; 525-9479. Selection of antique jewelry is bought and sold here.

Moss Antiques, 411 Royal St.; 522-3981. Antique estate diamond and gold jewelry and some reproductions.

Royal Antiques, 307-9 Royal St.; 524-7033, and 321 Royal St.; 523-2281 (see Antiques).

Waldhorn & Adler Antiques, (see Antiques).

LACE

Baltazor Bridal Fabrics & Laces, 3262 Severn Ave., Metairie; 889-0333. New lace for dressmaking and bridal needs is available.

Lylian Shop, 1514 St. Charles Ave.; 525-2020. Lace-trimmed lingerie, blouses, children's clothing, and linens are the specialty here.

Meisel Fabrics, 8225 Oak St.; 866-9438. New laces for bridal gowns and evening dresses.

LEATHER

Rapp's, 604 Canal St.; 568-1953, Uptown Square; 861-1453, and New Orleans Centre; 566-0700. Rapp's also has other locations, each offering leather luggage, leather repair, and gift items.

LINENS

Lylian Shop (see Lace).

Sutton's, 501 Royal St.; 581-3666. Sutton's has a large selection of imported lace tablecloths and table linens.

Town and Country Shop (see Women's Clothing).

MARKETS

Crescent City Market, Girod at Magazine Street. Saturday morning only. Fresh fruits and vegetables, garden plants, and sometimes demos by chefs.

The French Market. A New Orleans tradition since the French, Spanish, and Indians traded there in the early days of the city, today the French Market is still a place to shop for fresh produce, strings of garlic, sugarcane, herbs, and spices. The farmer's marketplace is located at Decatur and St. Philip, just behind the U.S. Mint. This busy market has rows of stalls where farmers present the best from their gardens, sunup until dark. Daily. It's a great place to pick out your Halloween pumpkin!

MUSIC AND VIDEOS

Smith's Record Center, 2019 St. Charles Ave.; 522-7969, 522-4843. Classical and popular music recordings can be found at this shop.

Tower Records, Videos, & Books, 408 N. Peters; 529-4411, www.towerrecords.com. CDs, of course, with a good selection of South Louisiana music.

Watermelons in the French Market — *Cecilia Casrill Dartez*

Virgin Megastore, 620 Decatur St.; 671-8100. CDs, videos, books, and software.

Video Blast, 377 W. Esplanade Ave.; 469-5447. Current and favorite movies in stock; special-order services. Helpful and personal service.

Video Connection, 3331 St. Charles Ave.; 891-4213. Video Connection rents or sells movies on videotape with a complete selection.

Werlein's for Music, 214 Decatur St.; 883-5080. This is a New Orleans landmark music store; several locations.

OFFICE SUPPLIES

Cambias Office Equipment, 332 Baronne St.; 523-3915. Come here for any needs or supplies to complete your office.

Office Depot, several locations; 889-6661. Suburban office supermarket supplying virtually every office need at discount prices.

US Office Products, 5307 Toler St., Jefferson; 736-0505. Has a complete selection of office supplies and furniture, with design and space planning services.

PHOTOGRAPHIC SUPPLIES

Bennett's Camera and Video, 3230 Severn Ave., Metairie; 885-9050. For film, developing, and camera needs. Equipment is bought, sold, and traded.

The Camera Shop, 7505 Maple St.; 861-0277. Color print developing services, camera equipment, gift albums, and accessories are available.

Lakeside Camera & Imaging, 3508 21st St., Metairie; 885-8660. Total camera and video store with film services and digital photo services.

Moldaner's, 622 City Park Ave.; 486-5811. Camera sales and repair, projector sales and rental, and all film and slide services at in-house lab facility. Very helpful and personal service.

PRINTS AND PAINTINGS

Didier Inc., 3439 Magazine St.; 899-7749. Beautiful 18th- and 19th-century paintings and American furniture as well as prints and museum framing are available. Specializing in Southern artists.

Dixon & Dixon, 237 Royal St.; 524-0282. Dixon & Dixon is a collector of 18th- and 19th-century paintings.

Sports Art Gallery, 521 Decatur St.; 525-3846. A sportsman's dream shop. Every type of sports art is available. Prints and original oils. Also located in Uptown Square.

RUGS

Dombourian Oriental Rugs, 2841 Magazine St.; 891-6601. Large selection of Oriental rugs.

Sarouk Shop, 1601 St. Charles Ave.; 522-3260. The St. Charles streetcar passes right in front of the Sarouk Shop. Many large antique and new Oriental carpets.

SHOES

Feet First, 518 Chartres St.; 566-7525, and 5500 Magazine St.; 899-6800. Ladies' name-brand shoes at discount prices. Unique styles.

Gentlemen's Quarter, 232 Royal St.; 522-7139. Men's shoes and accessories.

Haase's Shoe Store and Young Folks Shop, 8119 Oak St.; 866-9944. Shoes for the family; an uptown tradition.

Juanita's Name Brand Discount Shoes, 721 Veterans Blvd., Metairie; 834-9511. All brands of discount shoes for women.

Porter-Stevens, 3301 Veterans Blvd.; 834-3771. Men's shoes. Several mall store locations.

SKIN CARE

Albert Brown Salon, 7217 Perrier St.; 861-0090. Makeup and skin care, as well as facials and massages, are taken care of at Albert Brown Salon.

Body Joys, 3423 St. Charles Ave.; 895-4400. Total body pampering, from facials to massages to pedicures.

Earth Savers, 5501 Magazine St.; 899-8555. Spa services, aromatherapy, and a unique variety of beauty and skin-care products. Several other locations.

John Jay's, 540 Robert E. Lee Blvd.; 282-7234. Makeup and skin-care consultations are available. Several other locations.

Lulu Buras Skin Care, 7818 Maple St.; 865-7322. Skin-care program and makeup consulting.

SPORTS EQUIPMENT

Academy Sports & Outdoors, Westbank Expressway at Stumpf Boulevard; 363-8283.

Adventure Sports, 333 N. Service Rd., Metairie; 835-1932. Rugged outdoor clothing.

Athlete's Foot, 8110 Hampson St.; 866-7478, and four other city locations. Shoes of all types and clothing for the athlete are sold.

Massey's, 3363 Severn Ave., Metairie; 885-1144. Complete sporting needs for the entire family at Massey's.

Nevada Bob's, 4029 Veterans Blvd.; 887-4544. Discount golf and tennis equipment.

Oshman's Sports, 4329 Veterans Blvd.; 887-4700.

St. Bernard Sporting Goods, 3509 Ames Blvd., Marrero; 340-4700. Gun, fishing, hunting, and marine supplies are available.

Sports Authority, 2801 Veterans Blvd.; 443-5111. Sports buffs will find just what they need with the wide variety of choices here.

TOBACCO

Dos Jefes Uptown Cigar Shop, 5700 Magazine St.; 899-3030, 1-800-233-8907. Everything for the cigar and pipe smoker.

Epitome in Fine Tobacco, 729 St. Louis St.; 523-2844. A pipe and cigar shop, there is a large selection of connoisseur cigars.

Ye Olde Pipe Shoppe, 306 Chartres St.; 522-1484. They have a wide selection of pipes, tobacco, and cigars.

TOYS

Hello Dolly, 815 Royal St.; 522-9948. Many beautiful dolls, especially for the doll collector, can be acquired at Hello Dolly.

Kid's Stuff, 714 Dublin St.; 866-8697. Excellent selection of imported and domestic toys. Located in the Riverbend area.

Le Jouet, 1700 Airline Hwy., Metairie; 837-0533. Le Jouet has a large assortment of toys and children's games.

Le Petit Soldier Shop, 528 Royal St.; 523-7741. Many military miniature collectibles and military artifacts.

The Little Toy Shoppe, 900 Decatur St.; 522-6588. Large selection of stuffed toys for tots and children.

Magic Box, Uptown Square, 200 Broadway; 866-2804. Fun toys, educational materials, and science kits for the creative child.

Toys R Us, 3609 Veterans Blvd., Metairie; 455-9513, 12250 I-10 Service Rd.; 245-8697, and 4800 Lapalco Blvd.; 347-8426. Everything in one place.

SPORTS

New Orleans is truly a sports town, with some of the greatest fans anywhere! The Crescent City offers pro football, the Sugar Bowl, horse racing, baseball, basketball, soccer, ice hockey, tennis, golf, sailing, marathons, excellent hunting and fishing—no wonder the city as well as the state has been christened "Sportsman's Paradise."

SPORTS TO SEE

The Sugar Bowl

For many years the Sugar Bowl Football Classic was played in the Sugar Bowl Stadium on the Tulane campus. Now it has moved downtown to the Louisiana Superdome. This colorful event, New Orleans' crown jewel of sports, is the most exciting sports spectacle of the year. The Sugar Bowl is much more than an annual great football game; it is a whole week of superior athletic events—basketball, sailing, tennis—leading up to the climax, the second-oldest bowl game in the United States.

Tickets for all events should be ordered in advance from:

The Sugar Bowl Classic
1500 Poydras St.
New Orleans, LA 70130
525-8573, www.nokiasugarbowl.com

Sugar Bowl Football, Superdome, 1500 Poydras St. The first Sugar Bowl football game, sponsored by an organization of far-sighted business and community leaders, took place in 1935 before a crowd of 24,000. Today, the games are played before a crowd of over 80,000 with a worldwide TV audience of millions.

Sugar Bowl Basketball, Superdome, 1500 Poydras St. The basketball tournament is played during the week between Christmas and New Year's Day. It draws the best of the nation's college teams to a three-day tournament in the Superdome. For information call 525-8603.

Louisiana Superdome in the evening — *Alex Demyan, New Orleans Metropolitan Convention & Visitors Bureau*

Sugar Bowl Sailing. The regattas take place December and January on Lake Pontchartrain with the Southern Yacht Club as the base of operations. Many Sugar Bowl sailors go on to participate in other world-class sailing competitions.

Sugar Bowl Tennis. The Tennis Classic during December and January attracts many fine high school and college players. The tournament is played at the City Park Tennis Center located in beautiful City Park.

Sugar Bowl and Mardi Gras Walk/Run Marathons. For information call 482-6682.

Other College Sports

Football

Tulane plays all its football games in the Superdome. Southern and Grambling universities also play some games there.

Basketball

Tulane, Southern, Dillard, and the University of New Orleans offer a wide variety of good games to watch.

Call the college ticket offices for more information:

Tulane ticket office (football, baseball, and men's and women's basketball); 865-5506

University of New Orleans ticket office (baseball and men's and women's basketball); 280-6239, www.uno.edu/-spin/men/menfront.htm

Southern ticket office; 286-5195

Dillard ticket office; 286-4767

Professional Baseball

The season for the New Orleans Zephyrs (AAA baseball) runs from April through September. All Zephyr home games are played at the beautiful new stadium at 6000 Airline Dr., Metairie, LA 70003. It is a short, easy ride from downtown New Orleans, with lots of parking. Call 734-5155 or check www.zephyrsbaseball.com.

Professional Football

The New Orleans Saints team has been the pride of New Orleans since 1967. Fans stay amazingly loyal whether the team has a winning or a losing season. You will see the fleur-de-lis, the Saints' symbol, displayed all over town. Home games are played in the Superdome, beginning with preseason exhibition games in August. For information call the Saints' Ticket Office, 731-1700 or check www.nfl.com/saints/.

The Saints' practice field is located at 5800 Airline Dr. in Metairie, about a 20-minute drive west on I-10 from the Central Business District. For information on visiting, call 731-1700.

Professional Ice Hockey

The season for the New Orleans Brass (minor-league hockey) runs from October through March. The new Sports Arena (next to the Superdome at 1500 Poydras St.) is now home for this exciting hockey team. For advance tickets or information, call 565-8081 or 522-7825. Also check www.nobrass.com.

Professional Soccer

The season for the New Orleans Storm (minor-league soccer) runs from April through September. The Storm, an A League soccer team, plays all home games in the new Zephyr Stadium at 6000 Airline Dr., Metairie (a short, easy drive from downtown New Orleans, with lots of parking). For information or tickets, call 734-5155. Also check www.stormsoccer.com.

Horse Racing

Fair Grounds, 1751 Gentilly Blvd.; 944-5515, 1-800-262-7983, www.fgno.com. New Orleans has loved racing since the first two horses raced into the area with Spanish explorers on their backs. Officially, the first organized horse races took place in 1804. Today, Louisiana is one of the three top horse-breeding states in the country. The venerable Fair Grounds, established in 1872, is the third oldest track in America. It traditionally opens on Thanksgiving Day and finishes the season with the New Orleans Handicap and the Louisiana Derby in March. These two races bring the best three-year-olds in the country to New Orleans.

The Fair Grounds is open Thursday through Monday with post time at 12:30 pm. Every creature comfort is provided at this beautiful, oak-shaded racetrack. The Grandstand and the clubhouse are comfortable and weatherproofed. Excellent lunches are served at the clubhouse, and there is ample parking.

In late 1987 the Louisiana Legislature passed a bill which allows off-track betting. Many cafes, lounges, and small parlors offer food and drink while guests relax and enjoy the fun of horse racing away from the Fair Grounds.

Evangeline Downs, US Hwy. 167, North Lafayette, Louisiana. Listed only for those of you who are truly dedicated racing fans, this lovely track is a 2½-hour drive from New Orleans in the Bayou Country. Races are held from April 1 through September 6. For information, write Box 90490, Lafayette, LA 70509 or call 318-896-6185.

SPORTS TO DO

You have time to relax while you are in town, or maybe you want to stay in shape. What is your pleasure? Tennis? Soccer? Running? Whatever it is, you will find ample opportunity to enjoy it in this year-round sports city. Here is an extensive list of possibilities for you to explore.

Cycling

New Orleans, being flat as a pancake, is a great cycling town. Everyone, from businessmen in coats and ties with briefcase on the back, riding down St. Charles Avenue on their way to work, to bike racers with their helmets strapped on, to families with babies in special seats, rides bikes. The parks, the lakefront, and the levees are delightful places to bike. Bike touring gives you a unique view of the city.

The following area bicycle shops can assist with repairs, rentals, parts, and path maps. The lakefront bicycle path is a local favorite.

GNO Cyclery, 1426 S. Carrollton Ave.; 861-0023.

Joe's Bike Shop, 2501 Tulane Ave.; 821-2350.

Pauli's Bicycle and Fitness Store, 4501 Veteran Blvd.; 887-0291.

Also check **New Orleans Bicycling Club;** www.gnofn.org/~nobc/

For a ride, walk, run, or roll "on the wild side"—the North Shore countryside—try the beautiful **Tammany Trace,** open daily from 7 am till dark. Call for information: 1-800-634-9443 ext. 149 or 504-892-0520.

Fencing

New Orleans has a history of duels fought with swords or pistols. Today, when such skills are developed, it is for pleasure, not business!

New Orleans Fencing Academy; 283-4198. Classes for adults or high-school students are taught by highly qualified instructors. The Academy was founded in the 1960s.

Flying

For sport, transportation, or a fun way to see the sights, call:

Air Reldan (FAA approved), Lakefront Airport near Seabrook Bridge; 241-9400.

SuWest Airways, Inc., Lakefront Airport; 242-4883. Medical transportation, valuable cargo delivered door to door.

Golf

In March, the Italian Open and the St. Pat's Day charity golf tournaments are held. In May the Arthritis Foundation sponsors a benefit golf tournament.

There are a number of public and private courses in the city. For information on fees and equipment, call:

Audubon Golf Club, 473 Walnut St., Audubon Park; 865-8260.

Bayou Barriere Golf Club, 2202 Belle Chasse Hwy.; 394-9500.

Bayou Oaks City Park Golf, City Park; 483-9397. Golf Shop; 483-9396. Driving Range; 483-9394.

Beau Chene Country Club, Mandeville; 504-845-3572.

Chateau Golf and Country Club, Kenner; 467-1351.

Eastover Country Club, New Orleans East; 245-7347.

English Turn Country Club, Westbank; 391-8019.

Hidden Oaks Golf Course, Braithwaite; 504-682-2685.

Plantation Golf and Country Club, 1001 Behrman Hwy.; 392-3363.

Royal Golf Club, Slidell; 1-800-643-3060.

Gymnastics

Jewish Community Center, 5342 St. Charles Ave.; 897-0143.

The New Orleans Acro-Gymnastics School, 5116 Magazine St.; 891-8634.

Riverbend Gymnastics Academy, 200 Academy Dr.; 486-6141.

YMCA, 920 St. Charles Ave.; 568-9622.

Health Clubs

The national chain health clubs and exercise centers are popular in New Orleans. Please check the yellow pages. Listed are some clubs convenient for visitors.

New Orleans Athletic Club, 222 N. Rampart; 525-2375.

Rivercenter Racquet & Health Club, Hilton Hotel, 2 Poydras St.; 587-7242.

YMCA, 920 St. Charles Ave.; 568-9622.

Hiking and Backpacking

Hiking in and around New Orleans can be great fun (see SELF-GUIDED TOURS).

The levee along the Mississippi River is a good place to hike. You might begin a hike behind the Audubon Park Zoo and hike upriver to Carrollton Avenue, at which point you can board the streetcar to return to your lodgings. Or you might leave the streetcar at that point and hike the levee upriver to Ochsner Foundation Hospital, at which point you can walk through the grounds of the hospital to Jefferson Highway and board a bus which will take you back to the beginning of the streetcar line at Claiborne and Carrollton avenues. There is no shade available along the levee, so be prepared with hats and canteens. There is an unparalleled view of "life along the Mississippi." The City Park area is also good for hiking.

For professional guidance, call the Sierra Club (482-9566), Adventure Sports (835-1932), or Delta Wilderness Outfitters (835-1932). These sources can also furnish information on trips to outlying areas.

Horseback Riding

To rent or board horses, call:

Cascade Stables, Audubon Park off Magazine Street; 891-2246. Riding in the front section of Audubon Park. Boarding available.

City Park Stables, 1001 Filmore Ave.; 483-9398.

Hunting

Louisiana is an outdoors paradise. The many bayous, waterways, and rice fields are great nesting places and landing spots for geese, ducks, and doves. The dove season opens in early September and has a split season in October, November, December, and January. Shooting hours during this time are one half-hour before sunrise to sunset. For information about hunting seasons, guides, licenses, or equipment, contact any of the following:

Academy Sports & Outdoors, Westbank; 363-8283.

Adventure Sports, Metairie; 835-1932.
Department of Wildlife and Fisheries, 504-568-5636, 504-765-2346.
www.hunting.net.com
www.outdoorguides.com
www.sportsmans-paradise.com
www.wlf.state.la.us

Polo

The Harvest Polo Classic takes place in October at the Innisfree Farm in Folsom. It is quite a festival and an afternoon of polo conducted by Covington's League Community Projects. For information call 504-626-0957.

Racquetball

Racquetball is growing in popularity with busy people who play on their lunch hours. The controlled environment can also be very pleasant in this tropical climate.

Kenner YMCA, 2124 Driftwood Blvd., Kenner; 443-6363.
Racquet Club, Fairmont Hotel, 123 Baronne St.; 529-7111.
Racquetball South, Inc., 100 W. Virtue; 277-8231.
Rivercenter Racquet & Health Club, Hilton Hotel, 2 Poydras St.; 587-7242.

Rifle and Pistol Ranges

Some take part for the sheer enjoyment of the sport; some are practicing for hunting season. Either way, target practice is popular with all ages.

Gretna Gun Works, 230 Lafayette; 361-5422.
St. Bernard Indoor Shooting Center, 212 Aycock; 277-4867.

Roller Skating/Blading and Ice Skating

Roller skating/blading is popular in Audubon and City parks as well as along the lakefront.

Airline Skate Center, 6711 Airline Hwy.; 733-2248.
Ice Skating Club of New Orleans; 831-6760.

Skate Country Westbank, 1100 Terry Pkwy.; 392-2272.
Skate World, Inc., 701 W. Judge Perez, Chalmette; 271-7036.

Running

Running has taken the country and New Orleans by storm. The city is made for runners—it is so flat! Also, since all the main streets have "neutral grounds," you don't even have to dodge cars while you run. Good running spots are Audubon Park (the section between St. Charles Avenue and Magazine Street is closed to vehicular traffic), City Park, the levees, and the lakefront. NOTE: The visiting runner should be aware of the effect of the heat and high humidity in New Orleans, and pace oneself accordingly. Check the local newspapers and magazines for races being held while you are in town.

The New Orleans Marathon, the Mardi Gras Marathon, and the Crescent City Classic (see SPECIAL EVENTS) all create a tremendous amount of interest in New Orleans. Even if you do not happen to be a runner or walker, it is well worth a trip to the finish line to cheer the competitors and join in the celebration.

For information contact any of the following:

The Greater New Orleans Runners Association, 6112 Magazine St.; 899-3333.

The New Orleans Track Club; 482-6682.

www.runningnetwork.com

There are indoor tracks available at:

Rivercenter Health Club, downtown Hilton; 587-7242.

YMCA, the Lee Circle and Superdome branches. For information, call 568-9622.

Skiing

Many families in New Orleans enjoy ski vacations during the long Mardi Gras weekend, which is in late February or early March. Check local publications for ski trip information, or a local ski shop:

Massey's Ski Shop, 3363 Severn Ave., Metairie; 1-800-SKI-SHOP (754-7467), 885-1144.

Soccer

Soccer, though relatively new to South Louisiana, is enjoying immense popularity. There are competitive leagues springing up all over the area.

For information, call:
Club Soccer, 4240 Williams Blvd., Kenner; 464-4661.
New Orleans Soccer Academy, 6803 Franklin Ave.; 280-3982.

Tennis

New Orleans tennis players enjoy tennis 12 months during the year with the exception of a few weeks in January and February when the outdoor courts are frozen. New Orleans has many clay courts because they are cooler in the summer. Courts in New Orleans are out of doors except the courts in the Hilton Hotel's Rivercenter.

Audubon Park Tennis, Tchoupitoulas Street and Audubon Park; 895-1042.

City Park Wisner Tennis Center; 483-9383.

Joe Brown Tennis, 5603 Read Blvd.; 246-9543.

Rivercenter Tennis, Hilton Hotel, 2 Poydras St.; 587-7242. Holds "clinic" weekends as well as regular programs. Consider spending a "tennis weekend" in New Orleans!

Water Sports

Here in the Isle d'Orleans, as Napoleon referred to our water-circled city, sailing, fishing, hunting, and other water-related activities are very popular. Boat shows are among the best-attended events at the Superdome. And notice as you tour that in this city where driveways and parking places are at a premium, even in residential neighborhoods people find the most amazing spots to tuck their fishing boats out of the way. New Orleanians joke about being born with webbed feet; they take to the water as though they really are born that way. Join them and find out just how pleasurable these water sports can be.

Boating

Boating of any type is popular in the metropolitan area, from a pirogue on the bayou to motorboats on the area lakes and rivers to sailboats on the lake. To safisfy any of your boating needs or questions, contact the following:

Blue Dot Marine, 2409 Paris Rd.; 277-777.

Gulf Outlet Marina Boat Launch, 5353 Paris Rd., Chalmette; 277-9980.

J.R.'s Boat Launch & Supply, 20846 Chef Menteur Hwy.; 254-4646.

Murray Yachts & Sailing Instruction, 402 S. Roadway St.; 283-2507.

Odyssey Sailing; 1-888-300-SAIL.
Schubert's Marine, 126 S. Roadway; 282-8136.
West Marine, 827 Harrison Ave.; 482-5090.

Canoeing

For information call:
Adventure Sports, 333 N. Service Rd., Metairie; 835-1932.

Delta Wilderness Outfitters, 333 N. Service Rd., Metairie; 835-1932. Expert advice. Custom trips and guided tours for school groups, office staffs, clubs, teams, or friends can be arranged. Trips listed include: Bayou Boeuf Canoe trip, Atchafalaya, Honey Island, and Blind River. Canoeing kid's camps for summer.

Louisiana Nature and Science Center; 246-5672.
Sierra Club; 400 Magazine St.; 482-9566.

Diving

New Orleans has several very active dive clubs. In addition to the popular dives around the oil rigs (the waters 25 miles out are very clear like the Destin, Florida area water), the members plan trips to the Florida keys.

For information call:

Adventure Quest, Inc., 3230 S. I-10 Service Rd. W., Metairie; 887-DIVE, 1-800-963-DIVE.

Caribbean Dive Shop, 1708 Lake Ave., Metairie; 831-7017.
Harry's Dive Shop, 4709 Airline Dr., Metairie; 888-4882.

Fishing

Fresh water fishing is available in both Audubon Park and City Park. Each year in April, there is a **Big Bass Fishing Rodeo** held in City Park, with prizes for young and old.

Coastal Louisiana is a great place for saltwater fishing. It has been made even better by the proliferation of oil rigs off the coast; they serve as protection reefs and breeding grounds for an amazing variety of fish. To charter deep-sea fishing boats, call:

Captain Nick's Fishing Charters, New Orleans; 361-3004.
Charter Boat Early Bird, New Orleans; 581-4401.

Fishing Guide Services, New Orleans; 243-2100, pager 595-0727, toll free 1-800-SPECK36.

Jean Lafitte Fishing Charters, Gretna; 367-8353, Lafitte; 689-4120.
Joe's Landing, Barataria; 689-4304.
Sportsman's Paradise, Cocodrie; 594-2414.

Venice Marina, Inc., Venice; 534-9357, 534-7701.

For additional information about licenses, maps, weather, tournaments, or the Grand Isle Tarpon Rodeo, contact any of the following:

Academy Sports & Outdoors, Westbank; 363-8283.

Department of Wildlife and Fisheries; 504-568-5636.

Louisiana Nature and Science Center; 246-5672.

West Marine, New Orleans; 482-5090.

Or check the following Web sites:

www.nws.noaa.gov

www.rodnreel.com

www.sportmans-paradise.com

www.wlf.state.la.us

Scuba Lifesaving

Caribbean Dive Shop, 1708 Lake Ave., Metairie; 831-7017.

Harry's Dive Shop, 4709 Airline Hwy., Metairie; 888-4882.

Swimming

Your hotel, motel, or campground will, in all probability, have a fine swimming pool available.

For more extended use, we suggest that you investigate the excellent programs at all branches of the YMCA, the Jewish Community Center, and neighborhood centers.

Also, consider planning an all-day excursion to the beautiful beaches on the Mississippi Gulf Coast, about one and one-half hours' driving time from New Orleans on I-10 East (see ONE-DAY EXCURSIONS).

Tubing

Relax and float down the river on the Bogue Chitto and Tangipahoa rivers, on rented tubes or your own. Contact the **Bogue Chitto Tubing and Canoe Center,** Highway 16, north of Covington; 504-735-1173.

Windsurfing

Windsurfing is done mostly in New Orleans on Bayou St. John, and on Lake Pontchartrain.

SPECIAL EVENTS

All the world loves a party, and New Orleans is no exception. Almost any time of the year natives and visitors can find a special fun celebration to enjoy. Parades are a part of most of them, even if it's not Mardi Gras. But Mardi Gras is the supreme celebration.

MARDI GRAS

Mardi Gras in New Orleans is the annual rite of fantasy and pleasure, where for one delirious night, young and old, rich and poor, indulge in total revelry. It is the culminating crescendo of the 30- to 60-day Carnival season that begins January 6, on the Christian feast of the Epiphany (also known as Twelfth Night or King's Day), and ends on Ash Wednesday, the first day of Lent. New Orleanians anticipate the Carnival season and Mardi Gras with utter absorption; the social machinery of debutantes, masked balls, parades, and parties is shifted into high gear. Tuxedoes and gowns are readied, costumes are specially designed, hundreds of elaborate floats are constructed, bands are hired, and kings, queens, and courts are chosen for each ball.

The History of Mardi Gras

How did Carnival and Mardi Gras become such an overwhelming obsession with New Orleanians? It was on Mardi Gras March 3, 1699 that Frenchman Pierre Le Moyne, Sieur d'lberville (older brother of the founder of New Orleans), first broke camp upriver from the mouth of the Mississippi. The stream by this campsite is still named Bayou du Mardi Gras. The French expression "Mardi Gras" means, literally, "Fat Tuesday."

With this memory as a touchstone for New Orleans' growth, the Creole love of festival, dancing, feasting, masquerade, comedy, and theater produced a series of Carnival tableau balls and street parades. By 1857 a general rowdiness, and despair over the rowdiness, of Mardi Gras was dispelled by six young men originally from Mobile. They

Mardi Gras crowds on Canal Street — *Louisiana State Tourist Commission*

formed the Mystick Krewe of Comus, named after the pagan god of revelry and laughter, son of Bacchus and Circe. The krewe planned a parade, ball, and supper in the tradition of Mobile's New Year's Eve Cowbellion de Rakin. New Orleans had its first Carnival torchlight parade that February 24, 1857, with Comus on one float, Satan on the next accompanied by devils and bands, with fire and smoke from the flambeaux lighting up the spectacle. The following year all the gods of Olympus showed up, replete with marching bands. Success was noted in the *Illustrated London News* in May 1858.

After the Civil War, in 1872, the Twelfth Night Revelers picked up the leadership of Carnival and a new club was added to the list of Carnival personalities—Rex. When the Grand Duke Alexis of Russia, brother of the czar, announced he would arrive in New Orleans on Mardi Gras, the businessmen of the city sprang into action, organized the Rex organization, and put on a lavish parade honoring Alexis and the actress Lydia Thompson. Miss Thompson was performing at the Academy of Music in New Orleans at the time and her hit song (with the duke as well as the public), "If Ever I Cease to Love," became the official Mardi Gras song. Mardi Gras colors were initiated that year also, purple for power, green for faith, and gold for justice. In 1892 Rex used the "Symbolism of the Colors" as the theme of its parade.

Today's Carnival and Parades

There are approximately 60 parades during the 10 days immediately preceding Mardi Gras. Each parade consists of between 10 to 30 floats, interspersed with marching bands, both local and national. The parades take place in every section of the city, and each is financed by a group of private individuals, who spend countless hours and dollars throughout the year planning a spectacular show to share with the city. The metropolitan area's contributions, and certainly without them there could be no Mardi Gras, are a well-trained police force and a right-after-the-parade trash pick-up system. One way to judge the relative success of each year's Mardi Gras has been by how many tons of trash are picked up off the streets.

The floats are papier-mache masterpieces—wonderful, wobbly creations, brightly colored, trimmed with tiny pieces of foil to catch the light, each float portraying a particular facet of the parade's overall theme. They make their way slowly down the street with their crews of brightly costumed maskers on board, like towering ships sailing through a sea of surging spectators, all shouting, all waving their arms, all frantically trying to catch a "throw" from one of the maskers.

"Throw me something, mister"—this is the universal chant throughout the parade season. The New Orleans area Carnival, including Mardi Gras (also known as Shrove Tuesday), is one of the great world festivals with such close interaction between spectator and participant. Each masker boards the float with thousands of "throws," beads, necklaces, doubloons, whistles, plastic and stuffed animals, toys, and plastic cups, all of which are thrown to the crowd by the end of the parade.

What is a doubloon? It is a coin, about 1½" to 2" in diameter, minted with the crest of the krewe on one side and a representation of the theme of the parade on the other side. The idea came from H. Alvin Sharpe, master of intaglio, historian, poet, who first sold the Rex organization on the idea in 1959. He then continued to cut the dies for the most valuable doubloons until his death in 1983. Doubloons are made in gold and silver for special presents from the krewe to a favored few. The ones that are thrown by each krewe during its parade are aluminum, in a variety of colors to match the krewe's theme that year. They are the most sought-after throws, and for dedicated collectors, the success of the Carnival season may rest on whether or not a doubloon has been caught from every parade. Needless to say, doubloon trading has become a popular indoor sport in New Orleans.

Where to Stand

Your first Mardi Gras will be extra-special. Here are a few hints. If you are with children, see the parades on St. Charles Avenue, anywhere between Napoleon and Louisiana avenues. Stand toward the back of the crowd while the first few floats pass. By then you will have an idea of just how competitive you choose to be. Either come with snacks or eat a very early dinner, so that you arrive in time to find a place to park, or take the streetcar.

If you are a group of adults, you may choose the relative quiet of St. Charles Avenue or the brighter lights and larger crowds of Canal Street. Seeing the parade on Canal Street will give you time to eat dinner before the parade arrives. On Mardi Gras (Day), if you are in substantial shape, consider starting the day on St. Charles Avenue, somewhere between Napoleon and Louisiana avenues, about 9 am. Stroll slowly downtown, stopping to sit and rest whenever the spirit (or spirits) move you, watching the private marching groups waving their flowered canes as they pass, seeing the parade wherever it catches up with you, until you make your way back to Canal Street. For the hardiest, a plunge across Canal Street into the unbelievable Mardi Gras world of the French Quarter may be in order. But don't expect the

French Quarter to be in order! It will be shoulder to shoulder all the way, the crowd so thick in spots that you will move with it in spite of yourself. There will be maskers waving from balconies, streets paved with cans and bottles, and every imaginable elaborate costume, or lack of costume, on every imaginable type of person. A really whole-world experience.

In the past few years, suburban parades have increased in number. Parades held out of the city's limits are regularly attended by families with children. The crowds are not as compact, and the first-time parade goer may feel more at ease. Check local newspapers and magazines for parade times, routes, themes, and the reigning royalty of the day.

Another traditional treat on Mardi Gras (Day), but only for early risers, is the Zulu Parade, part of the Mardi Gras since 1909. Zulu is the oldest of the black krewes and the fifth oldest of all the krewes. The best place to see it is anywhere on St. Charles Avenue. Be there by 8 am. Zulu will also throw doubloons, but the real prize from a Zulu parade is a coconut. Only an honored few rate these, but shout for one anyway. It may be your lucky year. (These decorated coconuts are handed to spectators—not thrown.)

The traditional king of Carnival is Rex. One must never leave the Mardi Gras festivities without catching a glimpse of His Majesty. Rex is always a prominent New Orleans business and civic leader whose identity is kept secret until Mardi Gras morning.

The Rex parade, with its gorgeous floats, rolls on Mardi Gras morning. Early in the morning, families and groups of friends start "staking out" their spots along St. Charles Avenue to assure a good view of Rex and his float. Another highly anticipated Rex float is the Boeuf Gras, the fatted bull, which symbolizes the last meal eaten before Lent (which begins promptly at midnight, on Ash Wednesday). Rex doubloons, Mardi Gras-colored beads with crown pendant, and Rex signature cups are considered real treasures.

Masquerade

Wherever you decide to see it, be sure to mask (but only on Mardi Gras itself). It's not the same unless you do. Your costume can be a last-minute put-together of aluminum foil and face paint, a creation from one of the city's many costume shops, or a family costume project. Any way you choose, it will be the "you" you want to be on Mardi Gras. You will have a common bond as you laugh at yourself and admire others. Be sure to bring your camera and a lot of film; when you get home, your friends may not believe the stories unless you have pictures for proof.

MONTHLY EVENTS

January

Antiques Fair of Greater New Orleans, Pontchartrain Center; 875-9085, 465-9985. Dealers from around the country bring marvelous antiques, silver, porcelain, furniture, clothing, and more. Chipped crystal can even be restored on site.

Sugar Bowl Classic, 1500 Poydras St.; 587-3800. The Sugar Bowl, held on New Year's Day in the Superdome, is the football highlight that pits two of the top college teams in the nation against one another in an exciting match that will thrill even the nonfootball fan. The halftime show also holds the crowd's attention, quite a sight to see and hear! Uniformed marching school bands join local jazz high-step prancing bands while costumed coeds kick their heels to a variety of lively music.

The Feast of the Epiphany, the Feast of the Three Kings, King's Day, or Twelfth Night (January 6) is a lingering tradition popular in New Orleans. It is the day local bakeries begin to bake colorful King Cakes. These are yeast cakes baked in the round like a crown, decorated with sugar in the Carnival colors—purple, green, and gold. There is a tiny pink plastic baby hidden within; the person finding the baby is the host for the next King Cake party. Special masses are said on this feast day followed by a family breakfast consisting of King Cake and coffee. Christmas trees stay decorated until the day following the Twelfth Night Ball, the official opening of the Mardi Gras season.

The Battle of New Orleans; 589-4430. The Battle of New Orleans was fought in Chalmette, Louisiana. The historical site is about 20 minutes' drive from the Central Business District. This important battle was fought in 1815 (following the War of 1812). It united a motley group of Creoles, pirates, Indians, freemen of color, and backwoodsmen from Kentucky who knew how to fight in the marshy area. The British army, neatly dressed in fine uniforms, was unable to beat the 4,000 wilderness men fighting on their own ground or to cope with Louisiana weather and insects. Each year, the battle is re-enacted at Chalmette and there is a Mass of Thanksgiving at the Ursuline Convent.

February

Mardi Gras or Fat Tuesday (see MARDI GRAS) is the world's largest outdoor celebration and street costume party. This is the day when kings, dragons, clowns, and super heroes and heroines join arms and frolic in the streets, dancing, drinking, and entertaining their wildest fantasies. The 40-day pre-Easter fasting begins the following day on Ash Wednesday. Mardi Gras is a movable holiday based upon Easter's date. If Easter is later in the spring, Mardi Gras will take place in March.

Ash Wednesday is the day following Mardi Gras. Many Christians go to church and receive the blessed ashes on their foreheads and begin Lenten season. Again, as with Mardi Gras, this may have a March date.

Black Heritage & History Tributes, New Orleans Public Library; 596-2697. Exhibits and programs.

Live Stock Show and Championship Rodeo, Louisiana State University at Baton Rouge. For information, call 388-3201.

New Orleans Boat Show, Superdome; 587-3810. This fantastic show features the latest motorboats and sailboats, gadgets, and everything affiliated with boating.

March

Crescent City Depression Glass Show, St. Bernard Cultural Center; 278-4242.

St. Patrick's Day celebration, "the wearing of the green," March 17. Irish from all sections in New Orleans gather to drink toasts with green beer. Several bars in the "Irish Channel" have their special celebrations. Of course, the highlight is the St. Pat's Day Parade, which is held on Magazine Street in the Irish Channel the Saturday before, complete with floats, jazz bands, and politicians. Parade watchers are anxious to catch the traditional cabbages or green doubloons, potatoes, carrots, and other fresh vegetables. If you catch enough, your St. Patrick's Day dinner is complete! There is also an enormous Irish/Italian-American parade in neighboring Jefferson Parish. These celebrations add to the "joie de vivre" for locals. Check local newspapers and magazines for times and places.

St. Joseph's Day, March 19. New Orleans is blessed with lots of people of Italian descent, happy people ready to celebrate. Just two days following the Irish, they take over the city to celebrate their special day. Many families have St. Joseph altars in their homes, covered with special feast-day foods—home-baked breads, meat, fish, candies, and sweets all prepared and beautifully decorated to give to the poor of the city at the end of the day. In the Central Business District, at the Piazza d'ltalia, 300 Poydras St., a large altar is filled with many Italian edibles displayed for visitors and locals to see and enjoy. Each person visiting the altar receives a piece of blessed bread, a "lucky" bean, and the picture of St. Joseph with a prayer to recite. There is also a large altar at St. Joseph's Church, at 1802 Tulane Ave., and a boisterous parade through the French Quarter on St. Joseph's evening. Another extremely large altar is held by the Sisters of St. Joseph at the St. Joseph

Provincial House, 1200 Mirabeau Ave.; 288-3171. Check local newspapers and magazines for schedules.

The Italian Open Golf Tournament. The Italian Open Golf Classic, City Park Golf Course; 483-9396. The Italian Open Golf Classic is a tournament like no other. There is a prize given for the highest as well as the lowest score! Two golf courses are needed to take care of all the players, who are surely the best-fed golfers in the world. During one recent tournament, the *Times-Picayune* reported that players and spectators consumed 2000 pounds of sausage, four cases of olives, 1,000 muffuletta sandwiches (and they are big), 10 crates of grapes, 6 crates of apples, 300 pineapples, 200 cases of wine, a truck of beer, 400 pounds of ham, 600 pounds of Italian cheese, and a 250-pound Italian cake. Lifeguards are posted at the waterholes, just in case. All proceeds go to charity.

Louisiana Sports and Car Shows, Superdome; 587-3810. Check the local newspapers for dates, times, and fees.

Because of the warm climate and flat surfaces, New Orleans hosts the famous **Mardi Gras Marathon** and many other world-class road races. The annual **Jackson Day Race** is one of the oldest road races in the nation. Both the Mardi Gras Marathon and the Crescent City Classic attract world-famous runners who come by the hundreds. Famous race tee shirts and posters are collectors' items. The distances designated as 5K equals 3.1 miles, a half-marathon equals 13.1 miles, and a marathon equals 26.2 miles. Most road races have wheelchair and walking divisions. All races end with a food celebration—Creole jambalaya, po' boys, red beans and rice, beer, root beer, and cool spring water. Warm-weather races celebrate with watermelon and orange slices. For information call 482-NOTC or 482-6682 or write: Greater New Orleans Runners' Association, P.O. Box 6524, Metairie, LA 70009.

New Orleans Home & Garden Show, Superdome; 587-3810. This super showcase has everything concerning homes and gardens today and even homes of the future.

Tennessee Williams-New Orleans Literary Festival. One of New Orleans' illustrious writers is honored during a three-day festival of plays, panel discussions, lectures, workshops, literary walking tours, and socializing, ending with "Tea with Tennessee." For information call 581-1144, fax 529-2430, or e-mail twfest@gnofn.org.

April

Baseball season, Zephyr Field, 6000 Airline Hwy.; 734-5155. With the new AAA baseball team, the New Orleans Zephyrs, and their beautiful new field and stadium, you can see exciting baseball games from April through September. Baseball games here are enjoyed "New Orleans style"—with a variety of food and drink booths, singing, and dancing in the stands. A baseball game here is truly different from anywhere else.

Compaq Golf Classic, English Turn Golf Course; 831-4653.

Crescent City Classic Road Race; 861-8686, 891-9999, 482-NOTC. This is the city's best-known road race. The newspaper recently described it as the "largest aerobic participatory sporting event in the history of the city." The colorful 10-kilometer race begins in the French Quarter at Jackson Square and finishes in Audubon Park. The finish area becomes a drink and food fest, with competitors and their fans dancing under the oak trees to the sound of music, and feasting on sausage jambalaya, washed down with Perrier, Miller Lite, and Coca-Cola. Outstanding world-class runners arrive from such faraway places as Tanzania, Kenya, Botswana, Colombia, Austria, Switzerland, and Great Britain to compete against the best in the United States.

Easter Sunrise Service on the shores of Lake Pontchartrain. Check newspapers and magazines for time.

French Quarter Festival, www.frenchquarterfestivals.org. 100 Conti St.; 522-5730. During this marvelous music, food, and cultural festival, much of the French Quarter is blocked off to vehicular traffic. There are 14 stages throughout the Quarter, Jackson Square, and the Riverfront featuring a variety of music day and night. Food for many tastes is also available. A variety of events includes fireworks, children's activities, a second-line parade, and a 5K race.

The Jazz and Heritage Festival, mailing address: 1205 N. Rampart, New Orleans 70116; 522-4786. *CH*. Open-air and tent concerts and delicious local foods are available. Also, many Louisiana artists and craftspeople display their wares. Location is the New Orleans Fair Grounds, with evening concerts all around town. Check the newspapers for times and entrance fees. A shuttle bus runs from citywide areas to the Fair Grounds. There is an official poster issued for the Festival each year; those from earlier years have become collectors' items. The Festival lasts about 10 days, running through two weekends. Dress comfortably!

Open-Air Concerts at the Zoo with the New Orleans Symphony. Check with the local newspapers and zoo information (861-2537) for dates and times. The concert is for the price of zoo admission.

The Spring Fiesta. Many old homes in the Garden District, uptown, French Quarter, and River Road are open to the public. Beautiful gardens and patios are open both day and evening. The special "Patios by Candlelight" and Spring Fiesta Parade are highlights. Check with the local Spring Fiesta Headquarters, 826 St. Ann St.; 581-1367. Bayou and River Road tours are arranged for special groups; call ahead and make arrangements.

Symphony Book Fair is a fantastic feast for bookworms of all ages. Call 861-2004 or check the local papers.

World Championship Pirogue Races, Lafayette, Louisiana. Pirogues are narrow, light canoe-type boats, originally handhewn by the Indians out of cypress logs. Call 318-233-2705.

May

Asian-Pacific American Festival, UNO, Lakefront Campus; 280-6000, 525-5225. This festival celebrates Asian and Pacific Rim heritage and culture with food, crafts, dance, music, demonstrations, and a variety of activities.

Greek Festival, Hellenic Cultural Center, 1200 Robert E. Lee Blvd.; 282-0259. Greek food, music, dancing, and a variety of activities are featured to celebrate Greek heritage and culture.

The Jazz and Heritage Festival continues through the first weekend in May.

Walt Disney World on Ice, Superdome; 587-3810. Favorite Disney characters along with costumed ice skaters sing, dance, and skate to delight the entire family.

June

June finds many natives traveling to vacation spots and children beginning summer camp. A good time to plan your own sailing, biking, or hiking tour of New Orleans. (See SELF-GUIDED TOURS.)

French Quarter Tomato Festival, French Market; 522-2621. Food, music, and activities celebrate the tomato.

The New Orleans Science Fiction and Fantasy Festival features a weekend of favorite SciFi authors, exhibits, books, movies, and meetings. Check local periodicals for dates, times, and places.

Pepsi Super Fair, Superdome; 587-3860. Activities and rides inside the Dome.

July

Annual Grand Isle Tarpon Rodeo, at the eastern end of the island. This is a weekend of fishing-rodeo fun involving 100 trophies. It is approximately a three-hour drive from New Orleans. For information, call 504-787-2559.

Blessing of the Fleet, Delacroix; 676-3719, 676-3337. There is a ceremony and boat parade to bless fishing boats, with reception.

Degas Days. The weekend of activities honoring the French impressionist Edgar Degas—who lived and painted in New Orleans for a brief time—includes music, costumes, ballet, sidewalk chalk drawings, and a can can cabaret in the New Orleans Museum of Art, its surrounding City Park grounds, and other locations on Esplanade Avenue.

Essence Fest, Superdome; 587-3810, 1-800-ESSENCE. Sponsored by the national magazine, concerts and seminars highlight the best of African-American culture.

La Fete de Nouvelle Orleans. Check local papers and magazines. Great local chefs share their secrets and everyone gets to taste—by admission.

Fourth of July Celebration and Fireworks, at the Moon Walk in the French Quarter, at Torres Park, Chalmette, and at the lakefront. Check newspapers and magazines for details.

New Orleans Bastille Day Celebration. Complete with flag raisings in Jackson Square, this honors the French culture and heritage of New Orleans. Call the French consul; 523-5772, or check local periodicals.

Ringling Brothers Barnum and Bailey Circus comes to the Superdome; 587-3810.

August

International Fishing Rodeo at Houma; 851-1600.

Pro-football Exhibition Games at the Superdome.

Seafood Festival, Lafayette, Louisiana.

White Linen Night, Contemporary Arts Center, 900 Camp St.; 523-1216. This is an open-air celebration of the Warehouse District's art galleries. Also, various art organizations present previews of the upcoming season.

September

Festivals Acadiens, Lafayette, Louisiana; 1-800-346-1958. Marvelous celebration of Cajun culture and heritage.

Madisonville Wooden Boat Festival, Madisonville. This is a showplace for lovingly-cared-for wooden boats. It makes for a wonderful day in a quaint small town with beautifully restored houses. There is lots of Louisiana food, music, and culture.

Pirate's Alley Faulkner Society's Literary and Writers' Conference, Faulkner House Books, 624 Pirate's Alley; 524-2940, and other French Quarter locations. Several wonderful days are dedicated to "providing realistic assistance to promising writers and promoting the art of the written word." There are readings, seminars, lectures, master classes, panel discussions, meetings with authors, music, and parties. It concludes with presentations of prizes to adult and student winners of the Faulkner Creative Writing Competition. E-mail: Faulkhouse@aol.com, Web site: http://members.aol.com/Faulkhouse.

Pirogue Races, Jean Lafitte, Louisiana; 1-800-689-3525. Races in these unique Louisiana boats, sponsored by the Jean Lafitte Yacht Club.

Pro-football and College Games at the Superdome. For information, call 587-3810.

Renaissance Festival is held during the last two weekends of the month, at Lafreniere Park, just off Veterans Boulevard, and David Drive in Metairie. Song, dance, pageantry, extra-special food, and games are offerings here. For information, call the Jefferson Performing Arts Society; 885-2000.

Weindorf New Orleans, Washington Square, Faubourg Marigny. This festival celebrates German culture and heritage in a neighborhood where many German immigrants settled.

WYES-Channel 12 Educational TV Bid-by-Phone Auction, 916 Navarre Ave.; 486-5511. Excellent artwork is auctioned, along with every other imaginable thing! Just tune in your television and have the phone handy and you are "there."

October

Boo at the Zoo is a family Halloween night celebration at the Audubon Zoo. Call 861-2537.

Celtic Nations Heritage Festival, City Park, Marconi Meadow; 529-1391. This is a weekend of revelry in the heritage, games, music, dance, language, sports, crafts, and good-time nature of the Celtic culture. It is a fun time for the entire family, with many children's activities.

Jeff Fest and Kid's Fest, Lafreniere Park, Metairie; 888-2900. Family music festival with Louisiana music, food, and crafts.

New Orleans Film & Video Festival, Canal Place, Southern Repertory Theater, and Prytania Theater; 523-3818. Film screenings by Louisiana filmmakers as well as international classics and independent films.

Octoberfest, Deutsches Haus, 200 S. Galvez St.; 522-8014. Celebrate each weekend in October with German food, drink, music, dance, and sing-a-longs. Special family rates.

Official Opening of the Opera and the Symphony; 529-2278, 523-6530.

Overture to a Cultural Season Gala is an elegant benefit evening. Call 821-9300.

Pumpkin Time at the French Market in the Quarter. See the colorful painted and unpainted pumpkins, as well as corn, sugarcane, pecans, and long strings of garlic to keep the evil spirits away. Savor the smells and taste treats. A flea market is held in the Market area.

November

All Saints Day, November 1. This is the day when the cemeteries are filled with beautiful fresh flowers, and tombs are freshly white washed by faithful family and friends. The Los Islenos Heritage & Cultural Society holds an outdoor mass; 682-0862.

Cajun Christmas, Heymann Convention Center, Lafayette, Louisiana; 318-796-5853.

Celebration in the Oaks, City Park; 483-9415. About one million lights are lit to celebrate the holidays, through New Year's Day. A Cajun Christmas village, a Santa and candy village, Christmas trees decorated by area schoolchildren, walking and/or driving tours, and a variety of holiday activities are offered. Call for schedule.

Civil War Re-Enactment, Oak Alley Plantation, Vacherie; 1-800-44ALLEY, 504-265-2151.

Destrehan Plantation Festival, 13034 River Rd., Destrehan; 504-764-9315, 504-524-5522. Come here for local crafts, food, music, and tours of a beautiful plantation house.

The Opening Race at the Fair Grounds, 1751 Gentilly Blvd.; 944-5515. Held on Thanksgiving Day. Live racing then continues for four months.

Shrine Circus, Pontchartrain Center; 465-9985. The Shriners' delightful annual circus.

December

Annual Mid-Winter Sports Association Sugar Bowl Classic Activities, Superdome and Lake Pontchartrain; 587-3810. Basketball, tennis, and sailing.

Annual "Tea Party for the Dolls," Beauregard-Keyes House, 1113 Chartres; 523-7257. This is a special treat for children (bring your favorite doll!), complete with storytelling.

Bayou Christmas Festival, Jean Lafitte, Louisiana; 1-800-TO-BAYOU. Lights along the bayou, a *fais-do-do* (Cajun dance), and Santa arriving by pirogue.

Bonfire & Fireworks, Tezcuco Plantation, Darrow; 504-562-3929. Complete with dinner and candlelight tours.

Bonfires on the Levee. Bonfires are lit on the river in the New Orleans area to show Papa Noel the way. There is caroling too. Check local newspapers and magazines for schedules.

Celebration in the Oaks continues from November through December and to the New Year.

College basketball games. Check the newspaper or Ticketmaster; 522-5555.

Giant Menorah Lighting by a local rabbi on the Riverfront, by Riverwalk Marketplace and the Spanish Plaza.

New Year Countdown, Jackson Square; 566-5044.

Nutcracker Ballet. Check local newspapers and magazines for times and dates.

Oak Alley Plantation Christmas Bonfire Party, Vacherie; 1-800-44ALLEY, 504-265-2151.

Patio Planters Carols by Candlelight. Held at Jackson Square, this is a New Orleans tradition, held the Sunday night before Christmas at dusk. Candles and song sheets are distributed just prior to event. It is fun for all.

Yuletide Celebration on the River, Chalmette National Park; 589-4430, 589-4428. Traditional bonfires, caroling, and costumed guides. Beauregard House is decorated with fresh greens. This is a treat for the entire family.

SELF-GUIDED CITY TOURS

We include five tours that will enable you to see New Orleans on your own. The three walking tours include the French Quarter (the original French section), the Faubourg Marigny Historic District (the first suburb of the original French city), and the Garden District (the American section). The two driving tours include Esplanade/Lakefront/Cemeteries and a St. Charles Avenue driving or streetcar tour. These are excellent ways to see New Orleans up close.

Please also remember, as in any large city, do not conduct your personal walking tours after dark. In the French Quarter, Bourbon, Royal, Chartres, and North St. Peter streets are all good for nighttime sightseeing—there's a tremendous amount of people and vehicular traffic. Just use caution on the dark side streets. We want you to have a wonderful and trouble-free trip.

FRENCH QUARTER WALKING TOUR

Starting at Jackson Square

Vieux Carre means, literally, "Old Square." It is the only section of New Orleans that is laid out in such a neat, square pattern. Later, the Americans referred to it as the *French Quarter*. Today, New Orleanians refer to it simply as "*the Quarter.*"

Jackson Square is the spot where New Orleans was founded and has been the heart of the city ever since. The square was laid out by the French engineer de Pauger, in 1721 as a drill field. Flags were raised and lowered here with great ceremony as New Orleans became French, then Spanish, then French, then American, then Confederate, then part of the United States again. When French and Spanish soldiers

FRENCH QUARTER (VIEUX CARRE) WALKING TOUR

1. Jackson Square
2. The Presbytere
3. Saint Louis Cathedral
4. The Cabildo
5. The Louisiana State Arsenal
6. The Pontalbas
7. Le Petit Theatre du Vieux Carre
8. David Home (Petit Salon)
9. The Historical Pharmacy Museum
10. Napoleon House
11. Pierre Maspero's Exchange
12. The Old Bank of Louisiana
13. The Old Bank of the United States
14. Courthouse
15. The Old Louisiana State Bank
16. Casa Faurie
17. Hermann-Grima House
18. Merieult House
19. Maison Seignouret
20. The Court of the Two Lions
21. The Casa de Comercio
22. Le Monnier House
23. Maison de Flechier
24. Pirates Alley
25. The Cathedral Garden
26. Pere Antoine Alley
27. Orleans Ballroom
28. Madame John's Legacy
29. The Miltenberger House
30. The Cornstalk Fence
31. Lafitte's Blacksmith Shop
32. Gallier House
33. The Haunted House
34. The Thierre House
35. The Clay House
36. The Soniat House
37. Beauregard House
38. The Old Ursuline Convent
39. The Old United States Mint (Jazz Museum)
40. French Market
41. Moonwalk
42. Woldenberg Park

marched in the square it was called the Place d'Armes, and Indians and backwoods people who had come to town to peddle their wares often gathered around to watch the show. Not until 1851 was the name changed to Jackson Square in honor of general and president Andrew Jackson, whom local residents viewed as the "savior of the city"—since he defeated the British in the Battle of New Orleans in 1815. The cornerstone of the monument in the center of the square was laid by Jackson himself. The delicately balanced equestrian statue of Andrew Jackson is one of three cast by sculptor Clark Mills in his own foundry (1810-83). The others are in Lafayette Square, opposite the White House in Washington, D.C., and in Nashville, Tennessee. These were the first equestrian statues cast in the U.S.

Begin at Jackson Square, in front of St. Louis Cathedral (see SIGHTS). *The Presbytere* is just to the right of St. Louis Cathedral. The word Presbytere means "dwelling place for parish clergy," which was to be its original function. The first two buildings on this site burned in the fires of 1788 and 1794. This building was completed by the United States government in 1813 and used as a courthouse; it has never housed the clergy. Ownership was transferred from the Cathedral to the city of New Orleans in 1853. It is now part of the *Louisiana State Museum* and houses an excellent gift shop and many fine exhibits—such as an interesting Mardi Gras collection and a delightful exhibit of antique toys.

The first church on the site of the St. Louis Cathedral was designed by the young French engineer de Pauger and dedicated on Christmas 1727. It lasted 60 years, then burned in the great fire of 1788. The present church was constructed with funds donated by wealthy Don Andres Almonaster y Roxas, as were the Cabildo and the Presbytere (which were destroyed in the fire of 1794). The church was designated a cathedral in 1793, and is the second oldest cathedral in the United States. In 1851, the St. Louis Cathedral underwent major remodeling, in addition to being enlarged. In 1964, it was given the status of minor basilica, one of just 15 churches so designated in the United States. The floor-to-ceiling multi-colored stained-glass windows tell the visual life story of King Louis.

The Cabildo

The *Cabildo* is to the left of the St. Louis Cathedral. The word cabildo means "governing council." This building was constructed to house the Spanish administration. Like its neighbors on the square, it was rebuilt by Don Andres after the great fire of 1788. During its lengthy history, it has served as a library, a court, a fire station, a small holding jail, the site of the signing of the Louisiana Purchase agreement, and a very elegant though temporary home for the Marquis de Lafayette of Revolutionary War fame. It is now part of the *Louisiana State Museum*.

The *Louisiana State Arsenal* sits just behind the Cabildo, facing

St. Peter Street. It was built in 1839 in elegant Greek Revival design, and was originally the site of the Spanish prison, or "calabozo" in Spanish, which became "calaboose" to the Kentucky flatboaters or "kaintucks," who often found their way there after celebrating too well the arrival of their flatboats in New Orleans. In the wrought-iron balcony facing Pirates Alley you will see crossed cannons, with the monogram LL, above a pile of cannonballs. This was the insignia of the Louisiana Legion, an elite military organization of the early 1800s. The arsenal later served as Confederate general Beauregard's headquarters and as a Union military prison during the occupation of New Orleans. It is now part of the *Louisiana State Museum*.

The Pontalbas

The *Pontalbas* are a matched pair of red brick buildings on either side of the square, on St. Ann and St. Peter streets, begun in 1849 and said to be among the first "row houses" in America. Note the beautiful cast-iron railings, designed by Micaela Leonard Almonaster, Baroness de Pontalba, daughter of Don Andres Almonaster y Roxas, with her initials AP entwined in the center of each section. There are 16 houses in each row. Jenny Lind lived here at one time, as did William Faulkner.

The *1850 House*, at *525 St. Ann St. in the lower Pontalba*, is a beautifully restored and authentically furnished section of the Pontalba, well worth a visit (see SIGHTS). *Le Petit Theatre du Vieux Carre, 616 St. Peter St.*, is just across St. Peter Street from the Cabildo. This building, which was rebuilt as a faithful copy of the original, houses one of the oldest local theater groups in the country and the oldest in New Orleans, founded in 1916. Look into the beautiful patio and check on the availability of tickets for the current production. The theater produces excellent side-by-side seasons of both adult and children's plays.

Just next door at *620 St. Peter St.* is the *David Home*, built in 1838 as a Greek Revival city house. Note the beautiful entranceway and the bow and arrow design in the ironwork. It is now home of *Le Petit Salon*, one of the oldest women's clubs in the city.

Chartres Street

Return to the corner of Chartres Street, which was one of the main commercial streets of French New Orleans, **and walk left on Chartres from Jackson Square for two blocks.** In passing, note the house at *617 Chartres*, which was built in 1795 on the site of the house where the great fire of 1788 began. Peek into the courtyard and admire the lovely balconies.

Continue to 514 Chartres St., the Pharmacy Museum. "*La Pharmacie Francaise*" was built in 1837 in the French tradition of shop downstairs and home upstairs for Louis Dufilho, a pharmacist. Plan time to visit the restoration of the old apothecary shop, complete with medicines, medical instruments, pill-rolling machines, and even an old soda fountain. Be sure to enjoy the lovely patio while you are there (see SIGHTS).

Continue to 500 Chartres St., at the corner of St. Louis Street. The *Napoleon House*, built in 1814 by M. Nicholas Girod, mayor of New Orleans, has an interesting tile roof topped by an octagonal cupola which is a French Quarter landmark. Legend says that the home was built for Napoleon Bonaparte. Unfortunately, Napoleon died before the plan to rescue him from imprisonment on the Isle of St. Helena could be carried out. The building now houses the Napoleon House Restaurant and Bar, where recorded classical music is played exclusively (see DINING).

Just across St. Louis Street, on the left, is Pierre Maspero's Exchange. Slave auctions were held here, and upstairs in this building, Gen. Andrew Jackson and the pirate Jean Lafitte are said to have met to plan the Battle of New Orleans.

Royal Street

Walk one block farther, on Chartres; turn right on Conti Street and walk one block to 334 Royal St. The *Old Bank of Louisiana* is an elegantly columned building, dating from 1826. The bank issued bank notes that were as tastefully designed as its building, and by 1830 the bank had almost $5 million in assets. Just across the street at *339 Royal St.* is the *Old Bank of the United States*, built in 1800, the oldest bank building in New Orleans. It was designed by the architect Lafon. Note the excellent wrought-iron (or hand-forged iron) railings. It now houses *Waldhorn's Antiques*.

Turn back across Conti Street to 400 Royal St. The old *U.S. Civil Courts Building* at this address is on the site of old Spanish structures.

Across the street from the courthouse is the Old Louisiana State Bank at 401 Royal St. Designed by architect Benjamin Latrobe just before he died of yellow fever and chartered in 1818, this bank survived both the Panic of 1837 and the Civil War. The bank's monogram, LB, is part of the design of the wrought-iron balcony railing. It now houses *Manheim Galleries*.

Walk down Royal Street to 417 Royal St., Casa Faurie. This building was constructed in 1802 for the grandfather of the French impressionist painter Edgar Degas. It later housed the *Bank of Louisiana* and then, moving from business to pleasure, it became the home of a party-loving New Orleanian, the prosperous Martin Gordon. General Jackson was entertained here. At midcentury, it was the home of Paul Morphy, a world chess champion at the age of 21. It now houses the well-known *Brennan's Restaurant* (see DINING).

Excursions off Royal Street

Turn left on St. Louis Street, crossing Bourbon Street, to 820 St. Louis St., the Hermann-Grima House. The house was built in 1831 by German immigrant and businessman Samuel Hermann. It was designed by an American architect, William Brandt, in the Federal style—unusual for the French Quarter. The house and stables have been beautifully restored and are open to visitors. There is also an authentically restored kitchen building with special "cooking in the 1850s" demonstrations.

Return to Royal Street and turn left to 533 Royal St. Mid-block on the left, the *Merieult House* dates from 1792, a gift from Jean Francois Merieult to his beautiful red-haired wife, Catherine. It is said that Napoleon offered her a castle in exchange for her hair, which he wanted to give as a present to the Sultan of Turkey. Madame Merieult declined his offer. The house, having survived the fire of 1794, was remodeled in 1830. At this time, the granite pilasters were added, covering the original brick arches. The building now houses the *Historic New Orleans Collection* (part of the Kemper and Leila Williams Foundation) and is well worth a visit (see SIGHTS).

Continue on Royal Street. *Maison Seignouret, 520 Royal St.*, constructed in 1816, was the home of one of Louisiana's most talented furniture craftsmen, Francois Seignouret, who always carved an S into the design of his work. The patio, known as the *Brulator Court*, is one of the most photographed courtyards in New Orleans.

The Court of the Two Lions, 537 Royal St., dating from 1819, was owned by Vincent Nolte, on whose autobiography the story of Anthony Adverse was based. The two lions are over the gate facing Toulouse Street. The *Casa de Comercio, 536 Royal St.*, was built soon after the 1794 fire and is one of the best examples of Spanish architecture in New Orleans.

Turn left on St. Peter Street. *Le Monnier House* is located at *714 St. Peter St.* Dr. Yves LeMonnier, a respected physician, built this house in

New Orleans balcony garden *Cecilia Casrill Dartez*

1829. In 1860, it was bought by Antoine Alciatoire, founder of the famous Antoine's Restaurant, who operated a pension (or boarding house) here. At 718 St. Peter St. is the *Maison de Flechier.* A well-to-do-planter, Etienne Marie de Flechier, built this home soon after the fire of 1794. It is now occupied by one of New Orleans' best-known partying spots, Pat O'Brien's. There is a lovely courtyard at the end of the carriageway. Just down the block is Preservation Hall, a landmark for jazz enthusiasts (see NIGHTLIFE).

Pirates Alley

Retrace your steps to Royal Street and turn left to Pirates Alley, the name given to the walkway that runs alongside the Cathedral and the Cathedral Garden on the Cabildo side. Although the alley was not cut through until later, legend persists that this was one of the many places that General Jackson and Lafitte plotted together before the great battle. (It is quite possible that if those two had conferred in all the spots that legend says they did, they would have never found time to do any fighting—and New Orleans might be a British colony today.) Pause in front of Faulkner House Books, 624 Pirates Alley, a building where William Faulkner once lived and wrote during a Louisiana sojourn.

To Royal Street

Return to Royal Street and turn right. At the corner of Royal and Orleans is *The Cathedral Garden.* Note the monument in the center. It was erected during the time of Napoleon III to honor 30 French Marines who lost their lives serving as volunteer nurses during a Louisiana yellow fever epidemic. The garden is also known as St. Anthony's Garden. It is said that there were many duels fought here over the lovely quadroons of New Orleans. **On the other side of the Cathedral Garden is Pere Antoine Alley.** The name honors the Spanish Capuchin monk who was the much-beloved pastor of St. Louis Cathedral. He was sent to New Orleans from Spain as a commissary of the Inquisition, but never made any move to establish it here. He periodically fell in and out of favor with his superiors, but always had his congregation on his side. **Proceed up Orleans Street to number 717.** Here, across from the Cathedral Garden, is the site of the *Orleans Ballroom,* where the famous *Quadroon Balls* were held. The ballroom has been restored to a hotel which now occupies the site.

To Dumaine Street

Return to Royal Street, turn left, and walk a block and a half to Dumaine Street. Turn right. At *632 Dumaine St.* is *Madame John's Legacy*. This is one of two New Orleans buildings which vie for the honor of being the oldest in the Mississippi Valley. The contract for the construction of this West Indian-style building is still intact and dates the building at 1788-89. It is said to be the fictional house referred to in the George Washington Cable story, "Tite Poulette." Cable, who worked as a reporter for the *Picayune*, was famous for his stories describing New Orleans' Creole life, most of them published first in *Scribner's Magazine*.

Turn left as you leave the house and walk back to Royal Street and turn right. Proceed to 900 Royal St. The *Miltenberger Houses, 900-906-910 Royal St.*, were built by a widowed mother for her three sons in 1838. Madame Miltenberger's granddaughter, Alice Heine, became the first American Princess of Monaco. Taken to Paris at age 16 to snare a rich husband, she succeeded quite well, for first she married the Duc de Richelieu, and, 10 years after his death, in 1890, she married Prince Albert of Monaco. Her influence brought ballet, opera, and theater to Monaco, so that its fame now rests not only on gambling, but on the arts as well. After 20 years as Princess of Monaco, she decided it was not the life for her and divorced the prince. Located at *915 Royal St.*, the *Cornstalk Fence* is cast iron, made in Philadelphia and shipped by sea to New Orleans in 1834.

Turn left at St. Philip Street and walk a block to Lafitte's Blacksmith Shop, 941 Bourbon St. This small building is French "brick between posts" construction, dating from at least 1772. It is another one of the legendary haunts of the pirate Jean Lafitte, who reputedly used the Blacksmith Shop as a "front" for his lucrative but illegal contraband-trading ventures. The shop is now a piano bar (see NIGHTLIFE).

Walk back to St. Philip Street and to Royal Street, turn left, and continue to 1132 Royal St. The *Gallier House* was designed and built by famed New Orleans architect James Gallier, Jr., as his family's home. It was built in 1857-58 and has been meticulously restored and authentically furnished with a superb collection of period furnishings and artworks that reflect the gracious New Orleans lifestyle of the 1860s. It is open to the public. Don't fail to tour; it is a treat for all ages (see SIGHTS). The *Haunted House*, located at *1140 Royal St.*, is famous for tragedy. It was the home of the LeLaurie family, affluent and on the surface most respectable. However, there are many stories of tortured slaves, mysterious fires, and owners who fled to France when their

Cornstalk Fence, French Quarter *Cecilia Casrill Dartez*

crimes were discovered. It is said that, on certain nights, you will still hear the sound of ships and chains, and the groans and screams of the victims. Note the elaborate doorway of this very tall, French Empire-style house.

Governor Nicholls

Turn left on Governor Nicholls to number 721. The *Thierry House* was designed by the well-known architect Henry Latrobe, when he was 19 years old. This is the house, built in 1814, which is responsible for beginning the Greek Revival Period, so very important in Louisiana architecture.

Return down Governor Nicholls and cross Royal Street to the 600 block. The *Clay House, 618-20 Governor Nicholls*, was built in 1828 by John Clay, brother of the famous United States senator and statesman Henry Clay (one of the men honored in New Orleans' famous "funeral for three"). St. Frances Xavier Cabrini (the first American saint) used the house as a school in the 1890s.

Back to Chartres Street

Continue down Governor Nicholls and turn right on Chartres to 1133 Chartres St. The *Soniat House* is an elegant townhouse built for the aristocratic planter Joseph Soniat du Fossat. The balcony railings are cast iron which, as the "latest thing," replaced the original wrought iron in the 1860s.

Beauregard/Keyes House is located at *1113 Chartres*. Dating from 1827, it was originally the beautiful home of Joseph LeCarpentier, built on land purchased from the Ursuline Nuns. During the first mournful winter after the Civil War, Gen. P.G.T. Beauregard, who reputedly fired the first shot of the war at Fort Sumter in Charleston, South Carolina, rented a room here while he looked for a job. It was more recently home to the well-known author Frances Parkinson Keyes, who restored it and left it in the care of a foundation so that it could be enjoyed by future generations. Be sure to stop and tour.

1114 Chartres is the address of the *Old Ursuline Convent*. This structure (along with Madame John's Legacy) competes for the title of the oldest building in the Mississippi Valley. It was built for the Ursuline Nuns who arrived in New Orleans in the fall of 1726. They lived in a house on Chartres and Bienville streets while their convent was being completed. They came to care for the many settlers who were being struck down by yellow fever. These brave women arrived in their heavy gray religious habits, totally unprepared for the subtropical climate. They stayed to nurse, educate, and exert an influence on the community. They began the first Catholic, Negro, and Indian schools and first orphanage in the state. Their influence is felt even to this day.

The Old United States Mint

Turn left on Ursulines Street, and two blocks down, left again at Decatur Street. The *Old United States Mint, 300 Esplanade,* was designed by William Strickland and built in 1835. It was erected on the site of old *Fort St. Charles,* built by the Spanish in 1792 to protect the lower boundary of the city. General Jackson reviewed his hastily gathered army here before the Battle of New Orleans. Coins were minted here from 1838 to 1862, and later from 1879 to 1910. The mint-mark was "O" (coin collectors take note!). When Louisiana seceded from the Union, the Mint was seized by the state. A hanging took place there in 1862, the ultimate punishment for a too-enthusiastic New Orleanian who tore down the Union flag as it was being raised over the defeated city. The Mint has been restored and has become part of the *Louisiana State Museum.* Note the *"Streetcar Named Desire"* of Tennessee Williams fame which is on display just behind the Mint. Tennessee Williams was one of New Orleans' most unique habitués.

The French Market

The French Market runs from Barracks Street to Jackson Square along Decatur Street. The *French Market* was begun by the Spanish (a typical New Orleans twist) in 1791, but immediately named La Halle des Boucheries (the Butcher's Market) by the Creoles. When the original building was destroyed in 1812, an arcade was designed by the city surveyor. By 1823, the market boasted over 100 stalls and stretched along the levee from Dumaine Street to St. Philip Street. For decades, the women of New Orleans (and/or their servants) gathered here to "make groceries." *Harper's Weekly,* in 1882, described the "antique appearance" of the market and marveled at the many languages spoken there. By the early 1900s, the French Market had become Italian, as the immigrants who were small farmers on the outskirts of the city brought their produce to the market to sell. One of the young Italians who began by peddling fruit at the market ended up as president of Standard Fruit and Steamship Company. His name was Joseph Vaccaro. The Market underwent extensive restoration in the 1970s. Today, you will find the French Market is a joyous place to wander, to shop the Flea Market, to people-watch, to sniff exotic fragrances, to watch pralines and beignets being made, and to enjoy your choice of breakfast, lunch, dinner, or "just dessert."

Finish at the River

Continue on Decatur Street to Jackson Square. On the levee opposite Jackson Square is the *Moon Walk*, named after Mayor Moon Landrieu (mayor during the 1970s), who was responsible for its construction. It is a perfect place to finish any tour. Find a bench, relax, and let the breeze from the river refresh you while you watch the ever-changing procession of boats and ships working their way up and down the river. You may also wish to continue to the right (upriver) to *Woldenberg Riverfront Park*, a tree- and shrub-filled urban park which connects the Moon Walk to the *Aquarium of the Americas* and the *Entergy IMAX Theatre*.

Across the river is *Algiers*, where the French established the powder magazine for the colony. It was also used as the debarkation point for slaves as they were brought in from Africa.

The twin spans for the *Crescent City Connection* are to your right (upriver) and you will see the shiny white Canal Street Ferry plying its way back and forth across the river somewhat closer upstream. Just to the right is the dock from which many of the excursion boats depart. If you are lucky, you may catch a glimpse of the *Delta Queen* or the *Mississippi Queen* resting between voyages up and down the length of the Mississippi.

To the left (downriver), you will see wharves stretching around the bend in the river, with ships from many nations moored alongside. You return to the pivotal point in the French Quarter, where the city was laid out in French rationale, an orderly grid on a bend in the mighty Mississippi.

FAUBOURG MARIGNY WALKING TOUR

Introduction

The Faubourg Marigny Historic District is the first Creole suburb of the original French city of New Orleans. It all began with the subdivision

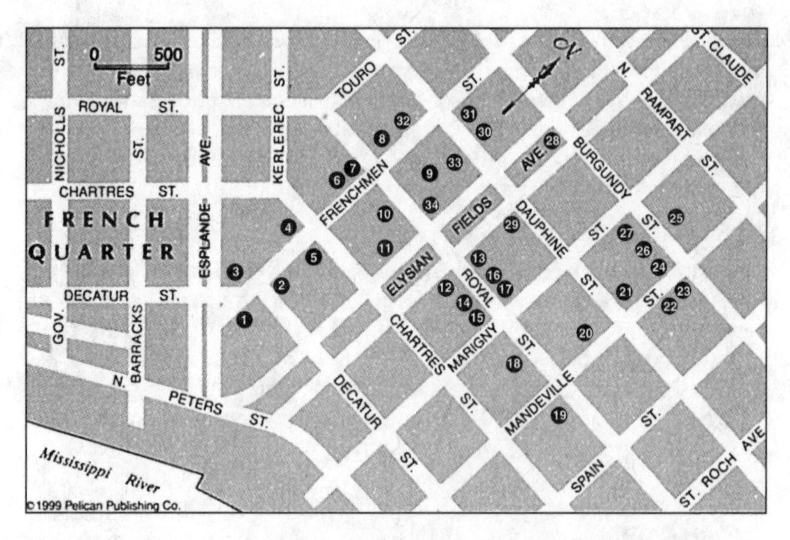

FAUBOURG MARIGNY HISTORIC DISTRICT WALKING TOUR

1. Esplanade Fire Station
2. Frenchmen Street
3. 501 Frenchmen
4. 542 Frenchmen (Praline Connection)
5. 2100 Chartres Street (Cafe Brasil)
6. 626 Frenchmen (Snug Harbor)
7. 634 Frenchmen Street (P J's Coffee & Tea Cafe)
8. 700-702 Frenchmen Street
9. Washington Square
10. Royal Street/Washington Square
11. "Smokey Mary" tracks
12. 635 Elysian Fields Avenue (Old Nolting Bakery Building)
13. 707 Elysian Fields Avenue
14. 2216-2218 Royal Street
15. 2228 Royal Street
16. 2231 Royal Street
17. 704 Marigny Street
18. 2318 Royal Street
19. 639 Mandeville Street (Belachi Building)
20. 708-710 Mandeville Street
21. 820-822 Mandeville Street
22. 823 Mandeville Street
23. 825 Mandeville Street
24. 826-828 Mandeville Street
25. 2300 Burgundy Street (Saints Peter and Paul Complex)
26. 2318 Burgundy Street
27. 2310 and 2308 Burgundy Street
28. Elysian Fields
29. 2204-2212 Dauphine Street
30. 2111 Dauphine Street (Claiborne Mansion)
31. 801 Frenchmen Street (Santa Fe Restaurant)
32. Frenchmen Street/Washington Square
33. Vieux Carré Bus Stop

of the plantation of Count Bernard Xavier Phillipe de Marigny de Mandeville, an extremely wealthy Creole who wished to develop a Creole residential area.

Within this historic district is a varied collection of 18th- and 19th-century structures built on the typical narrow lot. There are raised cottages, Creole cottages, single and double shotgun houses, and two-story Creole stores built in typical European fashion—one right next to the other. Houses are separated by either a wall or narrow alley, and the courtyards are small. There are very few exceptions.

This was eventually inhabited by the Irish, Italian, and German immigrants to New Orleans. As a result, Faubourg Marigny became a closely knit community with a fine neighborhood feeling. That pride is quite evident today, and you'll notice the wonderful neighborhood spirit as you explore the first Creole suburb.

Beginning the Tour

Begin the Faubourg Marigny Historic District Tour at the Old U.S. Mint on Decatur Street and Esplanade Avenue. Cross Esplanade to the left of the fire station, which is situated on a small piece of property between Decatur and Frenchmen streets. Pass the fire station and proceed on Frenchmen Street.

Frenchmen Street

Frenchmen Street is so named for a group of heroic Frenchmen who led a rebellion against the new Spanish takeover of the 1760s. The Frenchmen were executed by a Spanish firing squad on the area that is the beginning of Frenchmen Street. Bernard de Marigny immortalized these men with the street name.

These next two blocks of Frenchmen Street have become the "in" blocks for moderate-priced dining and good jazz and other music.

As you make the curve to the left, look across the street to *501 Frenchmen St.* This is a three-story, four-bay brick Creole townhouse which has a three-story separate service building—similar to the 1830s style. The second to third levels have the long French windows which open onto balconies with a delicate railing of wrought iron.

Then pass the *Praline Connection* at *542 Frenchmen,* which has gained a reputation for good local cuisine.

Across the street at *2100 Chartres* (corner of Frenchmen) is *Cafe Brasil.* Light refreshments, drinks, and live contemporary music can be found here in the evenings.

Cross Chartres and continue on to *Snug Harbor, 626 Frenchmen,* home of terrific jazz and some good food. It does become somewhat crowded here on weekends.

Now you arrive in front of *P J's Coffee & Tea Cafe, 634 Frenchmen,* a popular local coffee shop. It is a good place for a snack and rest stop.

This particular block was a shopping mecca during the turn of the century.

As you come to the corner of Frenchmen and Royal streets, look across the street to *700-702 Frenchmen St.* Here are two four-bay Creole townhouses built between 1833 and 1836 with separate (to the left and in the rear) service buildings. Note the louvered shutters on the long French doors and the original wrought-iron balcony. Part of the first floor was used as a neighborhood cafe in the 1940s.

Royal Street

Turn to the right on Royal Street and walk toward Elysian Fields. The entire block, or square, on your left is *Washington Square* with its cast-iron fence. With the tiny neighborhood courtyards, Washington Square was the "backyard" of the Faubourg. The park has always been used for strolling, relaxing, and children's play. In the early 1900s there was even a large built-in wading pool for the children.

Elysian Fields

Walk next to the park till you come to Elysian Fields and cross the street to the wide expanse (median) called the neutral ground. Pause on the neutral ground, and with your back to the river, view Bernard de Marigny's Champs Elysees. During the 1800s, this was also an extremely busy place. It was here that the "Smokey Mary" followed her tracks to take the city dwellers to Milneberg, the lakefront amusement park and family area—for picnics, games, dances, jazz bands, restaurants, and that breath of fresh lake air—before returning to the city and its hot summer air.

Cross to the other side of Elysian Fields on Royal Street and note two corner buildings. At *635 Elysian Fields* is the two-story, plastered-brick *Old Nolting Bakery* building, which dates from approximately 1830. There are full-length openings on both levels and an arched carriageway in the rear of the building.

Now look across Royal Street to *707 Elysian Fields* at another plastered brick building, built in the mid-1850s. This three-story fine Creole store-house (store below, family residence above) was built for bakery owner Ferdinand Nolting. Note the excellent cast-iron galleries on two levels which also make the traditional Creole cornered walkway for customers and other pedestrians.

Continue on Royal Street

Continue along Royal Street to 2216-18 Royal. This double shotgun house in the Greek Revival style has a four-bay galleried frame and dates from the 1840s.

At *2228 Royal* is a single-framed shotgun house from the 1880s. Note the low hip roof which extends to cover the gallery.

Now look across the street to *2231 Royal St.* This three-bay house with the central entrance carriageway is quite unique to Faubourg Marigny. It is a fine example of a raised-basement house in the Greek Revival style. Sea captain Richard Lamb Robertson had this house built for his family in the early 1830s.

Continue on Royal to the next corner. At *704 Marigny St.* is another two-story Creole store-house. The second level cast-iron gallery, with its vining motif, also covered the walkway for customers.

Cross Marigny and continue on to *2318 Royal,* a well-kept late-19th-century bayed cottage. Note the shallow ell on the left which offers a unique side entry.

Mandeville Street

Continue on Royal to the next corner, which is Mandeville Street. Look across the street to 639 *Mandeville*. This corner building is known as the *Belachi Building*, and is an 1880s two-story store-house—in typical Creole fashion again with the first level a store and second level a residence. French doors open onto the brick banquette.

Take a left on Mandeville and walk toward Dauphine Street. At *708-710 Mandeville* is a very simple and austere example of an 1830s brick shotgun double. Note the steep hip roof and the Greek Revival style of the plastered facade. Continue to the corner of Mandeville and Dauphine and notice the tiled street names in the sidewalk.

Cross Dauphine and continue along Mandeville, noticing the varied styles of houses. This particular block looks like a typical late Victorian street scene. The shotgun double at *820-822 Mandeville* has a lovely stained-glass dormer.

Stop at *823 Mandeville* and look at this camelback-style house with lots of lovely gingerbread adorning the front. The camelback, with its single story in front and two-story rear, was a design which was used to avoid local taxes which were levied upon the number of windows and doors in the front of a house.

There is a typical Creole cottage at *825 Mandeville*. The *826-828*

Mandeville shotgun double has much gingerbread on its facade. Walk to the corner of Mandeville and Burgundy streets.

Burgundy Street

As you turn left on Burgundy Street again notice the tiled names in the sidewalk. The right side of the 2300 block of Burgundy Street is the *Saints Peter and Paul Roman Catholic Church Complex*—the center for the faithful Irish, German, and Italian immigrants new to the Faubourg Marigny. This congregation was formed in 1848, at which time it met in a small building on the corner of Dauphine and Marigny streets.

This present church was built in 1860 of red brick and on a foundation of cotton bales, which is the reason for the slight tilt in the building. The left tower, which was originally 177 feet high, was damaged by lightning in 1911 and had to be lowered.

The famous New Orleans architect Henry Howard designed this church, which was considered the most impressive in the downtown area. The magnificent floor-to-ceiling leaded, stained-glass windows depicting biblical stories are worth the visit inside. The imposing main altar comes from Grand Rapids, Michigan.

The church has quite an Irish tradition in that for the first 100 years, all pastors were natives of Ireland. In 1998, Saints Peter and Paul celebrated its 150th anniversary.

To the left of the church is the *Saints Peter and Paul Hall*, built in the 1850s—a raised-basement style which houses an enormous auditorium and beautiful staircase and was once the home of the church's elementary school.

Across the street from the church and school are some excellent examples of Faubourg Marigny renewal. At *2318 Burgundy* is a renovated single Victorian shotgun house. The basket-weave banquette is still, fortunately, intact.

Numbers 2310 and 2308 Burgundy are both cheerfully painted single shotguns. Continue on Burgundy toward Elysian Fields.

Elysian Fields and Dauphine Streets

Cross Elysian Fields and reminisce about "Smokey Mary." On the opposite side take a left toward Dauphine Street next to Washington Square. At Dauphine and Elysian Fields stop to look across the street.

Number 2204-2212 Dauphine St. is a two-story store and house built in the 1850s. It is a Greek Revival-style building once owned by W. C. C.

Claiborne II. Here is another example of a cast-iron gallery used to protect valued customers and pedestrians from the weather.

Take a right on Dauphine to a variety of houses built in the 1850s-60s with a select view of Washington Square. Amidst the Creole cottages and shotguns is *2111 Dauphine*, the *Claiborne Mansion*. W. C. C. Claiborne II, son of the first American governor of Louisiana, and his Creole wife moved into their new home on the fashionable square in approximately 1859. This house was built by an American builder, Samuel Stewart, and incorporated the Greek Revival and Classic styles in this urban version of the Louisiana plantation type.

Continue to the corner of Dauphine and Frenchmen streets to the *Sante Fe Restaurant* in a fine old house, *801 Frenchmen*. This could be a nice refreshment break.

Back to the Starting Point

Then walk along Frenchmen behind Washington Square toward Royal Street. Now you may consider your two return options.

On the corner of Royal Street and Elysian Fields (you may have already noticed), there is usually a mini Vieux Carre bus fashioned as a small streetcar. This is the only size bus authorized to traverse the historic French Quarter. You can take the minibus through the Quarter for various stops, and on to Canal Street and the downtown hotels.

Or you may want to backtrack on Frenchmen Street to the Old U.S. Mint in the French Quarter.

GARDEN DISTRICT WALKING TOUR

Introduction

The Garden District is the very beautiful, very elegant section of the city developed by the Americans during the first half of the 19th century. Streets were laid out and homes were built in the city of Lafayette and on what had once been the great plantation of the Livaudais family. The most spectacular homes were built in the 1850s, during the period in which New Orleans reached the height of its prosperity.

Today, this section of the city is cherished like a valuable family heirloom. Homes are constantly being restored and gardens made ever more beautiful.

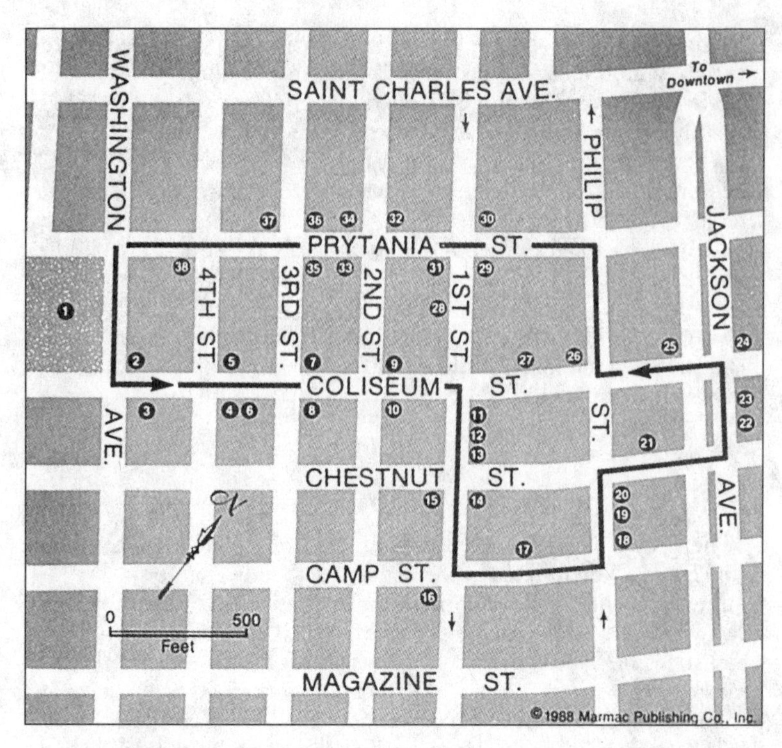

GARDEN DISTRICT WALKING TOUR

1. Lafayette Cemetery
2. Commander's Palace Restaurant
3. 2700-2726 Coliseum Street (Freret's Folly)
4. 2632 Coliseum Street
5. 2627 Coliseum Street
6. 2618 Coliseum Street
7. 1415 Third Street
8. 1331 Third Street
9. 2425 Coliseum Street
10. 1325 Second Street
11. 1331 First Street
12. 1315 First Street
13. 1312 First Street
14. 1239 First Street
15. 1236 First Street
16. 1134 First Street
17. 2325 Camp Street
18. 1208 Philip Street
19. 1220 Philip Street
20. 1238 Philip
21. "Raised Cottages"
22. 1305 Jackson Avenue
23. 1329 Jackson Avenue (Trinity Episcopal Church)
24. 1401 Jackson Avenue (Perkins-Lacoste House)
25. 1410 Jackson Avenue (Budever-Eustis House)
26. 1410 Philip Street
27. Seven Sisters or Brides' Row
28. 1420 First Street
29. 2340 Prytania Street Toby's Corner)
30. 2343 Prytania Street
31. 2406 Prytania Street
32. 2423 Prytania Street
33. 2504 Prytania Street
34. 2507 Prytania Street
35. 2520 Prytania Street
36. 2523 Prytania Street
37. 2605 Prytania Street
38. 1448 Fourth Street

Although some of the feeling of the Garden District can be absorbed by driving slowly up and down its one-way streets (by car only—buses are not allowed), we strongly recommend a leisurely walk as the best way to delight in the special atmosphere of the area.

As you walk, be aware of the elegant detailing—roof lines, cornices, recessed doorways with leaded glass or etched glass inserts, varied designs of capitals on columned houses, interesting lightning rods pointing skyward, delicately shaded flagstone or rosy brick sidewalks, and the intricate designs in iron railings and fences. Also, note the abundance and variety of plant life, from the familiar azaleas and camellias to huge live oaks, magnolias and palms, banana trees, Japanese plums, and elephant ears. Enjoy the delicate scent of sweet olive or jasmine.

Camera buffs, be prepared; the Garden District is a paradise for photographers!

Beginning the Tour

Leave the streetcar at Washington and St. Charles Avenue (Car Stop #16). Walk one block left (toward the river) on Washington Avenue to Prytania Street, or park your car close to that intersection, and begin.

Cross Prytania Street and on your right you will see: *Lafayette #1 Cemetery*, established in 1833, enclosed by the brick wall in 1858. Many of those buried here are Irish and German immigrants who fell victim to yellow fever. Gen. John B. Hood, of Civil War fame, and his wife are buried here. They also succumbed to yellow fever, dying within a day of each other. Note the interesting above-ground tombs and "oven" vaults belonging to special groups such as the Jefferson Fire Company No. 2. The cemetery originally belonged to the city of Lafayette. Because the sexton was paid a very small salary, he had a tomb-building business on the side, and he was often too busy to care for the cemetery properly. Today, the cemetary is well cared for and is a popular place for artists to set up their easels.

Across the street, on the corner of Washington Avenue and Coliseum Street, is *Commander's Palace Restaurant* (see DINING), built by Emile Commander in 1880, on the site of the old Livaudais Plantation. Today it is owned by the Brennan family and is a popular place for parties and jazz brunches as well as lunch and dinner.

Coliseum Street

Turn left on Coliseum Street, and on the right you will see *2700-2726 Coliseum St.* Times and the hazards of investing money never change! These five homes were built on speculation by architect William Freret. Unfortunately, he built them just before the Civil War, and because times were so bad, they were very difficult to sell. They came to be known as Freret's Folly.

Cross Fourth Street and continue on Coliseum. On each side of the street you will see two unusual architectural types for New Orleans. On the right is *2632 Coliseum St.*, a mansard-roofed house, and on the left is *2627 Coliseum St.* The latter, a Swiss chalet that has rarely seen snow, was designed by Julius Koch for James B. Eustis, United States Senator and Ambassador to France under Grover Cleveland. Today it is owned by one of the Brennan's Restaurant clan.

2618 Coliseum St. is an excellent example of a relatively new house built to harmonize with the area. It was once the home of Gen. and Mrs. Kemper Williams, through whose generosity we have the Historic New Orleans Collection on Royal Street in the French Quarter.

Third Street

Cross Third Street and look left to *1415 Third St.* Finished in 1865, at a cost of $80,000, it was the home of Walter Robinson, a Virginian who dealt in tobaccos. It is interesting to note that a home like this could be built during the waning days of the Civil War. Each story is 15 feet 8 inches high. The interior boasts fine frescoes, cornices, and medallions, and a magnificent winding staircase. Rumor has it that it was one of the first houses in the city to have indoor plumbing. Note the lovely iron fence and tassel trim on the side balconies.

Just across Coliseum Street is an 1850s home, *1331 Third St.*, designed by architect James Gallier, Sr., for Michael Musson, a prominent cotton merchant and uncle of French Impressionist Edgar Degas, who visited and painted here. The cast-iron gallery was added later. The residence at *2425 Coliseum* was built in 1850. The house originally had slave quarters in the rear, but these were removed in favor of a Greek Revival addition in 1883. There are beautiful Waterford crystal chandeliers inside.

As you cross Second Street, note *1325 Second St.*, an 1880 cottage, reminiscent of both Swiss and Gothic styles.

First Street

When you reach First Street, turn right and note *1331 First St.*, designed by Samuel Jamison in 1869; and *1315 First St.*, also designed by Samuel Jamison in Italianate style. Note the lovely cast-iron gallery. The house is cement over brick construction.

The home at *1312 First St.* was originally a one-story home, built to face Chestnut Street in 1849. During the 1880s the house was raised and turned to face First Street, and a new first floor was built underneath. *1239 First,* an 1857 Greek Revival house, is the home of Albert Brevard. Note the three different styles of columns, and interesting rose design in the balcony ironwork.

A classic Greek Revival house, *1236 First St.* was built in 1847 by John Gayle for his bride. It was designed to have all the important rooms on the south side.

At the corner of Camp Street is *1134 First St.* This house was built before 1850 by Mr. Jacob Payne, who probably designed it. It was built by slaves from Mr. Payne's plantation in St. Landry Parish, and through the years, only two families have owned it. Jefferson Davis was a frequent visitor and finally died here, surrounded by friends. His daughter Winnie made her debut here.

Camp, Philip, and Chestnut Streets

Turn left on Camp Street, passing *2325 Camp,* which dates from 1852. **Walk one block to Philip Street. Turn left** to see *1208 Philip St.*, an 1857 Greek Revival house, and *1220 Philip St.*, an 1857 house of the Italianate style. It was the home of Isaac Delgado, an art collector and founder of what is now the New Orleans Museum of Art.

The house at *1238 Philip St.* (corner of Chestnut Street) was built in 1854 for John Rodenburg, a feed merchant, out of cypress and heart pine, with 18-inch-thick brick-bearing walls. The ceilings are 14 feet high. The property is noted for its beautiful gardens.

Turn left on Chestnut Street and while walking one block to Jackson Avenue, note the handsomely converted shotgun double house and the interesting row of "raised cottages."

Jackson Street

A Greek Revival house with Italianate details, *1305 Jackson Ave.* was built by Augustus Tardy, a cotton broker, in 1871. It is currently the *Parish House of Trinity Episcopal Church.*

Trinity Episcopal Church is located at *1329 Jackson Ave.* The congregation was formed in 1847, at which time it met in a small wooden building at the corner of Second and Constance streets. The present church was built in Gothic Revival style in 1852-53, with a new front and tower added in 1873. Trinity Church sponsors a fine elementary school (building on Chestnut Street). A famous early rector of Trinity Church was Leonidas Polk, a West Point graduate. He was Episcopal Bishop of Louisiana at the time that the Civil War began. His West Point classmate, Jefferson Davis, was in urgent need of trained officers, and he convinced Polk that he should "buckle the sword over the gown." Bishop Polk went off to war as a major general and was killed in Georgia in 1864 while on a reconnaissance mission.

The *Perkins-Lacoste House*, at *1401 Jackson Ave.*, is an antebellum home, designed in the Palladian manner by L. E. Reynolds. Reynolds and his brother, also an architect, are buried in an interesting silver-painted cast-iron tomb in Metairie Cemetery (see Cemeteries Driving Tour). The *Budever-Eustis house, 1410 Jackson Ave.*, was also designed and built by Reynolds.

Walk one block on Coliseum Street to Philip Street.

Shotgun Houses

The residence at *1410 Philip St.* is a classic New Orleans "shotgun" cottage that has been remodeled and the front entrance moved from Coliseum to Philip Street. It was featured in *House and Garden* magazine.

Continue along Coliseum Street to view a row of "shotgun" cottages, of which *1410 Philip* was the first, known locally as "the Seven Sisters" or "Brides' Row." Legend has it that these houses were built for the seven daughters of a doting father as they married. They are built on lots that are only 30 feet wide, as are many houses in New Orleans.

Prytania Street

Turn right on First Street and walk one block to Prytania Street. *1420 First St.* is the location of a lovely Greek Revival house, currently the home of former Saints' quarterback Archie Manning. The raised cottage at *2340 Prytania St.* is a very practical style of building in the frequently flooded New Orleans of this period, and is probably the oldest house in the Garden District. It was built in 1820 by a Philadelphian, Mr. Thomas Toby, a well-to-do merchant who began as manager of the Livaudais Plantation. Most of the Garden District is built on what was once the Livaudais Plantation, and the large live oak behind the house, a member of the Live Oak Society, is known as the Livaudais Oak. Mr. Toby later lost his fortune helping finance the Texas Revolution. The house is known as "Toby's Corner."

Just across the street is *2343 Prytania St.*, a palatial home which, even when it was built in 1870, cost $100,000. It was built as a townhouse for a sugar planter, Bradish Johnson. The house, a free Renaissance-style design of architect James Freret, boasts 18-foot ceilings, fluted Corinthian columns, and a magnificent oak spiral staircase. It is currently the main building of the *Louise S. McGehee School*, a private school for girls.

Turn left and continue up Prytania for four blocks, passing a relatively modern house, *2400 Prytania*, now the *French Consulate* in New Orleans. Across the street is the *Adams-Jones House, 2423 Prytania*, built for a prosperous merchant who purchased his lot from the Livaudais Plantation. It was at one time the home of the first president of Tulane University. This is a good example of a Louisiana cottage, with a particularly beautiful doorway. The house at *2504 Prytania St.* was built in 1858, with Tiffany windows added later. It is now the *Women's Opera Guild House*, open to the public. The interior is embellished with beautiful cornices and medallions, and furnished with antiques of the antebellum period.

Built in the 1850s, *2507 Prytania St.* was carefully restored after a fire 100 years later. The rooms are 22 feet square, with a ballroom that is 22 by 44 feet. It is currently owned by one of the Brennan's Restaurant family.

James Gallier, Jr., designed the structure at *2520 Prytania St.* It was the home of John M. Parker, former governor of Louisiana. Note the lovely iron lace gallery. The interesting carriage house, now a residence, faces Third Street.

Chapel of Our Mother of Perpetual Help, 2523 Prytania St., was originally a congregation for French-speaking Catholics which met on Jackson Avenue. It is currently housed in the old Lonsdale-McStea home, one of the larger houses in the Garden District. Note the unusual stepped gable.

Don't miss *2605 Prytania St.*, an interesting Gothic Revival-style home with a carriage house to the side. An Italianate-style home, *1448 Fourth St.*, at the corner of Prytania, was designed by architect Henry Howard and built in 1859. It was the home of a real Kentucky colonel, Col. Robert Henry Short. Note the beautiful entrance, the ironwork balconies, with Spanish-type supports, and, of course, the "cornstalk" fence, with its iron morning glories blooming amid the iron. Such "rustic" ironwork was part of the "Picturesque" period of architecture, begun in the 1830s in New York. Such "natural" subjects as grape arbors, tree stumps, and holly were reproduced in iron. This house is one of the most photographed houses in the Garden District.

Back to the Starting Point

The tour ends as it began, at the corner of Washington Avenue and

Prytania Street. The large gray frame building across the street was originally the Southern Athletic Club, where the gentlemen of the Garden District took their exercise and also held meetings of their volunteer military units. To the right is the Rink, originally a skating rink and now a unique shopping center.

ESPLANADE/LAKEFRONT/ CEMETERIES DRIVING TOUR

This tour will begin at the Mississippi River, take you up the broad Esplanade Avenue, then along the banks of Bayou St. John to Lake Pontchartrain, and back into the French Quarter via Canal Street. See NEW ORLEANS AREA MAP pp. 6-7.

Esplanade Avenue is a living museum, a showcase of 19th-century architecture. As early as 1721, when Pauger the surveyor arrived, maps show the Esplanade or City Commons laid out to be two arpents, 12 toises wide (an arpent is about 0.85 acre). By the 1830s, the area from Decatur to Rampart streets was being developed as a residential area. It was paved as far as Royal Street, had red brick sidewalks, and was lit at night by gas streetlamps.

Begin at the Foot of Esplanade

The foot of Esplanade is one of the most interesting spots in the city for, within view, you see represented many of the things that give New Orleans its unique flavor. First, there is the *Mississippi River,* hidden from view, but very much present through the booms and superstructure of the ocean-going cargo ships and liners visible over the tops of the wharves. Next, there are the railroad tracks, a link between the busy port and the rest of the continental United States. To one side is the Old Mint, occupying land that has been owned successively by French, Spanish, and American governments. Behind the Mint, you are conscious of the bustle of the French Market. To the other side, just half a block away, you glimpse Elysian Fields Avenue, a main artery leading to the Gentilly section of the city. And straight ahead stretches the Esplanade itself with its broad, treelined, and unique New Orleans "neutral ground" and its old homes, shops, and restaurants. Relax and savor the ambience while we guide you on a pleasant driving tour beginning at the foot of Esplanade in the 400 block.

Esplanade from the River to Rampart Street

On the 400 block is the *Old U.S. Mint* (see SIGHTS). The 500 block is occupied by French-style commercial/residential buildings. The building at *500 Esplanade* was built by Julien Lacroix, a free man of color. *524 Esplanade* was built by Hermann Weysham in 1845, after securing a loan of $5,000 (what would that be today?) from the Merchants Insurance Company. The five-layer foundation was designed to keep dampness out of the house. This is a constant challenge in New Orleans. The house at *602 Esplanade* dates from 1834. Note iron balconies that "wrap" around the corner. Note the four-room "brick between post" Creole cottage, *638 Esplanade*; most of the original structures along Esplanade were of this type. *The Gauche Stream House, 700 Esplanade*, was built in 1856, after removing an earlier house. It cost $20,000 at the time, and construction was supervised by Monsieur Gauche, owner of a prosperous crockery business.

During the 1850s, New Orleans City Railroad cars began traveling out Esplanade to Bayou St. John and back. Upon reaching the end of the line, passengers could visit the St. Louis No. 3 Cemetery, enjoy the Tivoli Gardens, or climb aboard a mule-drawn boat to ride along Bayou St. John to Lake Pontchartrain.

The Fisk family home was built at *740 Esplanade* in the mid-19th century. In 1860, elaborate gardens were planted, and the low brick building (now *730 Esplanade*) was added toward the back of the lot to accommodate a library and billiard room for the gentlemen. During the Civil War Colonel Fisk was killed in the battle of Murfreesboro, the ladies of the family removed themselves to North Carolina, and the home was occupied by Federal troops.

The building at *820 Esplanade* is a three-and-a-half-story Italianate-style structure. The land was purchased by Jean Pierre Dufour in 1816 and stayed in the same family for 98 years.

The oldest documented house on Esplanade, *833 Esplanade* dates from 1810, and at one time was the home of William C. Claiborne, the American governor. The present front door occupies the space that once was the carriageway. There is a beautiful patio in the rear.

The *900 block*, as a whole, is well preserved and gives a feeling for the Esplanade in its heyday. Note in particular numbers 906 and 908, which were designed by James Gallier, Jr., and 937, which is designed in Second Empire style.

Built in 1851, *1016 Esplanade* was remodeled in 1874. It is Greek Revival in style with cast-iron railings. This lot was first owned by a free man of color.

Lately renamed *Le Renaissance*, the building at *1020 Esplanade* has been known locally for years as the *Italian Hall*. It was built in 1835 by the Nott family, a three-story house with a side garden, designed by James Gallier, Sr. Mr. Nott was the first Dutch counsel in New Orleans, as well as an aid-de-camp to Governor Claiborne. As a director of the Bank of Orleans, he fought a duel with M. Saul, the cashier, who was accused of questionable banking practices. He won. Later it was the home of John Slidell, distinguished attorney, statesman, and United States senator, who resigned his seat in the Senate when Louisiana seceded from the Union. He then became Commissioner to France from the Confederate States. Slidell chose to remain in exile after the war and died in France. Frances Parkinson Keyes, the well-known novelist, refers to this house in her book, *Mme. Castel's Lodger*. In 1912, the Italian Hall Association bought the property and in 1920, additions were made and the outside redesigned by the Unione Italiana.

From Rampart Street to Bayou Road

Rampart Street was the original "back wall" of the city. The corner of Rampart and Esplanade was the site of *Fort St. John*, which along with the "rampart" was built during the Spanish era.

From Rampart Street on, development was slower as plantation owners often demanded higher prices before they would consider subdividing their property. *1240 Esplanade* is a three-bay brick American-style house with recessed entrance and cast-iron balcony. Note the cast-iron canopy supported by double iron brackets. In 1865, the year the Civil War ended, the house was bought by the founder of one of New Orleans' fine clothing stores, Leon Godchaux. When *St. Anna's Episcopal Church, 1313 Esplanade*, was founded in 1843, it occupied a site at Esplanade and the river, No. 5. It moved to this location in 1869, the present church being the second one to be built here.

The house at *1338-40* is a classic Creole cottage with real gallery. It was built by John Healy, who had purchased the lot at a sheriff's sale for $800, from plans done by architect Henry Howard. The mantels in each room cost $10 apiece, and in the backyard, there were 2,000-gallon cisterns with wooden covers and brass locks. Just a few years later, John Healy lost the house at a sheriff's sale, but his wife rescued the family honor by buying it back in 1862.

The *Jumonville-Gambino House, 1418 Esplanade*, was built shortly before the Civil War on a very large lot (by New Orleans standards): 96 x 128 feet. Note the iron picket fence with its graceful arched gateway.

An original Creole cottage, *1500 Esplanade* is over 150 years old. There was once a two-story brick kitchen behind. At *1519 Esplanade* is an American center-hall house, older than the Pontalbas on Jackson Square with beautiful interior detail.

Claiborne Avenue is where a drainage ditch was once dug to keep Esplanade from flooding every time it rained. This section of Claiborne Avenue is now covered by I-10.

The house at *1622 Esplanade* was built in the 1850s. The second owner added a wine cellar. The house at *1631 Esplanade* once belonged to Gen. P. G. T. Beauregard, C.S.A., who died here in 1895. Before the Civil War, he and his wife lived at 1028 Esplanade while he was assigned to supervise repairs on the Mint. Beauregard was a West Point graduate and an engineer. *The Dufour-Baldwin House, 1707 Esplanade,* is one of the most important residences, architecturally, in the city. It was designed by architect Henry Howard, and built just before the Civil War, an excellent example of late Classic style. It was first owned by Cyprien Dufour, one-time district attorney of Orleans Parish. Later it was purchased by Albert Baldwin, who moved to New Orleans from Massachusetts to make a success in both banking and hardware. He filled this beautiful home with 13 children.

The *1800 block* was not developed until the 1870s. The house at *1824* is a typical "Esplanade Ridge" house which somehow blends a late Classic American style with a geometric Italianate facade. One of architect Henry Howard's last designs, *1914 Esplanade*, is a Victorian version of Italianate, built in 1884. By the time the house changed hands in 1912, the act of sale included lighting fixtures, mirrors, and bathtubs.

In the *2200 block*, we find one of the numerous triangular parks formed when Esplanade cut across earlier routes. *Gayarre Park*, named for a New Orleans historian, was embellished with a statue on an elaborate terra-cotta base from the World's Fair and Exposition of 1884, held in what is now Audubon Park.

The *2300 block* furnishes an interesting contrast in architectural styles. The building encompassing *2325-27-29-31 Esplanade* is a marvelous Creole cottage row, while *2337* and *2341* are classic late-19th-century shotgun houses. Note the lovely cast-iron canopies, held by double iron brackets.

From Bayou Road to Moss Street

The *2400 block* is where Bayou Road crosses Esplanade. Before the Esplanade was developed, this block was the site of the Old Indian Market. The Houmas Indians camped here, on the portage between Bayou St. John and the Mississippi. They were joined by the group of laborers who arrived with Bienville to build the city. This area was later called Place Bretonne. There was a public market in the area until after World War II.

The Dunbar house at *2453 Esplanade* was once one of a pair belonging to the same family, built about 1874. Mansard-roofed mansions were a rarity in New Orleans at this time. The interior is graced with a beautiful staircase. The lot at *2522 Esplanade* was purchased in 1873 by Capt. John W. Tobin, a prominent New Orleans steamboat owner, who built his family home and surrounded it with beautifully landscaped grounds (which are now unfortunately covered with concrete). *2936 Esplanade* is a Gothic raised cottage, a most unusual building style in New Orleans. A great place to break your trip, the *Whole Foods Market, 3135 Esplanade*, is an excellent natural-foods grocery and delicatessen. Stop for a snack or to buy a picnic lunch to take to the park or the lakefront. Tuesday is Senior Citizen's Day, when those who qualify are given a 10 percent discount. The house at *3330 Esplanade* is a Creole cottage with gallery, which was moved to this site in the 1870s and recently restored. It was probably built in the 1830s by a German carpenter, Joseph Klar.

The *3400 block* was the place where the cars of the New Orleans City Railroad turned around to begin their return trip to town. It is presently occupied by the *Cabrini High School*, which was built in 1905 as the *Sacred Heart Orphan Asylum*, and *Our Lady of the Rosary Church*, built in 1924. Across the way is *St. Louis No. 3 Cemetery*, designed in 1854. When the land for the cemetery was surveyed, it was measured as "two arpents wide by 14 arpents deep for one and 16 for the other arpent." In the cemetery are tombs of the Hellenic Orthodox Community, of Valcour Aime, the prince of Louisiana plantation owners, who died just after the Civil War. The famous architect James Gallier, Sr., and his wife were drowned at sea when the *Evening Star*, a ship carrying the Galliers and an opera company on its way to sing in New Orleans, foundered in a storm off the coast of Georgia. The striking cenotaph that you see was done by their son, the equally well known architect, James Gallier, Jr.

From Moss Street to City Park

Turn left onto Moss Street and follow along as it winds its way down the banks of Bayou St. John. The street was originally called Port Street until a city ordinance changed the name in 1894. Built about 1784, *1300 Moss St.* is a structure from the Spanish period. It is known locally as the *Spanish Customs House*. An excellent example of French West Indian architecture, it sits on the corner of Grand Route St. John, which was the original portage from Bayou St. John to the river.

The house at *1342 Moss St.* shows the Greek Revival influence on

Classic columns of the Pitot House

Cecilia Casrill Dartez

the bayou. This house, dating from 1834, is now the rectory of the *Our Lady of Rosary Catholic Church* (which you drove past on Esplanade). *1440 Moss St.* was the home of the second mayor of New Orleans, James Pitot, who bought the house in 1810. It was built in 1799 on the spot where the Catholic school now stands and was moved in 1964 by a preservationist group. The West Indies-style cottage at *924 Moss St.* has been looking out on the bayou since before 1800.

Turn right at Orleans Avenue and cross the bayou. Then turn right again and follow Bayou St. John back to the entrance to City Park, where an excellent equestrian statue of Gen. P. G. T. Beauregard will greet you. Turn left and enter the park. Straight ahead, at the end of the lovely mall, you will see the New Orleans Museum of Art.

City Park was originally the *Allard Plantation*, a working plantation at the time the Esplanade was being developed. M. Allard was a delightful gentleman, schooled in France, who unfortunately never learned how to manage money. His land was purchased by John McDonogh, the philanthropist for whom many of New Orleans' public schools were named, who left it to the cities of New Orleans and Baltimore. New Orleans bought out Baltimore's share so that the park could be developed at the end of the 19th century. The park is noted for its huge oak trees, most over 100 years old, under which many famous duels are said to have been fought. There was, also, a cafe where Esplanade meets the bayou which served coffee to groups of gentlemen before they crossed over the bayou to fight their duels under the spreading oaks. The beautiful lagoon, which is available for fishing and pedal boating, was originally part of Bayou Metairie. The park also offers excellent golfing and tennis facilities (see SPORTS). Note the New Orleans Museum of Art (see VISUAL ARTS). *Tivoli Gardens*, once located on Bayou St. John, was for many years New Orleans' finest park.

From City Park to the Spanish Fort

As you leave the park, bid General Beauregard goodbye and turn left onto Wisner Boulevard. *Bayou St. John*, bordered by a lovely grassy area perfect for badminton, frisbees, and picnics, will be on your right. Since this bayou has no banks built up over centuries as most streams do, it is believed to be the result of an ancient geological fault in the earth. This is also true of Chef Menteur, a narrow waterway at the northwest end of Lake Pontchartrain.

Today, as you drive Wisner Boulevard, note the *Louisiana State University Dental School* across the bayou at DeSaix Boulevard, and the *Hellenic Orthodox Center* across the bayou at Robert E. Lee Boulevard.

The *Spanish Fort* area is on the banks of Bayou St. John, on Wisner Boulevard just after you cross Robert E. Lee Boulevard. It was originally called *Fort San Juan* and was built by the Spanish in 1769. General Jackson stationed a small garrison there before the Battle of New Orleans, to protect the city from British ships that had found their way into Lake Pontchartrain. By 1823, the land was sold to a Mr. Elkins who built New Orleans' *first Pontchartrain Hotel* there. The present-day very elegant hotel by that name is on St. Charles Avenue (see LODGING). By 1874, the railroad had been built which connected the Spanish Fort to the city. It became the city's most popular resort. Oscar Wilde lectured here in the 1880s. In the 1930s, the land from the fort out to the lakefront was "reclaimed." Spanish Fort lost its important location on the shores of the lake, while the area around it turned into a dignified residential neighborhood.

Along Lake Pontchartrain

Turn left onto Lakeshore Drive. In the 1930s, the State Legislature gave the go-ahead to a plan for the development of the New Orleans lakefront. Under the supervision of the Orleans Levee Board, an important group in this lowland city, a seawall was built 3,000 feet out in the lake and the area behind it, where you are now riding, was filled in. In this way, the city, which had always been short of dry land, acquired 2,000 brand-new acres. The area bordering the lake has been maintained through the years as a beautiful five-and-a-half-mile-long park for the enjoyment of all New Orleanians.

The *Mardi Gras Fountain*, sometimes lit at night with green, gold, and purple lights, is a landmark for anyone taking a relaxing evening sail on Lake Pontchartrain. Crests of the Carnival krewes form a circular wall around the fountain. Concerts and sunrise religious services are held here from time to time.

The Coast Guard Lighthouse, a favorite landmark in New Orleans, was originally set well out into the lake, but when the land was reclaimed, so was the lighthouse. Lake Pontchartrain, although very large (40 by 25 miles), is very shallow (approximate average depth is 15 feet) and it becomes very rough very quickly during a storm. The Coast Guard rescue boats have been a welcome sight to sailors in trouble.

West End

Lakeshore Drive ends at West End. West End was originally a large wooden platform built by the city out over the lake in 1871.

Constructed on this platform were a hotel, a restaurant, a bandstand, a pavilion, and even a scenic railway with a "tunnel of love" at one end! The trip from the city to West End was made by train, following the route of the present I-10, the tracks running along the edge of the New Basin Canal. It was at West End that the first movie was shown in the New Orleans area. Since that time, the land has been reclaimed from the lake, and the filled area has become a public park. During World War I, it was the site of an army training camp. Today, it is surrounded by seafood restaurants (see DINING), yacht harbors, and two of the city's yacht clubs, the *Southern Yacht Club*, one of the nation's oldest and best-known yacht clubs, and the *New Orleans Yacht Club*.

From West End to Cemeteries

Leaving West End retrace your route on Lakeshore Drive to Canal Boulevard. Turn right on Canal Boulevard and proceed to City Park Avenue.

At this intersection you will see a number of New Orleans cemeteries. At one time there were 14 cemeteries clustered around the "end" of Canal Street. In the early days of French New Orleans, the dead were buried along the riverbank. When the Spanish took possession of the colony, they brought with them the custom adopted in their other colonies of burying above the ground and enclosing the cemetery with a wall into which vaults were built. These came to be referred to as "oven vaults." The typical New Orleans tomb, which looks like a small house, is simply a number of vaults, one above the other. During the last century, some local fraternal and professional organizations have built large tombs to accommodate their members. One of the best examples is the *Volunteer Firefighters Memorial* at *Greenwood Cemetery*. Look for it as you **turn right onto City Park Avenue/Metairie Road.**

Turn right again on to the I-10 Service Road, bear left under I-10 itself, and continue on to the gates of Metairie Cemetery. This cemetery was founded in 1872 on the site of the *Old Metairie Jockey Club*, for years a popular racecourse. It is one of the most interesting and impressive cemeteries in the country, well worth some time to explore. Gen. P. G. T. Beauregard, whose statue you saw at the gate to City Park, is buried in the Army of Tennessee tomb. The most impressive monument in the cemetery, right in front, is the Moriarity tomb. New Orleans children for generations have called the four figures standing at the base "Faith, Hope, and Charity, and Mrs. Moriarity."

Longue Vue Gardens

Turn left onto the I-10 Service Road as you leave Metairie Cemetery, and go to the traffic light at the corner of Metairie Road. If you choose to visit Longue Vue Gardens during this tour, turn right, drive along Metairie Road alongside the cemetery (on the other side of the road is the golf course of the New Orleans Country Club) past three residential streets. You will then be at the corner of Bamboo Road, where you turn left and drive about half a block to the entrance to Longue Vue Gardens, a delightful oasis in the midst of the city (see SIGHTS).

At this point you have a choice to make. **If you are pressed for time, you may want to drive onto I-10 at Metairie Road and return quickly to your downtown hotel.** However, if you prefer a more leisurely route, we suggest that you **follow Metairie Road, crossing once more under I-10, and turn right onto Canal Street.** This wide, treelined thoroughfare will bring you past the cemeteries, through the heart of the Mid-City neighborhood, and back to the river and the business section.

Consider breaking your trip when you reach the intersection of Canal Street and Carrollton Avenue. If you turn left for just half a block and look carefully, you will see *Angelo Brocato's* ice-cream parlor. Inside this rather plain looking establishment is served some of the best ice cream in the city of New Orleans! There is wonderful Italian coffee to go with it (see DINING). After this break continue on Canal Street to your in-city destination.

ST. CHARLES DRIVING OR STREETCAR TOUR

Begin at Canal Street and St. Charles Street

St. Charles Avenue is bordered with old mansions and sights of historical interest, as well as two universities, a college, hotels, restaurants, shops, and parks. Relax and enjoy a leisurely drive from Canal Street up St. Charles to Carrollton Avenue. From Carrollton you can make a return trip on the St. Charles streetcar or, if driving, return to the Central Business District via Magazine Street. Those tourists who would rather "leave the driving to us" can board the streetcar (NEVER called a trolley in New Orleans) at the corner of Canal Street and St. Charles and enjoy the sights while swaying along on the track between the oak trees. See NEW ORLEANS AREA MAP.

Through Faubourg St. Mary/ The Central Business District

As you ride through the *Central Business District* of St. Charles Street between Canal and Lee Circle you will be in the *Faubourg St. Mary*, the first area of the city to be built by the Americans. Many of the original buildings are being restored and turned into elegant offices. You will cross Poydras Street, the modern masterpiece in the midst of the old faubourg. In the next block, at *545 St. Charles St.*, be sure to notice *Gallier Hall*, the Americans' answer to the Cabildo (the old government building on Jackson Square). Across from Gallier Hall is *Lafayette Square*, named for the French Revolutionary War general who later visited New Orleans. You are now approaching Lee Circle, at which point St. Charles Avenue officially begins.

From Lee Circle to Jackson Avenue

Lee Circle, the centerpiece of New Orleans' first "subdivision," was originally designed to accommodate a merry-go-round which never materialized. Union troops used it as a campground during the Civil War. A bronze 16½-foot statue of Robert E. Lee, weighing 7,000 pounds, stands atop a Doric column, facing north (never to turn its back on the enemy). The statue, executed by New York sculptor Alexander Doyle, was erected in 1884. During Mardi Gras, the circle is surrounded by a grandstand from which many Golden Age groups and other citizens have reserved seating to view the parades.

To continue our tour on the circle, *920 St. Charles* is the *Young Men's Christian Association*, which offers a wide variety of community facilities (see SPORTS and LODGING). At *615 Howard Ave.* will be the new Odgen Museum of Southern Art.

To the right is *K&B Plaza* at *1000 St. Charles*. The building, one of the finest modern structures in the city, was designed by Skidmore, Owings, and Merrill. The plaza surrounding the building is now a showcase for modern sculpture. The large water sculpture, *New Orleans as the Crescent City*, is by Isamu Noguchi, the renowned Japanese sculptor (see VISUAL ARTS).

The small building just across the street from the K&B Plaza is the only survivor of the private residences which bordered the circle in the late 1880s. Note the mansard roof and the elegant Italianate doorway.

Look to your right just before you pass under the I-10 bridge; in the distance is the glittering gold-leaf onion dome of *St. John the Baptist Church*, dating from 1871.

The *Jerusalem Temple, 1137 St. Charles*, built in 1916, is the home of the ancient Arabic Order Nobles of the Mystic Shrine, who are known for their support of the children's hospitals throughout the country.

St. Charles Avenue Shopping District

The section of St. Charles between the 1100 block and Jackson Avenue is largely commercial and contains many interesting shops and restaurants, all of which are described in greater detail in shopping and dining sections of this book.

You are now crossing streets named for the nine Muses of Greek mythology: Polymnia, Euterpe, Terpsichore, Melpomene, Thalia, Erato, Clio, Calliope, and Urania (the last no longer crosses St. Charles).

On the left at *1924 St. Charles* is the *Zion Lutheran Church*, built in 1871 in neo-Gothic design, the oldest church on the Avenue. The interior boasts a pressed-metal ceiling and tall flying buttresses adorn the exterior.

At *2031 St. Charles* is the *Pontchartrain Hotel*, neo-Spanish in style and typical of the early 20th century. It is one of the finest privately owned hotels in the country (see LODGING).

The Garden District

St. Charles Avenue from Jackson Avenue to Jena Street is part of the Historic Garden District of New Orleans, originally in the city of Lafayette. It is historically important as the main artery of the American sector of the city.

At *2265 St. Charles* is a home designed by Gallier and Turpin about 1856. This Greek revival home was originally the *Headquarters of the Episcopal Diocese of Louisiana*. The home with its beautiful side yard and patio has been faithfully restored and is a historical landmark.

A fine example of early Garden District style is *2336 St. Charles*. This Louisiana cottage, built in 1854, shows the Greek Revival influence of antebellum New Orleans.

Now a small hotel, *2427 St. Charles* is Queen Anne-Georgian Revival style and was built about 1890. This was the work of architect George Denegre.

Notice the tower on the asymmetrical home at *2503 St. Charles*, designed by Thomas Sully in Queen Anne style.

At *2525 St. Charles* is another beautifully preserved Queen Anne home by Thomas Sully, built about 1890 around a small cottage that had originally occupied the site.

Historically, *2701 St. Charles*, the *Grima House*, is one of the most important homes on the Avenue because of the detailing, ornamentation, interesting service wings, and outbuildings. It was built about 1850 for the Grima family and remodeled in the 1890s.

The *Christ Church Cathedral*, 2900 block of St. Charles, is the diocesan seat of the Episcopal Bishop of Louisiana, and was built in 1886. The English Gothic cathedral lost its steeple in the devastating hurricane of 1915. There are particularly beautiful stained-glass windows in both the main church and the chapel.

The residence at *3029 St. Charles* was home of the German Consul before World War II. It was built in 1880 in late Italianate style with Roman Doric columns.

Louisiana Avenue and St. Charles is an interesting solution to a space problem. *Bultman's Funeral Home* is made of three houses put together. Directly behind Bultman's is an old plantation house, now carefully restored.

Bouligny from Louisiana Avenue to Jefferson Avenue

To the left, one block off St. Charles, just past Louisiana Avenue, are the large buildings of *Touro Infirmary, 1401 Foucher St.* This private institution, under Jewish management, was founded in 1840, and moved to the present location in 1882. The hospital is famous as the site of the first heart and vascular surgery in the world, performed by the well-known Dr. Rudolph Matas.

At *3700 St. Charles* is *St. Charles General Hospital*, a proprietary institution.

The *Unity Temple*, designed by Leonard Spangenberg, a disciple of Frank Lloyd Wright, is at *3722 St. Charles Ave.* The circular design symbolizes eternity.

The Columns, 3811 St. Charles, was built in 1883 by a merchant prince who dealt in tobacco. It is a popular tourist attraction because *Pretty Baby* was filmed here. The home has a magnificent staircase with a stained-glass skylight. The Columns truly represents the spirit of opulence. For a time a boarding house, now a hotel, bar, and restaurant, this spot has become a favorite of sightseers to New Orleans.

At *3900 St. Charles Ave.*, the *Rayne Memorial Methodist Church*, built in 1875, is a memorial to a son killed at the Battle of Chancellorsville during the Civil War. Note the intricately carved brickwork and the graceful steeple, which is lit at night. The church is a fine example of Gothic Revival architecture.

The residences at *4010, 4020, 4114 St. Charles* were all done by the architectural firm of Sully and Toledano, who were responsible for more mansions on the Avenue than any other firm.

The home at *4101 St. Charles* was designed by Victor Bruno, another admirer of Frank Lloyd Wright.

On the left at the intersection of St. Charles and General Pershing Street is the *Touro Synagogue*, home of the oldest Jewish congregation in the Mississippi Valley. Named for Judah Touro, a merchant and hero of the Battle of New Orleans, it was designed in Byzantine style by architect Emil Weil, and consecrated in 1909. Centered in the dome is a blue stained glass, representing the Heaven of Heavens.

Across the Avenue, on the right, is the *First Baptist Church*, constructed in neo-California Mission style and dedicated in 1954.

At the crossing of *Napoleon Avenue* look left down the broad avenue for a vista toward the *Mississippi River*.

The Academy of the Sacred Heart is located at *4521 St. Charles*. Also known as "The Rosary," the religious order of the Sacred Heart, founded in France, came to New Orleans to educate young ladies. The main portion of this private girls' school was erected in 1899. Notice the lovely iron gates, circular drive, and beautiful fountain. The nuns established their first school in New Orleans in 1887 in the French Quarter. There is a feeling of quiet elegance when one steps within the Avenue gates. Architects Owen and Diboll created a design which even today reflects peace.

A 1906 Romanesque house at *4534 St. Charles* was built for the Mason-Smith family.

St. George's Episcopal Church is located at *4600 St. Charles*. When the congregation was first organized in 1859, this site was in the City of Jefferson.

The Georgian Revival *Schinak House* at *4631 St. Charles* is noted for the "gooseneck" railings on the upper galleries. The house was the *Japanese Consulate* from the early 1930s until December 7, 1941. On that day, all the private papers of the consulate were frantically thrown from an upstairs window into a bonfire burning in the driveway.

The nationally famous New Orleans architect H. H. Richardson was well known for his revival of the medieval Romanesque style. The *Brown House* at *4717 St. Charles* was designed by Favrot and Livaudais, after the style of Richardson, in 1902 for Mr. Perry Brown as a gift to his bride. He wanted her to have the largest and finest home on the Avenue. Note the marble steps, rounded arches, and detailed carving.

The *Hernandez House* at *4803 St. Charles* was moved forward from the back of the lot and restored. It is listed on the National Register of

Historic Places. Note the three-story tower and the mansard roof. The house was originally owned by Joseph Hernandez, president of the New Orleans and Carrollton Railroad, now the St. Charles streetcar line.

The *Orleans Club*, at *5005 St. Charles*, one of New Orleans' best-known women's organizations, is housed in this elegant building which was built in 1868 by Col. William Wynn as a wedding present for his daughter. Note the beautiful ironwork.

The Milton H. Latter Memorial Library, 5100 St. Charles, was donated to the city by Mr. and Mrs. Latter after their son was killed in World War II. The house was built in 1907, and was at one time the home of silent-film star Marguerite Clark, who became Mrs. Harry Williams of New Orleans. There are interesting frescoes on the ceilings of the downstairs rooms.

De La Salle School, 5300 St. Charles, formerly a private boys' school run by the Christian Brothers, is built on the site of the first black university in New Orleans. The parochial school is now coed.

At *5342 St. Charles* is the *Jewish Community Center*, a recreational learning center and club with family and neighborhood memberships. It was originally the site of *Jewish Orphans Home*. This building was designed by Curtis and Davis, with sculpture by Emery.

The 5400 Block to the University Section

On your right, the *5500 block, Danneel Park*, was given to the city by a reclusive but very successful cotton merchant, in memory of his parents. Generations of New Orleanians have spent their toddler years playing in Danneel Park.

The beautiful stone mansion at *5531 St. Charles* was built in 1912 for E. V. Benjamin in Italian Renaissance style. Notice the stone rail around the roof and the Ionic double columns.

The house at *5705 St. Charles* is a copy of "*Tara*," Scarlett O'Hara's home in *Gone with the Wind*, built in 1941 by George Palmer.

Number *5718 St. Charles*, built about 1890, is one of the finest Queen Anne houses in New Orleans.

The residences at *5800 and 5824 St. Charles* are a pair of Louisiana raised cottages, designed to protect against flooding. They are built of native cypress and date back to the 1860s, when this part of the Avenue was part of the town of Hurstville.

The home at *5809 St. Charles* is known as the *Wedding Cake House*, a fine white frame Victorian home with beautiful crystal leaded doors, elaborate layered trim, and a hand-carved dark wood interior.

Rosa Park is to the right, *Eleonore Street* to the left. Rosa Park was subdivided by two New Orleanians in 1891. Take a short drive around the circle of old Victorian homes. Magnolia trees line the center neutral ground.

St. Charles Presbyterian Church, 5900 block, is a Gothic landmark on the Avenue.

One of the most perfect Georgian Revival houses in the South, *6000 St. Charles* was designed by architect Thomas Sully.

At *6145 St. Charles* this stone Italian villa was built around 1920. A swimming pool and tennis court were added when the house had major renovations. The home and garden now cover two Avenue lots.

Temple Sinai stands on Calhoun and the Avenue, a modern interpretation of the Byzantine-style mosques of Constantinople. This is the first Reform Congregation in New Orleans. This temple was dedicated in 1928; the chapel and an addition were added in 1970. Beautiful needlepoint is displayed in the chapel.

The *Round Table Club, 6330 St. Charles*, was founded in 1902 by a group of men particularly interested in art, literature, and science. Many speakers of international note have lectured here.

The University Section/Uptown

On the right, *Loyola University*, which was established in 1911, occupies a 14-acre site. Calhoun and St. Charles mark the beginning of the Loyola University campus. It's easy to see why this uptown section of town is called the University Section. Operated by the priests of the Society of Jesus (S.J.s as they are called in New Orleans) this co-educational university's land extends back to Freret Street. The main building is *Marquette Hall*. The faculty home, *Thomas Hall*, is Tudor-Gothic red brick with terra-cotta trim.

Holy Name of Jesus Church is a Stone-Tudor Gothic, built in 1914 and inspired by Canterbury Cathedral. The Gothic interior is breathtaking with white marble floors, side, and center altars. Designed by DeBuys, Churchill and Labouisse, this church is a namesake of the mission church of the Jesuit priests.

Tulane University, next door to Loyola, was originally the Medical College of Louisiana, founded in 1834. The university adopted its present name in 1883, after a large bequest from Paul Tulane, a New Jersey-born philanthropist of French Huguenot background, who became a very successful New Orleans merchant. The buildings follow the Romanesque architectural style of Henry Richardson. The Medical School of Tulane University is located in downtown New Orleans.

Audubon Zoological Garden and Zoo is across the street from the universities. Handsome old oak trees shade the front section of Audubon Zoological Garden, once the 250-acre *Foucher Plantation* and *De Bore Estate*. Sugar was first granulated on the plantation in 1794. Etienne De Bore, mayor of New Orleans after the Louisiana Purchase, made Louisiana the center of sugarcane processing.

Stroll along the winding lagoon and enjoy watching the ducks being fed by toddlers under the watchful eyes of young matrons. Continue to the left of the lagoon and pass the Bandstand and Magazine Street. The entrance to the world-famous zoo is located one-half mile from the Avenue.

Audubon Park was the site of the World's Industrial and Cotton Centennial Exposition held in 1884-85.

Audubon Place is a privately owned street maintaining its own security guard at the front gate. Some call this "millionaires' row." Note the palm trees on the neutral ground. The large white columned home of the president of Tulane University is on the left side. The house is named after original owner Samuel Zemurry, co-owner of Cuyamel Fruit Company who gave millions to Tulane University.

On the right is *Number 1 Audubon Place*, neo-Italianate home; notice the dollhouse in the front garden.

St. Charles Baptist Church is located at Broadway and St. Charles. Dedicated in 1926, the bell tower and church reflect the California Mission style and Spanish Colonial style.

The Loyola Law School occupies the next two blocks on the left (the former Dominican College). The Administration building was designed by William Fitzner in the Italianate style. Six Dominican nuns from Ireland purchased this property at auction in 1863 for approximately $10,000. Their purpose was to found a school for Catholic girls in New Orleans. It was purchased by Loyola in the late 20th century to serve as an extension of the campus.

Across from the former Dominican College at Broadway and St. Charles, notice the stone and timber home with dollhouse replica in the side yard.

An unusual Steamboat Gothic style home, at *7717 St. Charles*, was built around 1880. This section was then within the town limits of Carrollton. Notice the roof and turret, which must be a good spot for viewing the Mississippi River just on the other side of the levee.

Riverbend Shops

St. Charles Avenue ends at Carrollton Avenue. Straight ahead is the levee, with the Mississippi River right on the other side. The superstructures of large ships are often visible as the ships move up- and downriver.

Where St. Charles Avenue meets Carrollton Avenue at the levee, there is the triangular area of *Riverbend* bounded by Carrollton Avenue, Dante Street, and the levee. This shopping neighborhood houses everything from ice-cream shops to nationally known jewelry designers. We recommend that you allow time to wander through this collection of interesting shops (see SHOPPING).

The Streetcar Return

If you are riding the streetcar, you can ride into Carrollton, the end of the line, or return directly from Riverbend via the streetcar to your downtown destination.

Driving Back via Magazine Street

If you are ready to resume your driving tour, **turn left going south in the direction of Canal Street, parallel to St. Charles Avenue on the street just next to the levee. This is Leake Avenue.** Continue on Leake, past the *Headquarters of the U.S. Army Corps of Engineers* (who are responsible for maintaining the levee system throughout the Mississippi Valley) and you will soon arrive at *Uptown Square* on your left, a chic shopping center built to resemble a medieval town (see SHOPPING).

Again, **continue on Leake, which will bend to the left through Audubon Park, following the contour of the river. Leake becomes Magazine Street when it crosses Broadway.**

Magazine Street is one of the city's most unusual streets, a potpourri of old and new, junk and treasure. The name comes from the French word *magasin*, which means store—the first store on the American side of Canal Street was at Magazine Street's beginning point. You will see that the name still applies, for as you drive you will pass glass, china, brass, tennis, flower, shoe, book, and antique shops, as well as neighborhood eating spots, art galleries, bakeries, and secondhand clothing stores. Many of the shops are housed in Victorian shotgun cottages which are interesting in their own right (see SHOPPING).

When you drive Magazine Street from the levee, through Audubon Park, you will see the golf course and a jogger's path to your left and the entrance to the *Audubon Zoological Garden,* the tennis courts, and the stables to your right. Two blocks farther on, at the corner of Henry Clay Avenue, you will pass the brick-walled monastery of the *Poor Clares,* a cloistered order of Roman Catholic nuns.

Four blocks farther on, at Nashville Avenue, you will find a good snacking place, *Chez Nous Charcuterie, 5701 Magazine*. At the corner of Jefferson Avenue, you will see, on your right, the *Poydras Home* (for Protestant ladies).

Continue down Magazine Street, stopping to browse when the spirit moves you. **You will cross Napoleon, Louisiana, Washington, and Jackson avenues. Shortly thereafter, signs will tell you to bear left and you will find yourself on Camp Street, driving through Coliseum Square.** Once the beginning of the Garden District and the showplace of the City of Lafayette, it is now being restored.

As you drive under the Crescent City Connection twin-span bridge, you will find yourself back in the downtown area, passing the impressive-looking brownstone building which houses the *Confederate Museum, 929 Camp St*. The *Contemporary Arts Center, 900 Camp St.*, one of the busiest creative spots in town, will be on your right, and two blocks farther on, also on your right, the gray plaster serenity of old *St. Patrick's Church, 724 Camp St.*, where Mass is still said in Latin each Sunday.

Just opposite *Lafayette Square*, the modern world begins with the *Fifth Circuit Court of Appeals, 600 Camp St.*, and the *Hale Boggs Building, 500 Camp St*. Be sure to note the interesting modern sculptures (see VISUAL ARTS). **Cross busy Poydras Street and proceed to your hotel.**

ONE-DAY EXCURSIONS

Life on a South Louisiana sugar plantation before the Civil War probably came as close as anything America ever had to life in a small European kingdom. The plantation owner was truly a king, having absolute decision making power over family, house servants, and field hands. Fortunes fluctuated frequently, depending on the cane crop, and since that crop depended on the weather and the spring flood stage of the Mississippi River, the plantation owners had to have a large streak of gambler's instinct in their makeup.

The homes they built reflected this—no "adding on" as they could afford it here! Rather, the homes were built with all the grandeur and amenities that were available at the time, were maintained by well-trained house servants, and were serviced by river packets that regularly stopped at their private landings.

Some of these houses have "gone into the Mississippi," as that capricious river periodically changed its course. Some have burned or, sadly, been abandoned during hard times and fallen victim to neglect and vandalism. There are a number, however, which have been lovingly restored and are now open to the public. Be sure to see one or more of them while visiting New Orleans.

If you must choose only one, we recommend a drive across the Huey Long Bridge to the West Bank, then upriver for lunch and a tour of Oak Alley at Vacherie, LA (New Orleans number; 523-4351). If you can allow a whole day, visit one or two more. An overnight stay at *Nottoway,* just below Baton Rouge at White Castle, LA, or at *Rosedown,* just above Baton Rouge in St. Francisville, LA, is a delightful treat. Following are a number of possible excursions.

PLANTATIONS ON THE MISSISSIPPI THE WEST BANK

(Four to Six Hours)

To Oak Alley

Take US 90 (South Claiborne Avenue, which becomes Jefferson Highway as it crosses the parish line) to the Huey Long Bridge. Cross the bridge and continue 13 miles on US 90 West to Boutte, then four miles farther to La. 3127. Turn right on Highway 3127, driving through the cane fields for about seven miles to La. 640. Turn right again to La. 18, River Road. You can't miss River Road; the levee will block your way. Turn left for about 15 winding miles, passing Evergreen Plantation and the towns of Edgard and Vacherie. Five and one-half miles past the Lutcher Ferry Landing, you will come to Oak Alley. Don't miss the first breathtaking view as you round the last curve on River Road. Then turn left into the grounds and enjoy.

Oak Alley's glory is the double line of 28 live oaks, planted in the early 1700s, which lead from the levee to the main house. This is undoubtedly one of the most spectacular vistas on the Mississippi. The house, a National Historic Landmark, was built in the early 1800s by Jacques Roman, a wealthy French planter, for his bride. It is a prime example of the opulent, antebellum lifestyle that existed along the Mississippi.

Lunch is served in an old cottage behind the main house. The food is authentic Creole and the price is reasonable. There are also cottages for overnight visitors, but be sure to make reservations ahead of time. Tours are daily, 9 am-5 pm, except Thanksgiving, Christmas, and New Year's Day. *CHG*. For information, write: Oak Alley Foundation, 3645 Hwy. 18, Vacherie, LA 70090. www.louisianatravel.com/oak.alley. Call 1-800-442-5539.

Laura: A Creole Plantation

Follow same directions to Oak Alley; however, when you come to the town of Vacherie (stay on River Road), continue till you see the Laura Plantation sign on your left.

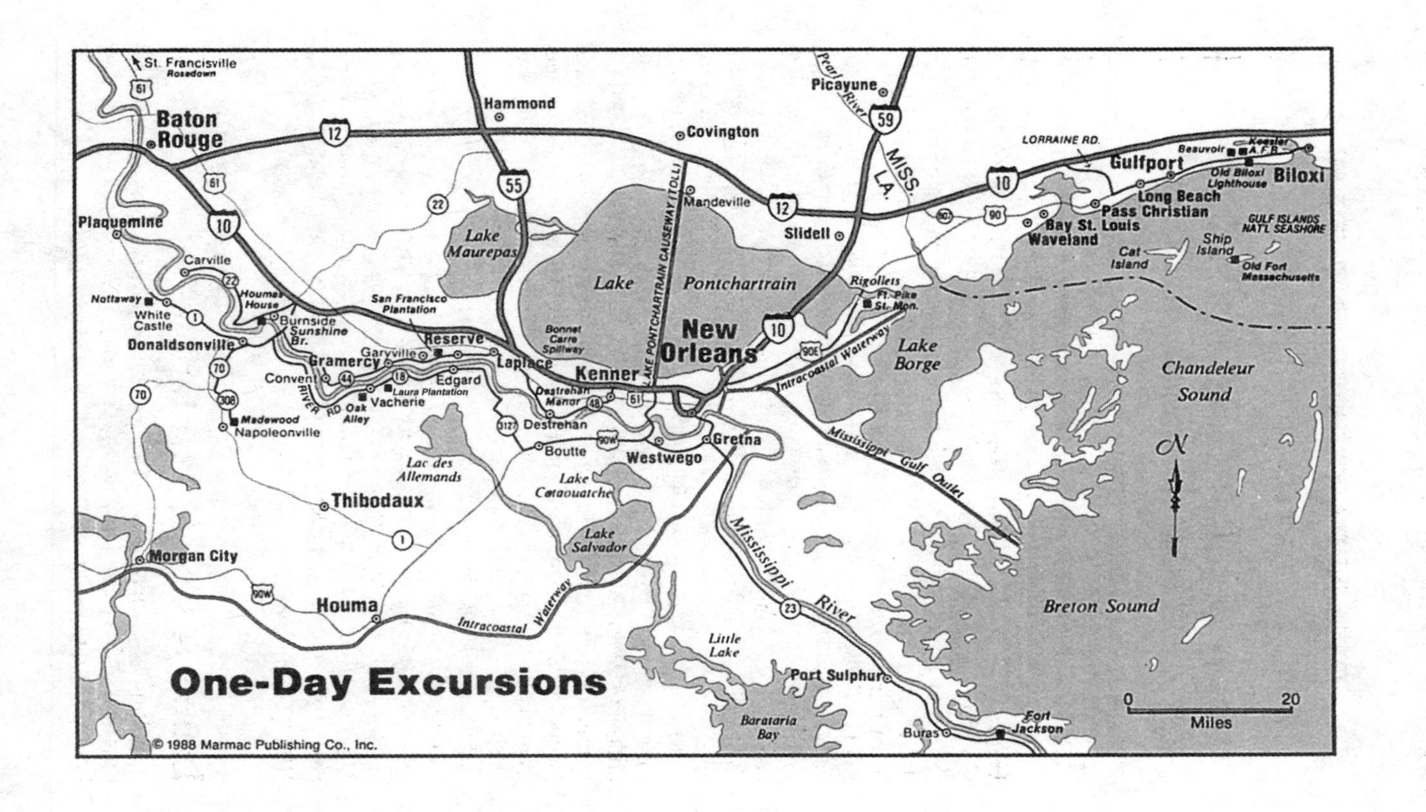

One-Day Excursions

Built in 1805, *Laura* has a total of 12 National Register buildings, including slave cabins where the "Br'er Rabbit" tales were recorded. Tours based on "Laura's Memoirs" detail 250 years of the lives of Creole plantation owners, women, children, and slaves. Laura is open daily, 9 am-5 pm. For information, write: Laura, 2247 La. Hwy. 18, Vacherie, LA 70090. Call 225-265-7690. www.lauraplantation.com.

Nottoway

As you leave Oak Alley, turn left onto River Road, La. 18, traveling 15 miles to the Sunshine Bridge junction, then another 15 miles on La. 1 through Donaldsonville to White Castle. Just past White Castle, you will reach *Nottoway*, built by Virginians but designed by architect Henry Howard of New Orleans. Nottoway is the largest plantation house in the South, tall enough to have a river view over the levee. Tours are well conducted and informative. CHG.

A couple can stay overnight and be awakened next morning to coffee, juice, and sweet potato biscuits. A leisurely champagne brunch follows. Lunch and dinner are also available to visitors in the ground-floor dining room. For reservations and tour information, call 504-346-8263.

After touring Nottoway, you must decide, depending on your time limit, whether to visit one more wonderful house or return to New Orleans. **If you must head for the city, turn right on River Road, cross the Sunshine Bridge, and follow the signs to I-10 East and, then, to New Orleans. You can also cross the river by taking the free ferry from White Castle to Carville. From Carville, follow River Road to the Sunshine Bridge, and proceed as marked to I-10 East into New Orleans.**

Madewood

If, as we hope, you would like to visit one more quality restoration, we suggest a pleasant 40-minute drive from Nottoway to *Madewood* plantation, on the banks of Bayou Lafourche. **Return to Donaldsonville on La. 1, turn right off the four-lane section onto La. 70, drive about five miles, then turn left onto La. 308, which follows Bayou Lafourche.** Madewood is on the Bayou at Napoleonville, LA.

Designed by Henry Howard, an Irish-American architect, and built by sugarcane planter Col. Thomas Pugh in 1846, the house has been superbly restored by the Marshall family. Period antique furnishings reflect lifestyles of the Old South's aristocracy. The National Historic Landmark is also a delightful bed and breakfast. The April 1999 issue of *National Geographic Traveler* rates Madewood in the top 55 of "Great Inns of the Southeast." CHG. For information, call 1-800-375-7151. www.madewood.com.

At the end of your tour, retrace your path to the Sunshine Bridge, then to I-10 East, and back to New Orleans.

A DAY ON THE EAST BANK

(Four to Six Hours)

There are three homes on the East Bank which are regularly open to the public and well worth seeing. They are *Houmas House*, just a few minutes upriver from the Sunshine Bridge, near Burnside, LA, *San Francisco*, and *Destrehan*, between the Sunshine Bridge and New Orleans.

Houmas House Plantation and Gardens

To begin your tour, leave New Orleans on I-10 West and travel along the edge of Lake Pontchartrain and across the Bonnet Carre Spillway to the Sunshine Bridge Exit, La. 22. Follow La. 22 left to River Road, and turn right, just a few miles to Houmas House. The levee will be on your right.

Houmas House, near Burnside, is especially interesting because both the original small cabin and the final Greek Revival home are beautifully restored. The house has a unique enclosed Widow's Walk on top, is furnished with fine antiques inside, and is surrounded by well-kept gardens and outbuildings. Guided tours are available. CHG. For information, call 504-473-7841, or the New Orleans number, 522-2262, or fax 504-474-0880.

Upon leaving Houmas House, turn left on River Road. At the intersection of La. 44 and La. 22, you will flnd the *Cabin*, a moderately priced restaurant housed in a former slave cabin of the Monroe Plantation. This is a good place to stop for lunch or a glass of iced tea. For information, call 504-473-3007.

San Francisco

Continue on River Road, La. 44, traveling downriver and passing the Sunshine Bridge. The levee will be on your right. Soon, you will pass *Tezcuco Plantation House*, an example of the raised cottage style, built in 1835. Eleven miles farther you will see *Jefferson College*, which was established in 1831 to educate the sons of the wealthy Mississippi

River planters. The imposing three-story Greek Revival building now belongs to the Jesuit order and is used as a men's retreat house. Another 15 miles and you will arrive at San Francisco.

San Francisco Plantation, dating from 1850, is located between Reserve and Garyville. Famous for its "Steamboat Gothic" exterior and its dramatic use of color in the interior, San Francisco is considered the most decorative house on the Mississippi. The interior is furnished with a collection of period antiques. Tours are available. *CHG*. For information, call 504-535-2341 or toll free 1-888-322-1756 or fax 504-535-5450. www.sanfranciscoplantation.org.

Ormond Plantation and Destrehan Manor

As you leave San Francisco, turn left on River Road, La. 44, into the town of La Place. The highway is forced to leave the river long enough to cross the *Bonnet Carre Spillway*, which was built to save the city of New Orleans from fearsome spring floods. When the gates of the spillway are opened, the water from the Mississippi is allowed to shortcut into Lake Pontchartrain and then into the Gulf of Mexico. The spillway was most recently opened during the Mississippi River floods of the Midwest in the mid-1990s. It was opened for approximately a month to ease the strain of rising river waters on the levee system. But, by 1998, Lake Pontchartrain had "come back" to its ideal brackish water salinity. So, you can now see brown pelicans and blue herons on the lake.

At La Place, bear right onto US 61, also known as Airline Highway. After crossing the spillway, you will arrive at a junction with La. 48; turn right and drive back to the levee. About four miles down the road, you will pass *Ormond Plantation*. Built during the 1780s, Ormond Plantation is one of the oldest and largest plantation houses. It is known for its Antique Doll Room and Antique Gun Room. A bed and breakfast is available in the manor itself. The plantation house is open daily for tours, 504-764-8544. *CHG*. Another mile or so and you will arrive at *Destrehan Manor*.

Built in 1787, Destrehan is an excellent example of the Greek Revival house. It was saved from ruin by a dramatic public outcry, which resulted in the formation of a foundation dedicated to restoration and maintenance of the structure. Insights into preservation techniques and processes are included in the tours. *CHG*. For information, write: P.O. Box 5, Destrehan, LA 70047 or call 504-764-9315, 504-524-5522.

Cajun music in the countryside *Louisiana State Tourist Commission*

There is an arts and crafts festival each fall at Destrehan Manor, complete with music, drama, good food, and boat rides up the Mississippi from New Orleans to the dock in front of the house.

Half an hour's drive from Destrehan will put you back in New Orleans. **Follow La. 48 to Williams Boulevard, La. 49, turn left to I-10 East, and return to downtown New Orleans.**

GLOBAL WILDLIFE CENTER

Louisiana's *Global Wildlife Center* was opened thanks to the progressive thinking of a Lafayette businessperson with high standards. There are 900 acres of free-roaming space for rare and not-so-rare hoofstock from around the globe. You can view all of these animals from within a tractor-drawn, canvas-topped wagon driven by a well-informed guide. The basic concepts for this center are conservation and education.

You will thoroughly enjoy the rare treat of observing more than 500 animals which represent 42 species from around the world—all roaming freely. Many of these animals are on the endangered species list, and some of them are even extinct in the wild. These animals all co-exist, grazing together, quite companionably. In fact, there are more hoof animals in the Global Wildlife Center than in all the Louisiana zoos combined.

Just a few of the animals that you will see from your covered wagon are Pere David's deer, emus, addax, gazelles, sitatunga antelope, Nile lechwe, giraffes, Indian zebra, and even American bison. There are no predators, or even overly aggressive animals. They will nibble on the food you can purchase at the *Safari Camp*.

Louisiana's Global Wildlife Center is only a 60-mile trip from downtown New Orleans, approximately one hour and 10 minutes (in off-peak traffic), and situated in the rolling hills of Tangipahoa Parish. **Take I-10 West to Causeway North, then take the Pontchartrain Causeway to the North Shore, then to Folsom. Follow La. 40 to the center's Safari Camp.**

The center is open daily from 10 am to sunset. There are even overnight accommodations and horseback riding. CHG. Call 504-796-3585.

MISSISSIPPI GULF COAST

The *Mississippi Gulf Coast* is a little over an hour's drive east on I-10 from New Orleans. There is a continuous public beach along the coast from Pass Christian to Biloxi. **Leave I-10 East at Pass Christian Exit and drive US 90 along the beach, enjoying one of the loveliest**

stretches of coast road in the United States. There are many fine old resort homes, strong survivors of numerous hurricanes, which preserve the traditional Gulf Coast ambience of gracious living.

At Biloxi, Mississippi, *Beauvoir,* the home of Jefferson Davis, president of the Confederate States of America, is open to the public. *CHG*. Other sites of interest in Biloxi are *Keesler Air Force Base* and the *Old Biloxi Lighthouse*, a landmark on the coast.

For real "sun and sand" people, there is an excursion boat which travels three times a day from Biloxi to *Ship Island*, one of a chain of barrier islands in the Mississippi Sound.

Motels and restaurants of all types are available along the coast. In fact, in the past few years, casinos have proliferated along the Mississippi Gulf Coast. So there are myriad places to visit, eat, and stay overnight. To obtain up-to-date listings of lodging, restaurants, entertainment, and shopping, stop at the Mississippi Visitor's Center just off the I-10 as you cross the state line from Louisiana.

OLD FORTS, ANYONE?

(Four Hours)

The Fort Pike State Commemorative Area is about 40 minutes from downtown New Orleans. **Take I-10 East to the US 90 East Exit and drive about 26 miles.** Fort Pike was begun in 1819 to guard the Lake Pontchartrain approach to the city. Visit the War of 1812 Museum, explore the fort, and bring provisions for a picnic on the grounds. *CHG*. For information, call 504-662-5703.

Another interesting old fort, *Fort Jackson*, is located on La. 23, south of Buras, LA. It was begun in 1822 to guard the river approach to the city, and was the site of a Civil War battle, when Admiral Farragut brought his Union gunboats up the river in 1862. Wander around the fort, visit the museum, and bring your picnic basket. *NCHG*. Fort Jackson is open daily from 10 am to sunset.

THE INTERNATIONAL VISITOR

New Orleans thoroughly enjoys its international visitors and does its best to make them feel quite at home. Spanish and French are spoken by key people in many stores, city offices, tourist attractions, and medical facilities. The consular offices and shipping companies are also good sources of advice and information. Many groups have been formed to preserve and continue the various cultural heritages represented in the city; they hold exuberant celebrations on national holidays and Saints' days throughout the year.

In the following section, we have listed a variety of resources available to international visitors.

The **World Trade Center,** 2 Canal St.; 529-1601, a privately owned nonprofit organization, offers a variety of services to international groups and individuals visiting the city. Group briefings on the city, its history, and its current commercial potential can be arranged. Trade groups are offered the use of offices, TELEX, secretarial services, meeting

rooms, and libraries, as well as assistance in setting up conferences. Spanish and French translations are readily available. Translations into other languages can be arranged for a fee. The World Trade Center is the only such privately owned trade organization in the country to offer this wide variety of services. The World Trade Center also offers the *Viewpoint* and *Top of the Mart Lounge* (see SIGHTS).

The **New Orleans Metropolitan Convention and Visitors Bureau,** 1520 Sugar Bowl Dr., in the Superdome; 566-5011, 1-800-672-6124, www.neworleanscvb.com, a visitor information center on 529 St. Ann St. in the French Quarter; 566-5031, has a colorful brochure available on request for visitors to the city, with general information and facts about the French Quarter printed in German, French, Italian, Spanish, and Japanese. Other brochures are available in French and Spanish only.

New Orleans Tourism Marketing Corp., 365 Canal St., One Canal Place, Ste. 2020, is extremely helpful to visitors and conventioneers. To obtain brochures and information, call 504-524-4784, fax 504-524-4780, or check www.neworleansonline.com.

The **New Orleans City Hall** handles intergovernmental and international issues. For information, call Intergovernmental Relations Division; 565-6419 or International Relations and Trade Development; 565-7230.

International and Ethnic Groups

Some are social, some are religious, some are educational, but all are well worth contacting.

Australia-New Zealand; 588-1926.

Austria Consulate, 755 Magazine St.; 593-0600.

China, Chinese Presbyterian Church, 2901 W. Esplanade Ave.; 461-0702.

Foreign Relations Association of New Orleans, 2 Canal St.; 523-2201.

France, French-American Chamber of Commerce, 2 Canal St.; 524-2042.

Germany, German Seamen's Mission, 6612 Canal Blvd.; 482-0465.
Deutsch Haus, 200 S. Galvez; 522-8014.

Greece, Greek Orthodox Cathedral of the Holy Trinity-Hellenic Cultural Center, 1200 Robert E. Lee Blvd.; 282-0259.
Greek Seaman's Tours, 428 Canal St.; 525-1610.

Ireland, Ireland-American Museum, O'Flaherty's Ballad Room, 508 Toulouse St.; 529-1317.

Italy, Italian American Federation of the Southeast, 1608 S. Salcedo; 891-1904. Italian-American Society of Jefferson, 1910 Monroe St., 362-0070.

Japan, Japan Business Tours, 365 Canal St.; 586-0502.

Korea, Korea House, 615 Orange St.; 488-0450.
Korean United Methodist Church, 3900 St. Charles Ave.; 897-3060.

Latin America, Latin Tours, 2 Canal St.; 524-1157, 524-4732.

Norway, Norwegian Seamen's Church, 1722 Prytania St.; 525-5570, 525-3602.

Spain, Spanish Seventh Day Adventist Church, 3907 Iroquois St.; 943-6851.

Consulates and Trade Offices

The Consular Corps has long held a position of high esteem in New Orleans. There have been consuls representing their countries here ever since New Orleans became part of the United States. Today they give a valuable added dimension to both the commercial and the social life of the city.

The following is the latest list of the Consular Corps of Louisiana. For additional information or answers to questions, write: World Trade Center, 2 Canal St., New Orleans, LA 70130-1507, or call 504-529-1601, fax 504-529-1691. Web site: http://www.wtc-no.org. E-mail: wtc-info@wtc-no.org.

Austria, Honorary Consul of Austria, 755 Magazine St., New Orleans, LA 70130; 581-5141, fax 566-1201.

Bangladesh, Honorary Consul General of Bangladesh, 321 St. Charles Ave., Second Floor, New Orleans, LA 70130; 586-8300, fax 525-9537.

Barbados, Honorary Consul of Barbados, 321 St. Charles Ave., 10th Floor, New Orleans, LA 70130; 586-1979, fax 525-9464.

Belgium, Honorary Consul of Belgium, 308 Citrus Rd., River Ridge, LA 70123; 837-5880, fax 849-2302.

Belize, Honorary Consul of Belize, 3601 Kent Ave., Metairie, LA 70006; 885-7704, fax 885-0156.

Bolivia, Honorary Consul of Bolivia, 643 Magazine St., New Orleans, LA 70130; 596-2720, fax 596-2760.

Brazil, Honorary Consul General of Brazil, Post Office Drawer 1030, New Iberia, LA 70562; 318-365-8101, fax 318-364-3742.

Burkina Faso, Honorary Consul of Burkina Faso, P.O. Box 3398, New Orleans, LA 70177; 945-3152, fax 945-0003.

Chile, Honorary Consul of Chile, P.O. Box 60046, New Orleans, LA 70160; 528-3364, fax 524-4156.

Colombia, Consul General of Colombia, 2 Canal St., Ste. 1844, New Orleans, LA 70130; 525-5580, fax 525-4903.

Costa Rica, Consul General of Costa Rica, 4532 W. Napoleon Ave., Ste. 112, Metairie, LA 70001; 887-8131, fax 887-0916.

Denmark, Honorary Consul of Denmark, 321 St. Charles Ave., New Orleans, LA 70130; 586-8300, fax 586-1967.

Dominican Republic, Consul General of the Dominician Republic, 2 Canal St., Ste. 1647, New Orleans, LA 70130; 522-1843, fax 522-1007.

Ecuador, Consul General of Ecuador, 2 Canal St., Ste. 1312, New Orleans, LA 70130; 523-3229, fax 522-9675.

El Salvador, Consul General of El Salvador, 2 Canal St., Ste. 1136, New Orleans, LA 70130; 522-4266, fax 523-5237.

Finland, Honorary Consul of Finland, 1100 Poydras, Ste. 3100, New Orleans, LA 70163; 523-6451, fax 524-3257.

France, Consul General of France, 300 Poydras St., Ste. 2105, New Orleans, LA 70130; 523-5772, fax 523-5725.

Germany, Honorary Consul of Germany, P.O. Box 61000, New Orleans, LA 70161-1000; 576-4289, fax 576-4782.

Great Britain, Honorary Consul of Great Britain, 321 St. Charles Ave., 10th Floor, New Orleans, LA 70130; 586-1979, fax 524-1736.

Greece, Consul of Greece, 2 Canal St., Ste. 2318, New Orleans, LA 70130; 523-1167, fax 524-5610.

Greek Maritime Section, Maritime Attaché and Vice Consul of Greek Maritime Section, 2 Canal St., Ste. 1946, New Orleans, LA 70130; 529-5288, fax 524-4522.

Guatemala, Honorary Consul of Guatemala, 1001 Howard Ave., Ste. 2504, New Orleans, LA 70113; 558-3751, fax 558-3755.

Honduras, Consul General of Honduras, 2 Canal St., Ste. 1641, New Orleans, LA 70130; 522-3118, fax 523-0544.

Hungary, Honorary Consul of Hungary, 1 Galleria Blvd., Ste. 1714, Metairie, LA 70001; 849-2739, fax 849-2740.

Iceland, Honorary Consul of Iceland, 210 Baronne St., Ste. 1022, New Orleans, LA 70112; 524-3342, fax 524-3344.

India, Honorary Consul of India, 201 St. Charles Ave., 50th Floor, New Orleans, LA 70170; 582-8106, fax 582-8549.

Italy, Honorary Consul of Italy, 201 St. Charles Ave., Ste. 2500, New Orleans, LA 70170-2500; 524-6887, fax 524-7979.

Japan, Consul General of Japan, 639 Loyola, Ste. 2050, New Orleans, LA 70113; 529-2101, fax 568-9847.

Korea, Honorary Consul General of Korea, 321 St. Charles Ave., 10th Floor, New Orleans, LA 70130; 586-1979, fax 566-0843.

Lesotho, Honorary Consul of Lesotho, 4 Grand Teton Ct., New Orleans, LA 70131; 391-0452, fax 433-4288.

Liberia, Honorary Consul Genral of Liberia, 333 St. Charles Ave., Ste. 806, New Orleans, LA 70130; 523-5300, fax 523-5303.

Luxembourg, Honorary Vice Consul of Luxembourg, P.O. Box 15803, New Orleans, LA 70175; 861-3743, fax 861-3973.

Mexico, Consul General of Mexico, 2 Canal St., Ste. 840, New Orleans, LA 70130; 522-3596, fax 525-2332.

Monaco, Honorary Consul General of Monaco, 199 Audubon Blvd., New Orleans, LA 70118; phone/fax 861-0103.

Netherlands, Honorary Consul of the Netherlands, 643 Magazine, New Orleans, LA 70130; 586-1200, fax 596-2800.

Nicaragua, Dean of the Consular Corps and Consul General of Nicaragua, 2 Canal St., Ste. 1937, New Orleans, LA 70130; 523-1507, fax 523-2359.

Norway, Honorary Consul of Norway, 650 Poydras St., Ste. 1700, New Orleans, LA 70130; 522-3526, fax 529-5745.

Panama, Consul General of Panama, 2 Canal St., Ste. 1324, New Orleans, LA 70130; 525-3458, fax 524-8960.

Peru, Honorary Consul of Peru, 333 St. Charles Ave., Ste. 1705, New Orleans, LA 70130; 525-2706, fax 525-2787.

Philippines, Honorary Consul General of the Philippines, 2 Canal St., Ste. 1843, New Orleans, LA 70130; 529-7561, fax 529-7562.

St. Vincent and the Grenadines, Honorary Consul of St. Vincent and the Grenadines, 650 Poydras St., Ste. 2100, New Orleans, LA 70130; 523-1385, fax 524-6891.

Senegal, Honorary Consul General of Senegal, 2 Canal St., Ste. 1843, New Orleans, LA 70130; 529-7561, fax 529-7562.

Spain, Consul General of Spain, 2 Canal St., Ste. 2102, New Orleans, LA 70130; 525-4951, fax 525-4955.

Sri Lanka, Honorary Consul General of Sri Lanka, P.O. Box 24818, New Orleans, LA 70184; 455-7600, fax 455-7605.

Sweden, Honorary Consul of Sweden, 2419 Broadway St., New Orleans, LA 70125; 861-2557.

Switzerland, Honorary Consul of Switzerland, 1620 Eighth St., New Orleans, LA 70115; 897-6510.

Thailand, Honorary Consul General of Thailand, 335 Julia St., New Orleans, LA 70130; 522-3400, fax 522-3434.

Uruguay, Honorary Consul of Uruguay, 2 Canal St., Ste. 2002, New Orleans, LA 70130; 525-8354, fax 524-8925.

Venezuela, Consul General of Venezuela, 2 Canal St., Ste. 1908, New Orleans, LA 70130; 522-3284, fax 522-7092.

Bank Hours

Banking hours in New Orleans are from 9 am to 3 pm Mon-Fri. Banks have drive-up windows that are open from 9 am to 6 pm. Also, cashiers in the major hotels can assist you. Of course, ATM machines are located in many places.

Currency Exchange and International Banking

The following banks have International Departments to serve you:

American Express Travel, 201 St. Charles Ave.; 586-8201.

Traveler's check 24-hour refund and purchase information; toll free 1-800-221-7282.

Bank One, numerous locations in the metro area. In the business district: Place St. Charles, 201 St. Charles Ave.; 558-1164, and World Trade Center, 2 Canal St.; 569-0482. For 24-hour account information; 822-0199, toll free 1-800-332-5950.

Hibernia National Bank, 313 Carondelet St. and many other branches.

International Division; 533-5801.

Whitney National Bank, 228 St. Charles Ave. and many other branches.

International Banking; 586-3636.

Evenings and Weekends; 838-4450.

For airport banking, the Whitney National Bank in Jefferson Parish operates a branch bank on the mezzanine level at New Orleans International Airport and on the Lobby Level as well. Foreign currency exchange, traveler's checks, and VISA/MC cash advances are available in the Lobby Office from 9 am to 6 pm Mon-Sat. Regular customer services are available in the Mezzanine Office from 9 am to 4 pm, Mon-Fri; 838-6492.

On the second floor of the airport, the **Convention and Visitors Bureau** operates an information booth with a multi-language staff.

Customs Allowances

If New Orleans is your point of entry, you will probably go through customs at New Orleans International Airport.

The growing global, free economy has dramatically changed customs restrictions, and more changes are forthcoming. Customs allowances now vary according to which part of the world you have visited or arrived from. Therefore, check for the most up-to-date information before you depart, at http://www.customs.ustreas.gov or call the Customs Service; 1-800-232-5378, the 24-hour information hotline; 202-927-6724, or general information; 504-670-2082.

Driving

In the United States, we drive in the right lane. On many rural highways and freeways, there is a 65 mph speed limit, while 55 mph is usually the maximum near urban areas.

It is wise to secure an international driver's license before leaving home. You are expected to turn on your headlights at dusk and when it is raining. You may turn right, after coming to a complete stop, at a red light in the state of Louisiana.

If you should be so unfortunate as to have an accident, leave the car as is, have someone call the police, and wait at the scene until the police arrive. Be sure to get name, address, phone, and name of insurance company from the opposite party.

Gasoline and service stations along the highway are usually open on weekends and in the evenings. Many are open 24 hours. There will be signs posted a mile or so before most of the exits on interstate highways indicating the types of gasoline and other services available there. Be aware that United States gallons are one-fifth smaller than those sold in the United Kingdom.

Education

The Ecole Franco-Americaine in Audubon Montessori School; 862-5103.

Jefferson Parish Public Schools Bi-Lingual Program and ESL (English as a Second Language) Program; 349-7776.

Orleans Parish Public Schools information; 365-8800.

Electricity

110 volts 60 cycles AC. You will need an adapter for your personal appliances.

Postage

Mail service is generally good, and letters can cross the country in one to three days. Zip codes must be used for guaranteed delivery. Express Mail is available. Check with the nearest post office for information on rates and hours. The main post office, 701 Loyola; 589-1111, has extended business hours: 7 am to 8 pm Mon-Fri, 7 am to 11 pm Sat, and 12 noon to 5 pm Sun.

International Publications and Newspapers

International newspapers may be available through consular offices and national groups. Other sources are:

In the French Quarter, **Sidney's Newsstand,** 917 Decatur St.; 524-6872, carries a selection of English, French, German, and Italian newspapers.

In the Central Business District, **The New Orleans Public Library International Department,** 219 Loyola Ave., corner of Tulane Ave., has a good selection of international newspapers and periodicals, bi-lingual librarians, and a most pleasant reading area.

In the uptown area, **The Tulane University Library,** corner of Freret Street and Audubon Boulevard; 865-5604, has a selection of international publications.

Medical

The United States has no national health service, so medical insurance should be arranged for in your home country. Most hospitals in New Orleans have bi-lingual staff members available. **Ochsner**

Foundation Hospital is particularly attuned to dealing with patients from other countries. The Ochsner Foundation also maintains **Brent House,** a hotel facility next door to the Clinic and Hospital, designed to accommodate families of out-of-town patients. For information, call 835-5411.

The Ronald McDonald House provides housing on a limited basis to families of hospitalized children. It is located at 4403 Canal St. For information, call 486-6668.

The **Tulane University Medical Center** provides in-house rooming for the immediate family. It is located at 1415 Tulane Ave. For information, call 588-5263.

Money

The U.S. dollar ($) is divided into 100 cents (¢). The coins are the penny, worth 1 cent (copper colored), nickel 5 cents, dime 10 cents, quarter 25 cents, half-dollar 50 cents (all silver colored), and occasionally a silver dollar coin. The bills or notes are all one color—green—and are in denominations of one dollar, five dollars, 10 dollars, 20 dollars, 50 dollars, 100 dollars, and 1,000 dollars.

Public Holidays

The following holidays are observed throughout the United States:

January 1, New Year's Day.

February 22, George Washington's Birthday, celebrated on closest Monday.

May 30, Memorial Day, celebrated on the closest Monday.

July 4, Independence Day.

September, Labor Day, first Monday after first Tuesday.

October 12, Christopher Columbus Day, celebrated on the closest Monday.

November 11, Veteran's Day.

November, Thanksgiving Day, fourth Thursday.

December 25, Christmas Day.

In New Orleans, many businesses are closed on Good Friday, the Friday before Easter Sunday, and Mardi Gras.

Telephone and Telegrams

Most public pay phones require a 35-cent coin deposit, but be sure to read instructions before inserting your coin. Some public telephones can be used only with telephone company credit cards. There is a coin return button to press in the event that your call cannot be completed. When calling long distance, dial 1, then the area code (found in the front section of the telephone book), then the number. Telephone numbers preceded by an 800 number are toll free in the United States. For information, dial 1-411.

To send a mailgram (guaranteed next-day delivery by mail and less expensive than a telegram), a telegram, an international message, or a charge-card money order, call **Western Union,** 1-800-325-6000 for an agent nearest you. For Spanish-speaking operators, call 1-800-325-4045. This is a toll-free number.

Time

Remember that in the United States, we count time from 1 am to 12 noon, and repeat numbers, going from 1 pm to 12 midnight. Businesses and stores remain open and functioning throughout the day. They do not close for a midday meal.

Tipping and Taxes

A tip (or a pourboire) is your means of saying "thank you" for a job well done. In the United States, the usual tip for restaurant service, hotel laundry and valet service, room service, bar bills, and taxi service is 15-20 percent. (You may sometimes see the word "gratuity" used instead of "tip.") Bellhops, skycaps, and porters usually receive 75 cents to $1 per bag. In New Orleans, there is a 9 percent tax on merchandise and food. In New Orleans, our taxes sometimes change from year to year. There is also a tax on hotel and motel rooms.

Tours

World Trade Center; 529-1601.

French Tours—**Harriet L. Martin;** 865-1894, **New Orleans Tours;** 592-0560; **Hotard Services;** 944-0253. All of these can refer local tour guides who speak different languages.

Also see the tour section of the TRANSPORTATION chapter in this book for the various tour companies, who all provide different language tours.

Translators

Contact your consulate general or one of the tour companies listed under "tours."

TV Channels and Radio Stations Broadcasting in Foreign Languages

There is some broadcasting in both French and Spanish in the New Orleans area.

TV:

WDSU-TV Channel 6—Sunday morning Spanish programs.
Channel 51 (cable)—Spanish-language station.

Radio:

WFNO-AM 830—Spanish-language station.
KGLA-AM 1540—Spanish-language station.
WWNO-FM 89.9—Saturday morning French programming.

Church Services

Chinese Presbyterian Church; 461-0702.
Grace Episcopal Church—Spanish Mass; 482-5242.
Iglesia Bautista Hispano-Americano; 525-2004.
Iglesia de Dios; 821-2339.
Korean United Methodist Church; 897-3060.
St. Anthony of Padua (Canal Street)—Spanish Mass; 488-2651.
St. Patrick's (downtown)—Latin Mass; 525-4413.
Spanish Seventh-Day Adventist Church; 943-6851.

METRIC CONVERSIONS

Length

1 millimeter	=	.039 inch (in.)	1 inch	=	2.54 cm.
1 centimeter	=	.39 in.	1 foot	=	0.30 m.
1 meter	=	3.28 feet (ft.)	1 yard	=	.91 m.
1 kilometer	=	.62 mile (mi.)	1 mile	=	1.61 km.

To convert miles to kilometers, multiply the number of miles by 8 and divide by 5.

Weight

1 gram	=	.04 ounce (oz.)	1 oz.	=	28.35 g.
1 kilogram	=	2.2 pounds (lb.)	1 lb.	=	.45 kg.
			1 ton	=	.91 metric ton

Liquid

		2.11 pints (pt.)	1 pt.	=	.47 liter
1 liter	=	1.06 quarts (qt.)	1 qt.	=	.95 liter
		.26 gallon (gal.)	1 gal.	=	3.79 liters

Temperature

To convert Fahrenheit temperatures to Centigrade (Celsius): Take the Fahrenheit temperature, minus 32, and divide by 1.8. This equals the Centigrade temperature.

CONVERSION CHARTS FOR CLOTHING

Dresses, coats, suits and blouses (Women)

British	10	12	14	16	18	20
American	8	18	12	14	16	18
Continental	40	42	44	46	48	50

Suits and overcoats (Men)

American/British	34	36	38	40	42	44
Continental	44	46	48	50	52	54

Shirts (Men)

American/British	14	14½	15	15½	16	16½	17	17½
Continental	36	37	38	39	40	41	42	43

Shoes (Men) for ½ sizes add ½ to preceding number

British	6	7	8	9	10	11
American	7	8	9	10	11	12
Continental	39½	40½	41½	42½	43½	44½

Shoes (Women) for ½ sizes add ½ to preceding number

British	3	4	5	6	7	8	9
American	4½	5½	6½	7½	8½	9½	10
Continental	35	36	37	38	39	40	41

SPECIAL PEOPLE

SENIOR CITIZENS

New Orleans is a great place for senior citizens—no hills, no snow to shovel, flowers blooming all year, good public transportation, and every imaginable kind of entertainment from relaxing to rambunctious! Many facilities offer senior citizen discounts. Wherever you go, be sure to ask.

The pursuit of physical fitness has taken the country by storm and senior citizens are part of the group. New Orleans is a good place for walking, running, or biking, but do adjust your distances to the high humidity. There are also numerous health clubs in the metropolitan area. See SPORTS for recommended places to pursue these activities.

The local transportation system is run by the **Regional Transit Authority (RTA),** which offers special fares for seniors. The red, white, and blue MediCare card can be used for identification, or a transit ID card can be obtained from the RTA office. For information, call 248-3900 or 242-2600.

Almost all concerts, sports events, museums, theaters, and Superdome activities give senior citizens a box office senior citizens discount. Call the following:

Ticketmaster of Louisiana, Inc. office, 1500 Poydras St.; 522-5572.
Louisiana Superdome, 1500 Poydras; 587-3800.
Saenger Performing Arts Center; 524-2490.
Jefferson Performing Arts Society; 885-2000.
Overture to the Cultural Season; 821-9300.

The public libraries, museums, and many civic organizations have many cultural programs of interest to older citizens. Refer to local newspapers and magazines for seniors activities. *New Orleans Prime* is "the monthly magazine for active mature adults in the metropolitan New Orleans area." Pick up a complimentary copy at coffeehouses, grocery stores, or family-type restaurants or write: *Prime*, 111 Veterans Blvd., Ste. 1810, Metairie, LA 70005, or call customer service; 832-3510, 834-9292. This is an excellent publication for area senior citizens, filled with pertinent information, articles, and a special events calendar.

When you're ready to go farther afield, check the airlines. Many give special rates to senior citizens. If you prefer to stay closer to the ground, ask about special fares from **Amtrak** (toll free 1-800-872-7245), **Greyhound** (828-3415), and **Hotard Travel** (944-0253).

The **American Association of Retired Persons** is a good organization to join whether you happen to be retired or not. They furnish a wealth of information in their magazines and other mailings regarding special offers and activities for senior citizens.

The metro-wide **Emergency Number** is 911.

The **Travelers Aid Society;** 525-8726, is available to help with emergencies or problems encountered while in New Orleans.

The **Red Cross Emergency** number is 586-8191.

VIA, Volunteer and Information Agency for metropolitan New Orleans, is a good source of information. If you need help, they can refer you to the proper agency. If you, as a senior citizen with a wealth of valuable experience, are willing to share that experience with others, they can assist in placing you in an interesting volunteer position. Call 488-4636.

All cities and parishes in the Greater Metropolitan Area have active recreation departments with senior citizens groups. Their numbers are listed in the blue pages of the telephone directory.

The **People Program** is a longtime successful program for "people of the third season." Weekday activities are offered that range from bridge to crafts, yoga, dancing, music, foreign languages, writing, and painting. Also arranged are group day trips, national tours, and an annual group trip abroad—all for a nominal fee. Members may even choose to participate in tournaments, exhibitions, performances, and lots of fun, all without the scrutiny of the under-50 crowd. "Live and let live" is the attitude of this mature group. For more information, contact: People Program, 1200 Mirabeau Ave.; 288-3171.

The **Council on Aging;** 821-4121, can furnish information on facilities and programs, including Meals on Wheels.

PHYSICALLY CHALLENGED POPULATION

Happily, physically challenged people are more mobile today than ever before. Improved electric and manual wheelchairs, laser care, sonic glasses for the blind, and public awareness have made it possible for the special traveler to move about with less difficulty than in the past. New Orleans, in compliance with the 1990 Americans with

Disabilities Act (ADA), provides wheelchair access to major tourist attractions. Large shopping centers are also barrier free. Even Uptown Square (Broadway at the river), with its multilevel medieval-village concept, is totally accessible.

The City of New Orleans operates the **LIFT,** a bus service for handicapped citizens. First call for an "eligibility form"; 827-7814. Then you will be able to call for a pickup with a specially equipped vehicle; 827-7433. The main RideLine information number is 248-3900.

Some regular city buses, operated by the **Regional Transit Authority,** have lifts to assist wheelchair riders. The buses are clearly marked with the handicapped symbol. For information on schedules, call 827-7433. Streetcars do not have lifts.

A special tram in the Audubon Zoological Garden also has a wheelchair lift; the zoo as a whole is planned for total access. The front part of Audubon Park is closed to vehicular traffic at all times, and with its wide asphalt roadway and convenient picnic areas provides an easy and delightful outdoor spot.

The lakefront area and City Park, as well as the grassy area on the City Park side of Bayou St. John, also provide easily accessible areas for outdoor relaxation.

American Rentals, 1400 Montegut St.; 947-9500, has junior-size wheelchairs available for office areas that are too small for regular-size wheelchairs. Special arm attachments are also available.

Delgado Community College Rehabilitation Human Resources; 483-4151, provides facilities for handicapped students.

Lamberts Orthotics and Prosthetics, 3627 Magazine St.; 897-6248, has special medical equipment and supplies such as chairs, crutches, etc., and also repairs orthopedic equipment.

Traveler's Aid; 525-8726, is available for advice and help.

University of New Orleans Rehabilitation Information; 280-6000, provides facilities for handicapped students.

The March of Dimes, New Orleans Metropolitan Chapter, 818 Howard Ave.; 522-0865, has a special Handi-Cab Minibus, equipped with a lift, to transport patients to and from hospitals.

For information and referrals concerning medical problems while visiting New Orleans, call the **Orleans Parish Medical Society,** 1450 Poydras St.; 523-2474.

Special information for the deaf can be obtained through the following numbers:

Deaf Action Center, Sign Language Interpreter Service; 525-0700.

Fire/Police; 911.

Local Transit Information for the hearing impaired; 827-7805.

Special information for the blind can be obtained through the following numbers:

American Council of the Blind; 1-800-424-8666.

Radio for the Blind and Print Handicapped Inc.; 899-1144.

Lighthouse for the Blind; 899-4501.

If you are having problems with accessibility, call the following for information or assistance.

Department of Justice; voice 1-800-514-0301; TTY 1-800-514-0383.

The Disability Business and Technical Assistance Center; voice/TTY 1-800-949-4232.

STUDENTS

Students traveling to New Orleans may take advantage of the many student discounts available with an ID at museums, theaters, and ticket offices.

Parking facilities in the uptown University Section are limited; students coming to Tulane, Loyola, or Newcomb may want to invest in a bicycle as a quick mode of transportation. There is excellent public transportation in this area as well as many shops, restaurants, and drugstores within walking distance. Vehicle parking permits are required for each university. If living off campus, you may want to check into carpools. Tulane and LSU medical schools are in the Central Business District, but the LSU Dental School is located in the Gentilly/City Park area. A car would be useful here.

The legal drinking age in New Orleans is 21. The driving age is 16. Be sure to have a current student ID and a valid driver's license. Also, be aware that illegally parked cars are towed (particularly in the French Quarter and the Central Business District), ticketed, or "booted" and that cars with out-of-state licenses are particularly tempting. The fee to redeem your car can range from $100 up (Auto Pound, Orleans Parish; 565-7236, Jefferson Parish; 364-5350).

To find out what's going on when you arrive, check your university student center for a campus newspaper, local newspapers, and local magazines. These publications all feature a "Calendar of Events" section. Also check the campus library and various campus bulletin boards for event notices.

Colleges and Universities

Delgado Community College, 615 City Park Ave.; 483-4114. This lovely City Park campus offers associate degrees that are accepted by local universities and applied toward a more advanced degree. This junior college also offers many courses not offered by a four-year institution.

Dillard University, 2601 Gentilly Blvd.; 283-8822. Dillard University dates back to 1869, with roots in both the Methodist Episcopal Church and the Missionary Association of the Congregational Church. In 1930, the name "Dillard" was officially adopted in honor of James Hardy Dillard, a distinguished educator of Negroes in the South. The first speech department in a black university was organized at Dillard in 1936. It is located on a beautiful 62-acre campus in the Gentilly area and has excellent residence halls and good sports facilities as well as a fine academic program.

Loyola University of the South, 6363 St. Charles Ave.; 865-2011. A Jesuit-run university, founded in 1911, it is well known for its communications and journalism departments, its music school, and its law school. Loyola is the largest Roman Catholic university in the South.

Louisiana State University Medical Complex is one of New Orleans' two fine side-by-side medical schools, with satellite programs in other locations around the state.

Administration, 1440 Canal St.; 568-4800.

School of Dentistry, 1100 Florida Ave.; 619-8700.

School of Medicine, 1542 Tulane Ave.; 568-4808.

Newcomb College (see Tulane University).

Nunez Community College, 3700 La Fontaine St., Chalmette; 278-7440. This accredited state community college meets the needs of suburban New Orleans residents. Associate degrees from this junior college are accepted at local four-year universities toward advanced degrees. Various classes are offered for personal enhancement or just fun.

Our Lady of Holy Cross College, 4123 Woodland Dr., West Bank; 394-7744. "Innovators in education since 1916," this Catholic-managed college has a varied curriculum and beautiful campus. The ambience is truly friendly and peaceful. The college is also very popular in the metropolitan area for education degrees and teacher certification.

Southern University of New Orleans, 6400 Press Dr.; 286-5000. This school is part of the Southern University system, with campuses in New Orleans, Baton Rouge, and Shreveport. The New Orleans campus, established in 1959, in New Orleans East, is primarily a commuter school. Southern is particularly known for its degree programs in social welfare and social work. Other fine programs include business, humanities, education, and health studies.

Tulane University, 6823 St. Charles Ave.; 865-5000. Tulane, first called the Medical College of Louisiana, was established in 1834. It merged with the University of Louisiana and changed its name when Paul Tulane left $1,000,000 to the school in 1883. It is noted for its excellent Law School, education programs, and University College; for

Sophie Newcomb College, an excellent women's college; and for its art, engineering, theater, and graduate business programs.

Tulane University Medical School, 1430 Tulane Ave.; 588-5263. Founded in 1834, it has long enjoyed an international reputation for excellence. Tulane Medical Center is attached to the Medical School.

University of New Orleans, at the lakefront, Leon C. Simon Boulevard at Elysian Fields Avenue; 280-6000. Part of Louisiana State University, the University of New Orleans, since the 1950s, has blossomed into an excellent university with fine graduate and undergraduate schools and nationally known basketball and baseball teams. The sports arena is quite active with games and concerts.

Xavier University, 7325 Palmetto St.; 486-7411. The first Roman Catholic college for blacks in the United States, it was founded by Sister Katherine Drexel in 1915 as a high school and in 1917 as a college. Today, it attracts a sizeable group of international students as well, and is particularly well known for its graduate programs and its Pharmacy School.

Theology Schools

New Orleans Baptist Theological Seminary, 3939 Gentilly Blvd.; 282-4455, teaches theology students.

Notre Dame Seminary School of Theology, 2901 S. Carrollton Ave.; 866-7426, educates students for Roman Catholic priesthood.

Lodging for Students

New Orleans is a mecca for students throughout the year, but especially during the Sugar Bowl, Mardi Gras, and the Jazz and Heritage Festival. The following suggestions for lodgings may be particularly convenient for student visitors:

Bed & Breakfast Inc., New Orleans, 1021 Moss St.; 1-800-749-4640, 488-4640. Call for reservations.

Bed and Breakfast of New Orleans, 671 Rosa Ave.; 838-0071.

Marquette House of New Orleans, a Youth Hostel, 2253 Carondelet St.; 523-3014. Call for information. Rooms let at 5:30 pm. Very reasonable, convenient to streetcar.

Park View Guest House, 7004 St. Charles Ave.; 861-7564. Convenient to uptown universities and Audubon Park. European and American plan.

St. Charles Guest House, 1748 Prytania St.; 523-6556. A European-style pension, with student discounts, bicycle rentals. Convenient to streetcar.

YMCA International Center Residence, 920 St. Charles Ave. at Lee Circle; 568-9622. Reasonable rates; short walk to train and bus stations.

Popular Student Hangouts

There are many popular student "hangouts" around the city. Within walking distance of the uptown campuses is Maple Street, which is lined with good informal restaurants, bars, gift shops, clothing stores, book stores, camera shops—almost anything you can think of. It's fun to explore.

The following is a list of some of the most popular meeting places. See DINING and NIGHTLIFE chapters for more detail.

Camelia Grill, 626 S. Carrollton Ave.; 866-9573. Fine food all day, as well as a traditional late night after-the-party stopping place.

Carrollton Station, 8140 Willow St.; 865-9190. Music, drinks.

Chinese Kitchen, 3327 S. Carrollton Ave.; 482-1122.

Ciro's Pizza and Spaghetti House, 7918 Maple St.; 866-9551. Good pizza within walking distance of uptown campuses.

College Inn, 3016 S. Carrollton Ave.; 866-3683. New Orleans specialties, reasonably priced. Also takeout orders.

Contemporary Arts Center Net Cafe, 900 Camp St.; 523-1216. Enjoy coffee, snacks, and music and surf the net.

Copeland's of New Orleans, 4338 St. Charles (on the streetcar line), 897-2325. Drinks and good Cajun food.

Cuco's, 1340 S. Carrollton; 861-3322. Cantina-style restaurant with festive Mexican food and atmosphere.

Dante Street Deli, 736 Dante; 863-3634. Drinks, sandwiches and specials, and takeout.

Fat Harry's, 4330 St. Charles Ave.; 895-9582. "The" all-night gathering place for the college set.

Hard Rock Cafe, 418 N. Peters St.; 529-5617. A popular crowded-with-loud-music restaurant with drinks, noted for hamburgers.

Italian Pie, 5219 Elysian Fields; 288-0888. Casual atmosphere with pizzas and a variety of Italian dishes.

La Madeleine French Bakery & Cafe, 601 S. Carrollton Ave.; 861-8661. French cafe with a variety of coffees, pastries, wonderful home-made whole-grain breads, and French-style meals.

Maple Leaf Club, 8316 Oak St.; 866-9359. Music, drinks.

Mid-City Lanes Rock 'n Bowl, 4133 S. Carrollton Ave.; 482-3133. Very popular for bowling in the 1950s lanes, eating at the bar counter, or dancing to live Cajun, zydeco, or rock bands, all in one space.

Pat O'Brien's, 718 St. Peter St.; 525-4823. A New Orleans tradition. Noted for its Hurricanes in souvenir glasses.

Plantation Coffeehouse, 5555 Canal Blvd.; 482-3164. A variety of coffees, pastries, and light meals, with weekend classical guitarist.

Tipitina's, 501 Napoleon Ave.; 894-8477. Music, drinks.

Vera Cruz, 7537 Maple St.; 866-1736. Mexican food and drink—good margaritas at Happy Hour.

Whole Foods Market, 3135 Esplanade Ave.; 943 1626. Great natural foods, deli.

Coffeehouses

New coffeehouses have sprouted everywhere. Here are some favorites of the student population—everything from the longtime to the new favorites.

Coffee and Company, 800 Harrison Ave.; 488-8946.

P.J.'s Coffee and Tea Cafes, several favorite locations: 637 N. Carrollton Ave.; 482-4847, 634 Frenchmen St.; 949-2292, 7624 Maple St.; 866-7031, 1532 Robert E. Lee Blvd.; 282-6154.

Plantation Coffeehouse, 5555 Canal Blvd.; 482-3164.

Rue de la Course, 1500 Magazine St.; 529-1455.

Starbucks Coffee, 7700 Maple St.; 864-0411.

True Brew Coffee, 3133 Ponce de Leon; 947-3948.

Christian Coffeehouses

Christian coffeehouses have recently begun to appear in the metropolitan area. In addition to coffee, live contemporary Christian music is "served." National and local Christian rock bands tour this coffeehouse circuit.

Amazing Grace Coffeehouse, 1041 Friscoville Ave., Arabi; 277-5520.

Coffee House of Faith, 400 Wiedman St., Gretna; 366-7811.

New Wine Coffee House, 1061 Oak Ave., Bridge City; 436-4820.

The Upper Room, 4057 Oregon Dr., Algiers; 364-1763.

FOR RESIDENTS

Bienvenu! Welcome! "The Crescent City," "the City that Care Forgot," "the Big Easy"—New Orleans is your new home.

Moving to New Orleans can be a challenging experience. You will have to learn the language, adapt to the lifestyle, and survive the humidity. Allow yourself time to relax and appreciate the differences. Develop your sense of adventure by trying new things. Be sure to costume for your first Mardi Gras! Read the local newspapers and magazines to be aware of all the things that are going on. There are the *Gambit* and *Times-Picayune (T-P)* newspapers. For magazines, look for *New Orleans Magazine*, *Gambit Weekly Native's Guide*, "Lagniappe" in Friday's *T-P,* and *New Orleans Vignettes*. Try new foods fixed new ways. And be a volunteer—it's an excellent way to learn about and become part of your new home.

New Orleans is the largest city in Louisiana, with a metropolitan population of approximately one million. It is a major port city, a tourist center (the second largest industry, after the port), and the trade mecca of the Central South. The ever expanding metropolitan area is defined by Orleans, Jefferson, St. Bernard, and St. Tammany parishes, with Plaquemines on one end of the city and St. Charles on the other growing fast.

We hope that the information in this chapter and in the rest of the book will make your move as pleasant and peaceful as possible. Come and join us and "laissez les bons temps rouler!" "Let the good times roll!"

New Orleans Rules of Thumb

1. ANYTHING is an excuse for a party.

2. Anything done with food and drink to accompany it is better than anything done without food and drink.

3. Coffee making is a cultural ceremony.

4. Mardi Gras or Carnival—the terms are somewhat interchangeable to the natives—is NOT a one-day event. It is talked about, planned for, reminisced about, and worked on all year long. The big

one-day "bash" for all this preparation is "Fat Tuesday"—English for the French "Mardi Gras."

5. Fine food is found EVERYWHERE in the city—not only in the well-known restaurants, but in the tiny neighborhood bars and seafood houses—and private homes, from the most pretentious to the plainest, are equally proud of their own special version of the local "national dish," red beans and rice.

6. There is no such thing as a compass direction in New Orleans. Don't ask whether a place is located north or south, east or west. You will get only blank stares from the natives. In New Orleans, you are told to go either "uptown" or "downtown," toward the river or toward the lake (meaning Lake Pontchartrain). You may hear, for example, that a store is located on the "uptown, river corner" of an intersection, or you may be told to go "three blocks uptown, then turn toward the lake and go two more blocks, and it will be in the middle of the block on the downtown side of the street"! Don't panic; you will get the hang of it sooner than you think.

This all started because of the way New Orleans is laid out. The streets tend to follow the curve of the river, so they may go in a north-south direction for a few blocks, then suddenly turn east-west. This makes "normal" direction giving an impossibility. Besides, say New Orleanians, it is not much fun anyway.

7. If you're planning a party, don't despair over rain; expect a bigger crowd. Rain doesn't keep people in—they consider it a challenge and go to twice as many places.

AN INTRODUCTION TO NEW ORLEANS LIVING

Geographical Profile

The physiographic characteristics of the state of Louisiana are much the same as those of the other Gulf Coast states—marshy, ever-changing coastlines slowly turning into flat pinelands, and then to gently rolling hills in the northern part of the state.

New Orleans is completely flat, below sea level, and located about 110 miles from the mouth of the Mississippi River and the Gulf of Mexico. It is surrounded by marshlands, bayous, and lakes. It is located at 90 degrees longitude and 29 degrees latitude, the same latitude as Cairo, Kuwait, and Delhi. It is dependent on the system of levees surrounding the city to protect it from periodic flood threats and channel shifts of the river. Also a necessity is the intricate system of pumping stations and canals which siphon the water off the city streets and out into Lake Pontchartrain every time it rains.

Streets that begin at the river are always numbered from the river out (or toward the lake). All these streets originally began with the 100 block right next to the river. Where the course of the river has shifted over the years, they may begin with 400 or 500, as some do in the French Quarter.

Street numbers in New Orleans move up 100 with each block; they do not just keep going until the possible numbers are used up as they do in New York, for example.

The Pontchartrain Causeway has opened up a whole new area of gracious living for "city-weary New Orleanians." The lovely old towns of Mandeville, Madisonville, Abita Springs, Covington, and Slidell are now surrounded with beautiful subdivisions and marinas. There are commuter services available for those who prefer not to drive to the city to work.

New Orleans is a subtropical city and has a year-round average temperature of 64 to 71 degrees. Most of the months are warm; there are some cold days during November, December, January, and February. However, the cold is usually short-lived, giving way to rain, heat, and high humidity. Summer heat is often tempered by afternoon rain showers.

New Orleans is lush and green all year round due to the abundant rainfall and high humidity. Because of the high water table, all kinds of plants flourish: camelias, azaleas, and banana plants, and magnolia, golden rain, and cherry laurel trees are popular garden starters. The soil is rich, fertile, and brownish-black.

The many lakes, bayous, and parks are available for relaxation. Lake Pontchartrain is a short drive from the downtown area; other getaway possibilities are the Gulf Coast, Slidell, Covington, Madisonville, Mandeville, Abita Springs and the River Road area. Consider short trips to discover the beauty of Louisiana and Mississippi.

People Profile

New Orleanians are a blend of Louisiana French (descendants of the Acadians), Europeans, French, Spanish, Latin Americans, Greeks, Italians, Irish, Germans, Africans, Jamaicans, Chinese, and most recently, Vietnamese. This creates a real gumbo (blend) of customs, traditions, and speech patterns. There is an amazing assortment of accents in different sections of the city, ranging from the classic "Brooklynese" to a true Southern drawl.

People are generally friendly and will party at the drop of a hat. Lots in the older sections are small and houses are close together, creating a neighborly mentality.

Among the loveliest residential areas are the Lakefront, the Garden District, Esplanade Ridge, the uptown area, and Old Metairie. Others are located on the West Bank (across the river) and in the Slidell/Covington/Mandeville area across Lake Pontchartrain.

Outdoor living and entertaining is a way of life in the area due to the sunny warm days and long summer evenings. Each ethnic group has contributed the best of its cooking and seasoning, resulting in the finest and tastiest food in the United States and probably the greatest number of gourmet cooks per square mile. There are many excellent cookbooks available to introduce you to the art of Creole or Cajun cooking, and any native will be more than happy to discuss (usually at length) his or her own special methods and shortcuts. In New Orleans, food is a favorite topic of conversation, along with city and state politics and who's related to whom. In order of importance, food ranks right up there with the latest gossip.

NEW ORLEANS INSIGHT

New Orleans loves "tradition" and commemorates every possible anniversary, from the Battle of New Orleans Day to Bastille Day, with pomp and ceremony. Anything old tends to be more important than anything new—furniture, houses, recipes, even families.

New Orleans likes to go formal. More formal attire for men is sold in one small uptown shop than in any other store of any size in the United States! Yet, at the same time, no place likes to "let its hair down" better—or can drop everything else and DO it better. You may find yourself dancing sedately in elegant evening clothes one night, then dancing in the street, in jeans, to the music of an impromptu jazz band the next day. For the men, spring and summer means white linen suits; they are de rigueur for all formal occasions, either daytime or evening.

To invite someone to your home for an informal visit, you either say "come have a cup of coffee" or "come have a drink"; never just "come." The "go cup," a plastic or paper cup containing a drink, is a New Orleans tradition. It allows people to move from party to party without ever leaving a drink behind and without using a glass container on public streets, which is prohibited by law.

New Orleanians don't like to drive very far. They tend to cluster all their activities in one small section of town and feel that anything beyond that is a major excursion. For a newcomer who is used to driving some distance for almost any activity (as is true in most cities), this attitude may come as a shock. But, bear with it—one thing it has produced is a plethora of marvelous small shops in every section of the city which are great fun to explore, and which manage to preserve that almost-forgotten tradition—good, old-fashioned, know-the-customer-by-name, personal service.

Also, true New Orleanians tend to drive like Parisians or Bostonians. They consider it a challenge to be first off from the traffic light, to find the best shortcut, to park, or double-park, in "No Parking" zones. The horn is merely an extension of their own voice, and is used almost as frequently; so if someone blasts away at you while you are trying to find your way around your new city, don't take it personally. It's part of the culture. Be aware, too, that New Orleans streets (and houses) tend to rise and fall slightly according to the amount of rainfall. Remember, the city is built on a swamp, and this makes for cracks and bumps in streets (as well as in ceilings). Maintaining the streets of this city is one of the world's most difficult jobs. So drive your favorite car gently.

Residents enjoy year-round outdoor sports; golf, tennis, walking, jogging, and roaming are among the most popular land-based activities. But surrounded as it is by water, sailing, boating, fishing, swimming, and duck hunting are probably the most popular sports of all.

Autos

Auto Insurance

Louisiana law requires drivers of automobiles to carry no-fault insurance, and drivers must have a valid driver's license, auto registration, and current brake tag (inspection sticker).

Auto Registration

Residents must purchase Louisiana license tag within 30 days of establishing residency. Residents must have proof of insurance, proof of ownership, and must pay ad valorem tax (personal property tax) at this time.

City of New Orleans, 8700 Lake Forest Blvd., Ste. 112; 243-7652.
Jefferson, 2150 Westbank Expwy., Room 101, Harvey; 361-6374.
Kenner, 3501 Chateau Blvd.; 465-3476.
St. Bernard, 1009 W. Moreau; 278-7406.

State of Louisiana Brake Tags

Residents must have motor vehicle registration. This safety inspection is required by law. For information call:

430 N. Lopez St.; 483-2519

3711 General Meyers Ave., Algiers; 364-4050.

13400 Old Gentilly Rd.; 244-9505.

Driver's Licenses

Out-of-state drivers have 60 days to obtain a Louisiana driver's license. A learner's license may be obtained at age 16 with parent's permission. The driver's license is valid for four years. Bring identification. Drivers are required to take an eye test and written test. Beginning drivers must also take a driving test. A new license is $18 ($10.50 for a replacement), payable in cash only. The following are Driver's License Examining and Renewal Offices:

East Bank, 102 Veterans Blvd.; 483-4610.

West Bank, 2001 Behrman Ave., Algiers; 361-6374, 2150 Westbank Expwy., Room 101, Harvey; 361-6374.

St. Bernard Parish, 1009 W. Moreau, Chalmette; 278-7406.

Reporting of Auto Accidents

In the case of an accident where there is personal injury, call the New Orleans Police immediately, 911. Non-emergency calls for service should be made to 821-2222. If the auto location is essential to determining the fault, leave autos in the position they were in at the time of the accident. Have driver's license, car registration, and insurance information available for the police.

Police will handle intoxicated or drugged drivers or emergency assistance.

If there is no personal injury, the involved parties may exchange insurance information and settle matters at the accident scene. However, a SR10 form must be filled out as soon as possible. This form may be obtained from any police headquarters.

Banking

The New Orleans scene is dominated by three major banks—Bank One, the Hibernia National Bank, and the Whitney National Bank.

Bank of Louisiana,
321 St. Charles Ave.; 899-9400.
Bank One, several locations;
504-561-8500, 1-800-826-3390.
Hibernia National Bank,
313 Carondelet St.; 538-5712.
People's Bank and Trust,
1615 E. Judge Perez Dr., Chalmette; 278-7918.
Whitney National Bank,
Main Office, 228 St. Charles Ave.; 586-7272.

The Chamber of Commerce

✓ **The Chamber/New Orleans and the River Region,** 601 Poydras St.; 527-6900. The metropolitan New Orleans civic and business life is represented by the Chamber, which does a great job of promoting the economy and growth of the city. The Chamber certifies certificates of origin and shipping documents on export shipments from the Port. It is an excellent source of information for newcomers, and both the Chamber and its Women's Auxiliary are good organizations with which to be involved.

$12

Area councils for Jefferson, East New Orleans, and St. Bernard can be reached at 527-6900.

no✓ The extremely helpful **New Orleans Metropolitan Convention & Visitors Bureau;** 566-5005, http://www.neworleansscvb.com, is wonderful in promoting all the positive aspects of the metropolitan New Orleans area, and the people at this agency respond very readily to all visitor and convention requests.

The New Orleans Tourism Marketing Corporation; 524-4784, http://www.neworleansonline.com, is another agency responding to the growing tourism and convention needs of metropolitan New Orleans.

Churches, Synagogues, and Temples

Louisiana was founded as a Roman Catholic colony and stayed that way until 1803, when it became part of the United States. Today, particularly in New Orleans, there are many denominations represented, but many of the local traditions and ideas are easily traceable to the Roman Catholic roots of the original settlers.

There are interesting church buildings, both modern and traditional, scattered throughout the city; New Orleans is a church-going community. A ride up St. Charles Avenue on Sunday morning will witness to this, as you will pass busy churches of almost every denomination.

Among the major denominations and ecumenical organizations are:

African Methodist Episcopal Church
Administrative Offices; 948-4251.
Archdiocese of New Orleans; 865-9521.
Assembly of God; 271-1696.
Baha'i New Orleans; 524-3931.
Baptist Association of Greater New Orleans; 282-1428.
Episcopal Diocese; 895-6634.

Greek Orthodox-Hellenic Center; 282-0259.
Islamic Center; 944-3758.
Jehovah's Witnesses, Central Unit; 488-9079.
Jewish Community Center; 897-0143.
Jewish Federation of Greater New Orleans; 828-2125.
Lutheran Church, Southern District; 282-2632.
Mennonite Central Committee; 524-3074.
Presbyterian Ministry; 943-8352.
St. Basil Orthodox Church; 888-8114.
St. Charles Avenue Christian Church; 899-6301.
United Methodist District Offices; 488-5430.

Clubs and Associations

After you locate you may be interested in joining one of the many golf, tennis, or social clubs in your neighborhood. There are many Mardi Gras clubs and marching groups which are of interest to new residents.

New Orleans has many private clubs, as do most other large cities, but even more interesting organizations, both business and cultural, with open membership policies. Also see SPORTS for organizations for sports recreation.

Crescent City Model Railroad Club; 737-3723.
Deutsches-Haus; 522-8014, fax 393-0333.
Friends of the Cabildo; 523-3939.
Irish Culture Society; 861-3746.
Jewish Community Center; 897-0143.
Junior Achievement of New Orleans; 832-0102.
League of Women Voters; 1-800-288-8683.
Lions Clubs:
Algiers 368-5466.
Metairie 837-4861.
West Bank 362-7500.
Louisiana Landmark Society; 482-0312.
New Orleans Opera Association; 529-2278.
New Orleans Symphony Book Fair; 861-2004.
New Orleans Women's Bowling Assn.; 486-3031.
Press Club of New Orleans; 523-1010.
Rotary Club of New Orleans; 525-6944.
Society for the Preservation and Encouragement of Barbershop Quartet Singing in America; 368-6390.

Education

Primary and Secondary Schools— Public, Private, and Parochial

New students must have proof of birth, doctor's certificate, immunization dates and records, and a final report card from the school last attended.

Public education is free for kindergarten through the 12th grade. There are four levels of education in the school system: kindergarten, one through six, juniors (grades seven through nine) or middle school (grades six through eight), and high school (grades nine through 12). Free all-day kindergarten is available in all elementary schools.

Private and parochial schools began in New Orleans in the early 1700s when the Ursuline nuns started teaching young women in the fledgling French colony. Today, many metropolitan New Orleans families choose only private or parochial education because of generations of tradition.

Accordingly, these excellent and fully accredited private and parochial schools often compete with the public schools for educational awards and acknowledgments.

Louisiana Department of Education; 504-342-3366, 342-3404.
Association for Gifted and Taleted Students—State Office; 1-800-626-8811.
Catholic Schools, Archdiocese of New Orleans; 861-9521, 861-6220.
Orleans Parish Public Schools; 365-8800, special education 365-8610, 365-8710.
Jefferson Parish Public Schools; 349-7600, special education East Bank Office; 736-1800, West Bank Office; 363-5300, Central Office; 349-7912.
St. Bernard Parish Public Schools; 271-2533, special education 277-8144.

There is a Child Search division which seeks to identify children with any exceptionality, from gifted to educable mentally handicapped. Call for information about testing and placement. Private testing results are also accepted. There is a list of rights for students in special education.

Jefferson Parish, East Bank; 736-1836, West Bank; 349-7935.
Orleans Parish; 365-8930.
St. Bernard Parish; 277-8144.

Within the Orleans Parish Public School System (288-6561), there are the following out-of the-ordinary facilities:

Guidance & Counseling; 365-5451.
Lusher Magnet Elementary; 862-5110.
McMain Magnet School; 562-5117.
The New Orleans Center for Creative Arts; 899-0055.
Rabouin Vocational High; 592-8398.
British Open Classroom:
Dibert; 483-6126.
Gordon Elementary; 286-2626.
Back to Basics:
Allen; 862-5154.
McDonogh #39; 286-2635.
Warren Easton Fundamental Senior High School; 827-4541.
College Preparatory:
Benjamin Franklin; 286-2600, gifted admissions; 286-2610.
McDonogh #35; 942-3592.

Universities and Colleges

New Orleans has many outstanding educational facilities at this level.

Delgado Community College; 483-4114.
Dillard University; 283-8822.
H. Sophie Newcomb College of Women (part of Tulane); 865-5000.
Louisiana State University and Tulane Medical Schools; 568-4008 (LSU), 588-5263 (Tulane).
Loyola University; 865-2011.
New Orleans Baptist Theological Seminary; 282-4455.
Notre Dame Seminary; 866-7426.
Nunez Community College; 278-7440.
Our Lady of Holy Cross College; 394-7744.
Southern University of New Orleans; 286-5000.
The University of New Orleans; 280-6000.
Tulane University; 865-5000.
Xavier University, 486-7411.

Government

City Government

The City of New Orleans is governed by a mayor and a seven-member City Council. Five council members are elected from single-member districts and two are elected as Council-at-Large. Elections for mayor and council are held every four years.

Parish Government

Orleans Parish boundaries coincide exactly with those of the City of New Orleans, so that most of the functions of government are handled by the City. The School Board is perhaps the most visible function of Orleans Parish government.

Congressional Districts

The New Orleans area is represented in the U.S. House of Representatives by:

Hon. William Jefferson; 589-2274.
Hon. Billy Tauzin; 271-1707.
Hon. David Vitter; 589-2753.

U.S. Senators From Louisiana

Sen. John Breaux, Democrat; 589-2531.
Sen. Mary Landrieu, Democrat; 589-2427.

Health Care

New Orleans is the medical center of the Central South, boasting two medical schools, a dental school, a number of fine teaching hospitals, and specialized care facilities. Tulane Medical Center sponsors a Primate Research Center that works with NASA.

For medical referrals we suggest: Foreign Travel Immunization, City Hall, 565-6919; **Jefferson Parish Medical Society;** 455-8282, **Orleans Parish Medical Society;** 523-2474.

Most of the following hospitals have 24-hour emergency service:

Central Business District

Eye Ear Nose and Throat Hospital, 2626 Napolean Ave.; 896-1100.

Tulane Medical Center and University Hospital, 1415 Tulane Ave.; 588-5263. Emergency; 588-5711.

Veterans Hospital, 1601 Perdido; 568-0811.

Chalmette

Chalmette Medical Center, 9001 Patricia St.; 277-8011.

Jefferson Parish

Ochsner Foundation, 1516 Jefferson Hwy.; 838-3000.

River Oaks Psychiatric Center, 1525 River Oaks Rd. W., Jefferson; 733-CARE.

Marrero

West Jefferson Medical Center, 1101 Avenue D; 347-5511.

Metairie

East Jefferson General Hospital; 4200 Houma Blvd.; 454-4000.

Lakeside Hospital; I-10 and Clearview Pkwy.; 885-3333.

Mid City/Uptown

Baptist Memorial Medical Center, 2700 Napoleon Ave.; 899-9311.

Children's Hospital, 200 Henry Clay Ave.; 899-9511.

Mercy Memorial Medical Center, 301 N. Jefferson Davis Pkwy. Emergency; 483-5000.

St. Charles General Hospital, 3700 St. Charles Ave.; 899-7441.

Touro Infirmary, 1401 Foucher; 897-7011.

Medical Facilities for Special Treatment and Aid:

Alcoholics Anonymous; 525-1178.
Alzheimers Disease Assn., 1014 Calhoun St.; 895-6223.
Children's Hospital; 899-9511.
DePaul Hospital and Community Mental Health Center; 899-8282.
New Orleans Council on Aging, 2400 Canal St.; 821-4121.
Planned Parenthood of Louisiana, 4018 Magazine St.; 897-9200.
Poison Control and Information Center; 1-800-535-0525.
Rape Crisis Line—24 hours; 483-8888.
River Oaks Crisis Center; 733-2273.
Charity Hospital, 1523 Tulane Ave.; 568-2311. Charity Hospital, in the CBD, is the major hospital for the State Hospital System. There are several smaller charity hospitals throughout the state who send patients to metropolitan New Orleans. This is a 2,000-bed hospital which has the largest delivery unit in the state.

Home and Garden Shopping Needs

Here are just a few suggestions to get you started. Also see SHOPPING.

Air Conditioning Repairs—
Berner's; 944-8731.
Carrollton Refrigeration and Appliances; 861-2501.

Blinds and Shades and Drapes—
Probst; 895-2094.
Wren's Tontine; 525-7409.

Building Materials—
Harry's Ace Hardware, 5 locations; 895-1500.
Home Depot; 246-4572.

Carpet and Rug Cleaning—
Klein's; 899-1544.
Russell's; 482-3153.

Doors—
Hollywood Door Company; 837-5711.

Electrical Repairs—
Stuart's; 581-9080.

Furniture Rentals—
American Rentals; 947-9500.
Weiner Cort; 733-8381.

Furniture Repairs and Upholstery—
Kohlmaier & Kohlmaier; 895-6394.
Probst; 895-2094.

Glass (Auto and Home-Mirrors)—
Binswanger; 523-1364.

Home Accessories—
Home Furnishing Store; 566-1707.

Lamp Repairs, Lamps, and Lamp Shades—
Stewart's; 835-7193.

Landscaping Nursery—
Guillot's Nursery; 488-5526.
Perino's; 834-7888.
Talen's; 482-6233.

Leather Cleaning—
Imperial; 822-0631.

Locks—
ACME; 486-5305.

Painting—Residential—
Wayne the Painter; 899-1893.

Paintings—Restored—
New Orleans Museum of Art; 488-2631.

Pest Control—
Orkin; 464-6571.
Terminix; 834-7330.

Picture Frames—
Gordon's of Metairie; 837-9416.
House of 10,000 Frames; 865-7255.

Plumbing—
George's; 282-5591.

Pools Services—
Pelican Pools; 889-7600.

Remodeling—
Campbell Contractors; 246-0556.

Laws

Local Laws

For general questions, call the **Citizen Action Center,** City Hall; 565-7115.

For information on zoning regulations, call the **City Planning Commission;** 565-7000.

Liquor Laws

In the Greater New Orleans area, you must be 21 to buy alcohol. Liquor, wine, and beer are sold in grocery stores and package stores from 7 to 8 am until 12 midnight, seven days a week. Alcoholic beverages are served in restaurants and bars seven days a week.

Property Laws

For information on zoning regulations and work permits, call the City Planning Commission at 565-7000. New Orleans has many historic districts and strict zoning laws, so it is prudent to check the rules before beginning a project.

Zoning Laws

In 1976, the City of New Orleans created the Historic District Landmarks Commission. Today, there are seven historic districts in the city. Before beginning a restoration project, we suggest that you contact the **Preservation Resource Center,** 604 Julia St., 581-7032, for information on your particular area.

Legal Services

For referrals call: New Orleans Legal Association, Main Office, 529-1000.

Libraries

Jefferson Parish Library Department is headquartered at 4747 W. Napoleon, Metairie; 838-1100. Call for information on the closest branch library.

The New Orleans Public Library, Main Branch, is located at 219 Loyola Ave.; 529-READ. There are 12 branches located throughout the city. For locations and hours, check under NEW ORLEANS, CITY OF, PUBLIC LIBRARY in the blue pages of the telephone book.

Newspapers and Publications

Newspapers

New Orleans has one major daily newspaper with morning and evening editions, the ***Times-Picayune,*** 3800 Howard Ave.; 821-1455.

Weekly Newspaper—***Gambit,*** 4141 Bienville; 486-5900.

Neighborhood Newspapers—***St. Bernard News,*** 3010 Lausat St., Metairie; 832-1481, ***St. Bernard Voice,*** 234 Mehle Ave., Arabi; 279-7488.

Religious Newspapers—***Clarion Herald*** (Catholic), 1000 Harold, 596-3035, ***Jewish Voice*** (Jewish), 924 Valmont; 895-8784, ***Jewish News*** (Jewish), 3788 Veterans Blvd.; 455-8822.

Black Community Publications—***Data News Weekly,*** 3501 Napoleon Ave.; 822-4433, ***Louisiana Weekly,*** 822 Perdido St.; 524-5563.

Business Publications—***New Orleans City Business,*** 111 Veterans Blvd., Metairie; 834-9292, ***Daily Journal of Commerce,*** 118 Terry Pkwy., Gretna; 368-8900, ***Daily Shipping Guide,*** 118 Terry Pkwy., Gretna; 368-6111.

Magazines

Louisiana Life, 111 Veterans Blvd., Ste. 1810, Metairie; 834-9698, ***New Orleans Magazine,*** 111 Veterans Blvd., Metairie; 831-3731, ***Where Magazine,*** 528 Wilkinson; 522-6468.

Pets

Local laws require rabies vaccination for pets by a licensed veterinarian, or at periodic clinics sponsored by the City of New Orleans, which will be advertised in the newspaper. Pets must be confined to owner's property unless on a leash. Dogs running loose will be picked up. For information, call the **SPCA,** 1319 Japonica St.; 944-7445, **Jefferson Parish Animal Shelter;** 349-5111.

Veterinarians—**Lakeside Animal Hospital,** 3838 Veterans Blvd., Metairie; 887-0282, **Audubon Veterinary Hospital,** 731 Nashville

Ave.; 891-0685, **Animal Emergency Clinic,** 1955 Veterans Blvd.; 835-8508.

Public Services

The **City of New Orleans** is supplied by:

Gas and Electricity: Entergy; 1-800-368-3749.

Gas Emergency Service: 636-2020.

Electric Emergency Service: 1-800-968-8243.

Water: Sewerage and Water Board; 529-2837, Emergency; 942-3789, nights and weekends; 529-2837.

Trash Pick-up Schedule: New Orleans Sanitation Dept.; 826-1791.

New Orleans Legal Assistance Corp.; 529-1000.

For **Jefferson Parish** service, call:

Electricity: Entergy; 1-800-368-3749.

Gas: Louisiana Gas Service Company; 456-9882.

Water: Jefferson Parish Water Department; East Bank; 838-4362, West Bank; 349-5081.

Garbage and Trash Collection; 837-8950.

For **area-wide telephone service** contact: BellSouth, New Services; 557-6500.

Trouble Shooter:

New Orleans has a very productive television help line. Have a problem and can't get any action? Call **WWL, TV Action Hot Line;** 522-4404.

Taxes

Individual Income Tax

Louisiana requires a tax on all sources of income unless they are exempt by statute. Employers are required to withhold state income tax for both resident and nonresident employees.

Property Tax

Property taxes vary slightly from parish to parish, but, in general, they will probably be lower than they were in your former home.

For information call:

City of New Orleans Assessor's Office; 565-7050.

Jefferson Parish Assessor, East Bank; 736-6370.

Jefferson Parish Assessor, West Bank; 362-4100.

Check with the **Real Estate Board of New Orleans;** 486-7266, for more information.

Sales Tax

In the City of New Orleans, the sales tax is 9 percent. In Jefferson Parish, the sales tax is 8.75 percent.

Television and Radio

See MATTERS OF FACT for complete TV and radio listings.

Volunteerism

Once you have settled and met your neighbors and church members, you may enjoy volunteering your time and energy in one of the many civic organizations. It's a good way to make new friends, meet people, and help your community fill its needs.

Although there are many more agencies, we have listed a few to get you started. VIA is the local **Voluntary Center of Greater New Orleans,** listing thousands of interesting volunteer positions. For information, call 488-4636.

A few organizations of particular interest are:

American Cancer Society	522-0851
American Heart Association	456-7224
Audubon Zoological Garden	861-2537
Big Brothers	283-2291
Big Sisters	283-2291
Boy Scouts of America	887-0388
Cancer Association	529-2273
Catholic Charities	523-3755
Children's Hospital	899-9511
Girl Scouts of America	733-8220
Jewish Family & Children's Services	831-8475
Light House for the Blind	899-4501
Louisiana Nature Center	246-5672
Louisiana State Museum	568-6968
New Orleans Council on the Aging	821-4121
New Orleans Museum of Art	482-7219
Trinity Christian Community	482-7822
United Way	822-5540
Urban League of New Orleans	524-4667
Volunteers of America	525-2179
YWCA	482-9922

Voter Registration

To vote in Orleans or other parishes, state, and federal elections, you must be 18 years old, registered, a citizen of the United States, mentally sound, and not under conviction of a felony.

To register to vote, call:

Orleans Parish; 565-7135.

Jefferson Parish, East Bank; 736-6191.

Jefferson Parish, West Bank; 364-2670.

St. Bernard Parish; 278-4232.

For more information call:

League of Women Voters, New Orleans; 581-9106, Jefferson Parish; 828-4332, Louisiana; 1-800-288-8683, St. Bernard; 279-3146.

Republican Party of Jefferson; 888-4700.

Republican Party of New Orleans; 482-3281.

Jury Duty

Residents between the ages of 18 and 70 are called to serve on jury duty. Once jurors have served on Criminal duty, they will not be called again unless they wish to have their names placed back on the rolls. They may be called for Federal duty. Attorneys, doctors, residents with physical handicaps, and stay-at-home parents with very young children at home may ask for exemptions. Follow instructions on your jury-request form.

NEW ORLEANS REAL ESTATE

Information and Referrals

Local Boards of Realtors are good sources of general information and referrals:

Jefferson Board of Realtors, Inc.; 885-3200.

Real Estate of New Orleans; 525-4811.

Most real-estate agencies in the New Orleans area have branch offices in St. Tammany Parish, on the north shore of Lake Pontchartrain, as well as in the other developing parishes, such as St. Charles, just upriver from New Orleans.

Renting

Apartments in New Orleans may be part of a modern complex (if you choose suburbia) or a quaint set of rooms in an old house. Air conditioning is a necessity (either central or window units, which are used in many of the older houses); the heating system will probably be gas, many of the older houses using floor furnaces and space heaters. Ceiling fans work well with the high ceilings of the old houses, both to cool you in the summer and to blow the warm air down to "people level" in the winter. Check on whether or not the neighborhood is prone to flooding, what arrangements are available for parking (often, in the older sections, there is no driveway), and the proximity of public transportation.

Unfurnished apartments in New Orleans may or may not be equipped with stove and refrigerator, so be sure to ask.

For information, call **Apartment Association of New Orleans;** 888-2492, or the Board of Realtors in the appropriate parish.

Quick Overview of the Neighborhoods

The boundary lines of the City of New Orleans and of Orleans Parish (or county—remember?) are exactly the same. Why are there two political entities governing the same piece of ground? Two reasons come to mind immediately: no one likes to give up political clout once they have it, and it would be very time consuming to sort things out and rearrange them. So at the moment, the public schools are run by Orleans Parish, as is the Sheriff's Office, but police and fire departments and libraries are run by the city. The main thing you need to be aware of at this point is that you will see both names used, but they refer to exactly the same land area.

Neighborhoods in New Orleans are referred to as being "above Canal Street" or "below Canal Street." Those "above Canal Street" include the lower Garden District, the Garden District, Uptown, and Carrollton. Those "below Canal Street" include the French Quarter, Creole Faubourgs, Gentilly, and New Orleans East. Mid-City and Lakeview sort of straddle the line.

The **Garden District** is delightful, famous, close to the Central Business District, and very expensive. It includes the area from Jackson Square to Louisiana Avenue and from St. Charles Avenue to Magazine Street (see SELF GUIDED CITY TOURS chapter).

The **Lower Garden District** is even older, closer to the Central Business District, and is currently the "in" area for restoration. You may also hear it referred to as the Coliseum Square Section. The Friends of the Cabildo, a support group for the Louisiana Museum Complex, did an excellent book on this section, which is available in bookstores or at the public library.

Between Magazine Street and the river, and from the Lower Garden District to Audubon Park, is an area loosely called the **Irish Channel.** (The section was originally considered to extend only to Louisiana Avenue.) Most of the Irish have become quite affluent and moved away. Today, it has become a checkerboard of black families who have lived there for years and young, white executives who relish the challenge of restoring the shotgun cottages. The area contains everything from Kingsley House, the oldest settlement house in the city which was founded by Trinity Episcopal Church, to St. Alphonsus Church, from Hansen's, which is reputed to be the best "snoball" stand in New Orleans, located across from the wharves on Tchoupitoulas Street, to Clancy's, a fine restaurant complete with black-coated waiters and gleaming white linen. Don't try to figure out this section without a good real-estate agent as a guide.

In the **uptown** section most of the houses are turn-of-the-century or older. Many have been carefully restored and painted in marvelous pastel colors. Gardens are well kept. Audubon Park is close by, and three of the city's institutions of higher learning, as well as many of its private elementary and secondary schools, are located in this section. It is close to the Central Business District and there is good public transportation. Prices range all the way from expensive to "a real find."

Along the shores of Lake Pontchartrain, you will find **Lake Vista, Lake Shore,** and **Lake Terrace.** These are all relatively new sections, built in the fifties and sixties on filled land that was once part of the lake. They are planned areas; the lots are small but there may be more of the feeling that you are used to in other cities. **Lakeview,** from City Park Avenue to Robert E. Lee Boulevard, is older but similar in feeling.

Gentilly is an old area of town with interesting houses and historic street names. Three of the city's finest predominantly black private schools, Dillard University, St. Augustine High School, and St. Mary's Academy, are located in this area. So is the historic Fair Grounds Racetrack.

The **Faubourg Marigny,** located below Esplanade Avenue, is the first New Orleans "subdivision," the first residential section to be built outside the wall of the Vieux Carre. Today, its historic value and its quaint atmosphere are once more being appreciated, and it is enjoying a resurgence in popularity. We again refer you to the books published by the Friends of the Cabildo, one of which is an excellent study of the Creole Faubourgs. This is currently a prime location for buying low and renovating.

New Orleans East is located between the Inner-Harbor Navigational Canal, the lake, the Orleans Parish line, and the Intracoastal Waterway. It is a new section of New Orleans, still building, full of new homes, apartments, and fine shopping centers. Lots are

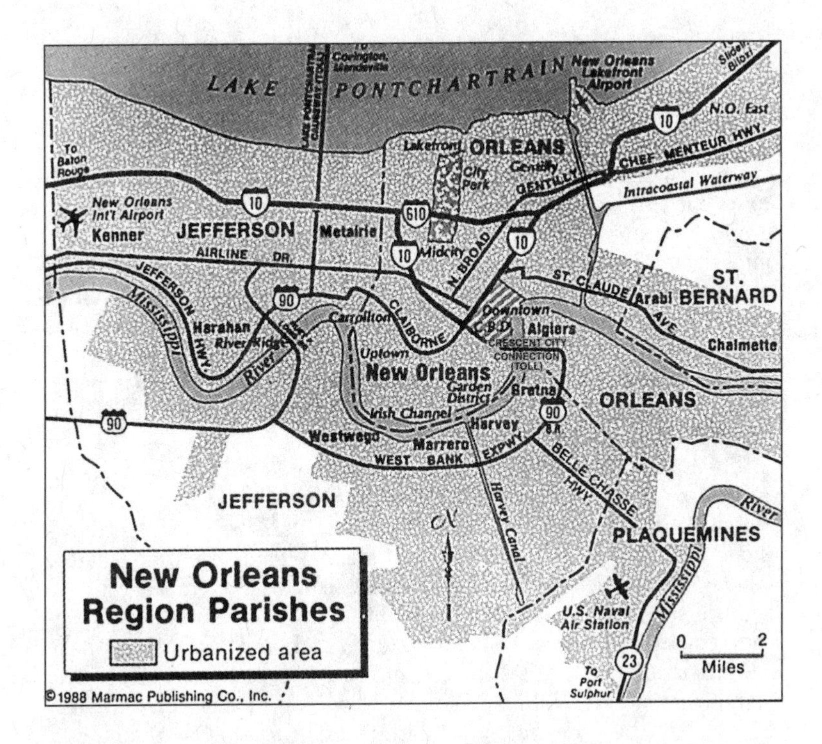

available—a scarce commodity in New Orleans. The Louisiana Nature Center and the Michoud Space Facility are located here.

The **West Bank** is currently accessible to New Orleans over the Huey Long Bridge in Jefferson Parish, the twin-span Crescent City Connection bridge, and numerous ferries. One of the ferries takes you right to the foot of Canal Street, a delightful ride.

Algiers is the oldest of the West Bank communities, and the only one in Orleans Parish. Others are Gretna, Harvey, Marrero, and Westwego, all in Jefferson Parish. These areas have grown so rapidly in the years since the first span of the Crescent City Connection was opened that you can no longer tell where one stops and the next starts.

Old Metairie is the area on the upriver side of Orleans Parish between the parish line and Causeway Boulevard and between Airline Highway and Veterans Boulevard. This is where the uptown people go if they move to the "suburbs." It was developed between the thirties and the fifties and is a stable area with homes ranging from practical to palatial. Many are on slightly bigger lots. It is a pleasant place to live.

New Metairie includes everything else between the Orleans Parish line and the city of Kenner and from Airline Highway to Lake Pontchartrain. This, since the 1970s, has been the fastest growing community in the metropolitan area. All of Metairie, Old and New, is an unincorporated area, governed by the Jefferson Parish Council. The homes are all new, almost all brick. Many neighborhoods have swim clubs. There is a choice of public, private, or parochial schools. It takes somewhat longer to get to the Central Business District during peak hours but you may decide that it is worth it. It is a short drive to the airport and to the Causeway over Lake Pontchartrain, which makes it quite convenient for those who do a lot of traveling.

Kenner, although it is hard to tell where it starts and stops, is one of the largest cities in Louisiana. It is the area around New Orleans International Airport, from river to the lake, and from David Drive to the St. Charles Parish line. Much of the city is new and includes everything from apartment complexes to elegant homes bordering a golf course.

Covington, Mandeville, and **Slidell** are three old communities on the north shore of Lake Pontchartrain. Since the 1970s, they have become bedroom communities for New Orleans. There is still a feeling of country, a slower pace. It is getting harder and harder to find a native as newcomers flock to the North Shore, searching for relief from the "culture shock" of moving to this area. There are a number of commuter buses and van pools which travel back and forth across Lake Pontchartrain each day. The Causeway serves Covington and Mandeville, and the I-10 Bridge from New Orleans East serves Slidell. The North Shore has many delightful small shops, good restaurants, state parks, and outdoor recreation opportunities. Slidell is also home of the Slidell Factory Stores shopping mall and Slidell's Olde Towne Antique District. The Slidell Chamber of Commerce publishes an extensive list of interest groups and clubs on the North Shore. This area is definitely worth a good look.

Another neighboring suburb is **Chalmette** in St Bernard Parish, which is now conveniently connected to the I-10 with a new expressway extension, I-510. Since the early 1990s, many newlyweds and young families have moved into the area. There are numerous convenient stores, groceries, restaurants, movie theaters, churches, and much more. Next to the river, the "older" sections of St. Bernard and Orleans parishes abut each other, which made St. Bernard one of the city's first bedroom communities. It also has the reputation of being an extremely safe area with good public schools and even a junior college.

PARTYTIME AND ENTERTAINMENT

What better way to cement new friendships or honor "old" friends than by having a really bang-up party? Since New Orleans is a "party town," there are a whole lot of (*beaucoup!*) party and special-event resources. A few of these, for adults and children, are listed below for your consideration. For a catered party, if your chosen spot does not offer catering, check "caterers" in the telephone directory. It is also important to check local publications or "community information" in the telephone directory to see that your planned date does not conflict with other events. After all, you would not want to miss another party!

If what you really want to do is go out, then we have a few suggestions of popular New Orleans party places and services.

All Aboard the Streetcar

On a typical Saturday morning, you will see streetcars trundling down St. Charles Avenue, filled with crepe paper streamers, balloons, cupcakes, and lively little people. Later in the day, the young may be replaced by their parents, the cupcakes by cocktails, and there may be a jazz band on board. Either way, the party will be a success. Call the **Regional Transit Authority (RTA);** 242-2600.

Aquarium Joys

The **Aquarium of the Americas,** Riverfront and Canal Street, Woldenberg Park; 861-2537. This is a wonderful party place for either adults or children. Part or all of the Aquarium can be rented for adult cocktail parties, with buffet tables and jazz bands placed among the beautifully lit tanks.

Children's parties are truly fun here—for day parties or sleepover events.

A Block-Long Bash

Block parties are popular in spring and fall. Get together with your neighbors, share expenses, have lots of friends, lots of food and drink, and a good band. The afternoon or evening will be a great success. Just be sure to: get permission from the city to close off your block during the party; hire an off-duty policeman to make sure that extra people aren't lured by the fun; plan a rain date—just in case. Call **Block Party Permits;** 565-6840.

Buggy Rides

Buggy rides are fun. Rent a buggy to tour the French Quarter, and follow the tour with a picnic in Jackson Square. Either do your own individual picnic baskets, buy muffulettas and baklava at the Central or Progress groceries, or order a basket prepared for you at **Chez Nous Charcuterie,** 5701 Magazine St.; 899-7303. To rent buggies, call either **Mid-City Carriages;** 581-4415, or **Old Quarter Tours;** 944-0446.

Carousel Party

The Last Carousel in City Park is an excellent and unique place to have a child's birthday party or an adult's cocktail party. Day or night, the fantasy ambience of the carousel pavilion provides a party background unequaled anywhere. Built in 1906, City Park's carousel and pavilion have been beautifully refurbished. Call 488-2896.

City Park also has its own catering service; 488-2896, or you can provide your own refreshments.

Charter a Boat

You may want to cruise on a riverboat to the Audubon Zoo on the *Cotton Blossom*, leaving from the foot of Canal Street. Or charter the *Natchez* steamboat. Both boats are available for private parties and food and drink can be catered on board. Call 586-8777.

Dreamy Meals and Such

Perhaps you'd like to host a dinner at **Antoine's** (581-4422), a brunch at **Commander's** (899-8221), or a breakfast at **Brennan's** (525-9711). It is just a phone call away. If you want something fun and informal try a snoball party at **Hansen's Sno-Blitz** on Tchoupitoulas Street (891-9788), or rent a snoball machine from **Snowizard** (1-800-366-9760, 832-3901). Either way, you can't go wrong. Other options are afternoon tea at **Windsor Court** (523-6000) or a children's tea party or Glamour Girl Party (471-0094).

Elegance Five Ways

When a special celebration, a romantic wedding, a chic cocktail party, or a formal reception is in the offing, consider entertaining at **Gallier Hall** (545 St. Charles Ave.; 565-7457), the beautifully restored Greek Revival gem that was once our City Hall; or perhaps you would prefer the **Opera Guild House,** a lovely Garden District mansion on Prytania Street (see SELF GUIDED TOURS, Garden District Tour). For information, call 899-1945.

There are two beautiful and meticulously restored historic houses in the French Quarter where a party or reception would be surrounded by the Old World elegance of the French Quarter's Victorian era. **The Gallier House** (1118-32 Royal St.; 525-5661), home of noted architect James Gallier, Jr., reflects life in the 1860s. The **Hermann-Grima House** (820 St. Louis St.; 525-5661), built in 1831, comes complete with an open-hearth kitchen, stable, and large French-styled hidden courtyard (see SELF GUIDED TOURS, French Quarter Tour).

The **Pitot House** (1400 Moss St.; 482-0312) and grounds on Bayou St. John is an excellent surviving example of a colonial Louisiana plantation house. In the spring, this is a popular place for weddings.

Flights of Fantasy

Why not invite one or two couples and tour the city by airplane? You will have a unique view of your new home or a brand-new perspective of your old one. We recommend late afternoon to dusk; the sight of the setting sun turning the river and lake to gold as the city's lights come flickering on is absolutely unforgettable. Call **Air Reldan;** 241-9400, or **Lakefront Airport;** 243-4010.

Games and Clowns

Celebration Station (5959 Veterans Blvd., Metairie; 887-7888) is extremely popular for children's parties. You can rent a private room for pizza, party food, and drinks, then pick a variety of activities for your guests. There are myriad choices—from putt-putt golf to rides, games, and mazes.

Laser Tag and Video Arcade (8916 Veterans Blvd., Metairie; 469-7475) is a special place for parties with its 7,000-square-foot multilevel laser-tag arena. Laser tag is quite popular with teens, but adults enjoy it too—"you don't just play the game . . . you are the game." Group rates are available.

Riverbend Gymnastics Parties (200 Academy Dr.; 486-6141, 1200 Veterans Blvd.; 486-6352) feature high-energy activities and exciting games. There are trampolines, beams, bars, and constant supervision. Children especially like the nonstop activity. Don't forget your camera.

JoJo the Clown and Magician is a skilled entertainer who can even juggle and make balloon animals and designs. Call 739-9400.

Gracious Getaways

Oak Alley Plantation, a pleasant drive upriver from New Orleans, provides a dreamy setting for large weddings, parties, picnics; or consider renting a cabin or two for the weekend and having a houseparty. For details, call 1-800-44-ALLEY.

Houmas House Plantation and Gardens (40136 Hwy. 942, Burnside; 504-473-7841, New Orleans number 522-2262) is a wonderful party or reception place, with its beautiful and imposing Greek Revival architecture and large gallery.

Happy Faces

Happy Face Creations offers face painting for all, even airbrush face painting with special designs. Call 271-4FUN (4386).

How About a Hayride or Pony Ride?

A leisurely ride along the Mississippi in a hay-filled wagon, a stop for games and refreshments, and a return trip enlivened by songs and stories make for a very popular young people's birthday party. Or have the hayride come to you: pony rides and stagecoach rides will complete any party. Call **Pony Tales** at 469-0148.

Mardi Gras Party

Have a party in a float warehouse or "den" of Blaine Kern's Mardi Gras World. Partygoers can have a marvelous meal while a jazz band plays on stage and costumed entertainers cavort among the tables. Then guests are treated to a true Carnival parade complete with minifloats, bands, and costumed riders tossing traditional "throws" to the delight of all. Even themed cocktail parties include parades here. Or a complete miniparade can be brought to you! Call or write for your options: **Mardi Gras World;** 233 Newton St.; 361-7821, 1-800-362-8213, fax 361-3164, www.mardigrasworld.com.

Parade Parties

If you live anywhere near a Mardi Gras parade route, this is an easy way to entertain. Invite your friends to come early and park close by, serve snacks and drinks and a meal, watch the parade go by, and have more snacks ready afterwards. Be sure to have "go cups" and bags for parade throws.

A Play-the-Ponies Party

Luncheon or dinner at the racetrack is another favorite way of entertaining in New Orleans. From November to March call the **Fair Grounds** for luncheon reservations, 1751 Gentilly Blvd.; 943-2200. Enjoy a good meal, a drink or two, and let the horses do the entertaining for you.

Psychic Powers

Psychic **Sister Teresa** will do "readings" and predictions with tarot cards and palm readings. Adults will definitely have fun with this. Call or write 1417 Center St., Arabi; 277-2336, 1-800-918-9972.

A River Respite

Reserve a campground (all or part of it), just an hour's drive across the Causeway. You will have 20 tree-shaded acres on the Tangipahoa River, complete with beach, canoes, an excursion boat, tubing, good food prepared for you, and cabins or tent camping. For information, call or write **Ponchatoula Beach,** Rt. 2, Box 45, Ponchatoula, LA 70454; 1-386-6844.

The **Riverview Room** in the Jackson Brewery is a large reception room with one side overlooking the mighty Mississippi River. Call 525-3000.

Rock 'n Bowl

Mid-City Lanes Rock 'n Bowl (4133 S. Carrollton Ave.; 482-3133) is a novel and highly successful combination of live music and open bowling. Lineups include top blues, rock, zydeco, Cajun, and swing acts. So rent a few lanes, bowl with your friends, then stay for the food, music, and dancing. You may even see a few visiting celebrities. Both teens and adults enjoy this combination.

Smashing Status Creators

Elegance at the **New Orleans Museum of Art** or casual chic at the **Audubon Zoo**—for hundreds of your closest friends—is costly, but definitely impressive.

Storyland Party and Storytelling

In City Park's **Storyland,** have a party with the Little Mermaid, Mother Goose, Jenny Giraffe, on a private ship, or by the crooked house. Situated under enormous live oak trees, Storyland has a magical quality and even a castle. You can bring your own cake and refreshments, or City Park Catering can do it for you. Call 483-9381, 488-2896.

Where else but in New Orleans will you experience stories that are dramatically different from anywhere else in the world? The **Storyteller of the Strange and Amusing** is a New Orleans native, author, and storyteller with years of experience who will entertain children or adults with age-appropriate stories; and, in the meantime, all will discover the uniqueness of this subtropical area and some of its unusual and delightful characters. A résumé can be sent upon request. Call or write 283-9358, fax 283-9463.

Sweets and Eats

Swiss Confectionery (747 St. Charles Ave.; 522-7788) is extremely popular with locals for a variety of novelty or custom-made cakes, with the best cake flavor and texture in the city. Generations of New Orleans brides have chosen Swiss Confectionery cakes for weddings and showers. Delivery service is available.

Gambino's Bakeries (3609 Toledano St.; 822-3340, 3821 Veterans Blvd.; 885-7500) make the best doberge cake in the city. This is a tall cake with many layers of special filling, all covered with a hard, thin icing.

Charlie's Deli (515 Harrison Ave.; 486-1766) provides catering of a variety of delicious local foods.

Swinging Skaters

Roller or ice skating parties are always fun, especially if you reserve the rink just for you and your friends. For roller skating, call **Skate World,** 701 W. Judge Perez Dr.; 271-7036, or **Airline Skate Center,** 6711 Airline Dr.; 733-2248.

CHILDREN

One of New Orleans' best-kept secrets (contrary to what many "grownup" people say) is that the New Orleans metropolitan area definitely is a place for children and their families to visit and truly have fun. This chapter will help you get started, then will continue to guide you to the treasures—contemporary and old—that have abounded since the French discovered this area 300 years ago. In addition, there are numerous specially scheduled events for children and families which will be listed in local newspapers and magazines. Look for these publications in local bookstores, coffeehouses, grocery stores, and family-type restaurants.

Several good Web sites list calendars of events: www.bestofneworleans.com, www.loveneworleans.com/kidspage/, and the New Orleans Public Library's kids page at www.gnofn.org/~nopl/kids/kids.htm.

Here are some beginning suggestions. These "starters" have been proven by local parents and educators who know that New Orleans really is for children and families.

One of the first things a visiting child should do is ride across the **Mississippi River** on the ferry, which you board at the foot of Canal Street (see SIGHTS). Once you get to the West Bank and Old Algiers, take the free shuttle to **Mardi Gras World**—an absolute delight for the entire family! Watch a colorful video about Mardi Gras, try on costumes, and see elaborate costumes on display. Then go into the float "den" and see float making in progress, view enormous completed floats, and climb into a minifloat. Don't forget your camera! Then, catch your breath, catch the shuttle and the ferry to return to the East Bank. Call Mardi Gras World for shuttle bus times: 361-7821.

After a relaxing ferry ride, walk across the plaza to the **World Trade Center** building. There is a special outside glass elevator which whisks passengers to the observation deck for a bird's-eye view of the ferry and West Bank and a panoramic view of the city as a whole.

Stroll through the **French Market** to see and smell all the fresh produce, and then through the **Flea Market** to shop for everything from masks to beads, jewelry, and clothing. Top it all off with a stop at **Cafe du Monde** for those wonderfully warm French doughnuts, *beignets*, laden with mounds of confectioner's sugar. Children can choose orange juice, chocolate milk, or maybe *cafe au lait* (mostly warm milk).

The **Jackson Square Pedestrian Mall** is completely closed to vehicular traffic, day and night, and is a constant source of wonderful street entertainers. All types of musicians, tap dancers, mimes, jugglers, magicians, and balloon sculptors perfomr usually just for applause and a donation of your choice tossed into their hats. Children love the circuslike atmosphere and the Lucky Dog hot dog stand. Also, don't forget to stroll around outside Jackson Square's iron fence and view the artists at work "on the fence" with their oils and pastels. You might even consider one of the five-minute caricature specials.

Another entertaining and delightful stroll is through the **Royal Street Promenade.** Royal Street from behind the Cathedral to Bienville Street is barricaded against vehicular traffic. Children are thrilled with the prospect of walking in the street (usually a "no-no"). They can experience street entertainment and shopping in this authentic 1800s "mall." Look for plaques on the buildings, and check SELF GUIDED CITY TOURS in this book, to have children discover the dates and uses of some of these old, yet well-preserved, buildings. Some T-shirt and souvenir shops are located among the antique shops and boutiques.

The **Audubon Zoological Garden** is one of the five best in the country! Plan at least half a day at the zoo. We recommend additional time for a streetcar ride to the park and at the end of the day, when it's time to relax, a boat ride back to Canal Street. We guarantee that everyone will sleep well that night.

Also an Audubon Institute facility is the **Aquarium of the Americas,** where children can easily spend half a day. There is a walk-through tunnel of fish, fish feeding in the giant Gulf of Mexico tank, alligators, snakes, penguins, otters, an Amazon rainforest, a petting section, and much more! Just next door is the **Entergy IMAX Theatre,** with a five-and-a-half-story screen with Surround Sound. Call for move title and showing times: 581-4629.

The **Louisiana Science and Nature Center** is another super place for children, with its planetarium and hands-on exhibits. Call to check on special programs and guided tours. We recommend allowing half a day for this excursion, too.

Frequently, navy ships from the United States and from foreign countries visit the port of New Orleans. They are open to visitors during their stay and offer interesting tours to adults and children alike. Check local publications or Riverwalk mall information.

Excellent children's theater is offered by **Le Petit Theatre du Vieux Carre;** check newspaper listings. The museums are full of exhibits that children will enjoy. Among them are the toys at the **Presbytere** and the

Mardi Gras costumes at the **U.S. Mint** (both part of the Louisiana State Museum Complex), the view of life in "the old days" at **Gallier House,** the Civil War exhibits at the **Confederate Museum,** both the historical figures and the "Chambers of Horrors" at the **Musee Conti Wax Museum,** and 1850s cooking demonstrations at the **Hermann-Grima House.**

The **Louisiana Children's Museum,** in the Warehouse District (see SIGHTS), is a must for parents and grandparents with excursions on their minds. You'll find yourself having as much fun as your young folks.

Also, don't miss the year-round activities, classes, good advice, and general fun offered by the **Parenting Center at Children's Hospital,** 200 Henry Clay Ave. at the river; 896-9591. There are also a parent support group, lunchtime seminars, community talks, and a "Warm Line" (895-KIDS) to help parents.

On those hectic days when young children and teens need an active change of pace, there are several alternatives. **Celebration Station** (887-7888) has rides, games, and putt-putt golf among its many activities. For teens, there is **Laser Tag and Video Arcade** (469-7475). Then, for everyone, bowling is fun at **Mid-City Lanes Rock 'n Bowl** (482-3133), with live music in the evenings.

OK, those are your "starters." Below are listed a few more kid-specific places.

St. Charles Avenue streetcar
Louisiana State Museum Complex
Jazzland Theme Park (when opened)
Jean Lafitte National Historical Park—Barataria and Chalmette units
Rivertown and LaSalle Landing (12 attractions)
Woldenberg River Park

Need more? In the SIGHTS section, adults may discover other areas of interest for their children. New Orleans has so much to offer!

Children's Tours

In the SELF GUIDED CITY TOURS chapter, refreshment and shopping stops are suggested among the places of interest. This should help to accommodate the interest and activity level of children touring with adults.

However, if there is a need for something different and more child specific, consider a company that will also conduct children's tours. Whether on foot or by bus, these are lots of fun and a little educational, too. **Melody's Tours** offers special children's or young people's tours of the New Orleans metropolitan area which are geared to your group's age and interest levels. For information call 361-5959 or 283-9358 or fax 361-0932. For some literary lagniappe, young children may wish to follow the jaunts of a local literary character, Jenny Giraffe, and discover New Orleans through these unique eyes.

Restaurants

The DINING chapter of this guide lists area restaurants by type of food, location, and price. Some restaurants are also designated with a CS—Children's Specials. There are many choices depending on the type of food you want to eat, in which part of the metro area you wish to eat, your cost considerations, and the type of ambience you desire. All CS-designated restaurants have a variety of offerings—everything from coloring-book menus with crayons or table coverings to draw on to special children's menu items. You may wish to call for a particular restaurant's children's specials - they will all be willing to help you have a wonderful dining experience with children.

Teens often gather in the area's many coffee shops (which also serve teas, soft drinks, juices, and light meals). These are great after-school meeting, socializing, and studying places. They are quite popular on the weekends with live music and/or poetry readings.

Mardi Gras for Children

If your trip coincides with the Carnival season, please see SPECIAL EVENTS for basic Mardi Gras information for families. This CHILDREN chapter will give the first timer with children a few extra tips.

Here are basic, common-sense rules to help everyone have a good, safe time:

Obey all parking signs, and never block anyone's driveway even a little.

Stand behind the barricades during a passing parade. Floats are beautiful but can be very dangerous if you get too close while they are moving.

Use ladders with caution.

Do not use glass containers.

Keep children close to you, and also establish an after-parade meeting spot (just in case).

Ambulances, first-aid stations, and lost-child stations are located along parade routes. Ask a police officer for directions.

For some literary lagniappe and good basic Mardi Gras information, purchase a copy of *Arthur Hardy's Mardi Gras Guide*. This indispensable guide details parade routes, times, and themes and offers a lot of Carnival trivia. There are several good children's picture books which delightfully explain Mardi Gras. *Jenny Giraffe's Mardi Gras Ride* gives an entertaining someone-new-in-the-city view of this holiday and its parades.

Uninitiated parade viewers might consider the neighboring parish parades, with their less intense crowds. The Jefferson Parish parades are viewed best from one of the mall areas—Clearview Mall or Lakeside Mall. The Chalmette parades are the least crowded and very family oriented. The parades travel alongside wide, parklike neutral grounds. These areas are popular with young children who can run and play, while families picnic and visit as they wait for the parade (or during it). Teens also enjoy being able to walk up and down these neutral grounds to visit with friends or just "be seen".

The weekend before Fat Tuesday is the time of the Superkrewe parades. With children, the Bacchus parade, put on by an all-men's organization (the original Superkrewe), is best viewed at the beginning of the parade's route along St. Charles Avenue. It really becomes crowd-intensive closer to downtown. The Orpheus parade, a bit more of a family-oriented parade put on by a newer krewe of both men and women, can be well viewed all along the parade route. Whatever your choice, have fun!

BITS AND PIECES

New Orleans has stories to tell, factual history that reads like tales of intrigue and fantasies that are reenacted annually at Carnival and in daily fais-do-dos. In this magical city the ordinary and extraordinary swap places as swiftly as masks are donned or dropped. The rich cultural mix, the hot delta climate, and the position as gateway to the Americas all provide a fertile ground where traditions live on and new legends flourish. Here are bits and pieces of both.

—Did you know that the word "craps"—as in the well-known game of chance—originated in New Orleans? Bernard Marigny, a flamboyant character of the turn of the century (the 19th century, that is) learned the game while visiting London, and couldn't wait to get home to teach it to all his French cronies here. It quickly became the Frenchmen's favorite game. The Americans were already referring to the Frenchmen as "crapauds," meaning "frogs" in French, because they ate frog legs, so it was only logical that the name of the game so popular with the "crapauds" would become "craps."

—The first play was presented in English in New Orleans in 1828.

—Camp Street, which runs from Canal Street to Audubon Park, was the site of the slave camp for the Gravier Plantation.

—The only hill in the city of New Orleans, located in the Audubon Zoological Garden, was built by the WPA (the Works Progress Administration of the 1930s) so that the children of New Orleans would know what a hill looked like!

—The Cajuns of South Louisiana, more than 900,000 strong, are the largest French-speaking minority in the United States.

—John Law's scheme of the 1700s to make paradise of the Louisiana Swampland was called "the Mississippi Bubble."

—"Mississippi Bandits" was the name given by the French to John Law's henchmen who kidnapped unwilling French citizens and sent them sailing off to the New World. The opera *Manon* tells of one such incident.

—New Orleans is below sea level in many places. When it rains, 14 huge pumps pull the water off the streets, through an intricate system of 165 miles of canals, and out into Lake Pontchartrain.

—New Orleanians have always had minds of their own. Way back during the Spanish regime, Governor Unzaga said that to deal with the citizens "an enlightened prudence and a good deal of toleration are necessary."

—The bayous of South Louisiana have long been a haven for smugglers who transported their goods by cart from their carefully hidden ships to New Orleans.

—Louisiana is the only state to have had French-language daily newspapers and a French-language state Constitution.

—New Orleans is protected from Mississippi River flooding by a system of levees, 18 miles long on each side of the river, designed and maintained by the U.S. Army Corps of Engineers. There are also levees on the Lake Pontchartrain side of the city and along parish boundaries. When the river is at flood stage, the water lapping the levees is higher than the streets and houses on the other side.

—Jackson Square became a "tent city" in 1794 in order to house the victims of the great fire. (At that time, it was still the "Place d'Armes.")

—Wherever and whenever you eat seafood in the United States today, chances are one in four that a South Louisiana Cajun caught it!

—Congo Square, now Louis Armstrong Park, was the site of weekly "bamboula" dances, held by slaves. Louis Moreau Gottschalk, a black Creole composer much performed today, adapted the rhythms of this dance music and turned it into symphonies.

—To get to the West Bank, you have to travel east across the Mississippi River.

—Tennessee Williams, America's premier modern playwright, attributed the flowering of his talent to living in the "freeing atmosphere of the French Quarter." He maintained a home here until his death. Other authors who have come under the spell of the French Quarter are William Faulkner, Ernest Hemingway, Lyle Saxon, George Washington Cable, Frances Parkinson Keyes, and Robert Tallant.

—The position of first governor of Louisiana was offered to the Marquis de Lafayette, the French hero of the American Revolution, by President Thomas Jefferson; Lafayette, although he had come upon hard times, said no. Then Andrew Jackson asked for the job and Jefferson said no.

—Dueling was popularized in New Orleans by officers from Napoleon's army. During the 1830s, New Orleans was the dueling capital of the world.

—Pepe Llulla, New Orleans' most famous instructor in the art of dueling, kept in practice by shooting eggs off his son's head! As a sideline, he owned and operated a private cemetery.

—Dorothy Dix, famous predecessor of "Dear Abby" and "Ann Landers," was, in real life, Elizabeth Merriweather Gilmer of New Orleans, and lived for many years on Exposition Boulevard overlooking Audubon Park.

—The statue of Benjamin Franklin, originally in Lafayette Square and now in Benjamin Franklin High School, was sculpted to repay a $5,000 loan. Hiram Powers, one of America's great sculptors, borrowed from friends in New Orleans when he found himself in financial straits, and did the statue when he realized he could not come up with the cash to repay them.

—Canal Street is the widest business/commercial street in the United States.

—Gen. P. G. T. Beauregard, the famous Confederate general who reputedly fired the first shot of the Civil War, was referred to locally as "Napoleon in Gray."

—Louisiana was the first state to legalize "glove contests," or boxing. At the Olympic Athletic Club on Royal Street, James J. Corbett knocked out John L. Sullivan to win the world's heavyweight championship and the huge sum of $25,000. The loser received nothing.

—In 1852, New Orleans had a triple funeral, attended by almost 50,000 people, at which none of the deceased were present. A funeral car carried three urns, which substituted for the bodies of Henry Clay, Daniel Webster, and John C. Calhoun. The parade was so elaborate that it took an hour and a half to pass any given spot.

—The longest bridge over an inland waterway in the world is the Pontchartrain Causeway.

—The Code Noir of 1724, along with giving rules for the proper treatment of slaves, banished all Jews and Protestants from the Louisiana Territory. It was in effect until the Louisiana Purchase in 1803.

—"Free Lunch," set out on the bar, was a tradition dear to the hearts of American men until Prohibition days. It began in the St. Louis Bar on Exchange Place in the French Quarter.

—Westwego, on the West Bank, is the only town in the United States whose name forms a complete sentence! It was named by survivors of a coastal hurricane who chose the site because it was higher ground.

—In 1982, a newspaper in Glasgow, Scotland, carried a feature story about alligators running loose in the streets of New Orleans! The fact is that Louisiana has about 1,000 licensed alligator hunters, but none of them hunt in New Orleans.

—Dixie, the popular name for the Confederate States of America, was originally the mispronunciation by the American customers of the "dix" (or 10-franc note) issued by the Citizens Bank of New Orleans.

—When Judah Touro, the well-known Jewish philanthropist, died, he left $30,000 a year to Canal Street, to keep it beautiful.

—John Davis, who built the first gambling casino in New Orleans, became known (for good or otherwise) as "the father of gambling in America."

—The intersection of Metairie Road and I-10 might still be occupied by the Metairie Race Course if the members of that exclusive group had not blackballed Charles Howard, who ran the last of the legal lotteries in the city. When he was refused admission to the club, he bought the property—and turned it into Metairie Cemetery!

—There are more sets of tails (full dress) and tuxedoes owned by men in New Orleans than anywhere else in the country.

—In the course of its history, 10 flags have flown over the state of Louisiana:

1541-1682—the Spanish
1682-1762—the French Fleur-de-Lis
1762—the British (briefly over Baton Rouge)
1762-1800—the Spanish
1800-1803—the Tri-Color of France
1803—the United States. At this time the flag had only 15 stars
1810—the flag of West Florida (briefly)
1861—Independent Lousisiana
1861—the Confederate States Stars and Bars
1868—Louisiana readmitted to the Union

—New Orleans has been home to two nuns who have been canonized saints of the Roman Catholic Church. St. Frances Xavier Cabrini operated a school in the French Quarter. Mother Elizabeth Seton, the first native-born American citizen to achieve sainthood in the Roman Catholic Church, was a Sister of Charity and devoted her life to nursing and education.

—The New Orleans Lawn Tennis Club, founded on Christmas Day 1876, is the oldest club for tennis players in the United States.

—The name Louisiana is a mix of the French "Louisiane" and the Spanish "Luisiana."

—World-famous Tabasco Sauce is made at Avery Island, Louisiana, and stored in casks for years. As each cask is opened in preparation for bottling, it must be taste-tested by a member of the founding family, the McIlhenneys.

—The nation's first trolley cars powered by overhead suspended wires were used on the line that carried passengers to New Orleans' City Park.

—It's hard to believe now, but in the early 1900s a law was passed that closed all the racetracks in the city in order to "redeem New Orleans from pillage by the nation's gamblers."

—There have been European ships sailing up and down the Mississippi ever since DeSoto first found it in 1541. The river was named by the Algonquin Indians, "miss" meaning "by" and "sipi" meaning "river."

—The capital of Louisiana is Baton Rouge, about two hours upriver from New Orleans. (The name means "red stick" in French.)

—The state flower is the magnolia, and the state bird is the pelican.

A GLOSSARY

New Orleans needs a glossary! Here is ours for you. New Orleans has a specialized vocabulary derived from its French, Spanish, Indian, and black heritage and its unique geographical location. This vocabulary has been handed down from generation to generation and remains in everyday usage.

Acadians—French from Nova Scotia who were driven out by the English during the French and Indian War. They began arriving in Louisiana about 1755 and settled in the bayou country. Longfellow's narrative poem, "Evangeline," tells the story of this group. The name has been shortened to "Cajun." They are descendants of the very first Europeans to arrive in North America. They established a colony in Canada in 1604, three years before the Jamestown, Virginia settlement and 16 years before the English came to Plymouth, Massachusetts.

Armoire—A two-door cabinet with shelves, usually quite large; a moveable closet.

"At the foot of"—Where a street meets the Mississippi River.

Bagasse—The residue left after the juice has been pressed out of the sugarcane; it is used in making insulation.

Banquette—Sidewalk. They were originally made of wood, often from flatboats which were broken up when they reached New Orleans. They were built a foot or so above the street; in rainy weather they were literally the "banks" of a stream.

Batture—The land built up by the silting action of the river. Usually as one bank is built up, the opposite bank is eaten away. Before the levees were built, a number of plantation houses "went into the river" because of such changes.

Bayou—A natural canal or secondary watercourse, whose water level is dependent on the overflowing of the major river or the marsh draining. The word is the Europeans' adaptation of the Choctaw Indian word *bayuk*, meaning small, sluggish stream.

Cajun—See Acadians.

Casket girls—Brought from France in the early days of Louisiana to be wives to men already here. They were cared for and chaperoned by the Ursuline Nuns until suitable husbands were found. The name comes from the small "casket" or chest full of belongings which was all they were allowed to bring with them.

Cast iron—Made by pouring molten iron into a mold; thus, the designs can be very ornate and can be reproduced many times. New Orleans is known for its elaborate ironwork in balconies and gates.

Craps—Name given by the "Americains" to the well-known game of chance when it was brought to New Orleans from London by Bernard de Marigny, scion of a wealthy planter. Bernard taught the game to all his French friends, who took to it most enthusiastically. The "Americains" had already christened the French "crapauds" (from the French word for "frogs") because they ate frog legs. Now, in continued derision, they called their favorite game "craps."

Creole—According to New Orleans historian John Chase, a Creole is a native-born Orleanian of French and/or Spanish extraction. It comes from the Spanish *criollo*, which means children born in the colonies. Today, it is used to describe everything New Orleans you can imagine, including people, customs, culture, and cuisine.

Doubloon—Originally the "pieces of eight" treasured by Spanish conquistadors. Today, they are the "collector's item" of Mardi Gras, an old tradition revived in 1960. The aluminum coins, about 1½ inches in diameter, are thrown from the floats in Mardi Gras parades. Lately, they have been thrown in St. Patrick's and St. Joseph's Day parades as well.

Fais-do-do—The exuberant Cajun version of the traditional American country dance or a feast before sleeping.

Galleries—Wide porches, often two-story, lined with wooden or lacy iron posts. They afford protection from both rain and heat in the subtropical climate.

Garconniere—Special living quarters built for the young men of the family so that they could "enjoy life" without disturbing the rest of the family.

Gardes de frise—Interesting fan-shaped braces on the ends of some of the iron balconies. They add both strength and afford protection from intruders.

Gris-gris—Charms, talismans, or spells used to conjure up good or evil by believers in Voodoo.

Ilet—The name French settlers gave to city blocks which, after a rain, often appeared to be "islands" surrounded as they were by the streets full of water.

Joie de vivre—The French term for "living with joyous abandon," the perfect way to describe the native New Orleanian's view of life.

Lagniappe—That little something extra, the 13th in a dozen, traditionally given to good customers; the Creole merchants' way of saying "merci," thank you.

Laissez les bon temps rouler!—A favorite Cajun French expression meaning "let the good times roll!"

Levee—A continuous wall of earth, either natural or artificial, which lines the banks of a bayou or river and helps prevent flooding.

Make groceries—To go grocery shopping. Its origin is an old French Louisiana expression of "making market" in the French Market.

Mardi Gras—Literally "Fat Tuesday," the day of wild celebration before Lent begins, on Ash Wednesday, the 40 days before Easter.

Neutral ground—Originally referred to the wide middle section of Canal Street, planned to separate the often warring French and American populations of the city. The term now applies to any of the medians that mark and lend beauty to the main streets of New Orleans.

Parish—The Louisiana equivalent of a county, used first by the Spanish.

Parrain—Godfather.

"Pass a good time"—The Cajun way of saying "have fun."

Picayune—An old Spanish coin worth 6¼ cents or half a "bit." It is the name of New Orleans' newspaper.

Pirogue—Originally long, narrowing shallow draft boats, handhewn from cypress logs by the Indians. They were adapted and renamed by the Cajuns and are still in use today.

Porte-cochere—An overhang or archway under which passengers can enter or alight from automobiles or carriages.

Shotgun house—Term applied to frame cottages built with four or five rooms in such a way that if a shotgun was fired through the front door, the shell would pass through every room before exiting the back door. You will see them all over town.

Soiree—An evening party.

"Throw me something, mister"—The universal shout at Mardi Gras parades.

Tignon—Turban made of bright-colored cotton cloth, once worn by the black women of New Orleans.

Vieux Carre—Literally "old square," it is the French Quarter, the original city of New Orleans.

Voodoo—A religious tradition brought to New Orleans by the blacks from Africa by way of the Caribbean Islands.

Where y'at?—A direct translation of "where are you at?" and a typical local neighborhood greeting. It means "how are you?" The "where are you at?" greeting began many years ago among laborers who would ask each other this question to find out where friends were working. Today it can mean "where y'at?" (which room in the house?) or "how ya doin'?"

Wrought iron—Made by bending heated iron rods; it is usually older and more delicate than cast iron.

INDEX